The Sacred Formulas of the Cherokees

CONTENTS

INTRODUCTION. 11
HOW THE FORMULAS WERE OBTAINED. 17
THE SWIMMER MANUSCRIPT. 18
THE GATIGWANASTI MANUSCRIPT. 21
THE GAHUNI MANUSCRIPT. 23
THE INÂLI MANUSCRIPT. 25
OTHER MANUSCRIPTS. 28
THE KANÂHETA ANI-TSALAGI ETI. 29
CHARACTER OF THE FORMULAS—THE CHEROKEE
    RELIGION. 31
THE ORIGIN OF DISEASE AND MEDICINE. 34
THEORY OF DISEASE—ANIMALS, GHOSTS, WITCHES. 38
SELECTED LIST OF PLANTS USED. 42
MEDICAL PRACTICE. 50
ILLUSTRATION OF THE TABU. 54
NEGLECT OF SANITARY REGULATIONS. 56
THE SWEAT BATH-BLEEDING—RUBBING—BATHING. 58
SHAMANS AND WHITE PHYSICIANS. 62
MEDICINE DANCES. 64
DESCRIPTION OF SYMPTOMS. 65
THE PAY OF THE SHAMAN. 66
CEREMONIES FOR GATHERING PLANTS AND PREPARING
    MEDICINE. 68
THE CHEROKEE GODS AND THEIR ABIDING PLACES. 70
COLOR SYMBOLISM. 74

IMPORTANCE ATTACHED TO NAMES. 76
LANGUAGE OF THE FORMULAS. 77
SPECIMEN FORMULAS. 79

MEDICINE.

DIDÛⁿLË'SKĬ ADANÛⁿ'WÂTĬ KANÂHË'SKĬ. 83
  FORMULA FOR TREATING THE CRIPPLER (RHEUMATISM).
HIÄ-NÛ' NASGWÛ' DIDÛⁿLË'SKĬ ADÂNÛ'ⁿWÂTĬ.....................90
  AND THIS ALSO IS FOR TREATING THE CRIPPLER.
HIÂ' I'NATÛ YUNISKÛ'LTSA ADÂNÛ'NWÂTÎ............................94
  THIS IS TO TREAT THEM IF THEY ARE BITTEN
    BY A SNAKE.
GÛⁿWÂNI'GISTÂ'Ĭ ADANU'ⁿWÂTÏ. 97
  TO TREAT THEM WHEN SOMETHING IS CAUSING
    SOMETHING TO EAT THEM.
GÛⁿWANI'GISTÛ'ⁿĬ DITANÛⁿWÂTI'YÏ.......................................101
  TO TREAT GÛⁿWANI'GISTÛ'ⁿĬ—(SECOND).
HIA' DU'NIYUKWATISGÛⁿÎ KANA'HÈHÛ. 104
  THIS TELLS ABOUT MOVING PAINS IN THE TEETH
    (NEURALGIA?).
UNAWA STÎ EGWA (ADANÛⁿWATÏ)..109
  TO TREAT THE GREAT CHILL.
HIÄ' TSUNSDI'GA DIL'TADI'NATANTI'YÏ..............................115
  THIS IS TO MAKE CHILDREN JUMP DOWN.
DALÂ'NI ÛⁿNÄGE'Ï ADANÛⁿWÂTÏ. 118
  TO TREAT THE BLACK YELLOWNESS.
TSUNDAYE'LIGAKTANÛ'HÏ ADANÛⁿWÂTÏ 122
  TO TREAT FOR ORDEAL DISEASES.

HUNTING.

GÛNÂ'HILÛⁿTA UGÛ'ⁿWA`LÏ..129
   CONCERNING HUNTING.
HIÄ' TSI'SKWA GANÂHILIDASTI'YÏ. 132
   THIS IS FOR HUNTING BIRDS.
INAGË'HÏ AYÂSTIⁿYÏ. 135
   TO SHOOT DWELLERS IN THE WILDERNESS.
(YÂ'NA TÏ'KANÂGI'TA.)..136
   BEAR SONG.
HIÄ' ATSÛ`TI'YÏ TSUN'TANÛ..138
   THIS IS FOR CATCHING LARGE FISH.

LOVE.

(YÛⁿWË'HÏ UGÛ'ⁿWA`LÏ I.) 143
   CONCERNING LIVING HUMANITY (LOVE).
HI'Ä ÄMA'YÏ Ä'TAWAST'YÏ KANÂ'HEHÛ. 148
   THIS TELLS ABOUT GOING INTO THE WATER.
(YÛ'ⁿWË'HÏ UGÛ'ⁿWA`LÏ II.) 150
   SONG FOR PAINTING.
ADALANI'STA`TI'YÏ. I..152
   TO ATTRACT AND FIX THE AFFECTIONS.
ADAYE'LIGA'GTA`TÏ'...154
   FOR SEPARATION (OF LOVERS).
(ADALANÏ'STÄ`TIYÏ II.) 156
   TO FIX THE AFFECTIONS.

MISCELLANEOUS FORMULAS.

SÛⁿNÂ'YÏ EDÂ'HÏ E'SGA ASTÛⁿTI'YÏ..161
   TO SHORTEN A NIGHT-GOER ON THIS SIDE.

GAHU'STÏ A'GIYAHU'SA..164
   I HAVE LOST SOMETHING.
HIA' UNÁLE (ATEST'YÏ)..166
   THIS IS TO FRIGHTEN A STORM.
DANAWÛ' TSUNEDÂLÛ'HÏ NUNATÛ'NELI'TALÛ"HÏ
   U'NALSTELTA"TANÛ'HÏ...168
   WHAT THOSE WHO HAVE BEEN TO WAR DID TO HELP
      THEMSELVES.
DIDA'LATLI"TÏ...173
   TO DESTROY LIFE.
HIÄ' A`NE'TSÂ UGÛ"WA`LÏ AMÂ'YÏ DITSÛ"STA`TÏ................180
   THIS CONCERNS THE BALL PLAY—TO TAKE THEM TO
      WATER WITH IT.

INTRODUCTION.

The sacred formulas here given are selected from a collection of about six hundred, obtained on the Cherokee reservation in North Carolina in 1887 and 1888, and covering every subject pertaining to the daily life and thought of the Indian, including medicine, love, hunting, fishing, war, self-protection, destruction of enemies, witchcraft, the crops, the council, the ball play, etc., and, in fact, embodying almost the whole of the ancient religion of the Cherokees. The original manuscripts, now in the possession of. the Bureau of Ethnology, were written by the shamans of the tribe, for their own use, in the Cherokee characters invented by Sikwâ'ya (Sequoyah) in 1821, and were obtained, with the explanations, either from the writers themselves or from their surviving relatives.

Some of these manuscripts are known to be at least thirty years old, and many are probably older. The medical formulas of all kinds constitute perhaps one-half of the whole number, while the love charms come next in number, closely followed by the songs and prayers used in hunting and fishing. The great number of love charms will doubtless be a surprise to those who have been educated in the old theory that, the Indian is insensible to the attractions of woman. The comparatively small number of war formulas is explained by the fact that the last war in which the Cherokees, as a tribe, were engaged on their own account, closed with the Revolutionary period, so that these things were well nigh forgotten before the invention of the alphabet, a generation later. The Cherokees who engaged in the Creek war and the late American civil war fought in the interests of the whites, and their leaders were subordinated to white officers, hence there was not the same opportunity for the exercise of shamanistic rites that there would have been had Indians alone been concerned. The prayers for hunting, fishing, and the ball play being in more constant demand, have been better preserved,

These, formulas had been handed down orally from a remote antiquity until the early part of the present century, when the invention of the Cherokee syllabary enabled the priests of the tribe to put them into writing. The same invention made it possible for their rivals, the missionaries, to give to the Indians the Bible in their own language, so that the opposing forces of Christianity and shamanism alike profited by the genius of Sikwâya. The pressure of the new civilization was too strong to be withstood, however, and though the prophets of the old religion still have much influence with the people, they are daily losing ground and will soon be without honor in their own country.

Such an exposition of the aboriginal religion could be obtained from no other tribe in North America, for the simple reason that no other tribe has an alphabet of its own in which to record its sacred lore. It is true that the Crees and Micmacs of Canada and the Tukuth of Alaska have so-called alphabets or ideographic systems invented for their use by the missionaries, while, before the Spanish conquest, the Mayas of Central America were accustomed to note down their hero legends and priestly ceremonials in hieroglyphs graven upon the walls of their temples or painted upon tablets made of the leaves of the maguey. But it seems never to have occurred to the northern tribes that an alphabet coming from a missionary source could be used for any other purpose than the transcription of bibles and catechisms, while the sacred books of the Mayas, with a few exceptions, have long since met destruction at the hands of fanaticism, and the modern copies which have come down to the present day are written out from imperfect memory by Indians who had been educated under Spanish influences in the language, alphabet and ideas of the conquerors, and who, as is proved by an examination of the contents of the books themselves, drew from European sources a great part of their material. Moreover, the Maya tablets were so far hieratic as to be understood, only by the priests and those who had received a special training in this direction, and they seem therefore to have been entirely unintelligible to the common people.

The Cherokee alphabet, on the contrary, is the invention or adaptation of one of the tribe, who, although he borrowed most of the Roman letters, in addition to the forty or more characters of his own devising, knew nothing of their proper use or value, but reversed them or altered their forms to suit his purpose, and gave them a name and value determined by himself. This alphabet was at once adopted by the tribe for all purposes for which writing can be used, including the recording of their shamanistic prayers and ritualistic ceremonies. The formulas here given, as well as those of the entire collection, were written out by the shamans themselves—men who adhere to the ancient religion and speak only their native language in order that their sacred knowledge might be preserved in a systematic manner for their mutual benefit. The language, the conception, and the execution are all genuinely Indian, and hardly a dozen lines of the hundreds of formulas show a trace of the influence of the white man or his religion. The formulas contained in these manuscripts are not disjointed fragments of a system long since extinct, but are the revelation of a living faith which still has its priests and devoted adherents, and it is only necessary to witness a ceremonial ball play, with its fasting, its going to water, and its mystic bead manipulation, to understand how strong is the hold which the old faith yet has upon the minds even of the younger generation. The numerous archaic and figurative expressions used require the interpretation of the priests, but, as before stated, the alphabet in which they are written is that in daily use among the common people.

In all tribes that still retain something of their ancient organization we find this sacred knowledge committed to the keeping of various secret societies, each of which has its peculiar ritual with regular initiation and degrees of advancement. From this analogy we may reasonably conclude that such was formerly the case with the Cherokees also, but by the breaking down of old customs consequent upon their long contact with the whites and the voluntary adoption of a civilized form of government in 1827, all traces of such society organization have long since disappeared, and at present each priest or shaman is isolated and independent, sometimes confining himself to a particular specialty, such as love or medicine, or even the treatment of two or three diseases, in other cases broadening his field of operations to include the whole range of mystic knowledge.

It frequently happens, however, that priests form personal friendships and thus are led to divulge their secrets to each other for their mutual advantage. Thus when one shaman meets another who he thinks can probably give him some valuable information, he says to him, "Let us sit down together." This is understood by the other to mean, "Let us tell each other our secrets." Should it seem probable that the seeker after knowledge can give as much as he receives, an agreement is generally arrived at, the two retire to some convenient spot secure from observation, and the first party begins by reciting one of his formulas with the explanations. The other then reciprocates with one of his own, unless it appears that the bargain is apt to prove a losing one, in which case the conference comes to an abrupt ending.

It is sometimes possible to obtain a formula by the payment of a coat, a quantity of cloth, or a sum of money. Like the Celtic Druids of old, the candidate for the priesthood in former times found it necessary to cultivate a long memory, as no formula was repeated more than once for his benefit. It was considered that one who failed to remember after the first hearing was not worthy to be accounted a shaman. This task, however, was not so difficult as might appear on first thought, when once the learner understood the theory involved, as the formulas are all constructed on regular principles, with constant repetition of the same set of words. The obvious effect of such a regulation was to increase the respect in which this sacred knowledge was held by restricting it to the possession of a chosen few.

Although the written formulas can be read without difficulty by any Cherokee educated in his own language, the shamans take good care that their sacred writings shall not fall into the hands of the laity or of their rivals in occult practices, and in performing the ceremonies the words used are uttered in such a low tone of voice as to be unintelligible even to the one for whose benefit the formula is repeated. Such being the case, it is in order to explain how the formulas collected were obtained.

HOW THE FORMULAS WERE OBTAINED.

On first visiting the reservation in the summer of 1887, I devoted considerable time to collecting plants used by the Cherokees for food or medicinal purposes, learning at the same time their Indian names and the particular uses to which each was applied and the mode of preparation. It soon became evident that the application of the medicine was not the whole, and in fact was rather the subordinate, part of the treatment, which was always accompanied by certain ceremonies and "words." From the workers employed at the time no definite idea could be obtained as to the character of these words. One young woman, indeed, who had some knowledge of the subject, volunteered to write the words which she used in her prescriptions, but failed to do so, owing chiefly to the opposition of the half-breed shamans, from whom she had obtained her information.

THE SWIMMER MANUSCRIPT.

Some time afterward an acquaintance was formed with a man named A`yûⁿ'inï or "Swimmer," who proved to be so intelligent that I spent several days with him, procuring information in regard to myths and old customs. He told a number of stories in very good style, and finally related the Origin of the Bear[1]. The bears were formerly a part of the Cherokee tribe who decided to leave their kindred and go into the forest. Their friends followed them and endeavored to induce them to return, but the Ani-Tsâ'kahï, as they were called, were determined to go. Just before parting from their relatives at the edge of the forest, they turned to them and said, "It is better for you that we should go; but we will teach you songs, and some day when you are in want of food come out to the woods and sing these songs and we shall appear and give you meat." Their

1   To appear later with the collection of Cherokee myths.

friends, after warning several songs from them, started back to their homes, and after proceeding a short distance, turned around to take one last look, but saw only a number of bears disappearing in the depths of the forest. The songs which they learned are still sung by the hunter to attract the bears.

When Swimmer had finished the story he was asked if he knew these songs. He replied that he did, but on being requested to sing one he made some excuse and was silent. After some further efforts the interpreter said it would be useless to press the matter then as there were several other Indians present, but that to-morrow we should have him alone with us and could then make another attempt.

The next day Swimmer was told that if he persisted in his refusal it would be necessary to employ some one else, as it was unfair in him to furnish incomplete information when he was paid to tell all he knew. He replied that he was willing to tell anything in regard to stories and customs, but that these songs were a part of his secret knowledge and commanded a high price from the hunters, who sometimes paid as much as $5 for a single song, "because you can't kill any bears or deer unless you sing them."

He was told that the only object in asking about the songs was to put them on record and preserve them, so that when he and the half dozen old men of the tribe were dead the world might be aware how much the Cherokees had known. This appeal to his professional pride proved effectual, and when he was told that a great many similar songs had been sent to Washington by medicine men of other tribes, he promptly declared that he knew as much as any of them, and that he would give all the information in his possession, so that others might be able to judge for themselves who knew most. The only conditions he made were that these secret matters should be heard by no one else but the interpreter, and should not be discussed when other Indians were present.

As soon as the other shamans learned what was going on they endeavored by various means to persuade him to stop talking, or failing in this, to damage his reputation by throwing out hints as to his honesty or accuracy of statement. Among other objections which they advanced was one which, however incomprehensible to a white man, was perfectly intelligible to an Indian, viz.: That when he had told everything this information would be taken to Washington and locked up there, and thus they would be deprived of the knowledge. This objection was one of the most difficult to overcome, as there was no line of argument with which to oppose it.

These reports worried Swimmer, who was extremely, sensitive in regard to his reputation, and he became restive under the insinuations of his rivals. Finally on coming to work one day he produced a book from under his ragged coat as he entered the house, and said proudly: "Look at that and now see if I don't know something." It was a small day-book of about 240 pages, procured originally from a white man, and was about half filled with writing in the Cherokee characters. A brief examination disclosed the fact that it contained just those matters that had proved so difficult to procure. Here were prayers, songs, and prescriptions for the cure of all kinds of diseases—for chills, rheumatism, frostbites, wounds, bad dreams, and witchery; love charms, to gain the affections of a woman or to cause her to hate a detested rival; fishing charms, hunting charms—including the songs without which none could ever hope to kill, any game; prayers to make the corn grow, to frighten away storms, and to drive off witches; prayers for long life, for safety among strangers, for acquiring influence in council and success in the ball play. There were prayers to the Long Man, the Ancient White, the Great Whirlwind, the Yellow Rattlesnake, and to a hundred other gods of the Cherokee pantheon. It was in fact an Indian ritual and pharmacopoeia.

After recovering in a measure from the astonishment produced by this discovery I inquired whether other shamans had such books. "Yes," said Swimmer, "we all have them." Here then was a clew to follow up. A bargain was made by which be was to have another blank book into which to copy the formulas, after which the original was bought. It is now deposited in the library of the Bureau of Ethnology. The remainder of the time until the return was occupied in getting an understanding of the contents of the book.

THE GATIGWANASTI MANUSCRIPT.

Further inquiry elicited the names of several others who might be supposed to have such papers. Before leaving a visit was paid to one of these, a young man named Wilnoti, whose father, Gatigwanasti, had been during his lifetime a prominent shaman, regarded as a man of superior intelligence. Wilnoti, who is a professing Christian, said that his father had had such papers, and after some explanation from the chief he consented to show them. He produced a box containing a lot of miscellaneous papers, testaments, and hymn-books, all in the Cherokee alphabet. Among them was his father's chief treasure, a manuscript book containing 122 pages of foolscap size, completely filled with formulas of the same kind as those contained in Swimmer's book. There were also a large number of loose sheets, making in all nearly 200 foolscap pages of sacred formulas.

On offering to buy the papers, he replied that he wanted to keep them in order to learn and practice these things himself—thus showing how thin was the veneer of Christianity, in his case at least. On representing to him that in a few years the new conditions would render such knowledge valueless with the younger generation, and that even if he retained the papers he would need some one else to explain them to him, he again refused, saying that they might fall into the hands of Swimmer, who, he was determined, should never see his father's papers. Thus the negotiations came to an end for the time.

On returning to the reservation in July, 1888, another effort was made to get possession of the Gatigwanasti manuscripts and any others of the same kind which could be procured. By this time the Indians had

had several months to talk over the matter, and the idea had gradually dawned upon them that instead of taking their knowledge away from them and looking it up in a box, the intention was to preserve it to the world and pay them for it at the same time. In addition the writer took every opportunity to impress upon them the fact that he was acquainted with the secret knowledge of other tribes and perhaps could give them as much as they gave. It was now much easier to approach them, and on again visiting Wilnoti, in company with the interpreter, who explained the matter fully to him, he finally consented to lend the papers for a time, with the same condition that neither Swimmer nor anyone else but the chief and interpreter should see them, but he still refused to sell them. However, this allowed the use of the papers, and after repeated efforts during a period of several weeks, the matter ended in the purchase of the papers outright, with unreserved permission to show them for copying or explanation to anybody who might be selected. Wilnoti was not of a mercenary disposition, and after the first negotiations the chief difficulty was to overcome his objection to parting with his father's handwriting, but it was an essential point to get the originals, and he was allowed to copy some of the more important formulas, as he found it utterly out of the question to copy the whole.

These papers of Gatigwanasti are the most valuable of the whole, and amount to fully one-half the entire collection, about fifty pages consisting of love charms. The formulas are beautifully written in bold Cherokee characters, and the directions and headings are generally explicit, bearing out the universal testimony that he was a man of unusual intelligence and ability, characteristics inherited by his son, who, although a young man and speaking no English, is one of the most progressive and thoroughly reliable men of the band.

THE GAHUNI MANUSCRIPT.

The next book procured was obtained from a woman named Ayâsta, "The Spoiler," and had been written by her husband, Gahuni, who died about 30 years ago. The matter was not difficult to arrange, as she had already been employed on several occasions, so that she understood the purpose of the work, besides which her son had been regularly engaged to copy and classify the manuscripts already procured. The book was claimed as common property by Ayâsta and her three sons, and negotiations had to be carried on with each one, although in this instance the cash amount involved was only half a dollar, in addition to another book into which to copy some family records and personal memoranda. The book contains only eight formulas, but these are of a character altogether unique, the directions especially throwing a curious light on Indian beliefs. There had been several other formulas of the class called Y'û'ⁿnwëhï, to cause hatred between man and wife, but these had been torn out and destroyed by Ayâsta on the advice of an old shaman, in order that her sons might never learn them. In referring to the matter she spoke in a whisper, and it was evident enough that she had full faith in the deadly power of these spells.

In addition to the formulas the book contains about twenty pages of Scripture extracts in the same handwriting, for Gahuni, like several others of their shamans, combined the professions of Indian conjurer and Methodist preacher. After his death the book fell into the hands of the younger members of the family, who filled it with miscellaneous writings and scribblings. Among other things there are about seventy pages of what was intended to be a Cherokee-English pronouncing dictionary, probably written by the youngest son, already mentioned, who has attended school, and who served for some time as copyist on the formulas. This curious Indian production, of which only a few columns are filled out, consists of a list of simple English words and phrases, written in ordinary English script, followed by Cherokee characters intended to give the approximate pronunciation, together with the corresponding word in the Cherokee language and characters. As the language lacks a number of sounds which are of frequent occurrence in English, the attempts to indicate the pronunciation sometimes give amusing results. Thus we find: Fox (English script); *kwâgisï'* (Cherokee characters); *tsú`lû'* (Cherokee characters). As the Cherokee language lacks the labial *f* and has no compound sound equivalent to our *x*, *kwâgisï'* is as near as the Cherokee speaker can come to pronouncing our word fox. In the same way "bet" becomes *wëtï*, and "sheep" is *síkwï*, while "if he has no dog" appears in the disguise of *ikwï hâsï nâ dâ'ga*.

THE INÂLI MANUSCRIPT.

In the course of further inquiries in regard to the whereabouts of other manuscripts of this kind we heard a great deal about Inâ'lĭ, or "Black Fox," who had died a few years before at an advanced age, and who was universally admitted to have been one of their most able men and the most prominent literary character among them, for from what has been said it must be sufficiently evident that the Cherokees have their native literature and literary men. Like those already mentioned, he was a full-blood Cherokee, speaking no English, and in the course of a long lifetime he had filled almost every position of honor among his people, including those of councilor, keeper of the townhouse records, Sunday-school leader, conjurer, officer in the Confederate service, and Methodist preacher, at last dying, as he was born, in the ancient faith of his forefathers.

On inquiring of his daughter she stated that her father had left a great many papers, most of which were still in her possession, and on receiving from the interpreter an explanation of our purpose she readily gave permission to examine and make selections from them on condition that the matter should be kept secret from outsiders. A day was appointed for visiting her, and on arriving we found her living in a comfortable log house, built by Inâ'lĭ himself, with her children and an ancient female relative, a decrepit old woman, with snow-white hair and vacant countenance. This was the oldest woman of the tribe, and though now so feeble and childish, she had been a veritable savage in her young days, having carried a scalp in the scalp dance in the Creek war 75 years before.

Having placed chairs for us in the shade Inâ'li's daughter brought out a small box filled with papers of various kinds, both Cherokee and English. The work of examining these was a tedious business, as each paper had to be opened out and enough of it read to get the general drift of the contents, after which the several classes were arranged in separate piles. While in the midst of this work she brought out another box nearly as large as a small trunk, and on setting it down there was revealed to the astonished gaze such a mass of material as it had not seemed possible could exist in the entire tribe.

In addition to papers of the sort already mentioned there were a number of letters in English from various officials and religious organizations, and addressed to "Enola," to "Rev. Black Fox," and to "Black Fox, Esq," with a large number of war letters written to him by Cherokees who had enlisted in the Confederate service. These latter are all written in the Cherokee characters, in the usual gossipy style common among friends, and several of them contain important historic material in regard to the movements of the two armies in East Tennessee. Among other things was found his certificate as a Methodist preacher, dated in 1848. "Know all men by these presents that Black Fox (Cherokee) is hereby authorized to exercise his Gifts and Graces as a local preacher in M. E. Church South."

There was found a manuscript book in Inâ'li's handwriting containing the records of the old council of Wolftown, of which he had been secretary for several years down to the beginning of the war. This also contains some valuable materials.

There were also a number of miscellaneous books, papers, and pictures, together with various trinkets and a number of conjuring stones.

In fact the box was a regular curiosity shop, and it was with a feeling akin to despair that we viewed the piles of manuscript which had to be waded through and classified. There was a day's hard work ahead, and it was already past noon; but the woman was not done yet, and after rummaging about inside the house for a while longer she appeared with another armful of papers, which she emptied on top of the others. This was the last straw; and finding it impossible to examine in detail such a mass of material we contented ourselves with picking out the sacred formulas and the two manuscript books containing the town-house records and scriptural quotations and departed.

The daughter of Black Fox agreed to fetch down the other papers in a few days for further examination at our leisure; and she kept her promise, bringing with her at the same time a number of additional formulas which she had not been able to obtain before. A large number of letters and other papers were selected from the miscellaneous lot, and these, with the others obtained from her, are now deposited also with the Bureau of Ethnology. Among other things found at this house were several beads of the old shell wampum, of whose use the Cherokees have now lost even the recollection. She knew only that they were very old and different from the common beads, but she prized them as talismans, and firmly refused to part with them.

OTHER MANUSCRIPTS.

Subsequently a few formulas were obtained from an old shaman named Tsiskwa or "Bird," but they were so carelessly written as to be almost worthless, and the old mail who wrote them, being then on his dying bed, was unable to give much help in the matter. However, as he was anxious to tell what he knew all attempt was made to take down some formulas from his dictation. A few more were obtained in this way but the results were not satisfactory and the experiment was abandoned. About the same time A`wani'ta or "Young Deer," one of their best herb doctors, was engaged to collect the various plants used in medicine and describe their uses. While thus employed he wrote in a book furnished him for the purpose a number of formulas used by him in his practice, giving at the same time a verbal explanation of the theory and ceremonies. Among these was one for protection in battle, which had been used by himself and a number of other Cherokees in the late war. Another doctor named Takwati'hï or "Catawba Killer," was afterward employed on the same work and furnished some additional formulas which he had had his son write down from his dictation, he himself being unable to write. His knowledge was limited to the practice of a few specialties, but in regard to these his information was detailed and accurate. There was one for bleeding with the cupping horn. All these formulas obtained from Tsiskwa, A`wanita, and Takwtihi are now in possession of the Bureau.

THE KANÂHETA ANI-TSALAGI ETI.

Among the papers thus obtained was a large number which for various reasons it was found difficult to handle or file for preservation. Many of them had been written so long ago that the ink had almost faded from the paper; others were written with lead pencil, so that in handling them the characters soon became blurred and almost illegible; a great many were written on scraps of paper of all shapes and sizes; and others again were full of omissions and doublets, due to the carelessness of the writer, while many consisted simply of the prayer, with nothing in the nature of a heading or prescription to show its purpose.

Under the circumstances it was deemed expedient to have a number of these formulas copied in more enduring form. For this purpose it was decided to engage the services of Ayâsta's youngest son, an intelligent young man about nineteen years of age, who had attended school long enough to obtain a fair acquaintance with English in addition to his intimate knowledge of Cherokee. He was also gifted with a ready comprehension, and from his mother and uncle Tsiskwa had acquired some familiarity with many of the archaic expressions used in the sacred formulas. He was commonly known as "Will West," but signed himself W. W. Long, Long being the translation of his father's name, Gûnahi'ta. After being instructed as to how the work should be done with reference to paragraphing, heading, etc., he was furnished a blank book of two hundred pages into which to copy such formulas as it seemed desirable to duplicate. He readily grasped the idea and in the course of about a month, working always under the writer's personal supervision, succeeded in completely filling the book according to the plan outlined.

In addition to the duplicate formulas he wrote down a number of dance and drinking songs, obtained originally from A`yûⁿ'inï, with about thirty miscellaneous formulas obtained from various sources. The book thus prepared is modeled on the plan of an ordinary book, with headings, table of contents, and even with an illuminated title page devised by the aid of the interpreter according to the regular Cherokee idiomatic form, and is altogether a unique specimen of Indian literary art. It contains in all two hundred and fifty-eight formulas and songs, which of course are native aboriginal productions, although the mechanical arrangement was performed under the direction of a white man. This book also, under its Cherokee title, *Kanâhe'ta Ani-Tsa'lagï E'ti* or "Ancient Cherokee Formulas," is now in the library of the Bureau.

There is still a considerable quantity of such manuscript in the hands of one or two shamans with whom there was no chance for negotiating, but an effort will be made to obtain possession of these on some future visit, should opportunity present. Those now in the Bureau library comprised by far the greater portion of the whole quantity held by the Indians, and as only a small portion of this was copied by the owners it can not be duplicated by any future collector.

CHARACTER OF THE FORMULAS—THE CHEROKEE RELIGION.

It is impossible to overestimate the ethnologic importance of the materials thus obtained. They are invaluable as the genuine production of the Indian mind, setting forth in the clearest light the state of the aboriginal religion before its contamination by contact with the whites. To the psychologist and the student of myths they are equally precious. In regard to their linguistic value we may quote the language of Brinton, speaking of the sacred books of the Mayas, already referred to:

> Another value they have, * * * and it is one which will be properly appreciated by any student of languages. They are, by common consent of all competent authorities, the genuine productions of native minds, cast in the idiomatic forms of the native tongue by those born to its use. No matter how fluent a foreigner becomes in a language not his own, he can never use it as does one who has been familiar with it from childhood. This general maxim is tenfold true when we apply it to a European learning an American language. The flow of thought, as exhibited in these two linguistic families, is in such different directions that no amount of practice can render one equally accurate in both. Hence the importance of studying a tongue as it is employed by natives; and hence the very high estimate I place on these "Books of Chilan Balam" as linguistic material—an estimate much increased by the great rarity of independent compositions in their own tongues by members of the native races of this continent.[1]

The same author, in speaking of the internal evidences of authenticity contained in the Popol Vuh, the sacred book of the Kichés, uses the following words, which apply equally well to these Cherokee formulas:

> To one familiar with native American myths, this one bears undeniable marks of its aboriginal origin. Its frequent puerilities and inanities, its generally low and coarse range of thought and expression, its occasional loftiness of both, its strange metaphors and the prominence of strictly heathen names and potencies, bring it into unmistakable relationship to the true native myth.[2]

These formulas furnish a complete refutation of the assertion so frequently made by ignorant and prejudiced writers that the Indian had no religion excepting what they are pleased to call the meaning less mummeries of the medicine man. This is the very reverse of the truth. The Indian is essentially religious and contemplative,

1   Brinton, D. G.: The books of Chilan Balam 10, Philadelphia, n. d., (1882).
2   Brinton, D. G: Names of the Gods in the Kiche Myths, in Proc. Am. Philos. Soc., Philadelphia, 1881, vol. 19, p. 613.

and it might almost be said that every act of his life is regulated and determined by his religious belief. It matters not that some may call this superstition. The difference is only relative. The religion of to-day has developed from the cruder superstitions of yesterday, and Christianity itself is but an outgrowth and enlargement of the beliefs and ceremonies which have been preserved by the Indian in their more ancient form. When we are willing to admit that the Indian has a religion which he holds sacred, even though it be different from our own, we can then admire the consistency of the theory, the particularity of the ceremonial and the beauty of the expression. So far from being a jumble of crudities, there is a wonderful completeness about the whole system which is not surpassed even by the ceremonial religions of the East. It is evident from a study of these formulas that the Cherokee Indian was a polytheist and that the spirit world was to him only a shadowy counterpart of this. All his prayers were for temporal and tangible blessings—for health, for long life, for success in the chase, in fishing, in war and in love, for good crops, for protection and for revenge. He had no Great Spirit, no happy hunting ground, no heaven, no hell, and consequently death had for him no terrors and he awaited the inevitable end with no anxiety as to the future. He was careful not to violate the rights of his tribesman or to do injury to his feelings, but there is nothing to show that he had any idea whatever of what is called morality in the abstract.

As the medical formulas are first in number and importance it may be well, for the better understanding of the theory involved, to give the Cherokee account of

THE ORIGIN OF DISEASE AND MEDICINE.

In the old days quadrupeds, birds, fishes, and insects could all talk, and they and the human race lived together in peace and friendship. But as time went on the people increased so rapidly that their settlements spread over the whole earth and the poor animals found themselves beginning to be cramped for room. This was bad enough, but to add to their misfortunes man invented bows, knives, blowguns, spears, and hooks, and began to slaughter the larger animals, birds and fishes for the sake of their flesh or their skins, while the smaller creatures, such as the frogs and worms, were crushed and trodden upon without mercy, out of pure carelessness or contempt. In. this state of affairs the animals resolved to consult upon measures for their common safety.

The bears were the first to meet in council in their townhouse in Kuwa'hï, the "Mulberry Place,"[1] and the old White Bear chief presided.

1   One of the high peaks of the Smoky Mountains, on the Tennessee line, near Clingman's Dome.

After each in turn had made complaint against the way in which man killed their friends, devoured their flesh and used their skins for his own adornment, it was unanimously decided to begin war at once against the human race. Some one asked what weapons man used to accomplish their destruction. "Bows and arrows, of course," cried all the bears in chorus. "And what are they made of?" was the next question. "The bow of wood and the string of our own entrails," replied one of the bears. It was then proposed that they make a bow and some arrows and see if they could not turn man's weapons against himself. So one bear got a nice piece of locust wood and another sacrificed himself for the good of the rest in order to furnish a piece of his entrails for the string. But when everything was ready and the first bear stepped up to make the trial it was found that in letting the arrow fly after drawing back the bow, his long claws caught the string and spoiled the shot. This was annoying, but another suggested that he could overcome the difficulty by cutting his claws, which was accordingly done, and on a second trial it was found that the arrow went straight to the mark. But here the chief, the old White Bear, interposed and said that it was necessary that they should have long claws in order to be able to climb trees. "One of us has already died to furnish the bowstring, and if we now cut off our claws we shall all have to starve together. It is better to trust to the teeth and claws which nature has given us, for it is evident that man's weapons were not intended for us."

No one could suggest any better plan, so the old chief dismissed the council and the bears dispersed to their forest haunts without having concerted any means for preventing the increase of the human race. Had the result of the council been otherwise, we should now be at war with the bears, but as it is the hunter does not even ask the bear's pardon when he kills one.

The deer next held a council under their chief, the Little Deer, and after some deliberation resolved to inflict rheumatism upon every hunter who should kill one of their number, unless he took care to ask their pardon for the offense. They sent notice of their decision to the nearest settlement of Indians and told them at the same time how to make propitiation when necessity forced them to kill one of the deer tribe.

Now, whenever the hunter brings down a deer, the Little Deer, who is swift as the wind and can not be wounded, runs quickly up to the spot and bending over the blood stains asks the spirit of the deer if it has heard the prayer of the hunter for pardon. If the reply be "Yes" all is well and the Little Deer goes on his way, but if the reply be in the negative he follows on the trail of the hunter, guided by the drops of blood on the ground, until he arrives at the cabin in the settlement, when the Little Deer enters invisibly and strikes the neglectful hunter with rheumatism, so that he, is rendered on the instant a helpless cripple. No hunter who has regard for his health ever fails to ask pardon of the deer for killing it, although some who have not learned the proper formula may attempt to turn aside the Little Deer from his pursuit by building a fire behind them in the trail.

Next came the fishes and reptiles, who had their own grievances against humanity. They held a joint council and determined to make their victims dream of snakes twining about them in slimy folds and blowing their fetid breath in their faces, or to make them dream of eating raw or decaying fish, so that they would lose appetite, sicken, and die. Thus it is that snake and fish dreams are accounted for.

Finally the birds, insects, and smaller animals came together for a like purpose, and the Grubworm presided over the deliberations. It was decided that each in turn should express an opinion and then vote on the question as to whether or not man should be deemed guilty. Seven votes were to be sufficient to condemn him. One after another denounced man's cruelty and injustice toward the other animals and voted in favor of his death. The Frog (walâ'sï) spoke first and said: "We must do something to check the increase of the race or people will become so numerous that we shall be crowded from off the earth. See how man has kicked me about because I'm ugly, as he says, until my back is covered with sores;" and here he showed the spots on his skin. Next came the Bird (tsi'skwa; no particular species is indicated), who condemned man because "he burns my feet off," alluding to the way in which the hunter barbecues birds by impaling them on a stick set over the fire, so that their feathers and tender feet are singed and burned. Others followed in the same strain. The Ground Squirrel alone ventured to say a word in behalf of man, who seldom hurt him because he was so small; but this so enraged the others that they fell upon the Ground Squirrel and tore him with their teeth and claws, and the stripes remain on his back to this day.

The assembly then began to devise and name various diseases, one after another, and had not their invention finally failed them not one of the human race would have been able to survive. The Grubworm in his place of honor hailed each new malady with delight, until at last they had reached the end of the list, when some one suggested that it be arranged so that menstruation should sometimes prove fatal to woman. On this he rose up in his place and cried: "Wata'ⁿ! Thanks! I'm glad some of them will die, for they are getting so thick that they tread on me." He fairly shook with joy at the thought, so that he fell over backward and could not get on his feet again, but had to wriggle off on his back, as the Grubworm has done ever since.

When the plants, who were friendly to man, heard what had been done by the animals, they determined to defeat their evil designs. Each tree, shrub, and herb, down even to the grasses and mosses, agreed to furnish a remedy for some one of the diseases named, and each said: "I shall appear to help man when he calls upon me in his need." Thus did medicine originate, and the plants, every one of which has its use if we only knew it, furnish the antidote to counteract the evil wrought by the revengeful animals. When the doctor is in doubt what treatment to apply for the relief of a patient, the spirit of the plant suggests to him the proper remedy.

THEORY OF DISEASE—ANIMALS, GHOSTS, WITCHES.

Such is the belief upon which their medical practice is based, and whatever we may think of the theory it must be admitted that the practice is consistent in all its details with the views set forth in the myth. Like most primitive people the Cherokees believe that disease and death are not natural, but are due to the evil influence of animal spirits, ghosts, or witches. Haywood, writing in 1823, states on the authority of two intelligent residents of the Cherokee nation:

> In ancient times the Cherokees had no conception of anyone dying a natural death. They universally ascribed the death of those who perished by disease to the intervention or agency of evil spirits and witches and conjurers who had connection with the Shina (Anisgi'na) or evil spirits. * * * A person dying by disease and charging his death to have been procured by means of witchcraft or spirits, by any other person, consigns that person to inevitable death. They profess to believe that their conjurations have no effect upon white men.[1]

On the authority of one of the same informants, he also mentions the veneration which "their physicians have for the numbers four and seven, who say that after man was placed upon the earth four and seven nights were instituted for the cure of diseases in the human body and the seventh night as the limit for female impurity."[2]

Viewed from a scientific standpoint, their theory and diagnosis are entirely wrong, and consequently we can hardly expect their therapeutic system to be correct. As the learned Doctor Berendt states, after an exhaustive study of the medical books of the Mayas, the scientific value of their remedies is "next to nothing." It must be admitted that many of the plants used in their medical practice possess real curative properties, but it is equally true that many others held in as high estimation are inert. It seems probable that in the beginning the various herbs and other plants were regarded as so many fetiches and were selected from some fancied connection with the disease animal, according to the idea known to modern folklorists as the doctrine of signatures. Thus at the present day the doctor puts into the decoction intended as a vermifuge some of the

1. Haywood, John: Natural and Aboriginal History of East Tennessee, 267-8, Nashville, 1823.
2. Ibid., p. 281.

red fleshy stalks of the common purslane or chickweed (Portulaca oleracea), because these stalks somewhat resemble worms and consequently must have some occult influence over worms. Here the chickweed is a fetich precisely as is the flint arrow bead which is put into the same decoction, in order that in the same mysterious manner its sharp cutting qualities may be communicated to the liquid and enable it to cut the worms into pieces. In like manner, biliousness is called by the Cherokees dalâ'nï or "yellow," because the most apparent symptom of the disease is the vomiting by the patient of the yellow bile, and hence the doctor selects for the decoction four different herbs, each of which is also called dalâni, because of the color of the root, stalk, or flower. The same idea is carried out in the tabu which generally accompanies the treatment. Thus a scrofulous patient must abstain from eating the meat of a turkey, because the fleshy dewlap which depends from its throat somewhat resembles an inflamed scrofulous eruption. On killing a deer the hunter always makes an incision in the hind quarter and removes the hamstring, because this tendon, when severed, draws up into the flesh; ergo, any one who should unfortunately partake of the hamstring would find his limbs draw up in the same manner.

There can be no doubt that in course of time a haphazard use of plants would naturally lead to the discovery that certain herbs are efficacious in certain combinations of symptoms. These plants would thus come into more frequent use and finally would obtain general recognition in the Indian materia medica. By such a process of evolution an empiric system of medicine has grown up among the Cherokees, by which they are able to, treat some classes of ailments with some degree of success, although without any intelligent idea of the process involved. It must be remembered that our own medical system has its remote origin in the same mythic conception of disease, and that within two hundred years judicial courts have condemned women to be burned to death for producing sickness by spells and incantations, while even at the present day our faith-cure professors reap their richest harvest among people commonly supposed to belong to the intelligent classes. In the treatment of wounds the Cherokee doctors exhibit a considerable degree of skill, but as far as any internal ailment is concerned the average farmer's wife is worth all the doctors in the whole tribe.

The faith of the patient has much to do with his recovery, for the Indian has the same implicit confidence in the shaman that a child has in a more intelligent physician. The ceremonies and prayers are well calculated to inspire this feeling, and the effect thus produced upon the mind of the sick man undoubtedly reacts favorably upon his physical organization.

The following list of twenty plants used in Cherokee practice will give a better idea of the extent of their medical knowledge than could be conveyed by a lengthy dissertation. The names are given in the order in which they occur in the botanic notebook filled on the reservation, excluding names of food plants and species not identified, so that no attempt has been made to select in accordance with a preconceived theory.

Following the name of each plant are given its uses as described by the Indian doctors, together with its properties as set forth in the United States Dispensatory, one of the leading pharmacopœias in use in this country.[1] For the benefit of those not versed in medical phraseology it may be stated that aperient, cathartic, and deobstruent are terms applied to medicines intended to open or purge the bowels, a diuretic has the property of exciting the flow of urine, a diaphoretic excites perspiration, and a demulcent protects or soothes irritated tissues, while hæmoptysis denotes a peculiar variety of blood-splitting and aphthous is an adjective applied to ulcerations in the mouth.

[1] Wood, T. B., and Bache, F.: Dispensatory of the United States of America, 14th ed., Philadelphia, 1877.

SELECTED LIST OF PLANTS USED.

1. UNASTE'TSTYÛ = "very small root "—Aristolochia serpentaria—Virginia or black snakeroot: Decoction of root blown upon patient for fever and feverish head ache, and drunk for coughs; root chewed and spit upon wound to cure snake bites; bruised root placed in hollow tooth for toothache, and held against nose made sore by constant blowing in colds. Dispensatory: "A stimulant tonic, acting also as a diaphoretic or diuretic, according to the mode of its application; * * * also been highly recommended in intermittent fevers, and though itself generally inadequate to the cure often proves serviceable as an adjunct to Peruvian bark or sulphate of quinia." Also used for typhous diseases, in dyspepsia, as a gargle for sore throat, as a mild stimulant in typhoid fevers, and to promote eruptions. The genus derives its scientific name from its supposed efficacy in promoting menstrual discharge, and some species have acquired the "reputation of antidotes for the bites of serpents."
2. UNISTIL'Û"ISTÎ[2] = "they stick on"—Cynoglossum Morrisoni—Beggar lice: Decoction of root or top drunk for kidney troubles; bruised root used with bear oil as an ointment for cancer; forgetful persons drink a decoction of this plant, and probably also of other similar bur plants, from an idea that the sticking qualities of the burs will thus be imparted to the memory. From a similar connection of ideas the root is also used in the preparation of love charms. Dispensatory: Not named. C. officinale "has been used as a demulcent and sedative in coughs, catarrh, spitting of blood, dysentery, and diarrhea, and has been also applied externally in bums, ulcers, scrofulous tumors and goiter."

2. The Cherokee plant names here given are generic names, which are the names commonly used. In many cases the same name is applied to several species and it is only when it is necessary to distinguish between them that the Indians use what might be called specific names. Even then the descriptive term used serves to distinguish only the particular plants under discussion and the introduction of another variety bearing the same generic name would necessitate a new classification of species on a different basis, while hardly any two individuals would classify the species by the same characteristics.

3. ÛⁿNAGÉI = "olack"—Cassia Marilandica—Wild senna: Root bruised and moistened with water for poulticing sores; decoction drunk for fever and for a disease also called ûⁿnage'i, or "black" (same name as plant), in which the hands and eye sockets are said to turn black; also for a disease described as similar to ûⁿnage'i, but more dangerous, in which the eye sockets become black, while black spots appear on the arms, legs, and over the ribs on one side of the body, accompanied by partial paralysis, and resulting in death should the black spots appear also on the other side. Dispensatory: Described as "an efficient and safe cathartic, most conveniently given in the form of infusion."

4. KÂSD'ÚTA = "simulating ashes," so called on account of the appearance of the leaves—Gnaphalium decurrens—Life everlasting: Decoction drunk for colds; also used in the sweat bath for various diseases and considered one of their most valuable medical plants. Dispensatory: Not named. Decoctions of two other species of this genus are mentioned as used by country people for chest and bowel diseases, and for hemorrhages, bruises, ulcers, etc., although "probably possessing little medicinal virtue."

5. ALTSA'STI = "a wreath for the head"—Vicia Caroliniana—Vetch: Decoction drunk for dyspepsia and pains in the back, and rubbed on stomach for cramp; also rubbed on ball-players after scratching, to render their muscles tough, and used in the same way after scratching in the disease referred to under ûⁿnage'i, in which one side becomes black in spots, with partial paralysis; also used in same manner in

43

decoction with Kâsduta for rheumatism; considered one of their most valuable medicinal herbs. Dispensatory: Not named.

6. DISTAI'YÏ = "they (the roots) are tough"—Tephrosia Virginiana—Catgut, Turkey Pea, Goat's Rue, or Devil's Shoestrings: Decoction drunk for lassitude. Women wash their hair in decoction of its roots to prevent its breaking or falling out, because these roots are very tough and hard to break; from the same idea ball-players rub the decoction on their limbs after scratching, to toughen them. Dispensatory: Described as a cathartic with roots tonic and aperient.

7. U'GA-ATASGI'SKÏ = "the pus oozes out"—Euphorbia hypericifolia—Milkweed: Juice rubbed on for skin eruptions, especially on children's heads; also used as a purgative; decoction drunk for gonorrhœa and similar diseases in both sexes, and held in high estimation for this purpose; juice used as an ointment for sores and for sore nipples, and in connection with other herbs for cancer. Dispensatory: The juice of all of the genus has the property of "powerfully irritating the skin when applied to it," while nearly all are powerful emetics, and cathartics. This species "has been highly commended as a remedy in dysentery after due depletion, diarrhea, menorrhagia, and leucorrhea."

8. GÛ'NÏGWALÏ'SKÏ = "It becomes discolored when bruised"—Scutellaria lateriflora—Skullcap. "The name refers to the red juice which comes out of the stalk when bruised or chewed. A decoction of the four varieties of Gûnigwalï'skï—lateriflora, S. pilosa, Hypericum corymbosum, and Stylosanthes elatior—is drunk to promote menstruation, and the same decoction is also drunk and used as a wash to counteract the ill effects of eating food prepared by a woman in the menstrual condition, or when such a woman by chance comes into a sick room or a house under the tabu; also drunk for diarrhea and used with other herbs in decoction for breast pains. Dispensatory: This plant "produces no very obvious effects," but

some doctors regard it as possessed of nervine, antispasmodic and tonic properties. None of the other three species are named.

9. KÂ'GASKÛⁿTAGÏ = "crow shin"—Adiantum pedatum—Maidenhair Fern: Used either in decoction or poultice for rheumatism and chills, generally in connection with some other fern. The doctors explain that the fronds of the different varieties of fern are curled up in the young plant, but unroll and straighten out as it grows, and consequently a decoction of ferns causes the contracted muscles of the rheumatic patient to unbend and straighten out in like manner. It is also used in decoction for fever. Dispensatory: The leaves "have been supposed to be useful in chronic catarrh and other pectoral affections."

10. ANDA'NKALAGI'SKI = "it removes things from the gums"—Geranium maculatum—Wild Alum, Cranesbill: Used in decoction with Yânû Unihye stï (Vitis cordifolia) to wash the mouths of children in thrush; also used alone for the same purpose by blowing the chewed fiber into the mouth. Dispensatory: "One of our best indigenous astringents. * * * Diarrhea, chronic dysentery, cholora infantum in the latter stages, and the various hemorrhages are the forms of disease in which it is most commonly used." Also valuable as "an application to indolent ulcers, an injection in gleet and leucorrhea, a gargle in relaxation of the uvula and aphthous ulcerations of the throat." The other plant sometimes used with it is not mentioned.

11. ÛⁿLË, UKÏ'LTÏ = "the locust frequents it"—Gillenia trifoliata—Indian Physic. Two doctors state that it is good as a tea for bowel complaints, with fever and yellow vomit; but another says that it is poisonous and that no decoction is ever drunk, but that the beaten root is a good poultice for swellings. Dispensatory: "Gillenia is a mild and efficient emetic, and like most substances belonging to the same class occasionally acts upon the bowels. In very small doses it has been thought to be tonic."

12. SKWA'LĬ = Hepatica acutiloba—Liverwort, Heartleaf: Used for coughs either in tea or by chewing root. Those who dream of snakes drink a decoction of this herb and I'natû Ga'n`ka = "snake tongue"—(Camptosorus rhizophyllus or Walking Fern) to produce vomiting, after which the dreams do not return. The traders buy large quantities of liverwort from the Cherokees, who may thus have learned to esteem it more highly than they otherwise would. The appearance of the other plant, Camptosorus rhizophyllus, has evidently determined its Cherokee name and the use to which it is applied. Dispensatory: "Liverwort is a very mild demulcent tonic and astringent, supposed by some to possess diuretic and deobstruent virtues. It was formerly used in Europe in various complaints, especially chronic hepatic affections, but has fallen into entire neglect. In this country, some years since, it acquired considerable reputation, which, however, it has not maintained as a remedy in hæmoptysis and chronic coughs." The other plant is not named.
13. DA'YEWÛ = "it sews itself up," because the leaves are said to grow together again when torn—Cacalia atriplicifolia—Tassel Flower: Held in great repute as a poultice for cuts, bruises, and cancer, to draw out the blood or poisonous matter. The bruised leaf is bound over the spot and frequently removed. The dry powdered leaf was formerly used to sprinkle over food like salt. Dispensatory—Not named.
14. Â'TALĬ KÛLĬ' = "it climbs the mountain."—Aralia quinquefolia—Ginseng or "Sang:" Decoction of root drunk for headache, cramps, etc., and for female troubles; chewed root blown on spot for pains in the side. The Cherokees sell large quantities of sang to the traders for 50 cents per pound, nearly equivalent there to two days' wages, a fact which has doubtless increased their idea of its importance. Dispensatory: "The extraordinary medical virtues formerly ascribed to ginseng had no other existence than in the imagination of the Chinese. It is little more than a demulcent, and in this country is

not employed as a medicine." The Chinese name, ginseng, is said to refer to the fancied resemblance of the root to a human figure, while in the Cherokee formulas it is addressed as the "great man" or "little man," and this resemblance no doubt has much to do with the estimation in which it is held by both peoples.

15. Û'TSATÏ UWADSÏSKA = "fish scales," from shape of leaves—Thalictrum anemonoides—Meadow Rue: Decoction of root drunk for diarrhea with vomiting. Dispensatory: Not named.

16. K'KWË ULASU'LA = "partridge moccasin"—Cypripedium parviflorum—Ladyslipper: Decoction of root used for worms in children. In the liquid are placed some stalks of the common chickweed or purslane (Cerastium vulgatum) which, from the appearance of its red fleshy stalks, is supposed to have some connection with worms. Dispensatory: Described as "a gentle nervous stimulant" useful in diseases in which the nerves are especially affected. The other herb is not named.

17. A'HAWÏ' AKÄ'TÄ'—"deer eye," from the appearance of the flower-Rudbeckia fulgida—Cone Flower: Decoction of root drunk for flux and for some private diseases; also used as a wash for snakebites and swellings caused by (mythic) tsgâya or worms; also dropped into weak or inflamed eyes. This last is probably from the supposed connection between the eye and the flower resembling the eye. Dispensatory: Not named.

18. UTÏSTUGÏ'—Polygonatum multiflorum latifolium—Solomon's Seal: Root heated and bruised and applied as a poultice to remove an ulcerating swelling called tu'stï', resembling a boil or carbuncle. Dispensatory: This species acts like P. uniflorum, which is said to be emetic, In former times it was used externally in bruises, especially those about the eyes, in tumors, wounds, and cutaneous eruptions and was highly esteemed as a cosmetic. At present it is not employed, though recommended by Hermann as a good remedy in gout and rheumatism." This species in decoction has been found to produce nausea, a cathartic effect and either

diaphoresis or diuresis, "and is useful as an internal remedy in piles, and externally in the form of decoction, in the affection of the skin resulting from the poisonous exhalations of certain plants."

19. ÄMÄDITA`TÏ—"water dipper," because water can be sucked up through its hollow stalk—Eupatorium purpureum—Queen of the Meadow, Gravel Root: Root used in decoction with a somewhat similar plant called Ämäditá`tï ü'tanu, or "large water dipper" (not identified) for difficult urination. Dispensatory: "Said to operate as a diuretic. Its vulgar name of gravel root indicates the popular estimation of its virtues." The genus is described as tonic, diaphoretic, and in large doses emetic and aperient.

20. YÂNA UTSĚSTA = "the bear lies on it"—Aspidium acrostichoides—Shield Fern: Root decoction drunk to produce vomiting, and also used to rub on the skin, after scratching, for rheumatism—in both cases some other plant is added to the decoction; the warm decoction is also held in the mouth to relieve toothache. Dispensatory: Not named.

The results obtained from a careful study of this list maybe summarized as follows: Of the twenty plants described as used by the Cherokees, seven (Nos. 2, 4, 5, 13, 15, 17, and 20) are not noticed in the Dispensatory even in the list of plants sometimes used although regarded as not officinal. It is possible that one or two of these seven plants have medical properties, but this can hardly be true of a larger number unless we are disposed to believe that the Indians are better informed in this regard than the best educated white physicians in the country. Two of these seven plants, however (Nos. 2 and 4), belong to genera which seem to have some of the properties ascribed by the Indians to the species. Five others of the list (Nos. 8, 9, 11, 14, and 16) are used for entirely wrong purposes, taking the Dispensatory as authority, and three of these are evidently used on account of some fancied connection between the plant and the disease, according to the doctrine of signatures. Three of the remainder (Nos. 1,

3, and 6) may be classed as uncertain in their properties, that is, while the plants themselves seem to possess some medical value, the Indian mode of application is so far at variance with recognized methods, or their own statements are so vague and conflicting, that it is doubtful whether any good can result from the use of the herbs. Thus the Unaste'tstiyû, or Virginia Snakeroot, is stated by the Dispensatory to have several uses, and among other things is said to have been highly recommended in intermittent fevers, although alone it is "generally inadequate to the cure." Though not expressly stated, the natural inference is that it must be applied internally, but the Cherokee doctor, while he also uses it for fever, takes the decoction in his mouth and blows it over the head and shoulders of the patient. Another of these, the Distai'yĭ, or Turkey Pea, is described in the Dispensatory as having roots tonic and aperient. The Cherokees drink a decoction of the roots for a feeling of weakness and languor, from which it might be supposed that they understood the tonic properties of the plant had not the same decoction been used by the women as a hair wash, and by the ball players to bathe their limbs, under the impression that the toughness of the roots would thus be communicated to the hair or muscles. From this fact and from the name of the plant, which means at once hard, tough, or strong, it is quite probable that its roots are believed to give strength to the patient solely because they themselves are so strong and not because they have been proved to be really efficacious. The remaining five plants have generally pronounced medicinal qualities, and are used by the Cherokees for the very purposes for which, according to the Dispensatory, they are best adapted; so that we must admit that so much of their practice is correct, however false the reasoning by which they have arrived at this result.

MEDICAL PRACTICE.

Taking the Dispensatory as the standard, and assuming that this list is a fair epitome of what the Cherokees know concerning the medical properties of plants, we find that five plants, or 25 per cent of the whole number, are correctly used; twelve, or 60 per cent, are presumably either worthless or incorrectly used, and three plants, or 15 per cent, are so used that it is difficult to say whether they are of any benefit or not. Granting that two of these three produce good results as used by the Indians, we should have 35 per cent, or about one-third of the whole, as the proportion actually possessing medical virtues, while the remaining two-thirds are inert, if not positively injurious. It is not probable that a larger number of examples would change the proportion to any appreciable extent. A number of herbs used in connection with these principal plants may probably be set down as worthless, inasmuch as they are not named in the Dispensatory.

The results here arrived at will doubtless be a surprise to those persons who hold that an Indian must necessarily be a good doctor, and that the medicine man or conjurer, with his theories of ghosts, witches, and revengeful animals, knows more about the properties of plants and the cure of disease than does the trained botanist or physician who has devoted a lifetime of study to the patient investigation of his specialty, with all the accumulated information contained in the works of his predecessors to build upon, and with all the light thrown upon his pathway by the discoveries of modern science. It is absurd to suppose that the savage, a child in intellect, has reached a higher development in any branch of science than has been attained by the civilized man, the product of long ages of intellectual growth. It would be as unreasonable to suppose that the Indian could be entirely ignorant of the medicinal properties of plants, living as he did in the open air in close communion with nature; but neither in accuracy nor extent can his knowledge be compared for a moment with that of the trained student working upon scientific principles.

Cherokee medicine is an empiric development of the fetich idea. For a disease caused by the rabbit the antidote must be a plant called "rabbit's food," "rabbit's ear," or "rabbit's tail;" for snake dreams the plant used is "snake's tooth;" for worms a plant resembling a worm in appearance, and for inflamed eyes a flower having the appearance and name of "deer's eye." A yellow root must be good when the patient vomits yellow bile, and a black one when dark circles come about his eyes, and in each case the disease and the plant alike are named from the color. A decoction of burs must be a cure for forgetfulness, for there is nothing else that will stick like a bur; and a decoction of the wiry roots of the "devil's shoestrings" must be an efficacious wash to toughen the ballplayer's muscles, for they are almost strong enough to stop the plowshare in the furrow. It must be evident that under such a system the failures must far outnumber the cures, yet it is not so long since half our own medical practice was based upon the same idea of correspondences, for the mediaeval physicians taught that *similia similibus curantur*, and have we not all heard that "the hair of the dog will cure the bite?"

Their ignorance of the true medical principles involved is shown by the regulations prescribed for the patient. With the exception of the fasting, no sanitary precautions are taken to aid in the recovery of the sick man or to contribute to his comfort. Even the fasting is as much religious as sanative, for in most cases where it is prescribed the doctor also must abstain from food until sunset, just as in the Catholic church both priest and communicants remain fasting from midnight until after the celebration of the divine mysteries. As the Indian cuisine is extremely limited, no delicate or appetizing dishes are prepared for the patient, who partakes of the same heavy, sodden cornmeal dumplings and bean bread which form his principal food in health. In most cases certain kinds of food are prohibited, such as squirrel meat, fish, turkey, etc.; but the reason is not that such food is considered deleterious to health, as we understand it, but because of some fanciful connection with the disease spirit. Thus if squirrels have caused the illness the patient must not eat squirrel meat. If the disease be rheumatism, he must not eat the leg of any animal, because the limbs are generally the seat of this malady. Lye, salt, and hot food are always forbidden when there is any prohibition at all; but here again, in nine cases out of ten, the regulation, instead of being beneficial, serves only to add to his discomfort. Lye enters into almost all the food preparations of the Cherokees, the alkaline potash taking the place of salt, which is seldom used among them, having been introduced by the whites. Their bean and chestnut bread, cornmeal dumplings' hominy, and gruel are all boiled in a pot, all contain lye, and are all, excepting the last, served up hot from the fire. When cold their bread is about as hard and tasteless as a lump of yesterday's dough, and to condemn a sick man to a diet of such dyspeptic food, eaten cold without even a pinch of salt to give it a relish, would seem to be sufficient to kill him with, out any further aid from the doctor. The salt or lye so strictly prohibited is really a tonic and appetizer, and in many diseases acts with curative effect. So much for the health regimen.

In serious cases the patient is secluded and no strangers are allowed to enter the house. On first thought this would appear to be a genuine sanitary precaution for the purpose of securing rest and quiet to the sick man. Such, however, is not the case. The necessity for quiet has probably never occurred to the Cherokee doctor, and this regulation is intended simply to prevent any direct or indirect contact with a woman in a pregnant or menstrual condition. Among all primitive nations, including the ancient Hebrews, we find an elaborate code of rules in regard to the conduct and treatment of women on arriving at the age of puberty, during pregnancy and the menstrual periods, and at childbirth. Among the Cherokees the presence of a woman under any of these conditions, or even the presence of any one who has come from a house where such a woman resides, is considered to neutralize all the effects of the doctor's treatment. For this reason all women, excepting those of the household, are excluded. A man is forbidden to enter, because he may have had intercourse with a tabued woman, or may have come in contact with her in some other way; and children also are shut out, because they may have come from a cabin where dwells a woman subject to exclusion. What is supposed to be the effect of the presence of a menstrual woman in the family of the patient is not clear; but judging from analogous customs in other tribes and from rules still enforced among the Cherokees, notwithstanding their long contact with the whites, it seems probable that in former times the patient was removed to a smaller house or temporary bark lodge built for his accommodation whenever the tabu as to women was prescribed by the doctor. Some of the old men assert that in former times sick persons were removed to the public townhouse, where they remained under the care of the doctors until they either recovered or died. A curious instance of this prohibition is given in the second Didûⁿlë'skï (rheumatism) formula from the Gahuni manuscript (see page 350), where the patient is required to abstain from touching a squirrel, a dog, a cat, a mountain trout, or a woman, and must also have a chair appropriated to his use alone during the four days that he is under treatment.

In cases of the children's disease known as Gûⁿwani'gista'ï (see formulas) it is forbidden to carry the child outdoors, but this is not to procure rest for the little one, or to guard against exposure to cold air, but because the birds send this disease, and should a bird chance to be flying by overhead at the moment the flapping of its wings would fan the disease back into the body of the patient.

ILLUSTRATION OF THE TABU.

On a second visit to the reservation the writer once had a practical illustration of the gaktû'ⁿata or tabu, which may be of interest as showing how little sanitary ideas have to do with these precautions. Having received several urgent invitations from Tsiskwa (Bird), an old shaman of considerable repute, who was anxious to talk, but confined to his bed by sickness, it was determined to visit him at his house, several miles distant. On arriving we found another doctor named Sû'ⁿkï (The Mink) in charge of the patient and were told that he had just that morning begun a four days' gaktûⁿta, which, among other provisions, excluded all visitors. It was of no use to argue that we had come by the express request of Tsiskwa. The laws of the gaktûⁿta were as immutable as those of the Medes and Persians, and neither doctor nor patient could hope for favorable results from the treatment unless the regulations were enforced to the letter. But although we might not enter the house; there was no reason why we should not talk to the old man, so seats were placed for us outside the door, while Tsiskwa lay stretched out on the bed just inside and The Mink perched himself on the fence a few yards distant to keep an eye on the proceedings. As there was a possibility that a white man might unconsciously affect the operation of the Indian medicine, the writer deemed it advisable to keep out of sight altogether, and accordingly took up a position just around the corner of the house, but within easy hearing distance, while the interpreter sat facing the doorway within a few feet of the sick man inside. Then began an animated conversation, Tsiskwa inquiring, through the interpreter, as to the purpose of the Government in gathering such information, wanting to know how we had succeeded with other shamans and asking various questions in regard to other tribes and their customs. The replies were given in the same manner, an attempt being also made to draw him out as to the extent of his own knowledge. Thus we talked until the old man grew weary, but throughout the whole of this singular interview neither party saw the other, nor was the gaktûⁿta violated by entering the house. From this example it must be sufficiently evident that the tabu as to visitors is not a hygienic precaution for securing greater quiet to the patient, or to prevent the spread of contagion, but that it is simply a religious observance of the tribe, exactly parallel to many of the regulations among the ancient Jews, as laid down in the book of Leviticus.

NEGLECT OF SANITARY REGULATIONS.

No rules are ever formulated as to fresh air or exercise, for the sufficient reason that the door of the Cherokee log cabin is always open, excepting at night and on the coldest days in winter, while the Indian is seldom in the house during his waking hours unless when necessity compels him. As most of their cabins are still built in the old Indian style, without windows, the open door furnishes the only means by which light is admitted to the interior, although when closed the fire on the hearth helps to make amends for the deficiency. On the other hand, no precautions are taken to guard against cold, dampness, or sudden drafts. During the greater part of the year whole families sleep outside upon the ground, rolled up in an old blanket. The Cherokee is careless of exposure and utterly indifferent to the simplest rules of hygiene. He will walk all day in a pouring rain clad only in a thin shirt and a pair of pants. He goes barefoot and frequently bareheaded nearly the entire year, and even on a frosty morning in late November, when the streams are of almost icy coldness, men and women will deliberately ford the river where the water is waist deep in preference to going a few hundred yards to a foot-log. At their dances in the open air men, women, and children, with bare feet and thinly clad, dance upon the damp ground from darkness until daylight, sometimes enveloped in a thick mountain fog which makes even the neighboring treetops invisible, while the mothers have their infants laid away under the bushes with only a shawl between them and the cold ground. In their ball plays also each young man, before going into the game, is subjected to an ordeal of dancing, bleeding, and cold plunge baths, without food or sleep, which must unquestionably waste his physical energy.

In the old days when the Cherokee was the lord of the whole country from the Savannah to the Ohio, well fed and warmly clad and leading an active life in the open air, he was able to maintain a condition of robust health notwithstanding the incorrectness of his medical ideas and his general disregard of sanitary regulations. But with the advent of the white man and the destruction of the game all this was changed. The East Cherokee of to-day is a dejected being; poorly fed, and worse clothed, rarely tasting meat, cut off from the old free life, and with no incentive to a better, and constantly bowed down by a sense of helpless degradation in the presence of his conqueror. Considering all the circumstances, it may seem a matter of surprise that any of them are still in existence. As a matter of fact, the best information that could be obtained in the absence of any official statistics indicated a slow but steady decrease during the last five years. Only the constitutional vigor, inherited from their warrior ancestors, has enabled them to sustain the shock of the changed conditions of the last half century. The uniform good health of the children in the training school shows that the case is not hopeless, however, and that under favorable conditions, with a proper food supply and a regular mode of living, the Cherokee can hold his own with the white man.

THE SWEAT BATH-BLEEDING—RUBBING—BATHING.

In addition to their herb treatment the Cherokees frequently resort to sweat baths, bleeding, rubbing, and cold baths in the running stream, to say nothing of the beads and other conjuring paraphernalia generally used in connection with the ceremony. The sweat bath was in common use among almost all the tribes north of Mexico excepting the central and eastern Eskimo, and was considered the great cure-all in sickness and invigorant in health. Among many tribes it appears to have been regarded as a ceremonial observance, but the Cherokees seem to have looked upon it simply as a medical application, while the ceremonial part was confined to the use of the plunge bath. The person wishing to make trial of the virtues of the sweat bath entered the â'sï, a small earth-covered log house only high enough to allow of sitting down. After divesting himself of his clothing, some large bowlders, previously heated in a fire, were placed near him, and over them was poured a decoction of the beaten roots of the wild parsnip. The door was closed so that no air could enter from the outside, and the patient sat in the sweltering steam until he was in a profuse perspiration and nearly choked by the pungent fumes of the decoction. In accordance with general Indian practice it may be that he plunged into the river before resuming his clothing; but in modern times this part of the operation is omitted and the patient is drenched with cold water instead. Since the âsï has gone out of general use the sweating takes place in the ordinary dwelling, the steam being confined under a blanket wrapped around the patient. During the prevalence of the smallpox epidemic among the Cherokees at the close of the late war the sweat bath was universally called into requisition to stay the progress of the disease, and as the result about three hundred of the band died, while many of the survivors will carry the marks of the visitation to the grave. The sweat bath, with the accompanying cold water application, being regarded as the great panacea, seems to have been resorted to by the Indians in all parts of the country whenever visited by smallpox—originally introduced by the whites—and in consequence of this mistaken treatment they have died, in the language of an old writer, "like rotten sheep" and at times whole tribes have been almost swept away. Many of the Cherokees tried to ward off the disease by eating the flesh of the buzzard, which they believe to enjoy entire immunity from sickness, owing to its foul smell, which keeps the disease spirits at a distance.

Bleeding is resorted to in a number of cases, especially in rheumatism and in preparing for the ball play. There are two methods of performing the operation, bleeding proper and scratching, the latter being preparatory to rubbing on the medicine, which is thus brought into more direct contact with the blood. The bleeding is performed with a small cupping horn, to which suction is applied in the ordinary manner, after scarification with a flint or piece of broken glass. In the blood thus drawn out the shaman claims sometimes to find a minute pebble, a sharpened stick or something of the kind, which he asserts to be the cause of the trouble and to have been conveyed into the body of the patient through the evil spells of an enemy. He frequently pretends to suck out such an object by the application of the lips alone, without any scarification whatever. Scratching is a painful process and is performed with a brier, a flint arrowhead, a rattlesnake's tooth, or even with a piece of glass, according to the nature of the ailment, while in preparing the young men for the ball play the shaman uses an instrument somewhat resembling a comb, having seven teeth made from the sharpened splinters of the leg bone of a turkey. The scratching is usually done according to a particular pattern, the regular method for the ball play being to draw the scratcher four times down the upper part of each arm, thus making twenty-eight scratches each about 6 inches in length, repeating the operation on each arm below the elbow and on each leg above and below the knee. Finally, the instrument is drawn across the breast from the two shoulders so as to form a cross; another curving stroke is made to connect the two upper ends of the cross, and the same pattern is repeated on the back, so that the body is thus gashed in nearly three hundred places. Although very painful for a while, as may well be supposed, the scratches do not penetrate deep enough to result seriously, excepting in some cases where erysipelas sets in. While the blood is still flowing freely the medicine, which in this case is intended to toughen the muscles of the player, is rubbed into the wounds after which the sufferer plunges into the stream and washes off the blood. In order that the blood may flow the longer without clotting it is frequently scraped off with a small switch as it flows. In rheumatism and other local diseases the scratching is confined to the part affected. The instrument used is selected in accordance with the mythologic theory, excepting in the case of the piece of glass, which is merely a modern makeshift for the flint arrowhead.

Rubbing, used commonly for pains and swellings of the abdomen, is a very simple operation performed with the tip of the finger or the palm of the hand, and can not be dignified with the name of massage. In one of the Gahuni formulas for treating snake bites (page 351) the operator is told to rub in a direction contrary to that in which the snake coils itself, because "this is just the same as uncoiling it." Blowing upon the part affected, as well as upon the head, hands, and other parts of the body, is also an important feature of the ceremonial performance. In one of the formulas it is specified that the doctor must blow first upon the right hand of the patient, then upon the left foot, then upon the left hand, and finally upon the right foot, thus making an imaginary cross.

Bathing in the running stream, or "going to water," as it is called, is one of their most frequent medico-religious ceremonies, and is performed on a great variety of occasions, such as at each new moon, before eating the new food at the green corn dance, before the medicine dance and other ceremonial dances before and after the ball play, in connection with the prayers for long life, to counteract the effects of bad dreams or the evil spells of an enemy, and as a part of the regular treatment in various diseases. The details of the ceremony are very elaborate and vary according to the purpose for which it is performed, but in all cases both shaman and client are fasting from the previous evening, the ceremony being generally performed just at daybreak. The bather usually dips completely under the water four or seven times, but in some cases it is sufficient to pour the water from the hand upon the head and breast. In the ball play the ball sticks are dipped into the water at the same time. While the bather is in the water the shaman is going through with his part of the performance on the bank and draws omens from the motion of the beads between his thumb and finger, or of the fishes in the water. Although the old customs are fast dying out this ceremony is never neglected at the ball play, and is also strictly observed by many families on occasion of eating the new corn, at each new moon, and on other special occasions, even when it is necessary to break the ice in the stream for the purpose, and to the neglect of this rite the older people attribute many of the evils which have come upon the tribe in later days. The latter part of autumn is deemed the most suitable season of the year for this ceremony, as the leaves which then cover the surface of the stream are supposed to impart their medicinal virtues to the water.

SHAMANS AND WHITE PHYSICIANS.

Of late years, especially since the establishment of schools among them, the Cherokees are gradually beginning to lose confidence in the abilities of their own doctors and are becoming more disposed to accept treatment from white physicians. The shamans are naturally jealous of this infringement upon their authority and endeavor to prevent the spread of the heresy by asserting the convenient doctrine that the white man's medicine is inevitably fatal to an Indian unless eradicated from the system by a continuous course of treatment for four years under the hands of a skillful shaman. The officers of the training school established by the Government a few years ago met with considerable difficulty on this account for some time, as the parents insisted on removing the children at the first appearance of illness in order that they might be treated by the shamans, until convinced by experience that the children received better attention at the school than could possibly be had in their own homes. In one instance, where a woman was attacked by a pulmonary complaint akin to consumption, her husband, a man of rather more than the usual amount of intelligence, was persuaded to call in the services of a competent white physician, who diagnosed the case and left a prescription. On a second visit, a few days later, he found that the family, dreading the consequences of this departure from old customs, had employed a shaman, who asserted that the trouble was caused by a sharpened stick which some enemy bad caused to be imbedded in the woman's side. He accordingly began a series of conjurations for the removal of the stick, while the white physician and his medicine were disregarded, and in due time the woman died. Two children soon followed her to the grave, from the contagion or the inherited seeds of the same disease, but here also the sharpened sticks were held responsible, and, notwithstanding the three deaths under such treatment, the husband and father, who was at one time a preacher still has faith in the assertions of the shaman. The appointment of a competent physician to look after the health of the Indians would go far to eradicate these false ideas and prevent much sickness and suffering; but, as the Government has made no such provision, the Indians, both on and off the reservation, excepting the children in the home school, are entirely without medical care.

MEDICINE DANCES.

The Cherokees have a dance known as the Medicine Dance, which is generally performed in connection with other dances when a number of people assemble for a night of enjoyment. It possesses no features of special interest and differs in no essential respect from a dozen other of the lesser dances. Besides this, however, there was another, known as the Medicine Boiling Dance, which, for importance and solemn ceremonial, was second only to the great Green Corn Dance. It has now been discontinued on the reservation for about twenty years. It took place in the fall, probably preceding the Green Corn Dance, and continued four days. The principal ceremony in connection with it was the drinking of a strong decoction of various herbs, which acted as a violent emetic and purgative. The usual fasting and going to water accompanied the dancing and medicine-drinking.

DESCRIPTION OF SYMPTOMS.

It is exceedingly difficult to obtain from the doctors any accurate statement of the nature of a malady, owing to the fact that their description of the symptoms is always of the vaguest character, while in general the name given to the disease by the shaman expresses only his opinion as to the occult cause of the trouble. Thus they have definite names for rheumatism, toothache, boils, and a few other ailments of like positive character, but beyond this their description of symptoms generally resolves itself into a statement that the patient has bad dreams, looks black around the eyes, or feels tired, while the disease is. assigned such names as "when they dream of snakes," "when they dream of fish," "when ghosts trouble them," "when something is making something else eat them," or "when the food is changed," i.e., when a witch causes it to sprout and grow in the body of the patient or transforms it into a lizard, frog, or sharpened stick.

THE PAY OF THE SHAMAN.

The consideration which the doctor receives for his services is called ugista'`tï, a word of doubtful etymology, but probably derived from the verb tsï'giû, "I take" or "I eat." In former times this was generally a deer-skin or a pair of moccasins, but is now a certain quantity of cloth, a garment, or a handkerchief. The shamans disclaim the idea that the ugista'`tï is pay, in our sense of the word, but assert that it is one of the agencies in the removal and banishment of the disease spirit. Their explanation is somewhat obscure, but the cloth seems to be intended either as an offering to the disease spirit, as a ransom to procure the release of his intended victim, or as a covering to protect the hand of a shaman while engaged in pulling the disease from the body of the patient. The first theory, which includes also the idea of vicarious atonement, is common to many primitive peoples. Whichever maybe the true explanation, the evil influence of the disease is believed to enter into the cloth, which must therefore be sold or given away by the doctor, as otherwise it will cause his death when the pile thus accumulating reaches the height of his head. No evil results seem to follow its transfer from the shaman to a third party. The doctor can not bestow anything thus received upon a member of his own family unless that individual gives him something in return. If the consideration thus received, however, be anything eatable, the doctor may partake along with the rest of the family. As a general rule the doctor makes no charge for his services, and the consideration is regarded as a free-will offering. This remark applies only to the medical practice, as the shaman always demands and receives a fixed remuneration for performing love charms, hunting ceremonials, and other conjurations of a miscellaneous character. Moreover, whenever the beads are used the patient must furnish a certain quantity of new cloth upon which to place them, and at the close of the ceremony the doctor rolls up the cloth, beads and all, and takes them away with him. The cloth thus received by the doctor for working with the beads must not be used by him, but must be sold. In one instance a doctor kept a handkerchief which he received for his services, but instead sold a better one of his own. Additional cloth is thus given each time the ceremony is repeated, each time a second four days' course of treatment is begun, and as often as the doctor sees fit to change his method of procedure. Thus, when he begins to treat a sick man for a disease caused by rabbits, he expects to receive a certain ugista'`ti; but, should he decide after a time that the terrapin or the red bird is responsible for the, trouble, he adopts a different course of treatment, for which another ugista'`ti is necessary. Should the sickness not yield readily to his efforts, it is because the disease animal requires a greater ugista'`ti, and the quantity of cloth must be doubled, so that on the whole the doctrine is a very convenient one for the shaman. In many of the formulas explicit directions are given as to the pay which the shaman is to receive for performing the ceremony. In one of the Gatigwanasti formulas, after specifying the amount of cloth to be paid, the writer of it makes the additional proviso that it must be "pretty good cloth, too," asserting as a clincher that "this is what the old folks said a long time ago."

The ugista'`ti can not be paid by either one of a married couple to the other, and, as it is considered a necessary accompaniment of the application, it follows that a shaman can not treat his own wife in sickness, and vice versa. Neither can the husband or wife of the sick person send for the doctor, but the call must come from some one of the blood relatives of the patient. In one instance within the writer's knowledge a woman complained that her husband was very sick and needed a doctor's attention, but his relatives were taking no steps in the matter and it was not permissible for her to do so.

CEREMONIES FOR GATHERING PLANTS AND PREPARING MEDICINE.

There are a number of ceremonies and regulations observed in connection with the gathering of the herbs, roots, and barks, which can not be given in detail within the limits of this paper. In searching for his medicinal plants the shaman goes provided with a number of white and red beads, and approaches the plant from a certain direction, going round it from right to left one or four times, reciting certain prayers the while. He then pulls up the plant by the roots and drops one of the beads into the hole and covers it up with the loose earth. In one of the formulas for hunting ginseng the hunter addresses the mountain as the "Great Man" and assures it that he comes only to take a small piece of flesh (the ginseng) from its side, so that it seems probable that the bead is intended as a compensation to the earth for the plant thus torn from her bosom. In some cases the doctor must pass by the first three plants met until he comes to the fourth, which he takes and may then return for the others. The bark is always taken from the east side of the tree, and when the root or branch is used it must also be one which runs out toward the east, the reason given being that these have imbibed more medical potency from the rays of the sun.

When the roots, herbs, and barks which enter into the prescription have been thus gathered the doctor ties them up into a convenient package, which he takes to a running stream and casts into the water with appropriate prayers. Should the package float, as it generally does, he accepts the fact as an omen that his treatment will be successful. On the other band, should it sink, he concludes that some part of the preceding ceremony has been improperly carried out and at once sets about procuring a new package, going over the whole performance from the beginning. Herb-gathering by moonlight, so important a feature in European folk medicine, seems to be no part of Cherokee ceremonial. There are fixed regulations in regard to the preparing of the decoction, the care of the medicine during the continuance of the treatment, and the disposal of what remains after the treatment is at an end. In the arrangement of details the shaman frequently employs the services of a lay assistant. Id these degenerate days a number of upstart pretenders to the healing art have arisen in the tribe and endeavor to impose upon the ignorance of their fellows by posing as doctors, although knowing next to nothing of the prayers and ceremonies, without which there can be no virtue in the application. These impostors are sternly frowned down and regarded with the utmost contempt by the real professors, both men and women, who have been initiated into the sacred mysteries and proudly look upon themselves as conservators of the ancient ritual of the past.

THE CHEROKEE GODS AND THEIR ABIDING PLACES.

After what has been said in elucidation of the theories involved in the medical formulas, the most important and numerous of the series, but little remains to be added in regard to the others, beyond what is contained in the explanation accompanying each one. A few points, however, may be briefly noted.

The religion of the Cherokees, like that of most of our North American tribes, is zootheism or animal worship, with the survival of that earlier stage designated by Powell as hecastotheism, or the worship of all things tangible, and the beginnings of a higher system in which the elements and the great powers of nature are deified. Their pantheon includes gods in the heaven above, on the earth beneath, and in the waters under the earth, but of these the animal gods constitute by far the most numerous class, although the elemental gods are more important. Among the animal gods insects and fishes occupy a subordinate place, while quadrupeds, birds, and reptiles are invoked almost constantly. The uktena (a mythic great horned serpent), the rattlesnake, and the terrapin, the various species of hawk, and the rabbit, the squirrel, and the dog are the principal animal gods. The importance of the god bears no relation to the size of the animal, and in fact the larger animals are but seldom invoked. The spider also occupies a prominent place in the love and life-destroying formulas, his duty being to entangle the soul of his victim in the meshes of his web or to pluck it from the body of the doomed man and drag it way to the black coffin in the Darkening Land.

Among what may be classed as elemental gods the principal are fire, water, and the sun, all of which are addressed under figurative names. The sun is called Une″lanû'hï, "the apportioner," just as our word moon means originally "the measurer." Indians and Aryans alike, having noticed how these great luminaries divide and measure day and night, summer and winter, with never varying regularity, have given to each a name which should indicate these characteristics, thus showing how the human mind constantly moves on along the same channels. Missionaries have naturally, but incorrectly, assumed this apportioner of all things to be the suppositional "Great Spirit" of the Cherokees and hence the word is used in the Bible translation as synonymous with God. In ordinary conversation and in the lesser myths the sun is called Nû′ⁿtâ. The sun is invoked chiefly by the ball-player, while the hunter prays to the fire; but every important ceremony—whether connected with medicine, love, hunting, or the ball play—contains a prayer to the "Long Person," the formulistic name for water, or, more strictly speaking, for the river. The wind, the storm, the cloud, and the frost are also invoked in different formulas.

But few inanimate gods are included in the category, the principal being the Stone, to which the shaman prays while endeavoring to find a lost article by means of a swinging pebble suspended by a string; the Flint, invoked when the shaman is about to scarify the patient with a flint arrow-head before rubbing on the medicine; and the Mountain, which is addressed in one or two of the formulas thus far translated. Plant gods do not appear prominently, the chief one seeming to be the ginseng, addressed in the formulas as the "Great Man" or "Little Man," although its proper Cherokee name signifies the "Mountain Climber."

A number of personal deities are also invoked, the principal being the Red Man. He is one of the greatest of the gods, being repeatedly called upon in formulas of all kinds, and is hardly subordinate to the Fire, the Water, or the Sun. His identity is as yet uncertain, but he seems to be intimately connected with the Thunder family. In a curious marginal note in one of the Gahuni formulas (page 350), it is stated that when the patient is a woman the doctor must pray to the Red Man, but when treating a man he must pray to the Red Woman, so that this personage seems to have dual sex characteristics. Another god invoked in the hunting songs is Tsu'l`kalû', or "Slanting Eyes" (see Cherokee Myths), a giant hunter who lives in one of the great mountains of the Blue Ridge and owns all the game. Others are the Little Men, probably the two Thunder boys; the Little People, the fairies who live in the rock cliffs; and even the De'tsata, a diminutive sprite who holds the place of our Puck. One unwritten formula, which could not be obtained correctly by dictation, was addressed to the "Red-Headed Woman, whose hair hangs down to the ground."

The personage invoked is always selected in accordance with the theory of the formula and the duty to be performed. Thus, when a sickness is caused by a fish, the Fish-hawk, the Heron, or some other fish-eating bird is implored to come and seize the intruder and destroy it, so that the patient may find relief. When the trouble is caused by a worm or an insect, some insectivorous bird is called in for the same purpose. When a flock of redbirds is pecking at the vitals of the sick man the Sparrow-hawk is brought down to scatter them, and when the rabbit, the great mischief-maker, is the evil genius, he is driven out by the Rabbit-hawk. Sometimes after the intruder has been thus expelled "a small portion still remains," in the words of the formula, and accordingly the Whirlwind is called down from the treetops to carry the remnant to the uplands and there scatter it so that it shall never reappear. The hunter prays to the fire, from which he draws his omens; to the reed, from which he makes his arrows; to Tsu'l`kalû, the great lord of the game, and finally addresses in songs the very animals which he intends to kill. The lover prays to the Spider to hold fast the affections of his beloved one in the meshes of his web, or to the Moon, which looks down upon him in the dance. The warrior prays to the Red War-club, and the man about to set out on a dangerous expedition prays to the Cloud to envelop him and conceal him from his enemies.

Each spirit of good or evil has its distinct and appropriate place of residence. The Rabbit is declared to live in the broomsage on the hillside, the Fish dwells in a bend of the river under the pendant hemlock branches, the Terrapin lives in the great pond in the West, and the Whirlwind abides in the leafy treetops. Each disease animal, when driven away from his prey by some more powerful animal, endeavors to find shelter in his accustomed haunt. It must be stated here that the animals of the formulas are not the ordinary, everyday animals, but their great progenitors, who live in the upper world (galû'ⁿlati) above the arch of the firmament.

COLOR SYMBOLISM.

Color symbolism plays an important part in the shamanistic system of the Cherokees, no less than in that of other tribes. Each one of the cardinal points has its corresponding color and each color its symbolic meaning, so that each spirit invoked corresponds in color and local habitation with the characteristics imputed to him, and is connected with other spirits of the same name, but of other colors, living in other parts of the upper world and differing widely in their characteristics. Thus the Red Man, living in the east, is the spirit of power, triumph, and success, but the Black Man, in the West, is the spirit of death. The shaman therefore invokes the Red Man to the assistance of his client and consigns his enemy to the fatal influences of the Black Man.

The symbolic color system of the Cherokees, which will be explained more fully in connection with the formulas, is as follows:

East	red	success; triumph.
North	blue	defeat; trouble.
West	black	death.
South	white	peace; happiness.
Above?	brown	unascertained, but propitious.
—	yellow	about the same as blue.

There is a great diversity in the color systems of the various tribes, both as to the location and significance of the colors, but for obvious reasons black was generally taken as the symbol of death, while white and red signified, respectively, peace and war. It is somewhat remarkable that red was the emblem of power and triumph among the ancient Oriental nations no less than among the modern Cherokees.[1]

1   For more in regard to color symbolism, see Mallery's Pictographs of the North American Indians in Fourth Report of the Bureau of Ethnology, pp. 53-57, Washington, 1886; Gatschet's Creek Migration Legend, vol. 2, pp. 31-41, St. Louis, 1888; Brinton's Kiche Myths in Proceedings of the American Philosophical Society, vol. 19, pp. 646-647, Philadelphia, 1882.

IMPORTANCE ATTACHED TO NAMES.

In many of the formulas, especially those relating to love and to life-destroying, the shaman mentions the name and clan of his client, of the intended victim, or of the girl whose affections it is desired to win. The Indian regards his name, not as a mere label, but as a distinct part of his personality, just as much as are his eyes or his teeth, and believes that injury will result as surely from the malicious handling of his name as from a wound inflicted on any part of his physical organism. This belief was found among the various tribes from the Atlantic to the Pacific, and has occasioned a number of curious regulations in regard to the concealment and change of names. It may be on this account that both Powhatan and Pocahontas are known in history under assumed appellations, their true names having been concealed from the whites until the pseudonyms were too firmly established to be supplanted. Should his prayers have no apparent effect when treating a patient for some serious illness, the shaman sometimes concludes that the name is affected, and accordingly goes to water, with appropriate ceremonies, and christens the patient with a new name, by which he is henceforth to be known. He then begins afresh, repeating the formulas with the new name selected for the patient, in the confident hope that his efforts will be crowned with success.

LANGUAGE OF THE FORMULAS.

A few words remain to be said in regard to the language of the formulas. They are full of archaic and figurative expressions, many of which are unintelligible to the common people, and some of which even the shamans themselves are now unable to. explain. These archaic forms, like the old words used by our poets, lend a peculiar beauty which can hardly be rendered in a translation. They frequently throw light on the dialectic evolution of the language, as many words found now only in the nearly extinct Lower Cherokee dialect occur in formulas which in other respects are written in the Middle or Upper dialect. The R sound, the chief distinguishing characteristic of the old Lower dialect, of course does not occur, as there are no means of indicating it in the Cherokee syllabary. Those who are accustomed to look to the Bible for all beauty in sacred expression will be surprised to find that these formulas abound in the loftiest flights of poetic imagery. This is especially true of the prayers used to win the love of a woman or to destroy the life of an enemy, in which we find such expressions as—"Now your soul fades away—your spirit shall grow less and dwindle away, never to reappear;" "Let her be completely veiled in loneliness—O Black Spider, may you hold her soul in your web, so that it may never get through the meshes;" and the final declaration of the lover, "Your soul has come into the very center of my soul, never to turn away."

In the translation it has been found advisable to retain as technical terms a few words which could not well be rendered literally, such as ada'wëhï and ugistâ'`tï. These words will be found explained in the proper place. Transliterations of the Cherokee text of the formulas are given, but it must be distinctly understood that the translations are intended only as free renderings of the spirit of the originals, exact translations with grammatic and glossarial notes being deferred until a more extended study of the language has been made, when it is hoped to present with more exactness of detail the whole body of the formulas, of which the specimens here given are but a small portion.

The facsimile formulas are copies from the manuscripts now in possession of the Bureau of Ethnology, and the portraits are from photographs taken by the author in the field.

SPECIMEN FORMULAS.

NOTE ON THE ORTHOGRAPHY AND TRANSLATION.

In the Cherokee text both d and g have a medial sound, approximating the sounds of *t* and *k* respectively. The other letters are pronounced in regular accordance with the alphabet of the Bureau of Ethnology. The language abounds in nasal and aspirate sounds, the most difficult of the latter being the aspirate ʻl, which to one familiar only with English sounds like *tl*.

A few words whose meaning could not be satisfactorily ascertained have been distinctively indicated in the Cherokee text by means of italics. In the translation the corresponding expression has been queried, or the space left entirely blank. On examining the text the student can not fail to be struck by the great number of verbs ending in *iga*. This is a peculiar form hardly ever used excepting in these formulas, where almost every paragraph contains one or more such verbs. It implies that the subject has just come and is now performing the action, and that he came for that purpose. In addition to this, many of these verbs may be either assertive or imperative (expressing entreaty), according to the accent. Thus *hatûⁿ-gani'ga* means "you have just come and are listening and it is for that purpose you came." By slightly accenting the final syllable it becomes "come at once to listen." It will thus be seen that the great majority of the formulas are declarative rather than petitional in form-laudatory rhapsodies instead of prayers, in the ordinary sense of the word.

MEDICINE.

DIDÛⁿLË'SKÏ ADANÛⁿ'WÂTÏ KANÂHË'SKÏ.

Sgë! Ha-Nûⁿdûgiûⁿyï tsûl`dâ'histï, Gi`lï Gigage'ï, hanâ'gwa hatûⁿgani'ga usïnuli'yu. Hida'wëhi-gâgû', gahu'stï tsan'ultï nige'sûⁿna. Ha-diskwûlti'yû tï'nanugagï, ase'gwû nige'sûⁿna tsagista``tï adûⁿni'ga. Ulsg'eta hûⁿhihyûⁿstani'ga. Ha-usdig'iyu-gwû ha-e'la-wastûⁿ iyûⁿta dûhilâ'hïstani'ga.

Sgë! Ha-Uhûⁿtsâ`yï tsûl`dâ'histï Gi`lï Sa`ka'nï, hanâ'gwa hatûⁿgani'ga usïnuli'yu. Hida'wëhi-gâgû', gahu'stï tsanu'ltï nige'sûⁿna. Diskwûlti'yû ti'nanugaï', ase'gwû nige'sûⁿna tsagista``tï adûⁿni'ga. Ulsge'ta hûⁿhihyûⁿstani'ga, Ha-usdigi'yu-gwû ha-e'la-wastûⁿ iyû'ta dûhitâ'hïstani'ga.

Sgë! (Ha)-Usûhi'(-yï) tsûl`dâ'histï, Gi`l'ï Gûⁿnage'ï, hanâ'gwa hatûⁿgani'ga usïnuli'yû. Hida'wëhi-gâgû', gahu'sti tsanu'ltï nige'sû'ⁿna. Diskwûlti'yû tinanugagï', ase'gwû nige'sûⁿna tsagista``tï adûⁿni'ga. Ulsg'eta hûⁿhihyûⁿstani'ga. Ha-usdigi'yu-gwû ha-e'la-wastûⁿ iyûⁿta dûhitâ'hïstani'ga.

Sgë! Wa'halä' tsûl`dâ'histï, Gi``lï Tsûne'ga, hanâ'gwa hatûⁿgani'ga usïliuli'yu. Hida'wëhi-gâgû', gahu'sti tsanû'ltï nige'sûⁿna. Diskwûlti'yû ti'nanugagï, ase'gwû nige'sûⁿna tsagista``tï adûⁿni'ga. Ha-ulsge'ta hûⁿhihyûⁿstani'ga. Ha-usdigi'yu-gwû e'lawastûⁿ iyûⁿta dûhità'hïstani'ga.

Sgë! Wa'halä tsûl`dâ'histï Tû'ksï Tsûne'ga, hanâ'gwa hatûⁿgani'ga usïnuli'yu. Hida'wëhi-gâgû', gahu'sti tsanu'ltï nige'sûⁿna. Ha-kâ'lû *gayûske'la* tsatûⁿneli'ga. Utsïna'wa nulatänûⁿta.

(Degâsisisgûⁿï.)—Tûksï uhya'ska gûnsta`tï` na'skï igahi'ta gûnstâ'ï hï'skï iyuntale'gï tsûntûngi'ya. Ûⁿskwû'ta kïlû' atsâ'tastï sâ'gwa iyûtsâ'tastï,

83

nû`̀kï igû*ⁿ*kta`tï, naski-gwû' diûⁿlë'nïskâhï igûⁿyi'yï tsale'nihû. Nû`̀kine ûⁿskwû'ta kïlû' nû`̀kï iyatsâ'tastï. Uhyaska'hi-`nû ade'la degû`laï tä'lï unine'ga-gwû' nûⁿ'wâti-`nû' higûnehâ'ï uhyaskâ'hï usdi'a-gwû. Une'lagi-`nû sâï' agadâ'ï agadi'dï ûⁿ'ti-gwû' yïkï' âsi'yu-gwû na'ski-`nû aganûⁿli'eskâ'ï da'gûⁿstanehûⁿ'ï ü`taâ'ta. Hiä`-nu:' nûⁿ'wâtï: Yâ'na-Unatsësdâ'gï tsana'sehâ'ï sâ'i-`nû Kâ'ga-Asgûⁿ'tagë tsana'sehâ'ï, sâi-`nû *Egûⁿlï*-gwû, sâi-nû' (U)wa'sgilï tsïgï' Egûⁿ'lï Usdi'a tsïgï', nûⁿyâ'hi-`nû tsuyë`dâ'ï Yâ'na-Utsësdâgï naskiyû' tsïgï', usdi'-gwû tsïgï'. Egûⁿ'lï (u)wa'sgilï tsïgï'; sâ'ï Wâ'tige Unas(te')tsa tsïgï', sâ'i-`nû Ûⁿage Tsunaste'tsa, Niga'ta unaste'tsa gesâ'ï.

Sunale'-gwû ale'ndï adanûⁿ'wâtï; tä'line e'ladï tsitkala'ï; tsâ'ine u'lsaladï'`satû'; nû`̀kine igû' ts'kalâ'ï. Yeli'gwû' igesâ'ï. Nû'lstâiyanû'na gesâ'ï akanûⁿ'wi'skï, nasgwû' nulstaiyanû'na.

Translation.

FORMULA FOR TREATING THE CRIPPLER (RHEUMATISM).

Listen! Ha! In the Sun Land you repose, O Red Dog, O now you have swiftly drawn near to hearken. O great ada'wëhï[1], you never fail in anything. O, appear and draw near running, for your prey never escapes. You are now come to remove the intruder. Ha! You have settled a very small part of it far off there at the end of the earth.

Listen! Ha! In the Frigid Land you repose, O Blue Dog. O now you have swiftly drawn near to hearken. O great ad'âw hï, you never fail in anything. O, appear and draw near running, for your prey never escapes. You are now come to remove the intruder. Ha! You have settled a very small part of it far off there at the end of the earth.

Listen! Ha! In the darkening land you repose, O Black Dog. O, now you have swiftly drawn near to hearken. O great ada'wëhï, you never fail in anything. O, appear and draw near running, for your prey never escapes. You are now come to remove the intruder. Ha! You have settled a very small part of it far off there at the end of the earth.

Listen! On Wa'halä you repose, O White Dog. Oh, now you have swiftly drawn near to hearken. O great ada'wëhï, you never fail in anything. Oh, appear and draw near running, for your prey never escapes. You are now come to remove the intruder. Ha! You have settled a very small part of it far off there at the end of the earth.

Listen! On Wa'halä, you repose, O White Terrapin. O, now you have swiftly drawn near to hearken. O great ada'wëhï, you never fail in anything. Ha! It is for you to loosen its hold on the bone. Relief is accomplished.

(Prescription.)—Lay a terrapin shell upon (the spot) and keep it there while the five kinds (of spirits) listen. On finishing, then blow once. Repeat four times, beginning each time from the start. On finishing the fourth time, then blow four times. Have two white beads lying in the shell, together with a little of the medicine. Don't interfere with it, but have a good deal boiling in another vessel—a bowl will do very well—and rub it on warm while treating by applying the hands. And this is the medicine: What is called Yâ'na-Utsë'sta ("bear's bed," the Aspidium acrostichoides or Christmas fern); and the other is called Kâ'ga-Asgû'ⁿtagï ("crow's shin," the Adianthum pedatum or Maidenhair fern); and the other is the common Egû'ⁿlï (another fern); and the other is the Little Soft (-leaved) Egû'ⁿlï (Osmunda Cinnamonea or cinnamon fern), which grows in the rocks and resembles Yâna-Utsë'sta and is a small and soft (-leaved) Egû'ⁿlï. Another has brown roots and another has black roots. The roots of all should be (used).

Begin doctoring early in the morning; let the second (application) be while the sun is still near the horizon; the third when it has risen to a considerable height (10 a. m.); the fourth when it is above at noon. This is sufficient. (The doctor) must not eat, and the patient also must be fasting.

1   *Ada'wëhï* is a word used to designate one supposed to have supernatural powers, and is applied alike to human beings and to the spirits invoked in the formulas. Some of the mythic heroes famous for their magic deeds are spoken of as *ada'wëhï* (plural *anida'wëhï* or *anida'we*), but in its application to mortals the term is used only of the very greatest shamans. None of those now belonging to the band are considered worthy of being thus called, although the term was sometimes applied to one, Usawï, who died some years ago. In speaking of himself as an ada'wëhï, as occurs in some of the formulas, the shaman arrogates to himself the same powers that belong to the gods. Our nearest equivalent is the word magician, but this falls far short of the idea conveyed by the Cherokee word. In the bible translation the word is used as the equivalent of angel or spirit.]

Explanation.

As this formula is taken from the manuscript of Gahuni, who died nearly thirty years ago, no definite statement of the theory of the disease, or its treatment, can be given, beyond what is contained in the formula itself, which, fortunately, is particularly explicit; most doctors contenting themselves with giving only the words of the prayer, without noting the ceremonies or even the medicine used. There are various theories as to the cause of each disease, the most common idea in regard to rheumatism being that it is caused by the spirits of. the slain animals, generally the deer, thirsting for vengeance on the hunter, as has been already explained in the myth of the origin of disease and medicine.

The measuring-worm (Catharis) is also held to cause rheumatism, from the resemblance of its motions to those of a rheumatic patient, and the name of the worm *wahïlï'* is frequently applied also to the disease.

There are formulas to propitiate the slain animals, but these are a part of the hunting code and can only be noticed here, although it may be mentioned in passing that the hunter, when about to return to the settlement, builds a fire in the path behind him, in order that the deer chief may not be able to follow him to his home. The disease, figuratively called the intruder (ulsgéta), is regarded as a living being, and the verbs used in speaking of it show that it is considered to be long, like a snake or fish. It is brought by the deer chief and put into the body, generally the limbs, of the hunter, who at once begins to suffer intense pain. It can be driven out only by some more powerful animal spirit which is the natural enemy of the deer, usually the dog or the wolf. These animal gods live up above beyond the seventh heaven and are the great prototypes of which the earthly animals are only diminutive copies. They are commonly located at the four cardinal points, each of which has a peculiar formulistic name and a special color which applies to everything in the same connection. Thus the east, north, west, and south are respectively the Sun Land, the Frigid Land, the Darkening Land, and Wä'halä', while their respective mythologic colors are Red, Blue, Black, and White. Wä'halä' is said to be a mountain far to the south. The white or red spirits are generally invoked for peace, health, and other blessings, the red alone for the success of an under taking, the blue spirits to defeat the schemes of an enemy or bring down troubles upon him, and the black to compass his death. The white and red spirits are regarded as the most powerful, and one of these two is generally called upon to accomplish the final result.

In this case the doctor first invokes the Red Dog in the Sun Land, calling him a great adáwehi, to whom nothing is impossible and who never fails to accomplish his purpose. He is addressed as if out of sight in the distance and is implored to appear running swiftly to the help of the sick man. Then the supplication changes to an assertion and the doctor declares that the Red Dog has already arrived to take the disease and has borne away a small portion of it to the uttermost ends of the earth. In the second, third, and fourth paragraphs the Blue Dog of the Frigid Land, the Black Dog of the Darkening Land, and the White Dog of Wä'halä' are successively invoked in the same terms and each bears away a portion of the disease and disposes of it in the same way. Finally, in the fifth paragraph, the White Terrapin of Wä'halä' is invoked. He bears off the remainder of the disease and the doctor declares that relief is accomplished. The connection of the terrapin in this formula is not evident, beyond the fact that he is regarded as having great influence in disease, and in this case the beads and a portion of the medicine are kept in a terrapin shell placed upon the diseased part while the prayer is being recited.

The formulas generally consist of four paragraphs, corresponding to four steps in the medical ceremony. In this case there are five, the last being addressed to the terrapin instead of to a dog. The prayers are recited in an undertone hardly audible at the distance of a few feet, with the exception of the frequent ha, which seems to be used as an interjection to attract attention and is always uttered in a louder tone. The beads—which are here white, symbolic of relief—are of common use in connection with these formulas, and are held between the thumb and finger, placed upon a cloth on the ground, or, as in this case, put into a terrapin shell along with a small portion of the medicine. According to directions, the shell has no other part in the ceremony.

The blowing is also a regular part of the treatment, the doctor either holding the medicine in his mouth and blowing it upon the patient, or, as it seems to be the case here, applying the medicine by rubbing, and blowing his breath upon the spot afterwards. In some formulas the simple blowing of the breath constitutes the whole application. In this instance the doctor probably rubs the medicine upon the affected part while reciting the first paragraph in a whisper, after which he blows once upon the spot. The other paragraphs are recited in the same manner, blowing once after each. In this way the whole formula is repeated four times, with four blows at the end of the final repetition. The directions imply that the doctor blows only at the end of the whole formula, but this is not in accord with the regular mode of procedure and seems to be a mistake.

The medicine consists of a warm decoction of the roots of four varieties of fern, rubbed on with the hand. The awkward description of the species shows how limited is the Indian's power of botanic classification. The application is repeated four times during the same morning, beginning just at daybreak and ending at noon. Four is the sacred number running through every detail of these formulas, there being commonly four spirits invoked in four paragraphs, four blowings with four final blows, four herbs in the decoction, four applications, and frequently four days' gaktu^{n}ta or tabu. In this case no tabu is specified beyond the fact that both doctor and patient must be fasting. The tabu generally extends to salt or lye, hot food and women, while in rheumatism some doctors forbid the patient to eat the foot or leg of any animal, the reason given being that the limbs are generally the seat of the disease. For a similar reason the patient is also forbidden to eat or even to touch a squirrel, a buffalo, a eat, or any animal which "humps" itself. In the same way a scrofulous patient must not eat turkey, as that bird seems to have a scrofulous eruption on its head, while ball players must abstain from eating frogs, because the bones of that animal are brittle and easily broken.

HIÄ-NÛ' NASGWÛ' DIDÛⁿLË'SKÏ ADÂNÛ'ⁿWÂTÏ.

Asga'ya yûkanû'ⁿwï
Agë`ya Giagage'ï atätï'; agë``ya-nû yûkanû'ⁿwï
Asga'ya Gigage'ï atätï'.

Yû! Higë'`ya Gigage'ï tsûdante'lûhï gese'ï. Ulsge'ta hi'tsanu'y`tani'leï. Ha-Nûⁿdâgû'ⁿyï nûⁿta'tsûdälenû'hï gese'ï. Gasgilâ' gigage'ï tsusdi'ga tetsadï'ilë' detsala'siditë-gë'ï. Hanâ'gwa usïnuli'yu detsaldisi'yûï.

Utsï(nä')wa nu'tatanû'ⁿta. Usû'hita nutanû'na. Utsïnä'wa-gwû nigû'ⁿtisge'stï.

(Degâ'sisisgû'ⁿï)—Hiä-gwû' nigaû' kanâhe'ta. Nû``kiha nagû'ⁿ-kwʔtisgâ' dagû'ⁿstiskû'ï. Sâ'gwa nûⁿskwiû'ta gûnstû'ⁿï agûnstagi's-kâï hûⁿtsatasgâ'ï nû``kine-`nû ûⁿskwû'ta nû``kï nûⁿtsâtasgâ'ï. Hiä`nû' nûⁿwâtï: Egû'ⁿlï, Yâ'na-`nû Utsësdâ'gï, (U)wa'sgili tsïgï' Egû'ⁿlï, tä'lï tsinu'dalë'ha, Kâ'ga-`nû Asgû'ⁿtagë tsiûⁿnâ'sehâ'ï, Da'yï-`nû Uwâ'yï tsiûⁿnâ'sehâ'ï. Su'talï iyutale'gï unaste'tsa agâ'tï, uga'nawû-`nû' dagûnsta'`tisgâ'ï nû'ⁿwâtî asûⁿga`la'ï. Usû'hï adanû'ⁿwâtï. nu'`kï tsusû'hita dulsi'nisû'ⁿ adanû'ⁿwâtï. Ä`nawa'gi-`nû dilasula'gï gesû'ⁿï ûlë' tsïkani'kaga'ï gûw`sdi'-gwû utsawa'ta ä`nawa'-gwû-nû'.

Hiä-nû' gaktû'ⁿta gûlkwâ'gï tsusû'hita. Gûⁿwädana'datlahistï' nige'sûⁿna—Salâ'lï, gi`li-`nû, wë'sa-'nû, ä'tatsû-nû', a'mä-'nû', ani-gë'`ya-nû. Uda`lï' ya'kanûⁿwi'ya nû'`kiha tsusû'hita unädanä'lâtsi-tustï nige'sûⁿna. Gasgilâ'gi-`nû uwä'suⁿ-gwû' u'skïladi'stï uwä'sû nû'`kï tsusû'hita'. Disâ'i-`nû dega'sgilâ ûⁿ'tsa nû`nä' uwa'`tï yigesûï nû'`kï tsusû'hita.

Translation.

AND THIS ALSO IS FOR TREATING THE CRIPPLER.

Yû! O Red Woman, you have caused it. You have put the intruder under him. Ha! now you have come from the Sun Land. You have brought the small red seats, with your feet resting upon them. Ha! now they have swiftly moved away from you. Relief is accomplished. Let it not be for one night alone. Let the relief come at once.

(Prescription)—*(corner note at top.)* If treating a man one must say *Red Woman*, and if treating a woman one must say *Red Man*.

This is just all of the prayer. Repeat it four times while laying on the hands. After saying it over once, with the hands on (the body of the patient), take off the hands and blow once, and at the fourth repetition blow four times. And this is the medicine. Egû'ⁿlï (a species of fern). Yâ'-na-Utsë'sta ("bear's bed," the Aspidium acrostichoides or Christmas fern), *two* varieties of the soft-(leaved) Egû'ⁿlï (one, the small variety, is the Cinnamon fern, Osmunda cinnamonea), and what is called Kâ'ga Asgû'ⁿtagë ("crow's shin," the Adiantum pedatum or Maidenhair fern) and what is called Da'yï-Uwâ'yï ("beaver's paw"—not identified). Boil the roots of the six varieties together and apply the hands warm with the medicine upon them. Doctor in the evening. Doctor four consecutive nights. (The pay) is cloth and moccasins; or, if one does not have them, just a little dressed deerskin and some cloth.

And this is the tabu for seven nights. One must not touch a squirrel, a dog, a cat, the mountain trout, or women. If one is treating a married man they (sic) must not touch his wife for four nights. And he must sit on a seat by himself for four nights, and must not sit on the other seats for four nights.

Explanation.

The treatment and medicine in this formula are nearly the same as in that just given, which is also for rheumatism, both being written by Gahuni. The prayer differs in several respects from any other obtained, but as the doctor has been dead for years it is impossible to give a full explanation of all the points. This is probably the only formula in the collection in which the spirit invoked is the "Red Woman," but, as explained in the corner note at the top, this is only the form used instead of "Red Man," when the patient is a man. The Red Man, who is considered perhaps the most powerful god in the Cherokee pantheon, is in some way connected with the thunder, and is invoked in a large number of formulas. The change in the formula, according to the sex of the patient, brings to mind a belief in Irish folk medicine, that in applying certain remedies the doctor and patient must be of opposite sexes. The Red Man lives in the east, in accordance with the regular mythologic color theory, as already explained. The seats also are red, and the form of the verb indicates that the Red Woman is either standing upon them (plural) or sitting with her feet resting upon the rounds. These seats or chairs are frequently mentioned in the formulas, and always correspond in color with the spirit invoked. It is not clear why the Red Woman is held responsible for the disease, which is generally attributed to the revengeful efforts of the game, as already explained. In agreement with the regular form, the disease is said to be put under (not into) the patient. The assertion that the chairs "have swiftly moved away" would seem from analogy to mean that the disease has been placed upon the seats and thus borne away. The verb implies that the seats move by their own volition. Immediately afterward it is declared that relief is accomplished. The expression "usû'hita nutanû'na" occurs frequently in these formulas, and may mean either "let it not be for one night alone," or "let it not stay a single night," according to the context.

The directions specify not only the medicine and the treatment, but also the doctor's fee. From the form of the verb the tabu, except as regards the seat to be used by the sick person, seems to apply to both doctor and patient. It is not evident why the mountain trout is prohibited, but the dog, squirrel, and cat are tabued, as already explained, from the fact that these animals frequently assume positions resembling the cramped attitude common to persons afflicted by rheumatism. The cat is considered especially uncanny, as coming from the whites. Seven, as well as four, is a sacred number with the tribe, being also the number of their gentes. It will be noted that time is counted by nights instead of by days.

HIÂ' I'NATÛ YUNISKÛ'LTSA ADANÛ'NWÂTÎ.

1. *Dûnu'wa*, dûnu'wa, dûnu'wa, dûnu'wa, dûnu'wa, dûnu'wa (*song*).
    Sgë! Ha-Walâ'sï-gwû tsûⁿlûⁿtani'ga.
2. Dayuha, dayuha, dayuha, dayuha dayuha (*song*).
    Sgë! Ha-*Usugï*-gwû tsûⁿ-lûⁿ-tani'ga.

(Degâ'sisisgû'ⁿï).—Kanâgi'ta nâyâ'ga hiä' dilentisg'ûⁿï. Ta'lï igûⁿ-kwʔta`tï, ûlë' talinë' tsutanûⁿna nasgwû' tâ'lï igûⁿkwʔta`tï. Tsâ'la aganûⁿlieskâï' tsâ'la yikani'gûⁿgû'âï' watsi'la-gwû ganûⁿli'yëtï uniskûl`tsûⁿï. Nûˊˋkï nagade'stisgâï' aganûⁿli'esgûⁿï. Akskû'nï gades-t'a`tï, nûû`kï nagade' sta hûⁿtsatasgâ'ï. Hiä-`nû' i'natû akti'sï udestâ'ï yigû'n`ka, naski-`nû' tsagadû'lägisgâ'ï iyu'stï gatgû'ⁿi.

Translation.

THIS IS TO TREAT THEM IF THEY ARE BITTEN BY A SNAKE.

1. Dûnu'wa, dûnu'wa, dûnu'wa, dûnu'wa, dûnu'wa, dûnu'wa.
    Listen! Ha! It is only a common frog which has passed by and put it (the intruder) into you.
2. Dayuha', dayuha, dayuha, dayuha, dayuha.
    Listen! Ha! It is only an *Us''gï* which has passed by and put it into you.

(Prescription.)—Now this at the beginning is a song. One should say it twice and also say the second line twice. Rub tobacco (juice) on the bite for some time, or if there be no tobacco just rub on saliva once. In rubbing it on, one must go around four times. Go around toward the left and blow four times in a circle. This is because in lying down the snake always coils to the right and this is just the same (*lit.* "means like") as uncoiling it.

Explanation.

This is also from the manuscript book of Gahuni, deceased, so that no explanation could be obtained from the writer. The formula consists of a song of two verses, each followed by a short recitation.

The whole is repeated, according to the directions, so as to make four verses or songs; four, as already stated, being the sacred number running through most of these formulas. Four blowings and four circuits in the rubbing are also specified. The words used in the songs are sometimes composed of unmeaning syllables, but in this case dûnuwa and dayuha seem to have a meaning, although neither the interpreter nor the shaman consulted could explain them, which may be because the words have become altered in the song, as frequently happens. Dûnu'wa appears to be an old verb, meaning "it has penetrated," probably referring to the tooth of the reptile. These medicine songs are always sung in a low plaintive tone, somewhat resembling a lullaby. Usu'`gï also is without explanation, but is probably the name of some small reptile or batrachian.

As in this case the cause of the trouble is evident, the Indians have no theory to account for it. It may be remarked, however, that when one dreams of being bitten, the same treatment and ceremonies must be used as for the actual bite; otherwise, although perhaps years afterward, a similar inflammation will appear on the spot indicated in the dream, and will be followed by the same fatal consequences, The rattlesnake is regarded as a supernatural being or ada'wehi, whose favor must be propitiated, and great pains are taken not to offend him. In consonance with this idea it is never said among the people that a person has been bitten by a snake, but that he has been "scratched by a brier." In the same way, when an eagle has been shot for a ceremonial dance, it is announced that "a snowbird has been killed," the purpose being to deceive the rattlesnake or eagle spirits which might be listening.

The assertion that it is "only a common frog" or" only an Usu'?gï brings out another characteristic idea of these formulas. Whenever the ailment is of a serious character, or, according to the Indian theory, whenever it is due to the influence of some powerful disease spirit the doctor always endeavors to throw contempt upon the intruder, and convince it of his own superior power by asserting the sickness to be the work of some inferior being, just as a white physician might encourage a patient far gone with consumption by telling him that the, illness was only a slight cold. Sometimes there is a regular scale of depreciation, the doctor first ascribing the disease to a rabbit or groundhog or some other weak animal, then in succeeding paragraphs mentioning other still less important animals and finally declaring it to be the work of a mouse, a small fish, or some other insignificant creature. In this instance an ailment caused by the rattlesnake, the most dreaded of the animal spirits, is ascribed to a frog, one of the least importance.

In applying the remedy the song is probably sung while rubbing the tobacco juice around the wound. Then the short recitation is repeated and the doctor blows four times in a circle about the spot.

The whole ceremony is repeated four times. The curious directions for uncoiling the snake have parallels in European folk medicine.

GÛⁿWÂNI'GISTÂ'Ï ADANU'ⁿWÂTÏ.

Sgë! Ha-tsida'wëiyu, gahus'tï aginúl`tï nige'sûⁿna. Gûⁿgwädaga'anadɂdiyû' tsida'wëi'yu. Ha-Wähuhu'-gwû hitagu'sgastanë`hëi. Ha-nâ'gwa hü`kikahûⁿnû' ha-dustü`'gahï digesûⁿ'ï, iyûⁿ'ta wûⁿ`kidâ'hïstani'ga.

Sgë! Ha-tsida'wëi'yu, gahu'stï aginu'l`tï nige'sûⁿna. Gûⁿgwädaga'nadɂdiyû' tsida'wëi'yu. Ha-Uguku'-gwû hitagu'sgastanë'hei' udâhi'yu tag'u'sgastanë'hëi'. Ha-na'gwadi'na hûⁿkikahûⁿnû'. Hanânâ'hï digesûⁿ'ï, iyûⁿ'ta wûⁿ`kidâ'hïstani'ga.

Sgë! Ha-tsida'wëi'yu, gahu'stï aginu'l`tï nige'sûⁿna. Gûⁿgwädaga'nadɂdiyû' tsida'wëi'yu. Ha-Tsistu-gwû hitagu'sgastanë'hë'ï udâhi'yu tagu'sgastanë'hëi'. Ha-nâ'gwadi'na hûⁿkikahûⁿ'nû. Ha-sunûⁿda'sï iyûⁿ'ta kane'skawâ'dihï digesûⁿ'ï, wûⁿ`kidâ'hïstani'ga.

Sgë! Ha-tsida'wëi'yu, gahu'stï aginu'l`tï nige'sûⁿna. Gûⁿgwädaga'nadɂdi'yûtsida'wëi'yu. Ha-De'tsata'-gwû (hi)tagu'sgastanë'hëi udâhi'yu tagu'sgastanë'hëi'. Ha-nâ'gwadi'na hûⁿkikahûⁿ'na. Ha-udâ'tale'ta digesûⁿ'ï, iyûⁿ'ta wûⁿ`kidâ'hïstani'ga.

(Degâ'sisisgûⁿ'ï)-Hiä'-skïnï' unsdi'ya dïkanûⁿwâtï tsa`natsa'yihâ'ï tsaniska'ihaɂï;gûⁿwani'gista'ïhi'anûdïɂsgaï'. Ämä' dûtsati'stïsgâ'ïnûⁿ`ki tsusûⁿhita dïkanûⁿwâtï Ulsinide'na dakanûⁿwïsgâ'ï. Ûⁿtsa iyûⁿta witunini'dastï yigesâ'ï.

Translation.

TO TREAT THEM WHEN SOMETHING IS CAUSING SOMETHING TO EAT THEM.

Listen! Ha! I am a great ada'wehi, I never fail in anything. I surpass all others-I am a great ada'wehi. Ha! It is a mere screech owl that has frightened him. Ha! now I have put it away in the laurel thickets. There I compel it to remain,

Listen! Ha! I am a great ada'wehi, I never fail in anything. I surpass all others—I am a great ada'wehi. Ha! It is a mere hooting owl that has frightened him. Undoubtedly that has frightened him. Ha! At once I have put it away in the spruce thickets. Ha! There I compel it to remain.

Listen! Ha! I am a great ada'wehi, I never fail in anything. I surpass all others—I am a great ada'wehi. Ha! It is only a rabbit that has frightened him. Undoubtedly that has frightened him. Ha! Instantly I have put it away on the mountain ridge. Ha! There in the broom sage I compel it to remain.

Listen! Ha! I am a great ada'wehi, I never fail in anything. I surpass all others—I am a great ada'wehi. Ha! It is only a mountain sprite that has frightened him. Undoubtedly that has frightened him. Ha! Instantly I have put it away on the bluff. Ha! There I compel it to remain.

(Prescription)—Now this is to treat infants if they are affected by crying and nervous fright. (Then) it is said that something is causing something to eat them. To treat them one may blow water on them for four nights. Doctor them just before dark. Be sure not to carry them about outside the house.

Explanation.

The Cherokee name for this disease is Guⁿwani'gistâĭ', which signifies that "something is causing something to eat," or gnaw the vitals of the patient. The disease attacks only infants of tender age and the symptoms are nervousness and troubled sleep, from which the child wakes suddenly crying as if frightened. The civilized doctor would regard these as symptoms of the presence of worms, but although the Cherokee name might seem to indicate the same belief, the real theory is very different.

Cherokee mothers sometimes hush crying children by telling them that the screech owl is listening out in the woods or that the De'tsata—a malicious little dwarf who lives in caves in the river bluffs—will come and get them. This quiets the child for the time and is so far successful, but the animals, or the De'tsata, take offense at being spoken of in this way, and visit their displeasure upon the *children born to the mother afterward*. This they do by sending an animal into the body of the child to gnaw its vitals. The disease is very common and there are several specialists who devote their attention to it, using various formulas and prescriptions. It is also called ätawi'nëhï, signifying that it is caused by the "dwellers in the forest," i. e., the wild game and birds, and some doctors declare that it is caused by the revengeful comrades of the animals, especially birds, killed by the father of the child, the animals tracking the slayer to his home by the blood drops on the leaves. The next formula will throw more light upon this theory.

In this formula the doctor, who is certainly not overburdened with modesty, starts out by asserting that he is a great ada'wehi, who never fails and who surpasses all others. He then declares that, the disease is caused by a more screech owl, which he at once banishes to the laurel thicket. In the succeeding paragraphs he reiterates his former boasting, but asserts in turn that the trouble is caused by a mere hooting owl, a rabbit, or even by the De'tsata, whose greatest exploit is hiding the arrows of the boys, for which the youthful hunters do not hesitate to rate him soundly. These various mischief-makers the doctor banishes to their proper haunts, the hooting owl to the spruce thicket, the rabbit to the broom sage. on the mountain side, and the, De'tsata to the bluffs along the river bank.

Some doctors use herb decoctions, which are blown upon the body of the child, but in this formula the only remedy prescribed is water, which must be blown upon the body of the little sufferer just before dark for four nights. The regular method is to blow once each at the end of the first, second, and third paragraphs and four times at the end of the fourth or last. In diseases of this kind, which are not supposed to be of a local character, the doctor blows first upon the back of the head, then upon the left shoulder, next upon the right shoulder, and finally upon the breast, the patient being generally sitting, or propped up in bed, facing the east. The child must not be taken out of doors during the four days, because should a bird chance to fly overhead so that its shadow would fall upon the infant, it would *fan the disease* back into the body of the little one.

GÛⁿWANI'GISTÛ'ⁿÏ DITANÛⁿWÂTI'YÏ.

Yû! Sgë! Usïnu'lï hatûⁿgani'ga, Giya'giya' Sa`ka'nï, ewʔsatâ'gï tsûl`dâ'histï. Usïnu'lï hatlasi'ga. Tsis'kwa-gwû' ulsge'ta uwu'tlani`lëʔ. Usïnuli'yu atsahilu'gïsi'ga. Utsïnä'wa nu'tatanûⁿta. Yü!

Yû! Sgë! Usïnu'lï hatûⁿgani'ga, Diga'tiskï Wâtige'ï, galûⁿlatï iyûⁿta ditsûl`dâ'histï. Ha-nâ'gwa usïnu'lï hatlasi'ga. Tsi'skwa-gwû dïtu'nila'-wʔitsû'hï higese'ï. Usïnûlï kë`'tati'gû`lahi'ga. Utsïnä'wa adûⁿni'ga. Yû!

Translation.

TO TREAT GÛⁿWANI'GISTÛ'ⁿÏ— (SECOND).

Yû! Listen! Quickly you have drawn near to hearken, O Blue Sparrow-Hawk; in the spreading tree tops you are at rest. Quickly you have come down. The intruder is only a bird which has, overshadowed him. Swiftly you have swooped down upon it. Relief is accomplished. Yû!

Yû! Listen! Quickly you have drawn near to hearken, O Brown Rabbit-Hawk; you are at rest there above. Ha! Swiftly now you have come down. It is only the birds which have come together for a council. Quickly you have come and scattered them. Relief is accomplished. Yû!

Explanation.

This formula, also for Gûⁿwani'gistû'ⁿï or Atawinë'hï, was obtained from A`wan'ita (Young Deer), who wrote down only the prayer and explained the treatment orally. He coincides in the opinion that this disease in children is caused by the birds, but says that it originates from the shadow of a bird. flying overhead having fallen upon the pregnant mother. He says further that the disease is easily recognized in children, but that it sometimes does not develop until the child has attained maturity, when it is more difficult to discern the cause of the trouble, although in the latter case dark circles around the eyes are unfailing symptoms.

The prayer—like several others from the same source—seems incomplete, and judging from analogy is evidently incorrect in some respects, but yet exemplifies the disease theory in a striking manner. The disease is declared to have been caused by the birds, it being asserted in the first paragraph that a bird has cast its shadow upon the sufferer, while in the second it is declared that they have gathered in council (in his body). This latter is a favorite expression in these formulas to indicate the great number of the disease animals.

Another expression of frequent occurrence is to the effect that the disease animals have formed a settlement or established a townhouse in the patient's body. The disease animal, being a bird or birds, must be dislodged by something which preys upon birds, and accordingly the Blue Sparrow-Hawk from the tree tops and the Brown Rabbit-Hawk (Diga'tiskï—"One who snatches up"), from above are invoked to drive out the intruders. The former is then said to have swooped down upon them as a hawk darts upon its prey, while the latter is declared to have scattered the birds which were holding a council. This being done, relief is accomplished. Yû! is a meaningless interjection frequently used to introduce or close paragraphs or songs.

The medicine used is a warm decoction of the bark of Kûnstû'tsï (Sassafras—Sassafras officinale), Kanûⁿsi'ta (Flowering Dogwood—

Cornus florida), Udâ'lana (Service tree—Amelanchier Canadensis), and Uni'kwa (Black Gum—Nyssa multiflora), with the roots of two species (large and small) of Da'yakali'skï (Wild Rose—Rosa lucida). The bark in every case is taken from the east side of the tree, and the roots selected are also generally, if not always, those growing toward the east. In this case the roots and barks are not bruised, but are simply steeped in warm water for four days. The child is then stripped and bathed all over with the decoction morning and night for four days, no formula being used during the bathing. It is then made to hold up its hands in front of its face with the palms turned out toward the doctor, who takes some of the medicine in his mouth and repeats the prayer mentally, blowing the medicine upon the head and hands of the patient at the, final *Yû!* of each paragraph. It is probable that the prayer originally consisted of four paragraphs, or else that these two paragraphs were repeated. The child drinks a little of the medicine at the end of each treatment.

The use of salt is prohibited during the four days of the treatment, the word (amä') being understood to include lye, which enters largely into Cherokee food preparations. No chicken or other feathered animal is allowed to enter the house during the same period, for obvious reasons, and strangers are excluded for reasons already explained.

HIA' DU'NIYUKWATISGÛⁿÎ KANA'HÈHÛ.

Sgë! Nûⁿdâgûⁿyï tsûl`dâ'histï, Kanani'skï Gigage. Usïnu'lï nûⁿnâ gi'gage hïnûⁿni'ga. Hïda'wëhi-gâgû', astï' digi'gage usïnû'lï dehïkssa'ûⁿtani'ga. Ulsge'ta kane'ge kayu'`ga gesûⁿ, tsgâ'ya-gwû higese'ï. Ehïstï' hïtuwa'saniy?teï'. Usïnu'lï astï' digi'gage dehada'ûⁿtani'ga, adi'na tsûlstai-yû'`ti-gwû higese'ï. Nâ'gwa gânagi'ta da'tsatane'lï. Utsïnä'wa nu'tatanûⁿta nûⁿtûneli'ga. Yû!

Hïgayûⁿlï Tsûne'ga hatûⁿgani'ga. "A'ya-gâgû' gatûⁿgisge'stï tsûngili'sï deagwûlstawïstitege'stï," tsadûnû'hï. Na'ski-gâgû' itsa'- wesû'hï nâ'gwa usïnu'lï hatûⁿgani'ga. Utsïnä'wa nútatanû'ta nûⁿtû'neli'ga. Yû!

Sgë! Uhyûⁿtlâ'yï tsûl`dâ'histï Kanani'skï Sa`ka'nï. Usïnu'lï nûⁿnâ sa`ka'nï hïnûⁿni'ga. Hïda'wëhi-gâgû', astï' (di)sa'ka'nï usïnu'lï dehïksa'ûⁿtani'ga. Ulsge'ta kane'ge kayu'`ga gesûⁿ, tsgâ'ya-gwû higese'ï. Ehïstï' hïtuwa'saniy?te(ï'). Usïnu'lï astï' disa`ka'nige dehada'ûⁿtaniga, adi'na tsûlstai-yû'`ti-gwû higese'ï. Nâ'gwa tsgâ'ya gûnagi'ta tsûtûneli'ga. Utsïnä'wa nu'tatanû'ⁿta nûⁿtûneli'ga. Yû!

Hïgayûⁿlï Tsûne'ga hatûⁿgani'ga. "A'ya-gâgû' gatûⁿgisge'stï tsûngili'sï deagwûlstawïstitege'stï," tsadûnû'hï. Nas'kigâgû' itsawesû'hï nâ'gwa usïnu'lï hatûⁿgani'ga. Utsïnä'wa nutatanûⁿta nûⁿtûneli'ga. Yû!

Sgë! Usûhi'yï tsûl`dâ'histï Kanani'skï Ûⁿnage. Usïnu'lï nûⁿnâ ûⁿnage hïnûⁿni'ga. Hïda'wëhi-gâgû', astï' digûⁿnage usïnu'lï dehïksa'ûⁿtani'ga. Ulsge'ta kane'ge kayu'`ga gesûⁿ, tsâgâ'ya-gwû higese'ï. Ehïstï' hïtuwa'saniy`teï'. Usïnu'lï astï' digûⁿnage dehada'ûⁿtani'ga, adi'na tsûlstai-yû'`ti-gwû higese'ï. Nâ'gwa tsgâ'ya gûnagi'ta tsûtûneli'ga. Utsïnä'wa nutatanû'ⁿta nûⁿtûneli'ga. Yû!

Hïgayû'ⁿlï Tsûne'ga hatûⁿgani'ga. "A'ya-gâgû' gatûⁿgisge'stï tsûngili'sï deagwûlstawï'stitege'stï," tsadûnû'hï. Na'skigâgû' itsawesû'hï nâ'gwa usïnu'li hatûⁿgani'ga. Utsïnä'wa nutatanûⁿta nûⁿtûneli'ga. Yû!

Sgë! Galûⁿlatï tsûl`dâ'histï, Kanani'skï Tsûne'ga. Usïnu'lï nûⁿnâ une'ga hïnûⁿni'ga. Hida'wëhi-gâgû', astï' tsune'ga usïnu'lï dehïksa'ûⁿ tani'ga. Ulsge'ta kane'ge kayu'`ga gesûⁿ, tsgâ'ya-gwû higese'ï. Ehïstï' hituwa'säniy`teï'. Usïnu'lï astï' tsune'ga dehada'ûⁿtani'ga, adi'na tsûlstai-yû'`ti-gwû higese'ï. Nâ'gwa tsgâ'ya gûnagi'ta tsûtûneli'ga. Utsïnä'wa nu'tatanûⁿta, nûⁿtûneli'ga. Yû!

Hïgayû'ⁿlï Tsûne'ga hatû'ⁿgani'ga. "A'ya-gâgû' gatûⁿgisge'stï tsûngili'sï deagwûlstawï'stitege'stï," tsadûnû'hï. Naski-gâgû' itsawesû'hï nâ'gwa usïnu'li hatûⁿgani'ga. U'tsïnä'wa nutatanûⁿta nûⁿtûneli'ga. Yû!

(Degasi'sisgûⁿï)—Hiä' duniyukwa'tisgûⁿï dïkanûⁿwâtï ätanûⁿsida'hi yi'gï. Na'skï digûⁿstanë'`ti-gwû ûlë' tsïtsâtû' yie'lisû. Nigûⁿ-gwû usû'na [*for* usûnda'na?] gûⁿtatï nayâ'ga nûⁿwatï unanûⁿskä`la'ï. Kane'ska dalâ'nige unaste'tla tsi'gï. Se'lu dïgahû`nû'hï tsuni'yahïstï' nû'`kï tsusû'hita, kanâhe'na-`nû naskï' iga'ï udanû'stï hi'gï nayâ'ga.

Translation.

THIS TELLS ABOUT MOVING PAINS IN THE TEETH (NEURALGIA?).

Listen! In the Sunland you repose, O Red Spider. Quickly you have brought and laid down the red path. O great ada'wehi, quickly you have brought down the red threads from above. The intruder in the tooth has spoken and it is only a worm. The tormentor has wrapped itself around the root of the tooth. Quickly you have dropped down the red threads, for it is just what you eat. Now it is for you to pick it up. The relief has been caused to come. Yû!

O Ancient White, you have drawn near to hearken, for you have said, "When I shall hear my grandchildren, I shall hold up their heads." Because you have said it, now therefore you have drawn near to listen. The relief has been caused to come. Yû!

Listen! In the Frigid Land you repose, O Blue Spider. Quickly you have brought and laid down the blue path. O great ada'wehi, quickly you have brought down the blue threads from above. The intruder in the tooth has spoken and it is only a worm. The tormentor has wrapped itself around the root of the tooth. Quickly you have dropped down the blue threads, for it is just what you eat. Now it is for you to pick it up. The relief has been caused to come. Yû!

O Ancient White, you have drawn near to hearken, for you have said, "When I shall hear my grandchildren, I shall hold up their heads." Because you have said it, now therefore you have drawn near to listen. The relief has been caused to come. Yû!

Listen! In the Darkening Land you repose, O Black Spider. Quickly you have brought and laid down the black path. O great ada'wehi, quickly you have brought down the black threads from above. The intruder in the tooth has spoken and it is only a worm. The tormentor has wrapped itself around the root of the tooth. Quickly you have dropped down the black threads, for it is just what you eat. Now it is for you to pick it up. The relief has been caused to come. Yû!

O Ancient White, you have drawn near to hearken, for you have said, "When I shall hear my grandchildren, I shall hold up their heads." Because you have said it, now therefore you have drawn near to listen. The relief has been caused to come. Yû!

Listen! You repose on high, O White Spider. Quickly you have brought and laid down the white path. O great ada'wehi, quickly you have brought down the white threads from above. The intruder in the tooth has spoken and it is only a worm. The tormentor has wrapped itself around the root of the tooth. Quickly you have dropped down the white threads, for it is just what you eat. Now it is for you to pick it up. The relief has been caused to come. Yû!

O Ancient White, you have drawn near to hearken, for you have said, "When I shall hear my grandchildren, I shall hold up their heads." Because you have said it, now therefore you have drawn near to listen. The relief has been caused to come. Yû!

(Prescription)—This is to treat them if there are pains moving about in the teeth. It is only (necessary) to lay on the hands, or to blow, if one should prefer. One may use any kind of a tube, but usually they have the medicine in the mouth. It is the Yellow-rooted Grass (kane'ska dalâ'nige unaste'tla; not identified.) One must abstain four nights from cooked corn (hominy), and kanâhe'na (fermented corn gruel) is especially forbidden during the same period.

Explanation.

This formula is taken from the manuscript book of Gatigwanasti, now dead, and must therefore be explained from general analogy. The ailment is described as "pains moving about in the teeth"—that is, affecting several teeth simultaneously—and appears to be neuralgia. The disease spirit is called "the intruder" and "the tormentor" and is declared to be a mere worm (tsgâ'ya), which has wrapped itself around the base of the tooth. This is the regular toothache theory. The doctor then calls upon the Red Spider of the Sunland to let down the red threads from above, along the red path, and to take up the intruder, which is just what the spider eats. The same prayer is addressed in turn to the Blue Spider in the north, the Black Spider in the west and the White Spider above (galûⁿ'lati). It may be stated here that all these spirits are supposed to dwell above, but when no point of the compass is assigned, galûⁿ'lati is understood to mean directly overhead, but far above everything of earth. The dweller in this overhead galûⁿ'lati may be red, white, or brown in color. In this formula it is white, the ordinary color assigned spirits dwelling in the south. In another toothache formula the Squirrel is implored to take the worm and put it between the forking limbs of a tree on the north side of the mountain.

Following each supplication to the spider is another addressed to the Ancient White, the formulistic name for fire. The name refers to its antiquity and light-giving properties and perhaps also to the fact that when dead it is covered with a coat of white ashes. In those formulas in which the hunter draws omens from the live coals it is frequently addressed as the Ancient Red.

The directions are not explicit and must be interpreted from analogy. "Laying on the hands" refers to pressing the thumb against the jaw over the aching tooth, the hand having been previously warmed over the fire, this being a common method of treating toothache. The other method suggested is to blow upon the spot (tooth or outside of jaw?) a decoction of an herb described rather vaguely as "yellow-rooted grass" either through a tube or from the mouth of the operator. Igawï', a toothache specialist, treats this ailment either by pressure with the warm thumb, or by blowing tobacco smoke from a pipe placed directly against the tooth. Hominy and fermented corn gruel (kanâhe'na) are prohibited for the regular term of four nights, or, as we are accustomed to say, four days, and special emphasis is laid upon the gruel tabu.

The prayer to the Spider is probably repeated while the doctor is warming his hands over the fire, and the following paragraph to the Ancient White (the Fire) while holding the warm thumb upon the aching spot. This reverses the usual order, which is to address the fire while warming the hands. In this connection it must be noted that the fire used by the doctor is never the ordinary fire on the hearth, but comes from four burning chips taken from the hearth fire and generally placed in an earthen vessel by the side of the patient. In some cases the decoction is heated by putting into it seven live coals taken from the fire on the hearth.

UNAWA STÎ EGWA (ADANÛⁿWATÏ).

Sgë! Galûⁿlatï' hinehi'(2) hinehi'yû(3) hinida'we(4), utsinâ'wa(5) adûⁿniga(6)

      1 2 1 2 2 2 3 4 3 3 5 6 6—Hayï!

Sgë! Uⁿwadâ'hi(1) hinehi'(2), hinehi'yû(3) hinida'we(4) utsinâ'wa(5) adûⁿni'ga(6)

      1 2 1 2 2 2 3 4 3 3 5 6 6—Hayï!

Sgë! Nâtsihi'(1) hinehi'(2) hinehi'yû(3) hinida'we(4) utsinâ'wa(5) adûⁿni'ga(6)

      1 2 1 2 2 2 3 4 3 3 5 6 6—Hayï!

Sgë! Amâyi'(1) hinehi'(2), hinehi'yû(3) hinida'we(4) utsinâ'wa(5) adûⁿni'ga(6)

      1 2 1 2 2 2 3 3 3 3 5 6 6—Hayï!

Sgë! Ha-nâ'gwa hatûⁿgani'ga, Agalu'ga Tsûsdi'ga, hida'wëhï, â'tali tsusdiga'hïduda'w?satûⁿditsûldâ'histï. (Hida'wëhï, gahu'stïtsanu'lûⁿhûⁿsgï' nige'sûⁿna.) Ha-nâ'gwa da'tûlehûⁿgû'. Usdi'gi(yu) utiya'stanûⁿ'(hï) (higese'ï). (Hûⁿ)hiyala'gistani'ga igä'tï usdigâ'hï usa'hilagï' Igâtu'ltï nûⁿnâ'hï wïte'tsatänûⁿ'ûⁿsï'. A`ne'tsâge'ta *getsatûnëhï* nûⁿgûlstani'gaigûⁿwûlstanita'stigwû. Ati'gale'yata tsûtû'neli'ga. Utsïnâ'wa (¹) nigûⁿtisge'stï.

Sgë! Ha-nâ'gwa hûⁿhatûⁿ'gani'ga, Agalu'ga Hegwahigwû'. Â'talï tsegwâ'hï duda'w?satûⁿ iyûⁿta ditsûldâ'histï. Agalu'ga He'gwa, hausïnu'lï da'tûlehûⁿgû. Usdi'giyu utiya'stanûⁿ'hï. Hiyala'gistani'ga ulsge'ta igâ'tegwâ'hï) usa'hïlagï'. (Igat-(egwâ'hï iyûⁿta nûⁿ-nâ'hï wïtetsatanûⁿ'ûⁿsï). A`ne'tsâge'ta *getsatûne'litise'sti* igûⁿ'wûlstanita'sti-gwû. Utsïnâ'wa-gwû nutatanûⁿta. Nigagï' Yû!

(Degâsi'sisgûⁿ'ï)—Unawa'stï e'gwa u'nitlûⁿgâ'ï. Ta'ya gûⁿtatï, ditsa'tista``ti. Tsâ'l-agayûⁿ'lï yä'hä ulûⁿkwati-gwû nasgwû'.

Translation.

TO TREAT THE GREAT CHILL.

Listen! On high you dwell, On high you dwell—you dwell, you dwell. Forever you dwell, you anida'we, forever you dwell, forever you dwell. Relief has come—has come. Hayï!

Listen! On Ûⁿwadâ'hï you dwell, On Ûⁿwadâ'hï you dwell—you dwell, you dwell. Forever you dwell, you anida'we, forever you dwell, forever you dwell. Relief has come—has come. Hayï!

Listen! In the pines you dwell, In the pines you dwell—you dwell, you dwell. Forever you dwell, you anida'we, forever you dwell, forever you dwell. Relief has come—has come. Hayï!

Listen! In the water you dwell, In the water you dwell, you dwell, you dwell. Forever you dwell, you anida'we, forever you dwell, forever you dwell. Relief has come—has come. Hayï!

Listen! O now you have drawn near to hearken, O Little Whirlwind, O ada'wehi, in the leafy shelter of the lower mountain, there you repose. O ada'wehi, you can never fail in anything. Ha! Now rise up. A very small portion [of the disease] remains. You have come to sweep it away into the small swamp on. the upland. You have laid down your paths near the swamp. It is ordained that you shall scatter it as in play, so that it shall utterly disappear. By you it must be scattered. So shall there be relief.

Listen! O now again you have drawn near to hearken, O Whirlwind, surpassingly great. In the leafy shelter of the great mountain there you repose. O Great Whirlwind, arise quickly. A very small part [of the disease] remains. You have come to sweep the intruder into the great swamp on the upland. You have laid down your paths toward the great swamp. You shall scatter it as in play so that it shall utterly disappear. And now relief has come. All is done. Yû!

1   So written and pronounced by A`yûⁿini instead of utsïnä'wa.

(Prescription.)—(This is to use) when they are sick with the great chill. Take a decoction of wild cherry to blow upon them. If you have Tsâ'l-agayûⁿlï ("old tobacco"—*Nicotiana rustica*) it also is very effective.

EXPLANATION.

Unawa'stï, "that which chills one," is a generic name for intermittent fever, otherwise known as fever and ague. It is much dreaded by the Indian doctors, who recognize several varieties of the disease, and have various theories to account for them. The above formula was obtained from A`yûⁿni (Swimmer), who described the symptoms of this variety, the "Great Chill," as blackness in the face, with alternate high fever and shaking chills. The disease generally appeared in spring or summer, and might return year after year. In the first stages the chill usually came on early in the morning, but came on later in the day as the disease progressed. There might be more than one chill during the day. There was no rule as to appetite, but the fever always produced an excessive thirst. In one instance the patient fainted from the heat and would even lie down in a stream to cool himself. The doctor believed the disease was caused by malicious tsgâ'ya, a general name for all small insects and worms, excepting intestinal worms. These tsgâ'ya—that is, the disease tsgâ'ya, not the real insects and worms—are held responsible for a large number of diseases, and in fact the tsgâ'ya doctrine is to the Cherokee practitioner what the microbe theory is to some modern scientists. The tsgâ'ya live in the earth, in the water, in the air, in the foliage of trees, in decaying wood, or wherever else insects lodge, and as they are constantly being crushed, burned or otherwise destroyed through the unthinking carelessness of the human race, they are continually actuated by a spirit of revenge. To accomplish their vengeance, according to the doctors, they "establish towns" under the skin of their victims, thus producing an irritation which results in fevers, boils, scrofula and other diseases.

The formula begins with a song of four verses, in which the doctor invokes in succession the spirits of the air, of the mountain, of the forest, and of the water. Galûⁿlatï, the word used in the first verse, signifies, as has been already explained, "on high" or "above everything," and has been used by translators to mean heaven. Ûⁿwadâ'hï in the second verse is the name of a bald mountain east of Webster, North Carolina, and is used figuratively to denote any mountains of bold outline. The Cherokees have a tradition to account for the name, which is derived from Ûⁿwadâ'lï, "provision house." Nâ'tsihï' in the third verse signifies "pinery," from nâ'ˋtsï, "pine," but is figuratively used to denote a forest of any kind.

In the recitation which follows the song, but is used only in serious cases, the doctor prays to the whirlwind, which is considered to dwell, among the trees on the mountain side, where the trembling of the leaves always gives the first intimation of its presence. He declares that a small portion of the disease still remains, the spirits invoked in the song having already taken the rest, and calls upon the whirlwind to lay down a path for it and sweep it away into the swamp on the upland, referring to grassy marshes common in the small coves of the higher mountains, which, being remote from the settlements, are convenient places to which to banish the disease. Not satisfied with this he goes on to direct the whirlwind to scatter the disease as it scatters the leaves of the forest, so that it shall utterly disappear. In the Cherokee formula the verb a`ne'tsâge'ta, means literally "to play," and is generally understood to refer to the ball play, a`ne'tsâ, so that to a Cherokee the expression conveys the idea of catching up the disease and driving it onward as a player seizes the ball and sends it spinning through the air from between his ball sticks. Niga'gï is a solemn expression about equivalent to the Latin consummatum est.

The doctor beats up some bark from the trunk of the wild cherry and puts it into water together with seven coals of fire, the latter being intended to warm the decoction The leaves of Tsâl-agayû'ⁿli (Indian tobacco—Nicotiana rustica) are sometimes used in place of the wild cherry bark. The patient is placed facing the sunrise, and the doctor, taking the medicine in his mouth, blows it over the body of the sick man. First, standing between the patient and the sunrise and holding the medicine cup in his hand, he sings the first verse in a low tone. Then, taking some of the liquid in his mouth, he advances and blows it successively upon the top of the head, the right shoulder, left shoulder, and breast or back of the patient, making four blowings in all. He repeats the same ceremony with the second, third, and fourth verse, returning each time to his original position. The ceremony takes place in the morning, and if necessary is repeated in the evening. It is sometimes necessary also to repeat the treatment for several—generally four—consecutive days.

The recitation is not used excepting in the most serious cases, when, according to the formula, "a very small portion" of the disease still lingers. It is accompanied by blowing *of the breath alone*, without medicine, probably in this case typical of the action of the whirlwind. After repeating the whole ceremony accompanying the song, as above described, the doctor returns to his position in front of the patient and recites in a whisper the first paragraph to the Little Whirlwind, after which he advances and blows his breath upon the patient four times as he has already blown the medicine upon him. Then going around to the north he recites the second paragraph to the Great Whirlwind, and at its conclusion blows in the same manner. Then moving around to the west—behind the patient—he again prays to the Little Whirlwind with the same ceremonies, and finally moving around to the south side he closes with the prayer to the Great Whirlwind, blowing four times at its conclusion. The medicine must be prepared anew by the doctor at the house of the patient at each application morning or evening. Only as much as will be needed is made at a time, and the patient always drinks what remains after the blowing. Connected with the preparation and care of the medicine are a number of ceremonies which need not be detailed here. The wild cherry bark must always be procured fresh; but the Tsâl-agayû'ⁿlĭ ("Old Tobacco") leaves may be dry. When the latter plant is used four leaves are taken and steeped in warm water with the fire coals, as above described.

HIÄ' TSUNSDI'GA DIL`TADI'NATANTI'YÏ.

I.

Sgë! Hïsga'ya Ts`sdi'ga ha-nâ'gwa da'tûlehûⁿgû' kïlû-gwû'. Iyûⁿta agayûⁿlinasï' taya'ï. Eska'niyü unayë'histï nûⁿta-yu'tanatï'. Sgë'! tinû'lïtgï! Tleki'yu tsûtsestâ'gï hwïnagï'. Yû!

Sgë! Hige'cya ts`sdi'ga ha-nâ'gwa da'tûlehûⁿgû' kïlû-gwû'. Iyûⁿta tsûtu'tunasï' täya'ï. Eska'niyü unayë'histï nûⁿtayu'tanatï'. Sgë! tinû'lïtgï! Tleki'yu tsûtsestâ' hwïnagï'. Yû!

Translation.

THIS IS TO MAKE CHILDREN JUMP DOWN.

Listen! You little man, get up now at once. There comes an old woman. The horrible [old thing] is coming, only a little way off. Listen! Quick! Get your bed and let us run away. Yû!

Listen! You little woman, get up now at once. There comes your grandfather. The horrible old fellow is coming only a little way off. Listen! Quick! Get your bed and let us run away. Yû!

Explanation.

In this formula for childbirth the idea is to frighten the child and coax it to come, by telling it, if a boy, that an ugly old woman is coming, or if a girl, that her grandfather is coming only a short distance away. The reason of this lies in the fact that an old woman is the terror of all the little boys of the neighborhood, constantly teasing and frightening them by declaring that she means to live until they grow up and then compel one of them to marry her, old and shriveled as she is. For the same reason the maternal grandfather, who is always a privileged character in the family, is especially dreaded by the little girls, and nothing will send a group of children running into the house more quickly than the announcement that an old "granny," of either sex is in sight.

As the sex is an uncertain quantity, the possible boy is always first addressed in the formulas, and if no result seems to follow, the doctor then concludes that the child is a girl and addresses her in similar tones. In some cases an additional formula with the beads is used to determine whether the child will be born alive or dead. In most instances the formulas were formerly repeated with the appropriate ceremonies by some old female relative of the mother, but they are now the property of the ordinary doctors, men as well as women.

This formula was obtained from the manuscript book of A`yû'ⁿinï, who stated that the medicine used was a warm decoction of a plant called Dalâ'nige Unaste'tsï ("yellow root"—not identified), which was blown successively upon the top of the mother's head, upon the breast, and upon the palm of each hand. The doctor stands beside the woman, who is propped up in a sitting position, while repeating the first paragraph and then blows. If this produces no result he then recites the paragraph addressed to the girl and again blows. A part of the liquid is also given to the woman to drink. A`yû'ⁿinï claimed this was always effectual.

II.

Hitsutsa, hitsu'tsa, tleki'yu, tleki'yu, ë'hinugâ'ï, ë'hinugâ'ï! Hi'tsu'tsa, tleki'yu, gûltsû'tï, gûltsû'tï, tinagâ'na, tinagâ'na!

Higë`yu'tsa, higë`yu'tsa, tleki'yu, tleki'yu, ë'hinugâ'ï, ë'hinugâ'ï!
Higë`yu'tsa, tleki'yu, gûⁿgu'stï, gûⁿgu'stï, tinagâ'na, tinagâ'na!

Translation.

THIS IS TO MAKE CHILDREN JUMP DOWN.

Little boy, little boy, hurry, hurry, come out, come out! Little boy, hurry; a bow, a bow; let's see who'll get it, let's see who'll get it!
Little girl, little girl, hurry, hurry, come out, come out, Little girl, hurry; a sifter, a sifter; let's see who'll get it, let's see who'll get it!

Explanation.

This formula was obtained from Takwati'hï, as given to him by a specialist in this line. Takwatihi himself knew nothing of the treatment involved, but a decoction is probably blown upon the patient as described in the preceding formula. In many cases the medicine used is simply cold water, the idea being to cause a sudden muscular action by the chilling contact. In this formula the possible boy or girl is coaxed out by the promise of a bow or a meal-sifter to the one who can get it first. Among the Cherokees it is common, in asking about the sex of a new arrival, to inquire, "Is it a bow or a sifter?" or "Is it ball sticks or bread?"

DALÂ'NI Û^{n}NÄGE'Ï ADANÛ'^{n}WÂTÏ.

Yuha'ahi', (yuha'ahi', yuha'ahi', yuha'ahi',)
Yuha'ahi', (yuha'ahi', yuha'ahi'), Yû!

Sgë! Û^{n}tal-e'gwâhi' didultâ'hïstï ulsge'ta. Usïnu'lï dâtitu'lene'ï. Usïnu'lï dunu'y?tani'leï.

Sgë! Ha-nâ'gwa statû'^{n}gani'ga, nû^{n}dâ'yï distûl`tâ'hïstï, Stisga'ya Dïst`sdi'ga, stida'wehi-gâgû. Û^{n}tal-e'gwa dâtitulene'(ï) ulsge'ta. Usïnu'lï detïstû'l`tani'ga ulsge'ta. Ditu'talenû'$^n$itsa nû$^n$nâ'hï $^w$i'de'tutanû'$^n$tatasï', nû$^n$tadu'ktahû'$^n$stï nige'sû$^n$na. Nû`gï iyayû'^{n}latägï' ayâwe'sâlû'^{n}ta de'dudûneli'sestï, Gû'^{n}tsatâtagi'yû tistadi'gûlahi'sestï. Tiduda'le`nû(ï) û'$^n$tale'gwâ $^w$ti'stûl'tati'nû$^n$tani'ga. Na'`nä witûl`tâ'hïstani'ga, tadu'ktahû'$^n$stï nige'sû$^n$na. Ha-na'`nä ^{w}id'ultâhiste'stï. (Yû!)

(Degasisisgû'^{n}ï)—Hïä' anine'tsï ga'`tïskï adanû$^n$wâtï. Ü'$^n$tla atsi'la tï'`tï yi'gï.

Translation.

TO TREAT THE BLACK YELLOWNESS.

Yuha'ahi', yuha'ahi', yuha'ahi', yuha'ahi',
Yuha'ahi', yuha'ahi', yuha'ahi' Yû!

Listen! In the great lake the intruder reposes. Quickly he has risen up there. Swiftly he has come and stealthily put himself (under the sick man).

Listen! Ha! Now you two have drawn near to hearken, there in the Sun Land you repose, O Little Men, O great anida'wehi! The intruder has risen up there in the great lake. Quickly you two have lifted up the intruder. His paths have laid themselves down toward the direction whence he came. Let him never look back (toward us). When he stops to rest at the four gaps you will drive him roughly along. Now he has plunged into the great lake from which he came. There he is compelled to remain, never to look back. Ha! there let him rest. (Yû!)

(Directions.)—This is to treat them when their breast swells. Fire (coals) is not put down.

Explanation.

This formula, from A`yûⁿinï's manuscript, is used in treating a disease known as Dalâni, literally, "yellow." From the vague description of symptoms given by the doctors, it appears to be an aggravated form of biliousness, probably induced by late suppers and bad food. According to the Indian theory it is caused by revengeful animals, especially by the terrapin and its cousin, the turtle.

The doctors recognize several forms of the disease, this variety being distinguished as the "black dalâni (Dalâni Ûⁿnage'ï) and considered the most dangerous. In this form of dalânï, according to their account, the navel and abdomen of the patient swell, the ends of his fingers become black, dark circles appear about his eyes, and the throat contracts spasmodically and causes him to fall down suddenly insensible. A`yûⁿinï's method of treatment is to rub the breast and abdomen of the patient with the hands, which have been previously rubbed together in the warm infusion of wild cherry (ta'ya) bark. The song is sung while rubbing the hands together in the liquid, and the prayer is repeated while rubbing the swollen abdomen of the patient. The operation may be repeated several times on successive days.

The song at the beginning has no meaning and is sung in a low plaintive lullaby tone, ending with a sharp *Yu!* The prayer possesses a special interest, as it brings out several new points in the Cherokee mythologic theory of medicine. The "intruder," which is held to be some amphibious animal—as a terrapin, turtle, or snake—is declared to have risen up from his dwelling place in the great lake, situated toward the sunset, and to have come by stealth under the sick man. The verb implies that the disease spirit creeps under as a snake might crawl under the coverlet of a bed.

The two Little Men in the Sun Land are now invoked to drive out the disease. Who these Little Men are is not clear, although they are regarded as most powerful spirits and are frequently invoked in the formulas. They are probably the two Thunder Boys, sons of Kanati.

The Little Men come instantly when summoned by the shaman, pull out the intruder from the body of the patient, turn his face toward the sunset, and begin to drive him on by threats and blows (expressed in the word gû'ⁿtsatatagi'yû) to the great lake from which he came. On the road there are four gaps in the mountains, at each of which the disease spirit halts to rest, but is continually forced onward by his two pursuers, who finally drive him into the lake, where he is compelled to remain, without being permitted even to look back again. The four gaps are mentioned also in other formulas for medicine and the ball play and sometimes correspond with the four stages of the treatment. The direction "No fire (coals) is put down" indicates that no live coals are put into the decoction, the doctor probably using water warmed in the ordinary manner.

Takwati'hï uses for this disease a decoction of four herbs applied in the same manner. He agrees with A`yûⁿinï in regard to the general theory and says also that the disease may be contracted by neglecting to wash the hands after handling terrapin shells, as, for instance, the shell rattles used by women in the dance. The turtle or water tortoise (seligu'gĭ) is considered as an inferior being, with but little capacity for mischief, and is feared chiefly on account of its relationship to the dreaded terrapin or land tortoise (tûksĭ'). In Takwatihĭ's formula he prays to the Ancient White (the fire), of which these cold-blooded animals are supposed to be afraid, to put the fish into the water, the turtle into the mud, and to send the terrapin and snake to the hillside.

TSUNDAYE'LIGAKTANÛ'HÏ ADANÛ'ⁿWÂTÏ

Sgë! Hanâ'gwa hatû'ⁿganiga, galû'ⁿlatï hetsadâ'histï, Kâ'lanû Û'ⁿnage, gahu'stï tsanu'lahû'ⁿsgï nige'sûⁿna. Ha-nâ'gwa (hetsatsa'ûⁿtani'ga. Hanigû'ⁿwatûⁿnigwälâe'stigwû tsalâsû'ⁿï. Asgin-u'danû higes'eï. Sanigala'gï gesû'ⁿï hastigtû'`lani'ga, duwâlu'wa'tû'tï nige'sûⁿna, nitûneli'ga. Ha-Usûhi'yï wititâ'hïstani'ga. Dadu'satahû'ⁿstï nige'sûⁿna nitû'neli'ga. Utsïnä'wa nu'tatanû'ⁿta.

Sgë! Ha-nâ'gwa hatû'ⁿgani'ga, Kâ'lanû Gïgage'ï, hidawëhi'yu. Ha-gahu'stï tsanu'lahû'ⁿsgï nige'sûⁿna, etsanetse'lûhï. Ha-galûⁿlati'tsa hetsatâ'histï. Nâ'gwa hetsatsâ'ûⁿtani'ga. Nigûⁿwatûⁿnigwalâe'sti-gwû tsalâsû'ⁿï. Asgin-udanû'hi-gwûhigese'ï. Ha-Sanigalâgïgesû'ⁿhâstigû'`lani'ga ulsge'ta, ha-utsïnä'wa-gwû' nigû'ⁿtisge'stï. Usûhi'yï wïntûnë'dû. Usûhi'yï wïtitâ'hïstani'ga. Utsïnä'wa adû'ⁿni'ga.

Sgë! Ha-nâ'gwa hatû'ⁿgani'ga, Kâ'lanû Sa'ka'ni; galû'latï hetsadâ'histï, hida'wëhï. Gahu'stï tsanu'lahûⁿsgï nige'sûⁿna, etsanetse'lûhï. Ha-nâ'gwa hetsatsâ'ûⁿtani'ga. Nigûⁿwatûⁿnigwalâe'sti-gwû tsalâsû'ⁿï. Sanigalâ'gï gesûⁿ hastigû'`lani'ga ulsge'ta. Duwâlu'watû'tï nige'sûⁿna, nitû'neli'ga. Usûhi'yï wititâ'hïstani'ga, dadu'satahû'ⁿstï nige'sûⁿna nitû'neli'ga. Utsïnä'wa adû'ⁿni'ga.

Sgë! Ha-nâ'gwa hatû'ⁿgani'ga, Wa'hïlï galûⁿlti'tsa hetsadâ'histï, Kâ'lanû Tsûne'ga, hida'wëhï. Gahu'stï tsanul`tï nige'sûⁿna. Hanâ'gwa hetsatsâ'ûⁿtani'ga. Nigûⁿwatûⁿnigwalâe'sti-gwû tsalâsû'ⁿï. Ha-nâ'gwa detal`tani'ga. Sanigalâ'gï gesûⁿ, hastig'û`lani'ga ulsge'ta, duwâlu'watu'`tï nige'sûⁿna nitû'neli'ga. Usûhi'yï wïtitâ'hïstani'ga. Dadu'satahû'ⁿstï nige'sûⁿna nitû'neli'ga. Utsïnä'wa adûⁿni'ga.

(Dega'sisisgû'ⁿï)—Hiä'agi`li'ya unitlûⁿgû'ⁿï adanû'wâtï. Askwanu'tsastï'. Tsâ'l(a) Agayûⁿlï unitsi'lûⁿnû'hï gûⁿtatï, anûⁿsga`lâ'-gwû; Kanasâ'la-`nû unali'gâhû, ade'la'-`nû nû'`gi-gwû ani'gage'ï dahâ'ï, Tsâliyu'stï-`nû Usdi'ga. Gahu'sti-'`nu yuta'suyû'ⁿna sâwatu'hi-gwû atï' dawâ'hila-gwû iyû'ⁿta.

Translation.

TO TREAT FOR ORDEAL DISEASES.

Listen! Ha! Now you have drawn near to hearken and are resting directly overhead. O Black Raven, you never fail in anything. Ha! Now you are brought down. Ha! There shall be left no more than a trace upon the ground where you have been. It is an evolute ghost. You have now put it into a crevice in Sanigalagi, that it may never find the way back. You have put it to rest in the Darkening Land, so that it may never return. Let relief come.

Listen! Ha! Now you have drawn near to hearken, O Red Raven, most powerful ada'wehi. Ha! You never fail in anything, for so it was ordained of you. Ha! You are resting directly overhead. Ha! Now you are brought down. There shall remain but a trace upon the ground where you have been. It is an evolute ghost. Ha! You have put the Intruder into a crevice of Sanigalagi and now the relief shall come. It (the Intruder) is sent to the Darkening Land. You have put it to rest in the Darkening Land. Let the relief come.

Listen! Ha! Now you have drawn near to hearken, O Blue Raven; you are resting directly overhead, ada'wehi. You never fail in anything, for so it was ordained of you. Ha! Now you are brought down. There shall be left but a trace upon the ground where you have been. You have put the Intruder into a crevice in Sanigalagi, that it may never find the way back. You have put it to rest in the Darkening Land, so that it may never return. Let the relief come.

Listen! Ha! Now you have drawn near to hearken; you repose on high on Wa'hïlï, O White Raven, ada'wehi. You never fail in anything. Ha! Now you are brought down. There shall be left but a trace upon the ground where you have been. Ha! Now you have taken it up. You have put the Intruder into a crevice in Sanigalagi, that it may never find the way back. You have put it to rest in the Darkening Land, never to return. Let the relief come.

(Directions)—This is to treat them for a painful sickness. One must suck. Use Tsâ'lagayû^n'-li ("Old Tobacco"—Nicotiana rustica), blossoms, and just have them in the mouth, and Kanasâ'la (Wild Parsnip), goes with it, and four red beads also must lie there, and Tsâliyu'sti Usdi'ga ("Little (plant) Like Tobacco"—Indian Tobacco—Lobelia inflata.) And if there should be anything mixed with it (i. e., after sucking the place), just put it about a hand's-length into the mud.

Explanation.

The Cherokee name for this disease gives no idea whatever of its serious nature. The technical term, Tsundaye'liga'ktanû'hï, really refers to the enthusiastic outburst of sociability that ensues when two old friends meet. In this instance it might be rendered "an ordeal." The application of such a name to what is considered a serious illness is in accordance with the regular formulistic practice of making light of a dangerous malady in order to convey to the disease spirit the impression that the shaman is not afraid of him. A`yû^{n}inï, from whom the formula was obtained, states also that the disease is sometimes sent to a man by a friend or even by his parents, in order to test his endurance and knowledge of counter spells.

As with most diseases, the name simply indicates the shaman's theory of the occult cause of the trouble, and is no clue to the symptoms, which may be those usually attendant upon fevers, indigestion, or almost any other ailment.

In some cases the disease is caused by the conjurations of an enemy, through which the patient becomes subject to an inordinate appetite, causing him to eat until his abdomen is unnaturally distended. By the same magic spells tobacco may be conveyed into the man's body, causing him to be affected by faintness and languor. The enemy, if bitterly revengeful, may even put into the body of his victim a worm or insect (tsgâya), or a sharpened stick of black locust or "fat" pine, which will result in death if not removed by a good doctor. Sometimes a weed stalk is in some occult manner conveyed into the patient's stomach, where it is transformed into a worm. As this disease is very common, owing to constant quarrels and rival jealousies, there are a number of specialists who devote their attention to it.

The prayer is addressed to the Black, Red, Blue, and White Ravens, their location at the four cardinal points not being specified, excepting in the case of the white raven of Wa'hilĭ, which, as already stated, is said to be a mountain in the south, and hence is used figuratively to mean the south. The ravens are each in turn declared to have put the disease into a crevice in Sanigala'gi—the Cherokee name of Whiteside Mountain, at the head of Tuckasegee River, in North Carolina, and used figuratively for. any high precipitous mountain—and to have left no more than a trace upon the ground where it has been. The adjective translated "evolute" (udanûhĭ) is of frequent occurrence in the formulas. but has no exact equivalent in English. It signifies springing into being or life from an embryonic condition. In this instance it would imply that whatever object the enemy has put into the body of the sick man has there developed into a ghost to trouble him.

The directions are expressed in a rather vague manner, as is the case with most of A`yûⁿini's attempts at original composition. The disease is here called by another name, agi`li'ya unitlûⁿgû'ⁿĭ, signifying "when they are painfully sick." The treatment consists in sucking the part most affected, the doctor having in his mouth during the operation the blossoms of Tsâ'l-agayû'ⁿlï (Nicotiana rustica), Kanasâ'la (wild parsnip,) and Tsâliyusti Usdiga (Lobelia inflata.) The first and last of these names signify "tobacco" and "tobacco-like," while the other seems to contain the same word, tsâ'la, and the original idea may have been to counteract the witchcraft by the use of the various species of "tobacco," the herb commonly used to drive away a witch or wizard. During the sticking process four red beads lie near upon a piece of (white) cloth, which afterward becomes the perquisite of the doctor. Though not explicitly stated, it is probable that the doctor holds in his mouth a decoction of the blossoms named, rather than the blossoms themselves. On withdrawing his mouth from the spot and ejecting the liquid into a bowl, it is expected that there will be found "mixed" with it a small stick, a pebble, an insect, or something of the kind, and this the shaman then holds up to view as the cause of the disease. It is afterward buried a "hand's length" (awâ'hilû)[1] deep in the mud. No directions were given as to diet or tabu.

1   This word, like the expression "seven days," frequently has a figurative meaning. Thus the sun is said to be seven awâ'hilû above the earth.

HUNTING.

GŪNÂ'HILÛ'ⁿTA UGÛ'ⁿWA`LÏ.

Una'lelü' eskiska'l`tasï'. Iskwa'lelü eskiska'l`tasï'. Yû! Ela-Kana'tï tsûldâ'hïstû'ⁿ, tsûwatsi'la astû'ⁿ detsatasi'ga. Ts?skwâ'lï uda'nisä'`testï, ugwala'ga udu'yaheti'dege'stï. Sunûsi'ya-gwû udanisä'`testï, ts`su'lti-gwû nige'sû'ⁿna.

Hïkayû'ⁿlï Gi'gage-gâgû', tsine'tsï gesû'ⁿ aw`stitege'stï. *Tsästû' utatiyi*, nâ'gwa *tsäs`tû gasû'hïsä`ti atisge'stï*. Ha-nâ'gwa nûⁿnâ tsusdi' tutana'wa-tegû' *digana'watû*ⁿ*ta* atisge'stï. Utalï' udaniû'hï ugwala'ga gûⁿwatuy'ahïti'tege'stï, hïlahiyû'ⁿta-gwû ʷustû'`stï nige'sû'ⁿna. D?stiskwâ'lï deudû'nisä`te'stï. Yû!

Translation.

CONCERNING HUNTING.

Give me the wind. Give me the breeze. Yû! O Great Terrestrial Hunter, I come to the edge of your spittle where you repose. Let your stomach cover itself; let it be covered with leaves. Let it cover itself at a single bend, and may you never be satisfied.

And you, O Ancient Red, may you hover above my breast while I sleep. Now let good (dreams?) develop; let my experiences be propitious. Ha! Now let my little trails be directed, as they lie down in various directions(?). Let the leaves be covered with the clotted blood, and may it never cease to be so. You two (the Water and the Fire) shall bury it in your stomachs. Yû!

Explanation.

This is a hunting formula, addressed to the two great gods of the hunter, Fire and Water. The evening before starting the hunter "goes to water," as already explained, and recites the appropriate formula. In the morning he sets out, while still fasting, and travels without eating or drinking until nightfall. At sunset he again goes to water, reciting this formula during the ceremony, after which he builds his camp fire, eats his supper and lies down for the night, first rubbing his breast with ashes from the fire. In the morning he starts out to look for game.

"Give me the wind," is a prayer that the wind may be in his favor, so that the game may not scent him. The word rendered here "Great Terrestrial Hunter," is in the original "Ela-Kana'tï." In this *e'la* is the earth and *kana'tï* is a term applied to a successful hunter. The great Kanatï, who, according to the myth, formerly kept all the game shut up in his underground caverns, now dwells above the sky, and is frequently invoked by hunters. The raven also is often addressed as Kanatï in these hunting formulas. Ela-Kana'tï, the Great Terrestrial Hunter—as distinguished from the other two—signifies the river, the name referring to the way in which the tiny streams and rivulets search out and bring down to the great river the leaves and débris of the mountain forests. In formulas for medicine, love, the ball play, etc., the river is always addressed as the Long Person (Yû^{n}wï Gûnahi'ta). The "spittle" referred to is the foam at the edge of the water. "Let your stomach be covered with leaves" means, let the blood-stained leaves where the stricken game shall fall be so numerous as to cover the surface of the water. The hunter prays also that sufficient game may be found in a single bend of the river to accomplish this result without the necessity of searching through the whole forest, and to that end he further prays that the river may never be satisfied, but continually longing for more. The same idea is repeated in the second paragraph, The hunter is supposed to feed the river with blood washed from the game. In like manner he feeds the fire, addressed in the second paragraph as the "Ancient Red," with a piece of meat cut from the tongue of the deer. The prayer that the fire may hover above his breast while he sleeps and brings him favorable dreams, refers to his rubbing his breast with ashes from his camp fire before lying down to sleep, in order that the fire may bring him dream omens of success for the morrow. The Fire is addressed either as the Ancient White or the Ancient Red, the allusion in the first case being to the light or the ashes of the fire; in the other case, to the color of the burning coals. "You two shall bury it in your stomachs" refers to the bloodstained leaves and the piece of meat which are cast respectively into the river and the fire. The formula was obtained from A`yûⁿinï, who explained it in detail.

HIÄ' TSI'SKWA GANÂHILIDASTI'YĬ.

Tsïgë'! Hĭkayû'ⁿl-Une'ga, tsûltâ'hïstû'ⁿ gûlitâ'hïstani'ga. Nâ'gwa tsûda'ntâ talehï'sani'ga. Sâ'gwa igûnsi'ya tsʔskwâli' udû'nisate'stï, tsʔsu'ltï nige'sûⁿna. Wane'(ï) tigi'gage(ï) tali'kanëli'ga. ᵁⁿtalï udanû'hï tsägista'`tï.

Hĭkayû'ⁿl-Une'ga, *anu'ya uwâtatâ'gï agi'stï tätsiskâ'ltane'lûhï.* ᵁⁿtalï u'danû' *te'tûlskewʔsi'ga.*

Hĭkayû'ⁿl-Une'ga, nûⁿnâ'(hï) kana'tï skwatetâ'stani'ga. Unigwalû'ⁿgï te'gatûⁿtsi'ga. Nûⁿnâ'(hï) kana'tï tati'kiyû'ⁿgwita'watise'stï. Unigwalû'ⁿgï tigûⁿwatû'tsanû'hï.

Hĭkayû'ⁿl-Une'ga, Kana'tï, skʔsalatâ'titege'stï, sa`ka'ni ginu'tʔtï nige'sûⁿna. Sgë!

Translation.

THIS IS FOR HUNTING BIRDS.

Listen! O Ancient White, where you dwell in peace I have come to rest. Now let your spirit arise. Let it (the game brought down) be buried in your stomach, and may your appetite never be satisfied. The red hickories have tied themselves together. The clotted blood is your recompense.

O Ancient White, * * * Accept the clotted blood (?).

O Ancient White. put me in the successful hunting trail. Hang the mangled things upon me. Let me come along the successful trail with them doubled up (under my belt). It (the road) is clothed with the mangled things.

O Ancient White, O Kanati, support me continually, that I may never become blue. Listen!

Explanation.

This formula, from A`yûⁿinï's manuscript, is recited by the bird-hunter in the morning while standing over the fire at his hunting camp before starting out for the day's hunt. A`yûⁿinï stated that seven blowgun arrows are first prepared, including a small one only a "hand-length" (awâ'hilû) long. On rising in the morning the hunter, standing over the fire, addresses it as the "Ancient White," rubbing his hands together while repeating the prayer. He then sets out for the hunting ground, where he expects to spend the day, and on reaching it he shoots away the short arrow at random, without attempting to trace its flight. There is of course some significance attached to this action and perhaps an accompanying prayer, but no further information upon this point was obtainable. Having shot away the magic arrow, the hunter utters a peculiar hissing sound, intended to call up the birds, and then goes to work with his remaining arrows. On all hunting expeditions it is the regular practice, religiously enforced, to abstain from food until sunset.

A favorite method with the bird-hunter during the summer season is to climb a gum tree, which is much frequented by the smaller birds on account of its berries, where, taking up a convenient position amid the branches with his noiseless blowgun and arrows, he deliberately shoots down one bird after another until his shafts are exhausted, when he climbs down, draws out the arrows from the bodies of the birds killed, and climbs up again to repeat the operation. As the light darts used make no sound, the birds seldom take the alarm, and are too busily engaged with the berries to notice their comrades dropping to the ground from time to time, and pay but slight attention even to the movements of the hunter.

The prayer is addressed to the Ancient White (the Fire), the spirit most frequently invoked by the hunter, who, as before stated, rubs his hands together over the fire while repeating the words. The expressions used are obscure when taken alone, but are full of meaning when explained in the light of the hunting customs. The "clotted blood" refers to the bloodstained leaves upon which the fallen game has lain. The expression occurs constantly in the hunting formulas. The hunter gathers up these bloody leaves and casts them upon the fire, in order to draw omens for the morrow from the manner in which they burn. A part of the tongue, or some other portion of the animal, is usually cast upon the coals also for the same purpose. This subject will be treated at length in a future account of the hunting ceremonies.

"Let it be buried in your stomach" refers also to the offering made the fire. By the red hickories are meant the strings of hickory bark which the bird hunter twists about his waist for a belt. The dead birds are carried by inserting their heads under this belt. Red is, of course, symbolic of his success. "The mangled things" (unigwalû"gĭ) are the wounded birds. Kana'tĭ is here used to designate the fire, on account of its connection with the hunting ceremonies.

INAGË'HÏ AYÂSTIⁿYÏ.

Usïnuli'yu Selagwû'tsï Gigage'ï getsû'ⁿneliga tsûdandâgi'hï aye`li'yu, usïnuli'yu. Yû!

Translation.

TO SHOOT DWELLERS IN THE WILDERNESS.

Instantly the Red Selagwû'tsï strike you in the very center of your soul—instantly. Yû!

Explanation.

This short formula, obtained from A`wani'ta, is recited by the hunter while taking aim. The bowstring is let go—or, rather, the trigger is pulled—at the final *Yû!* He was unable to explain the meaning of the word selagwû'tsï further than that it referred to the bullet. Later investigation, however, revealed the fact that this is the Cherokee name of a reed of the genus Erianthus, and the inference follows that the stalk of the plant was formerly used for arrow shafts. Red implies that the arrow is always successful in reaching the mark aimed at, and in this instance may refer also to its being bloody when withdrawn from the body of the animal. Inagë'hï, "dwellers in the wilderness," is the generic term for game, including birds, but A`wani'ta has another formula intended especially for deer.

(YÂ'NA TÏ'KANÂGI'TA.)

He +! Hayuya'haniwä', hayuya'haniwä', hayuya'haniwä', hayuya'haniwä'.
Tsistuyi' nehandu'yanû, Tsistuyi' nehandu'yanû—Yoho' +!
He +! Hayuya'haniwä', hayuya'haniwä', hayuya'haniwä', hayuya'haniwä'.
Kuwâhi' nehandu'yanû', Kuwâhi nehandu'yanû—Yoho' +!
He +! Hayuya'haniwä', hayuya'haniwä', hayuya'haniwä, hayuya'haniwä'.
Uyâ`ye' nehandu'yanû, Uyâ`ye' nehandu'yanû'—Yoho' +!
He +! Hayuya'haniwä', hayuya'haniwä', hayuya'haniwä, hayuya'haniwä'.
Gâtekwâ'(hï) nehandu'yanû', Gâtekwâ'(hï) nehandu'yanû'—Yoho' +!
Ûlë-`nû' asëhï' tadeya'statakûnï' gûⁿnage astû'tsïkï'.

Translation.

BEAR SONG.

He! Hayuya'haniwä', hayuya'haniwä', hayuya'haniwä', hayuya'haniwä'.
In Rabbit Place you were conceived (repeat)—Yoho' +!
He! Hayuya'haniwä', hayuya'haniwä', hayuya'haniwä', hayuya'haniwä'.

In Mulberry Place you were conceived (repeat)—Yoho' +!

He!   Hayuya'haniwä',   hayuya'haniwä',   hayuya'haniwä', hayuya'haniwä'.

In Uyâ'`yë you were conceived (repeat)—Yoho' +!

He!   Hayuya'haniwä',   hayuya'haniwä',   hayuya'haniwä', hayuya'haniwä'.

In the Great Swamp (?) you were conceived (repeat)—Yoho' +!

And now surely we and the good black things, the best of all, shall see each other.

Explanation.

This song, obtained from A`yû^{n}inï in connection with the story of the Origin of the Bear, as already mentioned, is sung by the bear hunter, in order to attract the bears, while on his way from the camp to the place where he expects to hunt during the day. It is one of those taught the Cherokees by the Ani-Tsâ'kahï before they lost their human shape and were transformed into bears. The melody is simple and plaintive.

The song consists of four verses followed by a short recitation. Each verse begins with a loud prolonged *He* +! and ends with *Yoho'* +! uttered in the same manner. Hayuya'haniwä' has no meaning. Tsistu'yï, Kuwâ'hï, Uyâ'`yë, and Gâte'kwâhï are four mountains, in each of which the bears have a townhouse and hold a dance before going into their dens for the winter. The first three named are high peaks in the Smoky Mountains, on the Tennessee line, in the neighborhood of Clingman's Dome and Mount Guyot. The fourth is southeast of Franklin, North Carolina, toward the South Carolina line, and may be identical with Fodderstack Mountain. In Kuwahi dwells the great bear chief and doctor, in whose magic bath the wounded bears are restored to health. They are said to originate or be conceived in the mountains named, because these are their headquarters. The "good black things" referred to in the recitation are the bears.

HIÄ' ATSÛ`TI'YÏ TSUN'TANÛ.

Sgë! Nâ'gwa hitsatû'ⁿgani'ga hitsiga'tugï'. Titsila'wisû'ⁿhï ᵘwâgi'`lï tege'tsûts`gû'`lawistï'. Tsuli'stana'lû ûlë' waktûï, agi'stï une'ka itsû'ⁿyatan ilû'ïstani'ga. Gûⁿwatu'hwïtû' nûⁿna'hï degûndâltsi'dâhe'stï. ᵘWâ'hisâ'nahï tigiwatsi'la. Tutsegû'`lawistï'tege'stï. Ûⁿtalï' degû'ⁿwatanûhï, uhisa'`tï nige'sûⁿna. Tsuwatsi'la dadâl`tsi'ga. A`yû A`yûⁿinï tigwadâ'ita. Yû!

Translation.

THIS IS FOR CATCHING LARGE FISH.

Listen! Now you settlements have drawn near to hearken. Where you have gathered in the foam you are moving about as one. You Blue Cat and the others, I have come to offer you freely the white food. Let the paths from every direction recognize each other. Our spittle shall be in agreement. Let them (your and my spittle) be together as we go about. They (the fish) have become a prey and there shall be no loneliness. Your spittle has become agreeable. I am called Swimmer. Yû!

Explanation.

This formula, from A`yûⁿinï's' book, is for the purpose of catching large fish. According to his instructions, the fisherman must first chew a small piece of Yugwilû' (Venus' Flytrap—Dionæa muscipula) and spit it upon the bait and also upon the hook. Then, standing facing the stream, he recites the formula and puts the bait upon the hook. He will be able to pull out a fish at once, or if the fish are not about at the moment they will come in a very short time.

The Yugwilû' is put upon the bait from the idea that it will enable the hook to attract and hold the fish as the plant itself seizes and holds insects in its cup. The root is much prized by the Cherokees for this purpose, and those in the West, where the plant is not found, frequently send requests for it to their friends in Carolina.

The prayer is addressed directly to the fish, who are represented as living in settlements. The same expression as has already been mentioned is sometimes used by the doctors in speaking of the *tsgâ'ya* or worms which are supposed to cause sickness by getting under the skin of the patient. The Blue Cat (*Amiurus, genus*) is addressed as the principal fish and the bait is spoken of as the "white food," an expression used also of the viands prepared at the feast of the green corn dance, to indicate their wholesome character. "Let the paths from every direction recognize each other," means let the fishes, which are supposed to have regular trails through the water, assemble together at the place where the speaker takes his station, as friends recognizing each other at a distance approach to greet each other, "Wâhisâ'nahï tigiwatsi'la, rendered "our spittle shall be in agreement," is a peculiar archaic expression that can not be literally translated. It implies that there shall be such close sympathy between the fisher and the fish that their spittle shall be as the spittle of one individual. As before stated, the spittle is believed to exert an important influence upon the whole physical and mental being. The expression "your spittle has become agreeable" is explained by A`yûⁿinï as an assertion or wish that the fish may prove palatable, while the words rendered "there shall be no loneliness" imply that there shall be an abundant catch.

LOVE.

(YÛⁿWË'HÏ UGÛ'ⁿWA`LÏ I.)

Ku! Sgë! *Alahi'yï* tsûl`dâ'histï, Higë``ya tsûl`di'yï, hatûⁿgani'ga. *Elahi'yï* iyûⁿta ditsûl`dâ'histï, Higë``ya Tsûne'ga. Tsisa``tï nige'sûⁿna. Tsâduhi'yï. Nâ'gwa-skïn'ï usïnuli'yu hûⁿskwane'`lûⁿgû' tsisga'ya agine'ga. Agisa``tï nige'sûⁿna. Nâ'gwa nûⁿâ une'ga hûⁿskwanûⁿneli'ga. Uhisa``tï nige'sûⁿna. Nâ'gwa skwade'tastani'ga. Sa`ka'ni u'tatï nige'sûⁿna. Nûⁿâ une'ga skiksa``ûⁿtaneli'ga. Elaye'`lï iyûⁿta skwalewistä``tani'ga E'latï gesûⁿ tsïtage'stï. Agisa``tï nige'sûⁿna. Agwâ'duhi'yu. Kûltsâ'te une'ga skiga``tani'ga. Uhisa``tï nige'sûⁿna, gûⁿkwatsâti'tege'sti. Tsi-sa`ka'ni agwä'tï nige'sûⁿna. Usïnuli'yu hûⁿskwane'`lûⁿgû'.

Ha-nâ'gwûlë *Elahi'yï* iyûⁿtä dûhiyane'`lûⁿgû' a'gë``ya sa`ka'ni. Nâ'gwa nûⁿâ'hï sa`ka'ni hûⁿtane'`laneli'ga. Uhisa``tï-gwû u'danû dudusa'gï tanela'sï. Nûⁿâ'hï sa`ka'nï tade'tâstani'ga. Nâgwûlë' hûⁿhiyatsâ'ûⁿtaniga. E'latï gesûⁿ tû'l`taniga. Dedu'laskûⁿ-gwû igûⁿwa`lawi'stï uhi'sa`ti'yï widaye'la`ni'ga. Dedulaskûⁿ-gwû igûⁿwa`lawi'stï uhi'sa`ti'yï nitûⁿneli'ga.

Ha-sâgwahi'yu itsilasta'agï + + uwä'sahi'yu, etsane'`laneli'ga. Agisa``tï nige'sûⁿna. Agwâ'duhï. A'yû agwadantâ'gï aye`li'yu d?ka``lani'lï duda'ntâ, uktahûⁿstï nige'sûⁿna. Yûⁿwï tsu'tsatûⁿ widudante'`tï nige'sûⁿna, nitûⁿneli'ga. Sâ'gwahï itsilasta'lagï, etsane'`laneli'ga kûlkwâ'gi-nasï' igûlstû'`lï gegane'`lanûⁿ.

Anisga'ya anewadi'stûⁿ unihisa`ti'yï. Tsu'nada'neilti'yï. Dï'la-gwû d egûⁿwänatsegû'`lawi'sdidegû'. Ayâ'ise'ta-gwû u'danû. Tsunada'neilti'yï. Utse'tsti-gwû degûⁿwänatsegû'`lawis'didegû'. Tsunada'neilti'yï. Ka'ga-gwû degûⁿwänatsegû'`awisdidegû'. Tsunada'neilti'yï. Da'l`ka-gwû degûⁿwänatsegû'`lawisdidegû'.

Kûlkwâ'gï igûlsta'lagï unihisa`ti'yu. Ige'ski-gwû nige'sûⁿna. Ayâ'ise'ta-gwû u'danû degû'ⁿwänatsûn`ti-degû'. K?si-gwû degû'ⁿwänatsûn`ti-degû'. A'yagâgû' tsisga'ya agine'ga ûⁿgwane''lanû'hï + + Nûⁿdâgû'ⁿyï iti'tsa ditsidâ'ga. Agisa'`tï nige'sûⁿna. Agwâduhi'yu. Tsi-sa`ka'nï agwä'tatï nige'sûⁿna. Kûltsâ'te une'ga ûⁿni'tagâgû' gûkwatsâ'nti-degû'. Agisä'`tï nige'sûⁿna. A'yû agwadantâ'gï aye`li'yu gûlasi'ga tsûda'ntâ, uktahû'ⁿstï nige'sûⁿna. A'yû tsï'gï tsûda'nta O O. Sgë!

Translation.

CONCERNING LIVING HUMANITY (LOVE).

Kû! Listen! In Alahi'yï you repose, O Terrible Woman, O you have drawn near to hearken. There in Elahiyï you are at rest, O White Woman. No one is ever lonely when with you. You are most beautiful. Instantly and at once you have rendered me a white man. No one is ever lonely when with me. Now you have made the path white for me. It shall never be dreary. Now you have put me into it. It shall never become blue. You have brought down to me from above the white road. There in mid-earth (mid-surface) you have placed me. I shall stand erect upon the earth. No one is ever lonely when with me. I am very handsome. You have put me into the white house. I shall be in it as it moves about and no one with me shall ever be lonely. Verily, I shall never become blue. Instantly you have caused it to be so with me.

And now there in Elahiyï you have rendered the woman blue. Now you have made the path blue for her. Let her be completely veiled in loneliness. Put her into the blue road. And now bring her down. Place her standing upon the earth. Where her feet are now and wherever she may go, let loneliness leave its mark upon her. Let her be marked out for loneliness where she stands.

Ha! I belong to the (Wolf) (+ +) clan, that one alone which was allotted into for you. No one is ever lonely with me. I am handsome. Let her put her soul the very center of my soul, never to turn away. Grant that in the midst of men she shall never think of them. I belong to the one clan alone which was allotted for you when the seven clans were established.

Where (other) men live it is lonely. They are very loathsome. The common polecat has made them so like himself that they are fit only for his company. They have became mere refuse. They are very loathsome. The common opossum has made them so like himself that they are fit only to be with him. They are very loathsome. Even the crow has made them so like himself that they are fit only for his company. They are very loathsome. The miserable rain-crow has made them so like himself that they are fit only to be with him.

The seven clans all alike make one feel very lonely in their company. They are not even good looking. They go about clothed with mere refuse. They even go about covered with dung. But I— I was ordained to be a white man. I stand with my face toward the Sun Land. No one is ever lonely with me. I am very handsome. I shall certainly never become blue. I am covered by the everlasting white house wherever I go. No one is ever lonely with me. Your soul has come into the very center of my soul, never to turn away. I—(Gatigwanasti,) (O O)—I take your soul. Sgë!

Explanation.

This unique formula is from one of the loose manuscript sheets of Gatigwanasti, now dead, and belongs to the class known as Yûⁿwë'hï or love charms (literally, concerning "living humanity") including all those referring in any way to the marital or sexual relation. No explanation accompanies the formula, which must therefore be interpreted from analogy. It appears to be recited by the lover himself—not by a hired shaman—perhaps while painting and adorning himself for the dance. (*See next two formulas.*)

The formula contains several obscure expressions which require further investigation. Elahiyĭ or Alahiyĭ, for it is written both ways in the manuscript, does not occur in any other formula met with thus far, and could not be explained by any of the shamans to whom it was submitted. The nominative form may be Elahĭ, perhaps from *ela*, "the earth," and it may be connected with Wa'hĭlĭ, the formulistic name for the south. The spirit invoked is the White Woman, white being the color denoting the south.

Uhisa'ʻtĭ, rendered here "lonely," is a very expressive word to a Cherokee and is of constant recurrence in the love formulas. It refers to that intangible something characteristic of certain persons which inevitably chills and depresses the spirits of all who may be so unfortunate as to come within its influence. Agisa'ʻtĭ nige'sûⁿna, "I never render any one lonely," is an intensified equivalent for, "I am the best company in the world," and to tell a girl that a rival lover is uhisa'ʻtĭ is to hold out to her the sum of all dreary prospects should she cast in her lot with him.

The speaker, who evidently has an exalted opinion of himself, invokes the aid of the White Woman, who is most beautiful and is never uhisa'ʻtĭ. She at once responds by making him a white—that is, a happy—man, and placing him in the white road of happiness, which shall never become blue with grief or despondency. She then places him standing in the middle of the earth, that he may be seen and admired by the whole world, especially by the female portion. She finally puts him into the white house, where happiness abides forever. The verb implies that the house shelters him like a cloak and goes about with him wherever he may go.

There is something comical in the extreme self-complacency with which he asserts that he is very handsome and will never become blue and no one with him is ever lonely. As before stated, white signifies peace and happiness, while blue is the emblem of sorrow and disappointment.

Having thus rendered himself attractive to womankind, he turns his attention to the girl whom he particularly desires to win. He begins by filling her soul with a sense of desolation and loneliness. In the beautiful language of the formula, her path becomes blue and she is veiled in loneliness. He then asserts, and reiterates, that he is of the one only clan which was allotted for her when the seven clans were established.

He next pays his respects to his rivals and advances some very forcible arguments to show that she could never be happy with any of them. He says that they are all "lonesome" and utterly loathsome—the word implies that they are mutually loathsome—and that they are the veriest trash and refuse. He compares them to so many polecats, oppossums, and crows, and finally likens them to the raincrow (cuckoo; *Coccygus*), which is regarded with disfavor on account of its disagreeable note. He grows more bitter in his denunciations as he proceeds and finally disposes of the matter by saying that all the seven clans alike are uhisa'˙tï and are covered with filth. Then follows another glowing panegyric of himself, closing with the beautiful expression, "your soul has come into the very center of mine, never to turn away," which reminds one forcibly of the sentiment in the German love song, "Du liegst mir im Herzen." The final expression, "I take your soul," implies that the formula has now accomplished its purpose in fixing her thoughts upon himself.

When successful, a ceremony of this kind has the effect of rendering the victim so "blue" or lovesick that her life is in danger until another formula is repeated to make, her soul "white" or happy again. Where the name of the individual or clan is mentioned in these formulas the blank is indicated in the manuscript by crosses + + or ciphers O O or by the word iyu'stï, "like."

HI'Ä ÄMA'YÏ Ä'TAWAST'YÏ KANÂ'HEHÛ.

Sgë! Ha-nâ'gwa usïnuli'yu hatû'ⁿgani'ga *Higë'`yagu'ga*, tsûwatsi'la gi'gage tsiye'la skïna'dû`'lani'ga. O O digwadâ'ita. Sa`ka'nï tûgwadûne'lûhï. Atsanû'ⁿgï gi'gage skwâsû'hisa`tani'ga. + + kûlstä'lagï + sa'ka'nï nu'tatanû'ⁿta. Ditu'nûⁿnâ'gï dagwû'laskûⁿ-gwû deganu'y`tasi'ga. Galâ'nûⁿtse'ta-gwû dagwadûne'lidise'stï. Sgë!

Translation.

THIS TELLS ABOUT GOING INTO THE WATER.

Listen! O, now instantly, you have drawn near to hearken, O Agë'`yagu'ga. You have come to put your red spittle upon my body. My name is (Gatigwanasti.) The blue had affected me. You have come and clothed me with a red dress. She is of the (Deer) clan. She has become blue. You have directed her paths straight to where I have my feet, and I shall feel exultant. Listen!

Explanation.

This formula, from Gatigwanasti's book, is also of the Yûⁿwë'hï class, and is repeated by the lover when about to bathe in the stream preparatory to painting himself for the dance. The services of a shaman are not required, neither is any special ceremony observed. The technical word used in the heading, ä'tawasti'yï, signifies plunging or going entirely into a liquid. The expression used for the ordinary "going to water," where the water is simply dipped up with the hand, is ämâ'yï dita`ti'yï, "taking them to water."

The prayer is addressed to Agë"yaguga, a formulistic name for the moon, which is supposed to exert a great influence in love affairs, because the dances, which give such opportunities for love making, always take place at night. The shamans can not explain the meaning of the term, which plainly contains the word agë"ya, "woman," and may refer to the moon's supposed influence over women. In Cherokee mythology the moon is a man. The ordinary name is nû"ndâ, or more fully, nû"ndâ sû"nâyë'hï, "the sun living in the night," while the sun itself is designated as nû"ndâ igë'hï, "the sun living in the day."

By the red spittle of Agë"yagu'ga and the red dress with which the lover is clothed are meant the red paint which he puts upon himself. This in former days was procured from a deep red clay known as ela-wâ'tï, or "reddish brown clay." The word red as used in the formula is emblematic of success in attaining his object, besides being the actual color of the paint. Red, in connection with dress or ornamentation, has always been a favorite color with Indians throughout America, and there is some evidence that among the Cherokees it was regarded also as having a mysterious protective power. In all these formulas the lover renders the woman blue or disconsolate and uneasy in mind as a preliminary to fixing her thoughts upon himself. (*See next formula*.)

(YÛ'ⁿWË'HÏ UGÛ'ⁿWA`LÏ II.)

Yû'ⁿwëhï, yû'ⁿwëhï, yû'ⁿwëhï, yû'ⁿwëhï.
Galû'ⁿlatï, datsila'ï—Yû'ⁿwëhï, yû'ⁿwëhï, yû'ⁿwëhï, yû'ⁿwëhï.
Nûⁿdâgû'ⁿyï gatla'ahï—Yû'ⁿwëhï.
Gë`yagu'ga Gi'gage, tsûwatsi'la gi'gage tsiye'la skïna'dû`lani'ga—Yû'ⁿwëhï, yû'ⁿwëhï, yû'ⁿwëhï.
Hiä-`nû' atawe'ladi'yï kanâ'hëhû galûⁿlti'tla.

Translation.

SONG FOR PAINTING.

Yû'ⁿwëhï, yû'ⁿwëhï, yû'ⁿwëhï, yû'ⁿwëhï.
I am come from above—Yû'ⁿwëhï, yû'ⁿwëhï, yû'ⁿwëhï, yû'ⁿwëhï.
I am come down from the Sun Land—yû'ⁿwëhï.

O Red Agë`yagu'ga. you have come and put your red spittle upon my body—Yû'ⁿwëhï, yû'ⁿwëhï, yû'ⁿwëhï!.
And this above is to recite while one is painting himself.

Explanation.

This formula, from Gatigwanasti, immediately follows the one last given, in the manuscript book, and evidently comes immediately after it also in practical use. The expressions used have been already explained. The one using the formula first bathes in the running stream, reciting at the same time the previous formula "Amâ'yĭ Ä'tawasti'yĭ." He then repairs to some convenient spot with his paint, beads, and other paraphernalia and proceeds to adorn himself for the dance, which usually begins about an hour after dark, but is not fairly under way until nearly midnight. The refrain, yû'ⁿwëhĭ, is probably *sung* while mixing the paint, and the other portion is recited while applying the pigment, or vice versa. Although these formula are still in use, the painting is now obsolete, beyond an occasional daubing of the face, without any plan or pattern, on the occasion of a dance or ball play.

ADALANI'STA`TI'YĬ. I.

Sgë! Ha-nâ'gwa hatû'ⁿgani'ga nihï'—

—Tsa'watsi'lû tsïkï' tsïkû' ayû'.
—Hiyelû' tsïkï' tsïkû' ayû'.
—Tsäwiyû' tsïkï' tsïkû' ayû'.
—Tsûnahu' tsïkï' tsïkû' ayû'.

Sgë! Nâ'gwa hatû'ⁿgani'ga, Hïkayû'ⁿlige. Hiä' asga'ya uda'ntâ tsa`ta'hisi'ga [Hïkayû'ⁿlige] hiye'lastûⁿ. Tsaskûlâ'hïsti-gwû' nige'sûⁿna. Dïkana'watûⁿta-gwû tsûtû'neli'ga. Hïlû dudantë'`tï nige'sûⁿna. Duda'ntâ dûskalûⁿ'tseli'ga. Astï' digûⁿ'nage tagu'talûⁿtani'ga.

Translation.

TO ATTRACT AND FIX THE AFFECTIONS.

Listen! O, now you have drawn near to hearken—

—Your spittle, I take it, I eat it.
—Your body, I take it, I eat it.   Each sung four times.
—Your flesh, I take it, I eat it
—Your heart, I take it, I eat it

Listen! O, now you have drawn near to hearken, O, Ancient One. This man's (woman's) soul has come to rest at the edge of your body. You are never to let go your hold upon it. It is ordained that you shall do just as you are requested to do. Let her never think upon any other place. Her soul has faded within her. She is bound by the black threads.

Explanation.

This formula is said by the young husband, who has just married an especially engaging wife, who is liable to be attracted by other men. The same formula may also be used by the woman to fix her husband's affections. On the first night that they are together the husband watches until his wife is asleep, when, sitting up by her side, he recites the first words: Sgë! Ha-nâ'gwa hatû'ⁿgani'ga nihï', and then sings the next four words: Tsawatsi'lû tsïkï' tsïkû' ayû', "Your spittle, I take it, I eat it," repeating the words four times. While singing he moistens his fingers with spittle, which he rubs upon the breast of the woman. The next night he repeats the operation, this time singing the words, "I take your body." The third night, in the same way, he sings, "I take your flesh," and the fourth and last night, he sings "I take your heart," after which he repeats the prayer addressed to the Ancient One, by which is probably meant the Fire (the Ancient White). A`yûⁿinï states that the final sentences should be masculine, i. e., His soul has faded, etc., and refer to any would-be seducer. There is no gender distinction in the third person in Cherokee. He claimed that this ceremony was so effective that no husband need have any fears for his wife after performing it.

ADAYE'LIGA'GTA`TÏ'.

Yû! Galûⁿlatï tsûl`dâ'histï, Giya'giya' Sa'ka'ni, nâ'gwa nûⁿtalûⁿ i'yûⁿta. Tsâ'la Sa`ka'ni tsûgistâ`'tï adûⁿni'ga. Nâ'gwa nidâtsu'l`tanûⁿ'ta, nûⁿ'tâtagû' hisa'hasi'ga. Tani'dâgûⁿ' aye`'li dehidâ'siga. Unada'ndâ dehiyâ'staneli'ga. Nidugale'ntanûⁿ'ta nidûhûⁿneli'ga.

Tsisga'ya agine'ga', nûⁿdâgûⁿyï ditsidâ`'stï. Gû'nï âstû' uhisa`'tï nige'sûⁿna. Agë`'ya une'ga hi'ä iyu'stï gûlstû`'li, iyu'stï tsûdâ'ita. Uda'ndâ usïnu'lï dâdatinilû'gûⁿeli'. Nûⁿdâgûⁿyitsû' dâdatinilugûstanelï. Tsisga'ya agine'ga, ditsidûstû'ⁿï nû`nû' kana'tlani'ga. Tsûnkta' tegä`la'watege'stï. Tsiye'lûⁿ gesû'ⁿï uhisa`'tï nige'sûⁿna.

Translation.

FOR SEPARATION (OF LOVERS).

Yû! On high you repose, O Blue Hawk, there at the far distant lake. The blue tobacco has come to be your recompense. Now you have arisen at once and come down. You have alighted midway between them where they two are standing. You have spoiled their souls immediately. They have at once become separated.

I am a white man; I stand at the sunrise. The good sperm shall never allow any feeling of loneliness. This white woman is of the Paint (iyustï) clan; she is called (iyustï) Wâyï'. We shall instantly turn her soul over. We shall turn it over as we go toward the Sun Land. I am a white man. Here where I stand it (her soul) has attached itself to (literally, "come against") mine. Let her eyes in their sockets be forever watching (for me). There is no loneliness where my body is.

Explanation.

This formula, from A`yûnini's book, is used to separate two lovers or even a husband and wife, if the jealous rival so desires. In the latter case the preceding formula, from the same source, would be used to forestall this spell. No explanation of the ceremony is given, but the reference to tobacco may indicate that tobacco is smoked or thrown into the fire during the recitation. The particular hawk invoked (giya'giya') is a large species found in the coast region but seldom met with in the mountains. Blue indicates that it brings trouble with it, while white in the second paragraph indicates that the man is happy and attractive in manner.

In the first part of the formula the speaker calls upon the Blue Hawk to separate the lovers and spoil their souls, *i. e.*, change their feeling toward each other. In the second paragraph he endeavors to attract the attention of the woman by eulogizing himself. The expression, "we shall turn her soul over," seems here to refer to turning her affections, but as generally used, to turn one's soul is equivalent to killing him.

(ADALANÏ'STÄ`TIYÏ II.)

Yû! Ha-nâ'gwa ada'ntï dätsâsi'ga, * * hïlû(stû'`lï), (* *) ditsa-(dâ'ita). A'yû O O tsila(stû'`lï). Hiye'la tsïkï' tsïkû'. (Yû!).

Yû! Ha-nâ'gwa ada'ntï dätsâsi'ga, * * hïlû(stû'`lï), (* *) ditsa-(dâ'ita). A'yû O O tsûwi'ya tsïkï' tsïkû'. Yû!

Yû! Ha-nâ'gwa ada'ntï dätsâsi'ga, * * hïlû(stû'`lï), (* *) ditsa-(dâ'ita). A'yû O O tsûwatsi'la tsïkï' tsïkû'. Yû!

Yû! Ha-nâ'gwa ada'ntï dätsâsi'ga, * * hïlû(stû'`lï), (* *) ditsa-(dâ'ita). A'yû O O tsûnahü' tsïkï' tsïkû'. Yû!

Sgë! "Ha-nâ'gwa ada'ntï dutsase', tsugale'ntï nige'sû^{n}na," tsûdûneï, Hïkayû^{n}lige galû'^{n}latï. Kananë'skï Û'^{n}nage galû'nlatï (h)etsatsâ'û^{n}tänile'ï. Tsänilta'gï tsûksâ'û^{n}tanile'ï. * * gûla(stû'`lï), * * ditsadâ'(ita). Dudantâ'gï uhani'latâ tïkwenû'$^n$tani'ga. Kûlkwâ'gï igûlsta'lagï iyû'$^n$ta yû'$^n$wï adayû'$^n$latawä' dudûne'lida'lû$^n$ uhisa'`tï nige'sû^{n}na.

Sgë! Ha-nâ'gwatï uhisa'`tï dutlû'$^n$tani'ga. Tsû'nkta daskâ'lû$^n$tsi'ga. Sâ'gwahï dï'kta de'gayelû$^n$tsi'ga. Ga'tsa igûnû'nugâ'ïstû uda'ntâ? Usû'hita nudanû'$^n$na ûltû$^n$ge'ta, gû$^n$wadûneli'dege'stï. Igû$^n$wûlsta'`ti-gwû duwâlu'wa`tû$^n$tï nige'sû$^n$na. Kananë'skï Û'$^n$nage'ï tsanildew`se'stï ada'ntâ uktû^{n}lesi'dastï nige'sûna. Gadâyu'stï tsûdâ'ita ada'ntï tside'atsasi'ga. A'ya a`kwatseli'ga.

Sgë! Ha-nâ'gwûlë' hû^{n}hatû^{n}ga'ga, Hïkayû^{n}lï Gi'gage. Tsetsûli'sï hiye'lastû^n a`ta'hisi'ga. Ada'ntâ hasû'gû'`lawï'stani'ga, tsa'skaláhistï nige'sû^{n}na. Hïkayû^{n}lige denätsegû`la'wïstani'ga. Agë'`ya gï'nsû^{n}gû`lawis'tani'ga uda'ntâ *uwahisï'sata*. Dïgïnaskûlâ'hïstï nige'sû^{n}na. Yû!

Hi'ä nasgwû' u`tlâ'yi-gwû dïgalû'ⁿwistan'tï snûⁿâ'yï hani'`lihûgûnasgi'stï. Gane'tsï aye'`lï asi'tadis'tï watsi'la, ganûⁿli'yetï aguwaye'nï andisgâ'ï. Sâi'yï tsika'nâhe itsu'laha'gwû.

Translation.

TO FIX THE AFFECTIONS.

Yû! Ha! Now the souls have come together. You are of the Deer (x x) clan. Your name is (x x) Ayâsta, I am of the Wolf (o-o) clan. Your body, I take it, I eat it. Yû! Ha! Now the souls have come together. You are of the Deer clan. Your name is Ayâsta. I am of the Wolf clan. Your flesh I take, I eat. Yû!

Yû! Ha! Now the souls have come together. You are of the Deer clan. Your name is Ayâsta. I am of the Wolf clan. Your spittle I take, I eat. I! Yû!

Yû! Ha! Now the souls have come together. You are of the Deer clan. Your name is Ayâsta. I am of the Wolf clan. Your heart I take, I eat. Yû!

Listen! "Ha! Now the souls have met, never to part," you have said, O Ancient One above. O Black Spider, you have been brought down from on high. You have let down your web. She is of the Deer clan; her name is Ayâsta. Her soul you, have wrapped up in (your) web. There where the people of the seven clans are continually coming in sight and again disappearing (i. e. moving about, coming; and going), there was never any feeling of loneliness.

Listen! Ha! But now you have covered her over with loneliness. Her eyes have faded. Her eyes have come to fasten themselves on one alone. Whither can her soul escape? Let her be sorrowing as she goes along, and not for one night alone. Let her become an aimless wanderer, whose trail may never be followed. O Black

Spider, may you hold her soul in your web so that it shall never get through the meshes. What is the name of the soul? They two have come together. It is mine!

Listen! Ha! And now you have hearkened, O Ancient Red. Your grandchildren have come to the edge of your body. You hold them yet more firmly in your grasp, never to let go your hold. O Ancient One, we have become as one. The woman has put her (x x x) soul into our hands. We shall never let it go! Yû!

(Directions.)—And this also is for just the same purpose (the preceding formula in the manuscript book is also a love charm). It must be done by stealth at night when they are asleep. One must put the hand on the middle of the breast and rub on spittle with the hand, they say. The other formula is equally good.

Explanation.

This formula to fix the affections of a young wife is taken from the manuscript sheets of the late Gatigwanasti. It very much resembles the other formula for the same purpose, obtained from A`yû"inï, and the brief directions show that the ceremony is alike in both. The first four paragraphs are probably sung, as in the other formula, on four successive nights, and, as explained in the directions and as stated verbally by A`yû"inï, this must be done. stealthily at night while the woman is asleep, the husband rubbing his spittle on her breast with his hand while chanting the song in a low tone, hardly above a whisper. The prayer to the Ancient One, or Ancient Red (Fire), in both formulas, and the expression, "I come to the edge of your body," indicate that the hands are first warmed over the fire, in accordance with the general practice when laying on the hands. The prayer to the Black Spider is a beautiful specimen of poetic imagery, and hardly requires an explanation. The final paragraph indicates the successful accomplishment of his purpose. "Your grandchildren" (tsetsûli'sï) is an expression frequently used in addressing the more important deities.

MISCELLANEOUS FORMULAS.

SÛⁿNÂ'YÏ EDÂ'HÏ E'SGA ASTÛⁿTI'YÏ.

Sgë! Uhyûⁿtsâ'yï galûnlti'tla tsûltâ'histï, Hïsgaya Gigage'ï, usïnu'lï di'tsakûni' denatlûⁿhi'sani'ga, Uy-igawa'stï duda'ntï. Nûⁿnâ'hï tatuna'watï. Usïnu'lï duda'ntâ dani'yûⁿstanilï'.

Sgë! Uhyûⁿtlâ'yï galûⁿlti'tla tsûltâ'histï, Hïsga'ya Të'halu, *hinaw?sü'?ki*. Ha-usïnu'lï nâ'gwa di'tsakûni' denatlûⁿhisani'ga uy-igawa'stï duda'ntï. Nûⁿnâ'hï tätuna'wätï. Usïnu'lï duda'ntâ dani'galïstani'.

Translation.

TO SHORTEN A NIGHT-GOER ON THIS SIDE.

Listen! In the Frigid Land above you repose, O Red Man, quickly we two have prepared your arrows for the soul of the Imprecator. He has them lying along the path. Quickly we two will take his soul as we go along.

Listen! In the Frigid Land above you repose, O Purple Man, * * * *. Ha! Quickly now we two have prepared your arrows for the soul of the Imprecator. He has them lying along the path. Quickly we two will cut his soul in two.

Explanation.

This formula, from A`yûⁿinïs' book, is for the purpose of driving away a witch from the house of a sick person, and opens up a most interesting chapter of Cherokee beliefs. The witch is supposed to go about chiefly under cover of darkness, and hence is called sûⁿnâ'yï edâ'hï, "the night goer." This is the term in common use; but there are a number of formulistic expressions to designate a witch, one of which, u'ya igawa'stï, occurs in the body of the formula and may be rendered "the imprecator," i. e., the sayer of evil things or curses. As the counteracting of a deadly spell always results in the death of its author, the formula is stated to be not merely to drive away the wizard, but to kill him, or, according to the formulistic expression, "to shorten him (his life) on this side."

When it becomes known that a man is dangerously sick the witches front far and near gather invisibly about his house after nightfall to worry him and even force their way in to his bedside unless prevented by the presence of a more powerful shaman within the house. They annoy the sick man and thus hasten his death by stamping upon the roof and beating upon the sides of the house; and if they can manage to get inside they raise up the dying sufferer from the bed and let him fall again or even drag him out upon the floor. The object of the witch in doing this is to prolong his term of years by adding to his own life as much as he can take from that of the sick man. Thus it is that a witch who is successful in these practices lives to be very old. Without going into extended details, it may be sufficient to state that the one most dreaded, alike by the friends of the sick man and by the lesser witches, is the Kâ'lana-ayeli'skï or Raven Mocker, so called because he flies through the air at night in a shape of fire, uttering sounds like the harsh croak of a raven.

The formula here given is short and simple as compared with some others. There is evidently a mistake in regard to the Red Man, who is here placed in the north, instead of in the east, as it should be. The reference to the arrows will be explained further on. Purple, mentioned in the second paragraph, has nearly the same symbolic meaning as blue, viz: Trouble, vexation and defeat; hence the Purple Man is called upon to frustrate the designs of the witch.

To drive away the witch the shaman first prepares four sharpened sticks, which he drives down into the ground outside the house at each of the four corners, leaving the pointed ends projecting upward and outward. Then, about noontime he gets ready the Tsâl-agayû'ⁿlï or "Old Tobacco" (*Nicotiana rustica*), with which he fills his pipe, repeating this formula during the operation, after which he wraps the pipe thus filled in a black cloth. This sacred tobacco is smoked only for this purpose. He then goes out into the forest, and returns just before dark, about which time the witch may be expected to put in an appearance. Lighting his pipe, he goes slowly around the house, puffing the smoke in the direction of every trail by which the witch might be. able to approach, and probably repeating the same or another formula the while. He then goes into the house and awaits results. When the witch approaches under cover of the darkness, whether in his own proper shape or in the form of some animal, the sharpened stick on that side of the house shoots up into the air and comes down like an arrow upon his head, inflicting such a wound as proves fatal within seven days. This explains the words of the formula, "We have prepared your arrows for the soul of the Imprecator. He has them lying along the path". A`yû'ⁿinï said nothing about the use of the sharpened sticks in this connection, mentioning only the tobacco, but the ceremony, as here described, is the one ordinarily used. When wounded the witch utters a groan which is heard by those listening inside the house, even at the distance of half a mile. No one knows certainly who the witch is until a day or two afterward, when some old man or woman, perhaps in a remote settlement, is suddenly seized with a mysterious illness and before seven clays elapse is dead.

GAHU'STÏ A'GIYAHU'SA.

Sgë! Ha-nâ'gwa hatû'ⁿgani'ga Nû'ⁿya Wâtige'ï, gahu'stï tsûtska'dï nige'sûⁿna. Ha-nâ'gwa dû'ⁿgihya'lï. Agiyahu'sa sï'kwa, haga' tsûⁿ-nû' iyû'ⁿta dätsi'waktû'hï. Tla-`ke' a'ya a'kwatseli'ga. O O digwadâi'ta.

Translation.

I HAVE LOST SOMETHING.

Listen! Ha! Now you have drawn near to hearken, O Brown Rock; you never lie about anything. Ha! Now I am about to seek for it. I have lost a hog and now tell me about where I shall find it. For is it not mine? My name is—.

Explanation.

This formula, for finding anything lost, is so simple as to need but little explanation. Brown in this instance has probably no mythologic significance, but refers to the color of the stone used in the ceremony. This is a small rounded water-worn pebble, in substance resembling quartz and of a reddish-brown color. It is suspended by a string held between the thumb and finger of the shaman, who is guided in his search by the swinging of the pebble, which, according to their theory, will swing farther in the direction of the lost article than in the contrary direction! The shaman, who is always fasting, repeats the formula, while closely watching the motions of the swinging pebble. He usually begins early in the morning, making the first trial at the house of the owner of the lost article. After noting the general direction toward which it seems to lean he goes a considerable distance in that direction, perhaps half a mile or more, and makes a second trial. This time the pebble may swing off at an angle in another direction. He follows up in the direction indicated for perhaps another half mile, when on a third trial the stone may veer around toward the starting point, and a fourth attempt may complete the circuit. Having thus arrived at the conclusion that the missing article is somewhere within a certain circumscribed area, he advances to the center of this space and marks out upon the ground a small circle inclosing a cross with arms pointing toward the four cardinal points. Holding the stone over the center of the cross he again repeats the formula and notes the direction in which the pebble swings. This is the final trial and he fiow goes slowly and carefully over the whole surface in that direction, between the center of the circle and the limit of the circumscribed area until in theory, at least, the article is found. Should he fail, he is never at a loss for excuses, but the specialists in this line are generally very shrewd guessers well versed in the doctrine of probabilities.

There are many formulas for this purpose, some of them being long and elaborate. When there is reason to believe that the missing article has been stolen, the specialist first determines the clan or settlement to which the thief belongs and afterward the name of the individual. Straws, bread balls, and stones of various kinds are used in the different formulas, the ceremony differing according to .the medium employed. The stones are generally pointed crystals or antique arrowheads, and are suspended as already described, the point being supposed to turn finally in the direction of the missing object. Several of these stones have been obtained on the reservation and are now deposited in the National Museum. It need excite no surprise to find the hog mentioned in the formula, as this animal has been domesticated among the Cherokees for more than a century, although most of them are strongly prejudiced against it.

HIA' UNÁLE (ATEST'YĬ).

Yuhahi', yuhahi', yuhahi', yuhahi', yuhahi',
Yuhahi', yuhahi', yuhahi', yuhahi', yuhahi'—Yû!

Sgë! Ha-nâ'gwa hïnahû"ski tayï'. Ha-tâ'sti-gwû gû"ska'ihû. Tsûtali'igwati'na halu'`nï. Kû'nigwati'na dula'ska galû'"lati-gwû witu'ktï. Wigû"yasë'hïsï. Â'talï tsugû'"yï wite'tsatanû'"û"sï' nû"nâhï tsane'lagï de'gatsana'wadise'stï. Kûnstû' dutsasû'"ï atû'"wasûtë'hahï' tsûtûneli'sestï. Sgë!

Translation.

THIS IS TO FRIGHTEN A STORM.

Yuhahi', yuhahi', yuhahi', yuhahi', yuhahi',
Yuhahi', yuhahi', yuhahi', yuhahi', yuhahi'—Yû!

Listen! O now you are coming in rut. Ha! I am exceedingly afraid of you. But yet you are only tracking your wife. Her footprints can be seen there directed upward toward the heavens. I have pointed them out for you. Let your paths stretch out along the tree tops (?) on the lofty mountains (and) you shall have them (the paths) lying down without being disturbed, Let (your path) as you go along be where the waving branches meet. Listen!

Explanation.

This formula, from A`yû"inï's book, is for driving away, or "frightening" a storm, which threatens to injure the growing corn. The first part is a meaningless song, which is sting in a low tone in the peculiar style of most of the sacred songs. The storm, which is not directly named, is then addressed and declared to be coming on in a fearful manner on the track of his wife, like an animal in the rutting season. The shaman points out her tracks directed toward the upper regions and begs the storm spirit to follow her along the waving tree tops of the lofty mountains, where he shall be undisturbed.

The shaman stands facing the approaching storm with one hand stretched out toward it. After repeating the song and prayer he gently blows in the direction toward which he wishes it to go, waving his hand in the same direction as though pushing away the storm. A part of the storm is usually sent into the upper regions of the atmosphere. If standing at the edge of the field, he holds a blade of corn in one hand while repeating the ceremony.

DANAWÛ' TSUNEDÂLÛ'HÏ NUNATÛ'NELI'TALÛ'ⁿHÏ U'NALSTELTA'`TANÛ'HÏ.

Hayï'! Yû! Sgë! Nâ'gwa usïnuli'yu A'tasû Gi'gage'ï hinisa'latani'ga. Usïnu'lï duda'ntâ u'nanugâ'tsidasti' nige'sûⁿna. Duda'ntâ e`lawi'nï iyûⁿta ä'tasû digûⁿnage'ï degûⁿlskwï'tahise'stï, anetsâge'ta unanugâ'istï nige'sûⁿna, nitinûⁿneli'ga. Ä'tasû dusa'ladanûⁿstï nige'sûⁿna, nitinûⁿneli'ga. E`lawi'nï iyûⁿta ä'tasû ûⁿnage' ugûⁿ'hatû ûⁿnage' sâ'gwa da`liyë'kû`lani'ga *unadutlâ'gï*. Unanugâ'tsida'stï nige'sûⁿna, nûⁿneli'ga.

Usïnuli'yu tsunada'ntâ kûl`kwâ'gine tigalûⁿ'nltiyûⁿ'ï iyûⁿta ada'ntâ tega'yë`ti'tege'stï. Tsunada'ntâ tsuligali'stï nige'sûⁿna dudûni'tege'stï. Usïnu'lï deniûⁿeli'ga galûⁿ'latï iyûⁿta widu'l`tâhïstï'tege'stï. Ä'tasû gigage'ï dëhatagûⁿyastani'ga. Tsunada'ntâ tsudastûⁿ'nilida'stï nige'sûⁿna nûⁿneli'ga. Tsunada'ntâ galûⁿ'latï iyûⁿta witë'`titege'stï. Tsunada'ntâ anigwalu'gï une'ga gûⁿwa'nadagûⁿyastitege'stï. Sa`ka'nï udûnû'hï nige'sûⁿna usïnuli'yu. Yû!

Translation.

WHAT THOSE WHO HAVE BEEN TO WAR DID TO HELP THEMSELVES.

Hayï'! Yû! Listen! Now instantly we have lifted up the red war club. Quickly his soul shall be without motion. There under the earth, where the black war clubs shall be moving about like ball sticks in the game, there his soul shall be, never to reappear. We cause it to be so. He shall never go and lift up the war club. We cause it to be so. There under the earth the black war club (and) the black fog have come together as one for their covering. It shall never move about (i. e., the black fog shall never be lifted from them). We cause it to be so.

Instantly shall their souls be moving about there in the seventh heaven. Their souls shall never break in two. So shall it be. Quickly we have moved them (their souls) on high for them, where they shall be going about in peace. You (?) have shielded yourselves (?) with the red war club. Their souls shall never be knocked about. Cause it to be so. There on high their souls shall be going about. Let them shield themselves with the white war whoop. Instantly (grant that) they shall never become blue. Yû!

Explanation.

This formula, obtained from A`wani'ta, may be repeated by the doctor for as many as eight men at once when about to go to war. It is recited for four consecutive nights, immediately before setting out. There is no tabu enjoined and no beads are used, but the warriors "go to water" in the regular way, that is, they stand at the edge of the stream, facing the east and looking down upon the water, while the shaman, standing behind them, repeats the formula. On the fourth night the shaman gives to each man a small charmed root which has the power to confer invulnerability. On the eve of battle the warrior after bathing in the running stream chews a portion of this and spits the juice upon his body in order that the bullets of the enemy may pass him by or slide off from his skin like drops of water. Almost every man of the three hundred East Cherokees who served in the rebellion had this or a similar ceremony performed before setting out—many of them also consulting the oracular ulû^{n}sû'tï stone at the same time—and it is but fair to state that not more than two or three of the entire number were wounded in actual battle.

In the formula the shaman identifies himself with the warriors, asserting that "we" have lifted up the red war club, red being the color symbolic of success and having no reference to blood, as might be supposed from the connection. In the first paragraph he invokes curses upon the enemy, the future tense verb *It shall be*, etc., having throughout the force of *let it be*. He puts the souls of the doomed enemy in the lower regions, where the black war clubs are constantly waving about, and envelops them in a black fog, which shall never be lifted and out of which they shall never reappear. From the expression in the second paragraph, "their souls shall never be knocked about," the reference to the black war clubs moving about like ball sticks in the game would seem to imply that they are continually buffeting the doomed souls under the earth. The spirit land of the Cherokees is in the west, but in these formulas of malediction or blessing the soul of the doomed man is generally consigned to the underground region, while that of the victor is raised by antithesis to the seventh heaven.

Having disposed of the enemy, the shaman in the second paragraph turns his attention to his friends and at once raises their souls to the seventh heaven, where they shall go about in peace, shielded by (literally, "covered with") the red war club of success, and never to be knocked about by the blows of the enemy. "Breaking the soul in two" is equivalent to snapping the thread of life, the soul being regarded as an intangible something having length, like a rod or a string. This formula, like others written down by the same shaman, contains several evident inconsistencies both as to grammar and mythology, due to the fact that A`wanita is extremely careless with regard to details and that this particular formula has probably not been used for the last quarter of a century. The warriors are also made to shield themselves with the white war whoop, which should undoubtedly be the red war whoop, consistent with the red war club, white being the color emblematic of peace, which is evidently an incongruity. The war whoop is believed to have a positive magic power for the protection of the warrior, as well as for terrifying the foe.

The mythologic significance of the different colors is well shown in this formula. Red, symbolic of success, is the color of the war club with which the warrior is to strike the enemy and also of the other one with which he is to shield or "cover" himself. There is no doubt that the war whoop also should be represented as red. In conjuring with the beads for long life, for recovery from sickness, or for success in love, the ball play, or any other undertaking, the red beads represent the party for whose benefit the magic spell is wrought, and he is figuratively clothed in red and made to stand upon a red cloth or placed upon a red seat. The red spirits invoked always live in the east and everything pertaining to them is of the same color.

Black is always typical of death, and in this formula the soul of the enemy is continually beaten about by black war clubs and enveloped in a black fog. In conjuring to destroy an enemy the shaman uses black beads and invokes the black spirits—which always live in the west—bidding them tear out the man's soul, carry it to the west, and put it into the black coffin deep in the black mud, with a black serpent coiled above it.

Blue is emblematic of failure, disappointment, or unsatisfied desire. "They shall never become blue" means that they shall never fail in anything they undertake. In love charms the lover figuratively covers himself with red and prays that his rival shall become entirely blue and walk in a blue path. The formulistic expression, "He is entirely blue," closely approximates in meaning the common English phrase, "He feels blue." The blue spirits live in the north.

White—which occurs in this formula only by an evident error—denotes peace and happiness. In ceremonial addresses, as at the green corn dance and ball play, the people figuratively partake of white food and after the dance or the game return along the white trail to their white houses. In love charms the man, in order to induce the woman to cast her lot with his, boasts "I am a white man," implying that all is happiness where he is. White beads have the same meaning in the bead conjuring and white was the color of the stone pipe anciently used in ratifying peace treaties. The white spirits live in the south (Wa'halä).

Two other colors, brown and yellow, are also mentioned in the formulas. Wâtige'ï, "brown," is the term used to include brown, bay, dun, and similar colors, especially as applied to animals. It seldom occurs in the formulas and its mythologic significance is as yet undetermined. Yellow is of more frequent occurrence and is typical of trouble and all manner of vexation, the yellow spirits being generally invoked when the shaman wishes to bring down calamities upon the head of his victim, without actually destroying him. So far as present knowledge goes, neither brown nor yellow can be assigned to any particular point of the compass.

Usïnuli'yu, rendered "instantly," is the intensive form of usïnu'lï "quickly," both of which words recur constantly in the formulas, in some entering into almost every sentence. This frequently gives the translation an awkward appearance. Thus the final sentence above, which means literally "they shall never become blue instantly," signifies "Grant that they shall never become blue, i. e., shall never fail in their purpose, *and grant our petition instantly.*"

DIDA'LATLI''TÏ.

Sgë! Nâ'gwa tsûdantâ'gï tegû'ⁿyatawâ'ilateli'ga. Iyustï (O O) tsilastû'`lï Iyu'stï (O O) ditsadâ'ita. Tsûwatsi'la elawi'nï tsidâ'hïstani'ga. Tsûdantâgï elawi'nï tsidâ'hïstani'ga. Nû'ⁿya gû'ⁿnage gû'ⁿyu'tlûⁿtani'ga. Ä`nûwa'gï gûⁿnage' gûⁿyû'tlûⁿtani'ga. Sûⁿtalu'ga gûⁿnage degûⁿyanu'galûⁿtani'ga, tsû'nanugâ'istï nige'sûⁿna. Usûhi'yï nûnⁿnâ'hï wite'tsatanû'ⁿû'ⁿsï gûne'sâ gûⁿnage asahalagï'. Tsûtû'neli'ga. Elawâ'tï asa'halagï'a'dûⁿni'ga. Usïnuli'yu Usûhi'yï gûltsâ'të digû'ⁿnagesta'yï, elawâ'tï gûⁿnage tidâ'hïstï wa`yanu'galûⁿtsi'ga. Gûne'sa gûⁿage sûⁿtalu'ga gûⁿnage gayu'tlûⁿtani'ga. Tsûdantâ'gï ûska'lûⁿtsi'ga. Sa'ka'nï adûⁿni'ga. Usû'hita atanis'se'tï, ayâ'lâtsi'sestï tsûdantâ'gï, tsû'nanugâ'istï nige'sûⁿna. Sgë!

Translation.

TO DESTROY LIFE.

Listen! Now I have come to step over your soul. You are of the (wolf) clan. Your name is (A`yûⁿinï). Your spittle I have put at rest under the earth. Your soul I have put at rest under the earth. I have come to cover you over with the black rock. I have come to cover you over, with the black cloth. I have come to cover you with the black slabs, never to reappear. Toward the black coffin of the upland in the Darkening Land your paths shall stretch out. So shall it be for you. The clay of the upland has come (to cover you). (?) Instantly the black clay has lodged there where it is at rest at the black houses in the Darkening Land. With the black coffin and with the black slabs I have come to cover you. Now your soul has faded away. It has become blue. When darkness comes your spirit shall grow less and dwindle away, never to reappear. Listen!

Explanation.

This formula is from the manuscript book of A`yû"inï, who explained the whole ceremony. The language needs but little explanation. A blank is left for the name and clan of the victim, and is filled in by the shaman. As the purpose of the ceremony is to bring about the death of the victim, everything spoken of is symbolically colored black, according to the significance of the colors as already explained. The declaration near the end, "It has become blue," indicates that the victim now begins to feel in himself the effects of the incantation, and that as darkness comes on his spirit will shrink and gradually become less until it dwindles away to nothingness.

When the shaman wishes to destroy the life of another, either for his own purposes or for hire, he conceals himself near the trail along which the victim is likely to pass. When the doomed man appears the shaman waits until he has gone by and then follows him secretly until he chances to spit upon the ground. On coming up to the spot the shaman collects upon the end of a stick a little of the dust thus moistened with the victim's spittle. The possession of the man's spittle gives him power over the life of the man himself. Many ailments are said by the doctors to be due to the fact that some enemy has by this means "changed the spittle" of the patient and caused it to breed animals or sprout corn in the sick man's body. In the love charms also the lover always figuratively "takes the spittle" of the girl in order to fix her affections upon himself. The same idea in regard to spittle is found in European folk medicine.

The shaman then puts the clay thus moistened into a tube consisting of a joint of the Kanesâ'la or wild parsnip, a poisonous plant of considerable importance in life-conjuring ceremonies. He also puts into the tube seven earthworms beaten into a paste, and several splinters from a tree which has been struck by lightning. The idea in regard to the worms is not quite clear, but it may be that they are expected to devour the soul of the victim as earthworms are supposed to feed upon dead bodies, or perhaps it is thought that from their burrowing habits they may serve to hollow out a grave for the soul under the earth, the quarter to which the shaman consigns it. In other similar ceremonies the dirt-dauber wasp or the stinging ant is buried in the same manner in order that it may kill the soul, as these are said to kill other more powerful insects by their poisonous sting or bite. The wood of a tree struck by lightning is also a potent spell for both good and evil and is used in many formulas of various kinds.

Having prepared the tube, the shaman goes into the forest to a tree which has been struck by lightning. At its base he digs a hole, in the bottom of which he puts a large yellow stone slab. He then puts in the tube, together with seven yellow pebbles, fills in the earth and finally builds a fire over the spot to destroy all traces of his work. The yellow stones are probably chosen as the next best substitute for black stones, which are not always easy to find. The formula mentions "black rock," black being the emblem of death, while yellow typifies trouble. The shaman and his employer fast until after the ceremony.

If the ceremony has been properly carried out, the victim becomes blue, that is, he feels the effects in himself at once, and, unless he employs the countercharms of some more powerful shaman, his soul begins to shrivel up and dwindle, and within seven days he is dead. When it is found that the spell has no effect upon the intended victim it is believed that he has discovered the plot and has taken measures for his own protection, or that, having suspected a design against him—as, for instance, after having won a girl's affections from a rival or overcoming him in the ball play—he has already secured himself from all attempts by counterspells. It then becomes a serious matter, as, should he succeed in turning the curse aside from himself, it will return upon the heads of his enemies.

The shaman and his employer then retire to a lonely spot in the mountains, in the vicinity of a small stream, and begin a new series of conjurations with the beads. After constructing a temporary shelter of bark laid over poles, the two go down to the water, the shaman taking with him two pieces of cloth, a yard or two yards in length, one white, the other black, together with seven red and seven black beads. The cloth is the shaman's pay for his services, and is furnished by his employer, who sometimes also supplies the beads. There are many formulas for conjuring with the beads, which are used on almost all important occasions, and differences also in the details of the ceremony, but the general practice is the same in all cases. The shaman selects a bend in the river where his client can look toward the east while facing up stream. The man then takes up his position on the bank or wades into the stream a short distance, where—in the ceremonial language—the water is a "hand length" (*awâ'hilû*) in depth and stands silently with his eyes fixed upon the water and his back to the shaman on the bank. The shaman then lays upon the ground the two pieces of cloth, folded into convenient size, and places the red beads—typical of success and his client—upon the white cloth, while the black beads—emblematic of death and the intended victim—are laid upon the black cloth. It is probable that the first cloth should properly be red instead of white, but as it is difficult to get red cloth, except in the shape of handkerchiefs, a substitution has been made, the two colors having a close mythologic relation. In former days a piece of buckskin and the small glossy seeds of the Viper's Bugloss (*Echium vulgare*) were used instead of the cloth and beads. The formulistic name for the bead is *sû'nĭkta*, which the priests are unable to analyze, the ordinary word for beads or coin being *adélâ*.

The shaman now takes a red bead, representing his client, between the thumb and index finger of his right hand, and a black bead, representing the victim, in like manner, in his left hand. Standing a few feet behind his client he turns toward the east, fixes his eyes upon the bead between the thumb and finger of his right hand, and addresses it as the Sû'nĭkta Gigäge'ï, the Red Bead, invoking blessings upon his client and clothing him with the red garments of success. The formula is repeated in a low chant or intonation, the voice rising at intervals, after the manner of a revival speaker. Then turning to the black bead in his left hand he addresses it in similar manner, calling down the most withering curses upon the head of the victim. Finally looking up he addresses the stream, under the name of Yû"wï Gûnahi'ta, the "Long Person," imploring it to protect his client and raise him to the seventh heaven, where he will be secure from all his enemies. The other, then stooping down, dips up water in his hand seven times and pours it upon his head, rubbing it upon his shoulders and breast at the same time. In some cases he dips completely under seven times, being stripped, of course, even when the water is of almost icy coldness. The shaman, then stooping down, makes a small hole in the ground with his finger, drops into it the fatal black bead, and buries it out of sight with a stamp of his foot. This ends the ceremony, which is called "taking to water."

While addressing the beads the shaman attentively observes them as they are held between the thumb and finger of his outstretched hands. In a short time they begin to move, slowly and but a short distance at first, then faster and farther, often coming down as far as the first joint of the finger or even below, with an irregular serpentine motion from side to side, returning in the same manner. Should the red bead be more lively in its movements and come down lower on the finger than the black bead, he confidently predicts for the client the speedy accomplishment of his desire. On the other hand, should the black bead surpass the red in activity, the spells of the shaman employed by the intended victim are too strong, and the whole ceremony must be gone over again with an additional and larger quantity of cloth. This must be kept up until the movements of the red beads give token of success or until they show by their sluggish motions or their failure to move down along the finger that the opposing shaman can not be overcome. In the latter case the discouraged plotter gives up all hope, considering himself as cursed by every imprecation which he has unsuccessfully invoked upon his enemy, goes home and—theoretically—lies down and dies. As a matter of fact, however, the shaman is always ready with other formulas by means of which he can ward off such fatal results, in consideration of a sufficient quantity of cloth.

Should the first trial, which takes place at daybreak, prove unsuccessful, the shaman and his client fast until just before sunset. They then eat and remain awake until midnight, when the ceremony is repeated, and if still unsuccessful it may be repeated four times before daybreak (or the following noon?), both men remaining awake and fasting throughout the night. If still unsuccessful, they continue to fast all day until just before sundown. Then they eat again and again remain awake until midnight, when the previous night's programme is repeated. It has now become a trial of endurance between the revengeful client and his shaman on the one side and the intended victim and his shaman on the other, the latter being supposed to be industriously working countercharms all the while, as each party must subsist upon one meal per day and abstain entirely from sleep until the result has been decided one way or the other. Failure to endure this severe strain, even so much as closing the eyes in sleep for a few moments or partaking of the least nourishment excepting just before sunset, neutralizes all the previous work and places the unfortunate offender at the mercy of his more watchful enemy. If the shaman be still unsuccessful on the fourth day, he acknowledges himself defeated and gives up the contest. Should his spells prove the stronger, his victim will die within seven days, or, as the Cherokees say, seven nights. These "seven nights," however, are frequently interpreted, figuratively, to mean seven years, a rendering which often serves to relieve the shaman from a very embarrassing position.

With regard to the oracle of the whole proceeding, the beads do move; but the explanation is simple, although the Indians account for it by saying that the beads become alive by the recitation of the sacred formula. The shaman is laboring under strong, though suppressed, emotion. He stands with his hands stretched out in a constrained position, every muscle tense, his breast heaving and voice trembling from the effort, and the natural result is that before he is done praying his fingers begin to twitch involuntarily and thus cause the beads to move. As before stated, their motion is irregular; but the peculiar delicacy of touch acquired by long practice probably imparts more directness to their movements than would at first seem possible.

HIÄ' A`NE'TSÂ UGÛ'ⁿWA`LĬ AMÂ'YÏ DITSÛ'ⁿSTA`TĬ.

Sgë! Ha-nâgwa ä'stï une'ga aksâ'ûⁿtanûⁿ usïnu'lï a`ne'tsâ, unatsâ'nûⁿtse'lahï akta'`tï adûⁿni'ga.

Iyu'stï utadâ'ta, iyu'stï tsunadâ'ita. Nûⁿnâ'hï anite'lahëhû' ige'skï nige'sûnna. Dû'ksi-gwû' dedu'natsgû`la'wate'gû. Da`'sûⁿ unilâtsi'satû. Sa`ka'ni unati'satû'.

Nûⁿnâ'hï dâ'tadu'nina'watï' a'yû-`nû' digwatseli'ga a`ne'tsâ unatsâ'nûⁿtse'lahï. Tla'mehû Gigage'ï sâ'gwa danûtsgû'`lani'ga. Igü"yï galûⁿlâ ge'sûⁿ i'yûⁿ kanûⁿlagï ᵘwâhâ'hïstâ'gï. Ta'line galûⁿlâ ge'sûⁿ i'yûⁿ kanûⁿlagï ᵘwâhâ'hïstâ'gï. He'nilû danûtsgû'`lani'ga. Tla'ma ûⁿni'ta a'nigwalu'gï gûⁿtla'`tisge'stï, ase'gwû nige'sûⁿna.

Du'talë a`ne'tsâ unatsâ'nûntse'lahï saligu'gi-gwû dedu'natsgû'`lawïstï't egû'. Elawi'nï da`'sûⁿ unilâtsi'satû.

Tsâ'ine digalûⁿlatiyûⁿ Sâ'niwä Gi'gageï sâ'gwa danûtsgû'`lani'ga, asë`gâ'gï nige'sûⁿna. Kanûⁿlagï ᵘwâhâ'hïstâ'gï nû'`gine digalûⁿlatiyûⁿ. Guli'sgulï' Sa`ka'ni sâ'gwa danûtsgû'`lani'ga, asë`gâ'gï nig'esuⁿna. Kanûⁿlagï ᵘwâhâ'hïstâgï hi'skine digalûⁿlatiyûⁿ. Tsütsü' Sa`ka'ni sâ'gwa danûtsgû'`lani'ga, asë`gâ'gï nige'sûⁿna.

Du'talë a`ne'tsâ utsâ'nûⁿtse'lahï. Tine'gwa Sa`ka'ni sâ'gwa danûtsgû'`lani'ga, ige'skï nige'sûⁿna. Da`'sûⁿ unilâtsi'satû. Kanûⁿlagï ᵘwâhâ'hïstâ'gï sutali'ne digalûⁿlatiyûⁿ. A'nigâsta'ya sâ'gwa danûtsgû'`lani'ga, asë`gâ'gï nige'sûⁿna. Kanûⁿlagï ᵘwâhâ'hïstâ'gï kûl`kwâgine digalûⁿlatiyûⁿ. Wâtatû'ga Sa`ka'ni sâ'gwa danûtsgû'`lani'ga, asë`gâ'gï nige'sûⁿna.

Du'talë a`ne'tsâ unatsâ'nûⁿtse'lahï, Yâ'na dedu'natsgû'`lawïstani'ga, ige'skï nige'suⁿna. Da`sûⁿ du'nïlâtsi'satû. Kanûⁿ'lagï de'tagaskalâ'ûⁿtanûⁿ', igûⁿ'wûlstanûhi-gwûdi'na tsuye'listi gesûⁿ'ï. Akta'`tï adûⁿni'ga.

Sgë! Nâ'gwa t?skï'nâne'lï ta'tädü' iyûⁿta a'gwatseli'ga, Wätatu'ga Tsûne'ga. Tsuye'listï gesûⁿ'ï skï'nâhûⁿsï' a'gwatseli'ga—kanûⁿ'lagï a'gwatseli'ga. Nä'`nâ utadâ'ta kanûⁿ'lagï dedu'skalâ'asi'ga.

Dedû'ndagûⁿ'yastani'ga, gûⁿwâ'hisâ'nûhï. Yû!

Translation.

THIS CONCERNS THE BALL PLAY—TO TAKE THEM TO WATER WITH IT.

Listen! Ha! Now where the white thread has been let down, quickly we are about to examine into (the fate of) the admirers of the ball play.

They are of—such a (iyu'stï) descent. They are called—so and so (iyu'stï). They are shaking the road which shall never be joyful. The miserable Terrapin has come and fastened himself upon them as they go about. They have lost all strength. They have become entirely blue.

But now my admirers of the ball play have their roads lying along in this direction. The Red Bat has come and made himself one of them. There in the first heaven are the pleasing stakes. Therein the second heaven are the pleasing stakes. The Pewee has come and joined them. The immortal ball stick shall place itself upon the whoop, never to be defeated.

As for the lovers of the ball play on the other side, the common Turtle has come and fastened himself upon them as they go about. Under the earth they have lost all strength.

The pleasing stakes are in the third heaven. The Red Tläniwä has come and made himself one of them, that they may never be defeated. The pleasing stakes are in the fourth heaven. The Blue Fly-catcher has made himself one of them, that they may never be defeated. The pleasing stakes are in the fifth heaven. The Blue Martin has made himself one of them, that they may never be defeated.

The other lovers of the ball play, the Blue Mole has come and fastened upon them, that they may never be joyous. They have lost all strength.

The pleasing stakes are there in the sixth heaven. The Chimney Swift has made himself one of them, that they may never be defeated. The pleasing stakes are in the seventh heaven. The Blue Dragon-fly has made himself one of them, that they may never be defeated.

As for the other admirers of the ball play, the Bear has just come and fastened him upon them, that they may never be happy. They have lost all strength. He has let the stakes slip from his grasp and there shall be nothing left for their share.

The examination is ended.

Listen! Now let me know that the twelve are mine, O White Dragon-fly. Tell me that the share is to be mine—that the stakes are mine. As for the player there on the other side, he has been forced to let go his hold upon the stakes.

Now they are become exultant and happy. Yû!

Explanation.

This formula, from the A`yûninï manuscript is one of those used by the shaman in taking the ball players to water before the game. The ceremony is performed in connection with red and black beads, as described in the formula just given for destroying life. The formulistic name given to the ball players signifies literally, "admirers of the ball play." The Tlä'niwä (sä'niwä, in the Middle dialect) is the mythic great hawk, as large and powerful as the roc of Arabian tales. The shaman begins by declaring that it is his purpose to examine or inquire into the fate of the ball players, and then gives his attention by turns to his friends and their opponents, fixing his eyes upon the red bead while praying for his clients, and upon the black bead while speaking of their rivals. His friends he raises gradually to the seventh or highest *galû"lati*. This word literally signifies height, and is the name given to the abode of the gods dwelling above the earth, and is also used to mean heaven in the Cherokee bible translation. The opposing players, on the other hand, are put down under the earth, and are made to resemble animals slow and clumsy of movement, while on behalf of his friends the shaman invokes the aid of swift-flying birds, which, according to the Indian belief, never by any chance fail to secure their prey. The birds invoked are the He'nilû or wood pewee (*Contopus virens*), the Tläniwä or mythic hawk, the Guli'sguli' or great crested flycatcher (*Myiarchus crinitus*), the Tsûtsû or martin (*Progne subis*), and the A'nigâsta'ya or chimney swift (*Chætura pelasgia*). In the idiom of the formulas it is said that these "have just come and are sticking to them" (the players), the same word (*danûtsgû'lani?ga*) being used to express the devoted attention of a lover to his mistress. The Watatuga, a small species of dragon-fly, is also invoked, together with the bat, which, according to a Cherokee myth, once took sides with the birds in a great ball contest with the four-footed animals, and won the victory for the birds by reason of his superior skill in dodging. This myth explains also why birds, and no quadrupeds, are invoked by the shaman to the aid of his friends. In accordance with the regular color symbolism the flycatcher, martin, and dragonfly, like the bat and the tlä'niwä, should be red, the color of success, instead of blue, evidently so written by mistake. The white thread is frequently mentioned in the formulas, but in this instance the reference is not clear. The twelve refers to the number of runs made in the game.

www.ingramcontent.com/pod-product-compliance
Ingram Content Group UK Ltd.
Pitfield, Milton Keynes, MK11 3LW, UK
UKHW021021210325
456568UK00006B/620

Space Clearing

VOLUME 2

BY THE SAME AUTHORS

Karen Kingston
Clear Your Clutter with Feng Shui

Karen Kingston & Richard Kingston
How to Clear Your Clutter
Space Clearing, Volume 1: The art of clearing and revitalizing energies in buildings

This book has been written with safety in mind. The utmost care has been taken to provide the information that is needed to do space clearing safely. However, the reader must understand that a range of energies can be found in buildings and space clearing may involve some risks. Some of the techniques also involve the use of lit candles, so the reader needs to be aware that these must be positioned with care and caution, and never left to burn unattended.

All guidelines need to be followed carefully and warnings heeded, and neither the authors nor the publisher can accept any responsibility for any injuries or damage, however they may arise. The authors and publisher also make no guarantees concerning the level of success the reader may experience by following the methods in this book, as the results will differ for each individual.

CONSCIOUS LIVING SERIES

Space Clearing

VOLUME 2:

How space clearing works

Karen Kingston & Richard Kingston

Clear Space Living

SPACE CLEARING, VOLUME 2: How space clearing works

Copyright © Clear Space Living Ltd 2024

First published in Great Britain in 2024 by Clear Space Living

Karen Kingston and Richard Kingston have asserted their rights to be identified as the authors of this work in accordance with the Copyright, Designs and Patents Act 1988.

The ALTMC definitions in the Glossaries section of this book have been included with the kind permission of the Clairvision School, copyright © Point Horizon Institute 1996–2023.

All rights reserved. No part of this book may be reproduced by any mechanical, photographic, or electronic process, or in the form of a photographic recording; nor may it be stored in a retrieval system, be transmitted in any form or by any means, or be otherwise copied for public or private use – other than for "fair use" as brief quotations embodied in articles and reviews – without the prior written permission of the publisher.

A CIP catalogue record for this book is available from the British Library.

Paperback ISBN: 978-1-8382504-2-3
Ebook ISBN: 978-8382504-6-1

Clear Space Living
www.clearspaceliving.com

Contents

How to use this book	viii
The terminology used in this book	ix

PART ONE: The evolution of space clearing — 1

1	My early years	2
2	Learning to do hand sensing	7
3	Discovering Bali	12
4	Discovering Balinese bells	26
5	Taking space clearing to the world	34
6	Meeting Richard	39
7	Richard's story	42

PART TWO: Deeper understandings of space clearing — 49

8	About spiritual connections	50
9	The main purposes of space clearing	63
10	Subtle body structures	67
11	Etheric awareness	72
12	Energetic protection	91
13	Superastral awareness	100
14	How hand sensing works	112
15	How flower offerings work	124
16	How space clearing water works	132
17	How clapping works	136
18	How belling works	139
19	How personal belling works	142
20	How harmony balls work	153

PART THREE: Energy clearing misconceptions — 157

21 Why there are so many misconceptions about
    energy clearing — 158
22 Intuitive energy clearing — 161
23 Intention and visualization — 164
24 Invocational energy clearing — 166
25 Distant energy clearing — 169
26 Purification with sound — 170
27 Purification with aromas — 177
28 Purification with light — 182
29 Negative energy absorbers, repellers, and banishers — 184
30 Dowsing — 187
31 Reiki — 190
32 Guardian spirits — 192

PART FOUR: Personal uses of space clearing — 197

33 The main personal uses of space clearing — 198
34 Space clearing to facilitate clutter clearing — 201
35 Space clearing to clear energies in objects — 203
36 Space clearing when moving home — 207
37 Space clearing guest rooms — 219
38 Space clearing when doing home improvements — 221
39 Space clearing for relationships — 228
40 Space clearing for health — 234
41 Space clearing at special times of the year — 241
42 Space clearing for major life events — 244
43 Space clearing after a disruptive experience — 255
44 Space clearing when travelling — 260
45 Space clearing to support personal development — 267
46 Space clearing for spiritual purposes — 273

PART FIVE: Business uses of space clearing — 277
47 Space clearing business premises — 278
48 Space clearing your own business — 285
49 Space clearing if you work for an employer — 289

PART SIX: Specialized uses of space clearing — 291
50 Other uses of space clearing — 292
51 Space clearing to complement feng shui — 293
52 Space clearing meeting rooms — 297
53 Space clearing treatment and therapy rooms — 303
54 Space clearing before and after an entity clearing — 307
55 The future of space clearing — 309

PART SEVEN: Resources — 311
56 What next? — 312
57 Recommended reading — 314

PART EIGHT: Glossaries — 317
58 ALTMC Glossary — 318
59 Space Clearing Glossary — 329
Index — 334

How to use this book

This book is designed to be read after *Space Clearing, Volume 1*, so except for Part One, you'll need to read Volume 1 first for it all to make sense.

Volume 2 is in eight parts, which can be read in any order:

Part 1: The evolution of space clearing
Part 2: Deeper understandings of space clearing
Part 3: Energy clearing misconceptions
Part 4: Personal uses of space clearing
Part 5: Business uses of space clearing
Part 6: Specialized uses of space clearing
Part 7: Resources
Part 8: Glossaries

Please be aware that this book is written in British English, which sometimes has different punctuation, spelling, and terminology to other styles of English.

The terminology used in this book

We explain in *Space Clearing, Volume 1* that a major challenge in writing a book about space clearing is a lack of vocabulary in the English language to describe the unseen worlds and how things work energetically. The words that do exist are also often vague or have different meanings to different people, depending on which spiritual school they have studied with or what they have read. This can lead to many misunderstandings, which we sincerely want to avoid. What's needed is a common vocabulary that everyone can understand.

We have therefore included in Part 7 of this book the same two glossaries that are in Volume 1, with a few additional entries:

ALTMC Glossary

This glossary is an abridged version of *A Language to Map Consciousness* (ALTMC for short, pronounced "alt-em-see"), which has been included with the kind permission of Samuel Sagan and the Clairvision School. The full version can be accessed online for free at clairvision.org.

Space Clearing Glossary

This glossary contains definitions of words we have coined ourselves that are specific to space clearing.

How to use the glossaries

Single asterisk

When you come across a term that has a single asterisk after it (like this*), flip to the ALTMC Glossary to get clarification.

Double asterisk

For a term that has a double asterisk after it (like this**), refer to the Space Clearing Glossary.

To avoid peppering the text with multiple asterisks, each term has only been asterisked once or twice at most, the first times we use it in the book.

PART ONE

The evolution of space clearing

1

My early years

by Karen Kingston

There were some very early signs that my life would take an unusual path.

I remember two defining moments of my childhood in particular. The first was at age 4, in the little attic bedroom my mother had created for me with its midnight-blue wallpapered ceiling, dotted with shiny silver stars. One day, as I sat there on the edge of my bed, I had a moment when I knew with certainty that, when I grew up, I was going to do something that no one had ever done before. I didn't know what it would be, but it was as if a veil lifted, and I could see the timeline of my life stretching out ahead of me and the potential it held.

The second defining moment was a few years later, when I realized I had existed before I was born. Again, it was as if a curtain had been pulled aside, and I could see clearly what I'd always known but never consciously thought. I realized I had existed as consciousness before I lived in my human body and would continue to exist as consciousness after it died. I began to look at people very differently after this, wondering if they knew this too. And I saw my life, from that moment on, as a finite period in which to accomplish something to the best of my ability before moving on.

My early years

Growing up

I spent the first 10 years of my life in the small town of Horsforth in West Yorkshire, England. I felt older than my years and in a hurry to get going, yet I knew I would have to be patient. I remembered having gone through childhood before and understood how essential it is to the incarnation process to put certain foundations in place during that time.

One of my most enduring childhood memories was that I never minded being sent to bed by my parents because as soon as my brother and I were asleep, we would meet up to fly above the garden of our house together. This didn't happen just once or twice. I remember our astral* travelling as a nightly occurrence for many years, as natural a part of our lives as exploring the physical world in our physical bodies during the day. Most of the images I have retained from that time are of looking down on our apple trees, lawns, greenhouse, and other garden features from above.

From an early age, I had an unquenchable curiosity and a desire to learn. By the time I was 4, I could already read and write. My father was a self-taught prodigy, having attained the status of amateur chess champion of Great Britain in his youth, so he helped me progress by buying me a typewriter to teach myself to type. It was an old, clunky, black metal Underwood with keys that would sometimes stick. I loved it and wore out ink ribbon after ink ribbon, spending many hours at my little attic desk, thumping away on those keys.

In those days in England, children didn't start school until they were 6 years old. I was so eager to get on and learn that, when I was 4, my father enrolled me in a posh private preparatory school nearby, where I wore a red blazer with a cream straw boater and a matching red hatband, like all the other kids. I don't know how he managed to afford to pay for this, but I'm very grateful that he did. I quickly devoured its entire library of books.

It was the same story when I began my regular education at infant school two years later. I rapidly exhausted the small collection of books and regularly traipsed across the black tarmacked playground to borrow books from the junior school library.

By the age of 11, I had read every book of interest to me in both school libraries and the local public library. From this, I concluded that much of the information in non-fiction books is not original but the product of the author having read other people's books, who in turn had read other people's books, and so it went on. I would see the same knowledge repeated again and again, with no insight into where it originally came from. I decided that I was going to have to find other ways to discern the truth of things for myself, rather than learning from books.

During my school years, I was very athletic and a first-rate student, top of the class in most subjects, with a wide range of interests. In reports, teachers described me as having an insatiable thirst for knowledge. They likened me to a sponge. They despaired somewhat that I would usually ignore whatever homework I was set and instead deliver essays of my own choosing, although they couldn't argue with the quality or quantity of the work I turned in. One essay I wrote at the age of 10 was based on a theory I explored for a few months that Jesus Christ was a time traveller from the future, which I felt might explain why he had such extraordinary healing skills. That certainly raised a few eyebrows.

This unconventional approach deepened as I went through my teens. When I was about 14, I undertook a lengthy study of the diseases that great classical composers had died of, as a way of understanding what was out of balance in their lives and how that was reflected in the music they wrote. I believed then, and still do to this day, that many of them tapped into magnificent archetypal* forces that they embodied in their music. Their state of health, and especially what they died of, was indicative of how well they were able (or not able) to hold the voltage of that. I remember being most impressed by Beethoven and the thunderous forces he was connected to, which I reckoned was the cause of his deafness. I especially admired the fact that he continued to compose regardless.

During this entire time, I was actively seeking answers to life's important questions. I wanted to know the real underlying reasons for things and was never satisfied with answers of convenience. I was sure there was more to life than the mundane levels that most people around me lived at.

Developing my subtle body structures

When I was 15, my father got sick and died of Hodgkin's disease. My mother embraced her new-found freedom from a marriage she'd felt trapped in from the start by consuming copious quantities of alcohol, inviting a local rock band to use our living room to practise in, and hosting loud parties in our house every night.

My life took a radical new turn as a result. Instead of the university education I had planned for, I wasn't able to study and didn't get the exam grades I needed. Instead, I left home and got a job. With hindsight, I can see this was fortunate as it saved me three years of my life. No degree course existed then or now for what I really wanted to study anyway.

In my teens, I selectively experimented with drugs for a year or so, hoping they would open new levels of consciousness to me. But I quickly concluded they weren't for me. I wanted permanent access to higher realms, not temporary false highs with random, unpredictable side-effects.

By my early twenties, I had reached the conclusion that everything has its origins in the unseen worlds of energy, and the answers to all things lie in those realms. I set about systematically awakening my subtle body* structures* to be able to perceive and interpret energies first-hand.

I started by visiting many churches and cathedrals in the UK. All bore testament to the fact that there had once been something special there. I could see that the people who designed and built those towering architectural structures were inspired to do so to create a place for lofty spiritual presences* to reside.

As often as I could, I also visited megalithic sites, stone circles, holy wells, and anywhere else I hoped to find sacred space of any kind. Sad to say, discoveries of note were far and few between. I did find some places that were more conducive to hosting spiritual presences than others, but I could see that as soon as humans started visiting, the disruption made it very difficult for these presences to stay. At best, I found interesting land energies. I enjoyed exploring castles, stately buildings, and the rich ethericity* of the English countryside, but I realized I needed to find more fruitful arenas for my explorations.

In 1978, when I was 24, I joined an esoteric theatre group and was a member of it for nine exciting and exuberant years. We explored the music, dance, and rituals* of many cultures, and it was there that I first came directly into contact with spiritual connections*.

2

Learning to do hand sensing

by Karen Kingston

It was also in 1978 that it first occurred to me that the London apartment I was living in might be affecting me more than I knew.

Located on the ground floor of an old Victorian house in West Hampstead, it was cold and gloomy. I assumed, when I first moved in, that it felt this way because it had no central heating and the windows were so small that very little sunlight came in. However, I noticed it still felt the same on the brightest and warmest sunny days. It was as if the walls themselves held melancholy. I started to wonder if there might be something more to know about this.

I had been developing my ability to sense energies with my hands for a couple of years. This was completely uncharted territory. I taught myself by trial and error, through many thousands of hours of practice. I had no idea what use hand sensing** might possibly have, just an unwavering enthusiasm to push the boundaries of energetic awareness and perception in every way I could. Little did I know how important it would be and where it would lead.

I had progressed to the point where I could run my hands close to a person's supine body and be able to feel, with a very high degree of accuracy, where there were stuck energies that were causing health issues. Then one day, I got the idea to apply this hand-sensing technique to the walls of my home.

The main entrance seemed the obvious place to start. I rolled up my sleeves, washed my face and hands, and positioned myself inside the front door. I raised my right hand and held it 3 centimetres (about an inch) away from the centre of the door, with my palm facing toward the door, at a right angle to my wrist, and my fingers pointing upward. I consciously relaxed the muscles in my hand and tuned into the energies in the door. I then walked around the inside perimeter of my apartment, reading the energies in the walls with my hand. I arrived back at the front door a few minutes later.

I was very surprised by the quantity of information that was embedded in the walls. My overall impression was of deeply ingrained feelings of sadness and loneliness, especially in the front room, which I had never liked and rarely used. Chatting to neighbours sometime later, I discovered that the previous occupant had been a lonely old woman who had spent most of her time in that room.

Developing hand sensing

I became so interested in hand sensing buildings that I started to seek out public places where I could do it, such as stately homes and meeting rooms. I would also browse the energy imprints of items in antique shops and charity shops. I progressed to animals, plants, and the food I purchased, using the technique to find the most etherically vibrant pieces of fruit, for example.

Then came the evening I described in Chapter 1 of *Space Clearing, Volume 1*, when I went to visit some friends in their new home and they allowed me to explore it blindfolded through hand sensing. There was no stopping me after that. I continued to develop deeper levels of the skill wherever I found opportunities to practise it.

Best of all was exploring the homes of friends who were willing to give me instant feedback about my findings. Each home revealed hidden aspects about the occupants that I had never suspected.

In one female friend's home, for example, I discovered through hand sensing that she had a deep longing to have a baby. When I mentioned this to her, her eyes welled with tears and she admitted it was true. I had no idea that was so important to her.

In another friend's home, I felt deep levels of stress imprinted in her bed, with pain in the area of the mattress that corresponded to her stomach. She confessed she was going through a period of serious financial difficulties that was badly affecting her sleep and had given her stomach ulcers. I'd been out of touch with her for some time, so I knew nothing about this until hand sensing revealed it.

How I developed space clearing

The more proficient I became at hand sensing, the more I noticed a correlation between the joyous, flowing energies in the homes of people whose lives were working well and the stagnant energies** in the homes of those who were stuck in some aspect of their life. I realized this was a huge unexplored arena of personal development that no one at that time seemed to be aware of (this was long before most westerners had heard of feng shui).

The obvious next step was not just to sense energies but to find ways to clear and revitalize them. The starting point had to be my own home, of course, which I wanted to be as energetically clear and vibrant as possible.

The next few years were a voyage of discovery as I developed the basic techniques for space clearing. Hand sensing turned out to be my greatest asset in this process because it allowed me to instantly perceive what worked and what didn't. I would never have been able to develop such an effective system without the ability to reliably check it in that way at each stage.

Also very helpful were the responses of friends who came to visit and were astonished by how different my home felt compared with the last time they had been there. This confirmed that my methods were producing tangible results, which spurred me to go further.

The first space clearing I did for a friend

The first space clearing I ever did for another person was in 1989. A friend had inherited a large Victorian house in London from his grandmother. He'd been unemployed for a few years, so he planned to rent out some of the rooms and become a landlord. Try as he might, though, he couldn't get anyone to live there. Many came to look. No one wanted to move in.

The problem continued for a while until one day he told me about it. This was long before anyone knew I did space clearing. I had been researching and developing it only for my own use, never thinking I would share it with anyone else. I felt so sorry for him that I went to take a look.

Sure enough, as soon as I walked into the house, there was a very spooky feeling that would immediately put prospective tenants off. Hand sensing the energy of the rooms, I discovered that his grandmother had lived there for most of her life, culminating in a very unhappy decade after her husband died. Her grief was deeply embedded in all the walls and furniture. Through hand sensing, I also discovered that she had had colon cancer and had died in the bed in her bedroom. My friend was able to confirm all these findings.

In those days, I didn't know if it was safe to conduct a space clearing ceremony with other people present, so I sent my friend out of the house while I did it. I hoped the clearing would help. And it did. Very soon all his rooms were full of paying tenants and he had a flow of income into his bank account. Even I was surprised by how fast it all changed for him.

I continued to develop space clearing, using it in each new home I lived in (I moved around a lot at that time). It still wasn't something I ever talked about, but I loved doing it.

Then my space clearing skills took a huge leap forward when I started travelling abroad.

3

Discovering Bali

by Karen Kingston

In 1990, at the age of 36, I was living in London and knew it was time for a change. I sold most of my possessions and made plans to travel to California with a friend. When it came to booking our tickets, we changed our minds and flew to India instead. From there we went to Thailand, where my friend announced he had run out of money and flew home to England. I decided to continue by myself and bought a ticket to Bali.

As it turned out, abandoning me in Thailand was the best favour my friend ever did for me. Arriving all alone in Bali allowed me to open to the place in a way I would never have done with an English-speaking companion at my side. I fell totally in love with the island, with its 25 volcanic peaks (most of them mercifully dormant, but two still active) and its unique spiritual culture, where purification practices are integrated into every aspect of their way of life. Many traditional cultures have a form of space clearing, but nowhere have they developed it to such a high level as in Bali, known as the island of the gods.

My first visit lasted two life-changing months. I returned six months later, and soon I was dividing my time equally between Bali and England.

Eventually, Bali became my permanent home, and I spent a total of 20 years there.

It's not easy to put into words what I learned during that time. I had no teacher. I learned directly from the spiritual connections that I encountered in temples, and it was mainly these interactions that developed and transformed my subtle body structures. I learned how to feel energies as tangibly as I could feel physical objects. I learned how to interact with forces woven into rocks. I became skilled at transforming ordinary rooms into sacred spaces. And most important of all, I learned how to commune with spiritual connections and how to land spiritual force into matter.

It was in Bali that I learned how to put depth and power into the space clearing methods I had developed by myself in the 12 years before I ever visited the island, and how to live a sacred way of life, not as a spiritual recluse but in a very down-to-earth way, just as Balinese people do.

Sometimes I would arrange to visit a Balinese priest or priestess, with a long string of questions to ask them. Often, not knowing I understood Balinese, they would turn to the Balinese friend who had introduced me and confide that my questions were beyond them.

I want to know and understand everything whereas Balinese people are happy to follow traditional practices without knowing how they work. However, because they have a deep connection to the spiritual presences that permeate every aspect of their way of life, I found I was able to learn something of value from each Balinese person I met, from the smallest child to the wisest sage. I felt I was living on an island of three million teachers.

Balinese wisdoms

I will always remember a young boy I met in a restaurant after I had been in Bali for just three weeks. He was the son of the restaurant owner. I had just ordered a meal and went to perch on the front steps of the restaurant to get the best view of the sunset over the ocean while I waited.

After a while, the boy came and sat beside me. He was a bright young thing, about 6 years old, with sparkling white teeth and a beautiful broad smile. His lithe brown body looked like one of those rubbery toys you can bend into any position. We exchanged names, and to pass the time I decided to practise my Balinese.

"What's that called?" I asked in Balinese, pointing to various objects in turn.

He told me the Balinese names.

Then I pointed to the black-and-white chequered cloth that was wrapped around each of the four corner pillars of the restaurant, which was open on three sides to the elements. "What's the Balinese name for that?" I asked.

"We call it *poleng*," he told me.

I had noticed this type of cloth before in many restaurants, temples, and shrines, as well as wrapped around sacred trees and sometimes worn as clothing.

"What's it for?" I asked, thinking to myself he surely wouldn't know.

He gave me a radiant smile and switched to broken English to explain.

"For protection," he said, unhesitatingly. "Black and white mean balance good and evil."

I don't know if I showed it on the outside, but my inner world started reeling. It had taken me over a dozen years of dedicated research to discover the esoteric significance of black-and-white chequers, and here was this six-year-old boy explaining it to me as if everybody knows that, don't they? In Bali, I was discovering, such wisdoms are a part of daily existence. The whole of life there is dedicated to maintaining energetic purity and the balance between good and evil, so that peace and harmony prevail.

An example of a Balinese shrine wrapped in poleng material

The Balinese spiritual way of life

Etheric* awareness and spiritual purification rituals are woven into every part of daily life in Bali. One of the easiest ways to see this is in the practice of making offerings.

Every village has three communal temples, and each home and business has a private temple within its grounds, containing several shrines. On an island that is slightly smaller than the US state of Delaware and a little larger than the county of Norfolk in England (it spans only 95 miles (153 km) from east to west and 70 miles (112 km) from north to south), there are over 20,000 public temples and countless private temples. Purification rituals are performed in each of these temples every day.

The simplest type of offering is a small coconut-leaf basket filled with brightly coloured flower heads, topped with a smoking incense stick and sprinkled with holy water. Millions of these are made each day, and many more when there are special ceremonies, as there frequently are. The range and breathtaking beauty of them all is amazing.

A Balinese flower offering

The Balinese consider themselves to be custodians of the land on which they live. They believe it is each person's sacred duty to maintain harmony in their own life by the way they interact with the energetic forces that support them from below and the gods who bless them from above.

This is where it gets really interesting. I once knew a Balinese man who was well educated and stylishly dressed, with one feature that stuck out as odd. He had a single, wiry black hair, about 4 inches (10 cm) long, growing from a mole on his upper arm. It made me ache to want to snip it, and one day I told him so. He smiled and explained to me gently, as if to a child, that he would never allow this to happen because it would cause the whole balance of nature to be cataclysmically disrupted.

The point is not whether he was right or wrong about this (and we'll never know), but the unswerving personal responsibility he felt to maintain balance in the world by his actions. It is this same belief that lies at the core of the Balinese practice of offerings. Come rain, come shine, they never miss a day. It's unthinkable that each person does not do their part in the cosmic scheme of things. How different the world would be if more people thought like this. It's one thing to intellectually discuss the concept of the butterfly effect – that everything in the world is interconnected, so small, seemingly trivial changes can have far-reaching consequences. In Bali, this is a consideration behind every action.

I've observed many Balinese people placing and activating offerings. To the casual observer, it appears that nothing much is happening. In the unseen worlds, however, the effect is remarkable. This is spiritual purification and presencing on a national scale, forming an energetic grid across the island that maintains the sacredness of the land and holds the people's connection to high spiritual presences intact.

A Balinese temple

The longer I lived in Bali, the more amazed I became by the know-how and practices of ordinary folk. I never met a Balinese person who could explain this to me in words, but what impressed me was that they all knew how to engage verticality* to connect with high spiritual forces. I saw an early clue to this in the pagoda-like roof structures of their temples, made from black coconut fibre and known as *meru*. They range from one tier for the humblest village temple to 11 tiers for the most exalted temples.

It was by tuning into these structures through my own verticality that I was able to access much of the information I sought about Balinese spiritual practices. They are believed to have been introduced in the 11th century by a Javanese priest called Mpu Kuturan, who clearly had highly developed verticality himself. When praying, many Balinese people naturally align the verticality of their personal column above* with the verticality of the temple roof, which gives them direct access to the spiritual presences housed within.

Another way I learned from Bali's spiritual culture was by plugging directly into the island-wide dragonweave that each person, young and old, is connected to. Dragonweave is a term coined by Samuel Sagan to describe a rare type of superastral* structure that rests on land energies. In Bali, it takes the form of an impeccably maintained energetic matrix that connects the temple of each home and business to a local village temple, which in turn is connected to a regional temple, which itself is connected to one of the eight *Sad Kahyangan* state temples, and ultimately to the mother temple in Besakih. The effect of this is that any Balinese person can go into any temple anywhere in Bali and have a direct connection through the dragonweave from there to the mother temple, where the highest spiritual forces of Bali's Hindu religion reside.

Balinese people learn from an early age (before they can walk) how to gear into this dragonweave, first through their column below* and later, as they grow up, through their column above. This is reinforced each night through the practice of each person sleeping with their head pointing toward the sacred mountains in the centre of the island or, in rare exceptional circumstances, toward the east, which is considered to be the next best thing because it's the direction of the rising sun.

In fact, Balinese people don't use the cardinal compass directions of north, south, east, and west. Instead, they use:
- *Kaja* – meaning toward the gods (in the direction of the mother temple or the mountains)
- *Kelod* – away from the gods (in the direction of the sea)
- *Kangin* – the direction of sunrise
- *Kauh* – the direction of sunset

Very confusingly for tourists, the geographical direction of *kaja* and *kelod* changes, depending on where you are located. For example, *kaja* is in a northern compass direction if you are located in the south of the island, in the south if you are located in the north, in the west if you are located in the east, in the east if you are located in the west, or in the direction of the mother temple if you are in the middle of the island.

Balinese people can become disorientated if they don't sleep with their head pointing toward *kaja*. It's as if their physical bodies become magnetized to the mountains where the spiritual presences reside. In fact, it is said that you can take a Balinese person, blindfold them, spin them around, then ask them the direction of *kaja*, and they will be able to tell you. I had great fun testing this theory on some willing volunteers and was very impressed by their accuracy.

If you go to Bali hoping to experience this type of sleeping arrangement, you'll find that most tourist accommodation is not built according to these principles because Balinese architects have long since realized that tourists don't know about it and don't care. I always slept with my head pointing toward *kaja* in my own home in Bali, and if ever I went travelling and stayed in a hotel, there would always be delighted smiles and willing hands to help me move my bed, if it needed to be repositioned.

I was very fortunate to live in Bali before modern technology and global influences began to impact too deeply and started to erode the spiritual way of life enjoyed there for so many centuries. I'm sorry to say that as the reliance on material possessions grows, the spiritual substance of the Balinese culture is being diluted and weakened. Sadly, I believe it's unlikely to survive in its present form much longer. I'm very grateful for the time I was able to spend there.

Then again, foreign writers who visited Bali in the 1930s said the same thing then and were proved wrong. I sincerely hope my prediction is proved wrong too.

Nyepi

There are five types of Balinese purification rituals:

- *Manusa yadnya* – rites of passage for human beings
- *Pitra yadnya* – rituals for the spirits of the dead
- *Dewa yadnya* – rituals for the gods
- *Rsi yadnya* – rituals for holy prophets
- *Bhuta yadnya* – rituals to appease lower spirits

The most impressive type of *bhuta yadnya* ritual is an annual event called *Nyepi,* which takes place during the new moon in March, at the beginning of the Balinese New Year, according to the *Saka* lunar calendar. This is always my favourite time of the year there because it begins with an energetic purification of the entire island, followed by a 24-hour period of complete silence. It's an annual, island-wide form of space clearing, followed by a day of deep involution*.

In the weeks before *Nyepi*, children randomly let off firecrackers all over the place, supposedly to frighten off *bhuta kala* (evil spirits). In the villages, giant papier mâché effigies of demons called *ogoh-ogoh* are created in garish colours with large fangs, dramatically long fingernails, and scary, predatory postures. Villages compete to create the best monster they can, with the added incentive that if they make two, the extra one can be entered into a competition to win a substantial cash prize, awarded nationally by the government and locally by the various regencies to keep the tradition alive. To make sure the effigies do not cause environmental pollution, the use of plastic and styrofoam has been banned.

Ceremonies take place at or near major crossroads around the island at dusk on the night before *Nyepi*, involving copious quantities of offerings to the *bhuta kala* that the *ogoh-ogoh* represent. In Bali, crossroads are understood to be intersections for energies as well as road traffic, and there is a widespread belief that accidents tend to happen at crossroads because noxious low-level elemental energies congregate there. The purpose of these offerings is to deter that from happening during the coming year.

Later in the evening, the *ogoh-ogoh* are paraded through the streets on bamboo frames to the accompanying clamour of crashing cymbals and drums from mobile gamelan *beleganjur* orchestras. Crowds of onlookers turn out to watch, and every kind of noise is encouraged. Then close to midnight, the effigies are set down at major crossroads and ritually burned. Many people stay up throughout the night making as much noise as possible until dawn, when stillness reigns throughout the land.

The next day is incredible. To my knowledge, it's the only place on earth where for one day a year everything comes to a complete standstill. Starting at 6 am, no traffic is allowed on the roads. No one can light fires or cook food. No electrical, mechanical, or digital equipment can be used, which means no TV, no music, no phones, and no electric lights, although quiet equipment such as refrigerators can be kept turned on. Apart from essential services such as those provided by hospitals, firefighters, and the police, no one is allowed to work. All activities stop and everyone stays quietly at home. No worldly pleasures are supposed to be indulged in (drinking, gambling, and so on). Talking, if necessary, is done in hushed tones. Children play quietly.

Even Bali's airport is closed for the day. No planes are allowed to take off or land. A friend who is a flight controller at Bali's airport tells me this creates havoc with international airline schedules each year, but I absolutely love the fact that Balinese people put their spiritual priorities first, regardless. It means that many of the planes are not where they need to be for onward flights but the world has to deal with it and sort it out. In 2018, for example, I read in a newspaper article that a total of 244 domestic and 238 international flights had to be cancelled.

Not everyone in Bali adheres strictly to the tradition of *Nyepi*, of course. There are always people who disregard rules, everywhere in the world. But many of the tens of thousands of priests and priestesses in Bali spend the day fasting and meditating, and security guards patrol the streets to make sure people at least stay at home, keep quiet, and don't turn on lights. Tourists in hotels are provided with food but are not allowed to go out, except if they need to go to hospital because of a medical emergency.

In the rural part of Bali where I used to live, such a deep level of stillness would descend that the dogs would stop barking and the cockerels stopped crowing. The only sounds that could be heard were the beautiful trills of birdsong, the wind rustling through the trees, and the soothing rhythm of waves lapping softly on the distant shore.

For one whole day, there is nothing you have to do and nowhere you can go. The busyness of modern life evaporates and everyone has a day of complete rest. It's perfect for meditation, taking stock of your life, and contemplating the year ahead. After nightfall, the effect is even more profound as you sit in complete darkness and silence, in the mellow companionship of those you love. It feels like it could go on forever, and you wish it would.

The next morning, the first car that passes sends shock waves through the air. It feels like a harsh intrusion into your peaceful haven. But soon the roads fill with people, bikes, cars, trucks, and buses, and the world returns to normal. *Nyepi* feels like it must have been a dream. Until next year.

Space clearing and Bali

If you visit Bali expecting to see people doing space clearing ceremonies in their homes, similar to the one described in *Space Clearing, Volume 1*, you're in for a big surprise. You will not find anything like it there. Only priests and shamans own bells, and the way they use them is very different to the way Richard and I use them for space clearing. Clapping** in corners has never crossed their minds, and they've never heard of harmony balls**.

It would be a huge mistake to think that the space clearing ceremony imitates any traditional purification practices that originate in Bali. It definitely does not. Balinese rituals work very well in the context of Bali's Hindu culture, but they do not translate well to usage in other parts of the world.

The only element that was directly inspired by Balinese purification practices is flower offerings**, and the way they are created and used is very different to the Balinese methods.

The only reason we sell space clearing equipment that is made in Bali is because it is by far the highest quality available anywhere in the world for that purpose. The space clearing ceremony originally consisted of a circuit of hand sensing, a circuit of clapping, and several circuits of bells. I used the best bells I could find in the UK, but their sound was mediocre, and I knew it.

Finding bells of the rare quality that are crafted in Bali gave me access to higher levels of space clearing, and adding flower offerings introduced the completely new dimension of landing spiritual connection during the ceremony. It was only then that I understood how important it is to do the steps in a precise order rather than intuitively or randomly, so that each step can build on the foundations put in place by the previous steps.

The space clearing ceremony that has evolved can be used by people all over the world to cleanse and purify the types of energies that are found in buildings today. Done regularly, space clearing can greatly add to the overall quality of your life. As any 6-year-old Balinese child can tell you, it's just as important to take care of the unseen worlds as the seen ones!

4

Discovering Balinese bells

by Karen Kingston

When I first started developing space clearing in 1978, the only piece of equipment I had was an English school bell that I had won in a raffle some years earlier.

I rarely enter competitions, and this is the only one I've ever won. I can still remember the surprise and joy I felt the first time I held the school bell in my hands. It was about 25 cm (10 inches) tall with a shiny brass dome and a brown mahogany handle, topped by a small brass bobble. I carried it home and put it in the centre of my mantelpiece, in pride of place.

It turned out to be just what I needed for space clearing. But it didn't take me long to realize that the results I could obtain with it were very limited. I wasn't able to find a better-quality English bell, so I started using bells from other countries. Instead of doing just one circuit of the inner perimeter of my apartment with my clangy school bell, I added several extra circuits, using progressively higher-pitched bells, refining the energy each time. This involved a lot more walking and the results were a little better, yet still very far from what I knew they could be. I gradually acquired a large collection of bells from around the world and was always looking for better-quality equipment.

Then I visited Bali and discovered Balinese bells. I quickly found that one circuit with a Balinese bell could do the same job as using all the other bells I had. And much, much more.

The first time I heard a Balinese bell

Acquiring my Balinese bell was such a milestone in the development of space clearing that the story is worth telling in full. I'm sure that if I hadn't discovered bells of such extraordinarily high calibre, Richard and I would not be writing this book today.

On my first ever visit to Bali in 1990, I was fortunate to be invited to a cremation ceremony in a remote Balinese village, high in the mountains. It was fascinating – a colourful, dramatic event attended by hundreds of people wearing their best sarongs. It culminated in setting fire to the ornate funerary tower in a small clearing near the temple.

I was the only non-Balinese person there and was given a very friendly welcome. Some of the children in the village had never seen a white person before and shyly asked if they could touch my nose. They were intrigued by how long it was compared with their own flat noses, and their curiosity was so innocent and genuine that of course I let them do it.

The most vivid memory I have of this occasion was not the people, though, but a bell I could hear being rung in the distance that had the purest sound I had ever heard. It was the last thing I had expected to hear that day, so deep in the jungle. I had to know what it was.

I made my way through the crowd and found a Balinese Hindu priestess sitting cross-legged on an elevated bamboo platform. She had a silver pot containing holy water in front of her and various pieces of ritual equipment made of brass.

She seemed to be in a deeply internalized world of her own, oblivious to the crowds around her. She repetitively dipped a bundle of grasses into the holy water and flicked it onto the offerings, while chanting mantras in what my friend told me was the High Balinese language.

Then time stood still for me as I saw her put down the grasses and pick up a beautiful bronze bell in her left hand. She rang it with a continuous ding-a-ling-a-ling rhythm, while chanting more mantras and performing a graceful series of mudras with her right hand that involved flower petals and more holy water. I watched with fascination as she used the sound of her bell as a vehicle to carry the spiritual essence of the words she was chanting.

I had tested hundreds of different types of bells at this point and had never heard one that was anything like this. I immediately realized that owning such a bell would allow me to take my space clearing work to an entirely new level.

I turned to the Balinese friend who had brought me to the ceremony and said, "I really want a bell like that. Where can I get one?"

He smiled a proud smile, pleased that I was so impressed with the bell, but said, as kindly as he could, that I should forget about wanting to own one because they are only ever made for Balinese priests and priestesses.

My quest to own a Balinese bell

In the days that followed, I checked among other Balinese friends and they all assured me that there was no possibility of a non-Balinese person ever being able to own such a bell. No one could even tell me where they were made. They spoke with reverence of what they called the magical powers of the bells, which only deepened my desire to have one.

Discovering Balinese bells

During the next year, I learned the local languages to be able to communicate better. I quickly became fluent in Indonesian and also immersed myself in learning Balinese, a much more complex language with three levels, numerous dialects, and no English to Balinese dictionaries at that time to help me. That opened a lot more doors for me because most of the older priests on the island had left school before Indonesian started being taught, so they only spoke Balinese.

I felt a special affinity with High Balinese. It's an extraordinary language, very close in frequency to Sanskrit and designed to carry spiritual frequencies in rituals. Balinese priests and priestesses are always addressed in High Balinese and they reply in Low, Middle, or High Balinese, according to the caste of the person they are talking to.

I continued to ask everyone I met who I hoped might be able to help me. Finally, I met a priest who understood why I wanted a bell. He was a masseur with remarkable etheric know-how and advanced healing skills. Over a period of months, he taught me how to do massage and we talked a lot about space clearing. He directed me to a village that was a day's journey from where I was staying. The return journey involved eight changes of buses on routes that had no timetables, and he couldn't give me a name or address, just an indication of the general area.

With such vague information, I didn't expect my first expedition to yield results. I was willing to make the trip as many times as necessary, and perhaps because of that, I didn't have to. Balinese people I met along the way helped me to switch from one bus to the next, and when I eventually arrived at my destination, I fortuitously met someone who took me to meet a family of bellmakers straight away. I later discovered I was lucky to have found the most highly respected and skilled bellmakers of them all.

I made that long journey by bus many times over the next year. I knew that I had to get to know them and they had to get to know me before I could even broach the topic of them making me a temple bell. No westerner had ever owned one before. This was going to be a very big ask.

Balinese people are wonderfully hospitable, so visitors are always offered refreshments. It may have changed a little since then, but at that time an unimportant guest would be given boiled tap water to drink and perhaps some peanuts. A more important guest would be offered tea and fruit. A highly esteemed guest would be given Balinese coffee and a local sweet delicacy. And a very honoured guest would receive a glass of Coca-Cola and a whole array of sweet cakes.

As a westerner, I didn't fit into any of the usual categories, so to be on the safe side they gave me the works each time I visited. For many years I'd had a completely sugar-free diet, but I wanted a bell so much that I was willing to drink Indonesian-style cola, which is much sweeter, and eat the sugary cakes offered by my gracious hosts, made with an alarming range of food colourings and strange textures that were alien to my English palate. This continued for about nine months until we knew each other well enough for them not to be offended when I admitted that I preferred a glass of water and some fruit.

Balinese temple bells

We talked in depth about my space clearing work and about bells. I learned that all bellmakers in Bali belong to a highly respected caste called *pandé*, which is deemed to be on the same level as the highest caste of priests and priestesses. Ordinary people are in awe of their skills.

They explained that a Balinese temple bell has an intricately carved brass handle, and the dome of the bell is made of a special type of bronze mixed with 22-carat gold, which is partly what gives it its superb resonance. The rest is down to the skills of the bellmakers, which have been handed down through generations. Immense care is taken to ensure that each bell is of the highest quality.

They explained that the crafting process for a temple bell is always begun at the full moon, which is the most potent time of the moon's cycle. Specific rituals are also performed at each stage to ensure the purity of the finished item. When a priest or priestess receives their bell, the first thing they do is to perform an elaborate consecration ceremony in their temple on an auspicious day determined according to the Balinese 210-day *Pawukon* calendar system.

When I felt I knew the bellmakers' family well enough, I asked if they would make me one of these bells to use for space clearing. To my delight they agreed, and I have used it ever since. I gave away all my other bells immediately.

That was in the latter part of 1991. I spent the next year visiting Balinese temples, observing the various ways that priests and priestesses use their bells to conduct purification rituals and invoke high-level spiritual connections during ceremonies. Of particular interest to me was the way that Balinese bells can be rung in such a way that they create a vehicle of sound on which a spiritual presence can ride.

At that time, I was living for six months of each year in Bali and six months in England. I took my temple bell back to England and began to use it in my space clearing work. Over the next year, the difference I observed in the space clearing ceremonies I conducted was immense. If I were to give an analogy, it would be akin to the difference between learning to play a violin on a basic instrument purchased in a local music shop and then suddenly having access to the levels of excellence facilitated by acquiring a Stradivarius. Balinese bells are in a completely different league to any other types of bells.

The techniques I have developed for space clearing are very different to those used in Hindu ceremonies in Bali. However, whenever I have shown Balinese priests or priestesses the way I ring my bell, they watch and listen intently, as only someone who is proficient in their art can do, and their faces spread into broad smiles of astonishment and delight that a westerner knows how to do that.

Balinese space clearing bells

What then happened in 1993 was an explosion of interest in people wanting to learn about space clearing. I started teaching workshops about it, and more and more people began asking me where they could buy a good-quality bell so they could put into practice what I was teaching them. I scoured the UK but still couldn't find any manufacturers of suitable bells there. At that time, all I could suggest to people was that they looked in oriental musical instrument shops or antique shops, which turned out to be a very unsatisfactory solution. Usually, the best they could find was Tibetan bells, which are not suited to space clearing at all.

That year I went back to Bali and, in a series of delicate overtures lasting several months, I put the problem to the bellmaker and his family. They thought the matter over and agreed to make temple bells for my students. This didn't work, though. All too soon it became clear that these bells were too expensive for most people and the crafting time was too long (two to three months for a single bell). There also weren't enough skilled bellmakers to make bells for my students and the Balinese priests and priestesses who needed them too. The most they could produce for me was about a dozen temple bells a year.

I felt increasingly uncomfortable teaching space clearing workshops without being able to offer people the tools to do the ceremony in their own homes. Then one day, in a flash of inspiration, I had the idea to ask the bellmaker if he could make a simpler version of a temple bell, with the same excellent purity of sound but a smaller dome and a wooden handle instead of an elaborately carved brass one. This reduced the cost and production time enormously.

It took a while to get everything right, but I'm happy to report that for many decades now the family has been producing the wonderful high-quality Balinese space clearing bells we sell through our online shop, at reasonable prices and in quantities that are usually enough to meet demand.

5

Taking space clearing to the world

by Karen Kingston

In 1991, on one of my visits from Bali back to the UK, I was invited to speak publicly about space clearing at an event in London. I was deluged with requests after the talk from people who wanted me to space clear their homes. This was how my professional work began.

By 1993, my knowledge and space clearing skills had developed to the level where I was ready to start teaching workshops. They immediately became very popular. I was featured in many national newspapers and radio shows, and appeared on major UK TV programmes, such as *This Morning*, watched by ten million viewers.

My first space clearing book

At that time, I had no intention of becoming an author. Then one day in 1994, someone who had attended one of my space clearing workshops sent me a copy of the notes she had typed up and circulated to all the other participants, whose names and addresses she had solicited. She meant well, but I was horrified to read what she had written and discover how much she had misunderstood.

I immediately improved the content of my workshop handouts. This helped a little, but it was clear to me that I really needed to write a book, primarily for workshop participants and also for anyone else who wanted to learn about space clearing.

Soon after, I was approached by Piatkus Books to do just that, and I wholeheartedly agreed. I wrote *Creating Sacred Space with Feng Shui* in 1995 and it was launched at the Mind Body Spirit Festival in London in May 1996. As a first-time author, I was naturally curious to see how it sold, so I went there that day to observe.

There were five or six bookstores at the event, each with huge piles of my book, stacked among all the other new titles. At the start of the day all the piles were of equal height. Imagine my surprise when I returned at lunchtime to discover that most of the other piles of books were still pretty much the same, but not mine. They had all gone.

My first thought was that my book must have been withdrawn from sale for some reason. But when I asked the booksellers, they told me it had sold out and they had sent for more copies from the warehouse.

This trend continued. The book quickly became an international bestseller, with sales of over a million copies in 15 languages, earning me a standing ovation when I spoke at the International Feng Shui Conference in Palm Springs in 1997. It had a wide appeal to anyone wanting to improve their quality of life and was also embraced by feng shui students worldwide.

It turned out that the timing for publishing this first book about space clearing was perfect. Many people were starting to become aware how much the energies in their home could affect them. Space clearing offered a completely new set of self-help tools they could use to change this. Articles by me and about me started to be published in newspapers and magazines around the world.

My clutter clearing book

In 1998, I published my second book, *Clear Your Clutter with Feng Shui*, to help people who had got stuck on Chapter 5 of the space clearing book, about clearing their clutter first.

This caused an even bigger sensation than the first book. To date, it has sold over two million copies in 26 languages. Not everyone wants to do space clearing, but it seems just about everyone has clutter of some kind. Until my book was published, no one had considered the energetic effects of keeping it. Clutter wasn't even mentioned in feng shui books at that time.

During the late 1990s and early 2000s, I travelled two or three times around the world each year, teaching workshops and doing consultations in the UK, the US, Australia, New Zealand, Singapore, Japan, Sweden, Norway, and many European countries. Soon I was teaching huge audiences and giving talks in such illustrious venues as the Stockholm Concert Hall.

In 2000, I used the royalties from my books to buy a piece of land in Bali and build a boutique hotel. Four years later, I added a two-storey octagonal conference centre with marble floors, spectacular ocean views, and a thatched roof that rose to a stunning 21-metre (69 feet) pinnacle. It became my favourite place on earth to teach, and many people travelled to take workshops and professional space clearing practitioner trainings with me there until I sold the property and left Bali in 2010. Richard co-led those events from 2005 on.

While living in Bali, I started to develop the art of creating high-level virtual spaces through which spiritual teachings could be passed. I used it primarily for working with space clearing practitioners around the world. This then led, in 2013, to teaching public online courses, which developed into all the online courses, classes, and personal sessions Richard and I offer today. They are very different to other types of online courses and services because of the consciously held virtual spaces we conduct them from.

Meeting Samuel Sagan

By 1999, I had reached a plateau in my own personal development work and was actively looking for a teacher to help me to move to the next level. I specifically wanted someone who had the perception to understand what I needed, the ability to facilitate my progress, and the wisdom not to require me to leave my own path and follow theirs. It was a tall order indeed. Yet, tuning in, it was clear to me that such a person did exist. He was male and located in either Australia or the United States. So, I set about finding him.

Later that year, while touring the US, I arrived half an hour early to do a talk in a bookstore in Seattle. The manager graciously offered to let me browse the bookshelves and pick any title I wished as a thank-you gift for my time. It was there that I came across Samuel Sagan's book *Entities: Parasites of the Body of Energy*. I expected it to be an amusing read, full of mystical nonsense. Instead, I was so intrigued by the depth of wisdom it contained that I stayed up most of that night reading it. It remains, to this day, the best book I have ever found on the topic. What impressed me the most was that the author knew considerably more about entities than I did. I had never come across that before.

I immediately made personal contact with Samuel Sagan. I read all his books and he read mine. Then in 2000, I flew to Australia to meet him and his students, who were members of the Clairvision School of meditation. Samuel and I became firm friends, and I stayed in close contact with him and participated in many of the intensives he led until his death in 2016.

Exactly as I'd hoped, he opened spaces for me to do my own personal development work and develop new levels of space clearing skills without requiring me to become one of his students. I owe him an immeasurable debt of gratitude on that account. Meeting and working with him felt to me like the spiritual equivalent of fortuitously meeting someone from your own country when travelling far from home in a foreign land. Although from different spiritual streams, we recognized and respected in each other an unwavering commitment to a life of high-level service, and we each did whatever we could to support the other's mission while incarnated here on earth.

6

Meeting Richard

by Karen Kingston

In 2002, Samuel Sagan took me to visit a property he had just purchased where he intended to build a meditation retreat centre. It was located about four hours from Sydney and consisted of 2,400 acres of fertile farmland and rocky outcrops, with a dilapidated old farmhouse and outbuildings at its centre. There was farmyard junk everywhere.

The next year, I heard about a man called Richard who was a newcomer to the Clairvision School and had taken over managing the property. He was doing exactly what I would have done if I lived there myself. He was systematically decluttering it, taking truckloads of junk to the local tip. He was also repairing the farmhouse, the perimeter fences, the machinery, and anything else that needed attention.

In 2004, I visited the property again to take part in a seven-day intensive and was amazed at how different the place felt. I was also very appreciative of the beautiful subterranean dragon* space that was being spread each night like a net beneath us, to hold us all in the space while we were sleeping. At first, I couldn't tell who was doing this. It took me until the third night to realize it was Richard, and that no one else had noticed this except me.

So that's how we first met – in the deep, infra-etheric* layers during the hours of the night, in spaces that are far beyond the comprehension of most people. I was surprised to discover he could do this, and he was equally surprised to discover I could perceive it.

Over the following month, we fell deeply in love and started living together at the retreat centre. In 2005, he moved to Bali to live with me there. We married in 2007 and have been together ever since. It has been the most extraordinary and fulfilling relationship of my life and continues to deepen with each passing year.

Not only is Richard a natural-born clutter clearer, but right from the start he was very interested to learn about space clearing too. I taught him how to do the ceremony and he immediately asked to train as a practitioner. By the time he flew to the UK in July 2005 to take my Professional Space Clearing Practitioner training, his skills were so advanced that he assisted me in teaching the training as well as participating in some sections as a student himself. Within months he was certified as a practitioner, having completed the most exacting training of any space clearer I've ever taught because I didn't want anyone to ever be able to say that I cut him any slack on account of our personal relationship.

Since then, he has achieved something that no one else I have trained ever has – he has developed his space clearing and clutter clearing skills to the same level as mine. In fact, in some aspects, he has surpassed me. All the examples of altar designs you can see on our websites were created by him. He has taken that aspect far beyond what I originally conceived it to be. He has also developed his own style of teaching and working with clients around the world through online classes and personal sessions. And it is now Richard, rather than me, who takes the lead in all the professional trainings we teach.

Meeting Richard

It was an obvious decision for us to write this new book together. This first part of the book has been written by me because it's about how I pioneered space clearing before meeting Richard. Most of the rest of the book has been co-authored because it's about how we have developed it together since then.

7

Richard's story

by Richard Kingston

In 2004, I was managing the meditation retreat centre belonging to the Clairvision School in Australia. One day, I was amused to see that the students living on the property started busily decluttering and tidying their rooms. "Karen Kingston is coming," they told me, which meant nothing to me, as I'd never heard of her.

I discovered she was an English woman who had written some books about space clearing and clutter clearing, and she would soon be arriving to take part in an intensive with some of the School's most senior instructors. This didn't change my behaviour at all as I had nothing that needed decluttering or tidying, and I wouldn't have joined in with the general commotion even if I had.

When someone lent me her book *Clear Your Clutter with Feng Shui* to read, I immediately resonated with what she'd written. It gave me many insights into why I used to completely declutter my life whenever I was feeling down or stuck, and why I'd find myself embarking on a new and exciting chapter of my life soon after.

Well, we met, and Karen has already told the story from there.

Richard's story

What she hasn't explained is how I came to be at that retreat centre at that time and how my life has changed so radically since the moment we met.

I was born in an outback town called Bourke, located in the middle of the Australian desert, about 750 km (470 miles) from Sydney, with a population of around 4,500 people at that time. Most people outside Australia have never heard of it, but for Aussies, when someone says they come from "the back o' Bourke", they immediately understand that they are from one of the remotest outposts there is. I lived there until I was 3 years old, when my family moved to Newcastle in New South Wales. I still have a deep affinity with the clear astrality* of remote, vast desert spaces.

I was fortunate to have a very good family upbringing, with my father's grounded, no-nonsense, hard-working approach to life, and my mother's unconditional love. She was a great teacher of how to remain emotionally open, regardless of whatever hardships came my way.

I knew from a very early age that there is more to life than the everyday level of existence. At 18 months old, I became known for my remarkable ability to waddle into a yard full of 30 or 40 chickens at my grandparent's farm, stop, pick one up, and walk around with it for as long as I chose to. Instead of running away or struggling to be let free, the chicken would calmly and contentedly rest in my arms. I later discovered this was an etheric know-how I had picked up at that very young age directly from my grandmother, who was able to do this too.

As I grew up, I found that most animals felt safe with me. Cats and dogs would follow me home. There was one particularly memorable occasion in my late twenties when the astonished owner of an ultra-vicious ex-police-trained German Shepherd guard dog emerged from his cabin to discover I had boarded his boat without permission, and instead of attacking me and ripping me to shreds, his dog was sitting next to me, calmly licking the palms of my hands.

I have always had the ability to connect with people at a higher level too, and to see beyond skin colour, culture, or status to the core of a person's being. The qualities of warmth, heartness, and human spirit are far more important to me than external appearances or accomplishments.

At the age of 14, I remember very clearly that a two-week time window opened up for me to decide which direction I wanted to take in life. The choice was between becoming a professional racing car driver or a chef. I had a natural talent for both, so it could have gone either way.

To help me decide, I went go-cart racing several times in the first week and worked with a top-level pastry chef the next week. I loved the adrenaline-fuelled buzz of driving, but in the end, I saw that the racing car driver path was limited (I'd surely die young in a fiery wreck). I chose the path of the chef because I knew it would open up the world for me and allow me to travel anywhere.

At 16, I took the entrance exam for a chef training course and was one of 24 people from 300 applicants who passed. By the age of 28, I had worked in a number of prestigious hotels in Europe and as Chef de Cuisine at two of the top restaurants in Australia. After that, I worked for over four years as the Executive Chef of one of the wealthiest European families, running the kitchens in their properties in St. Moritz, Portofino, Milan, and London. I also single-handedly provided all the catering for the family and their many celebrity guests on board their private luxury yacht, which cruised to exotic locations for up to six months each year.

By 2002, I was 32 years old and suffering from exhaustion and burnout. Most chefs work long hours, but for four years I had worked 17 hours a day, from 6 am till 11 pm in three-month stretches or more, with hardly any time off. I lived in hotel rooms or tiny bedrooms in the basements of the family's mansions, with no space for anything except a bed to sleep on. I had a glamorous job that was the envy of my chef friends, but no life of my own at all. I suppressed my loneliness with whisky and beer each night.

One day, in a moment of what I now believe was divinely inspired clarity, I realized it was time for change. I could feel that a whole new life was waiting for me if I just had the courage to walk away from this one. I resigned by email the next day, and again every day after that for six weeks until the family finally let me go. I walked away from my career as a chef and returned to Australia, with no idea what to do next.

I fell into a deep, dark, depressive pit for a while, consuming large quantities of alcohol and marijuana as an emotional coping mechanism. It was a really tough time, but one I still look back on as an invaluable experience. It taught me that taking alcohol and drugs only compounds the problems. It does not improve or resolve them. I would never go back to that again.

By 2003, I was ready for a fresh start and set up a wholesale organic food distribution company working with the organic and biodynamic farmers of the Hunter Valley in New South Wales. It was a wonderfully healing time, with much joy and laughter.

Then everything changed again later that year when I discovered the Clairvision School of meditation and met Samuel Sagan. I closed my new business and engaged in an 18-month period of inner exploration, doing full-time meditation, emotional deconstruction, and participating in intensives. With Samuel's guidance and the Clairvision School's tools for transformation, I discovered incredible inner worlds that pushed the boundaries of consciousness. It was utterly life-changing on all levels, mentally, emotionally, and spiritually. In the first four months, I also lost all the extra weight I had gained while cheffing – 35 kg (77 lb) – and I have maintained normal weight ever since.

The experience of those times has given me much more empathy for others. I deeply understand how it feels to be stuck in levels of depression, as well as the immense joys of discovering a whole new life beyond those dark spaces, enriched by more awareness.

It was at the end of this period, in 2004, that Karen and I met, and everything changed for me again.

Fairly early in our relationship, I was present when she did a beautiful space clearing ceremony and was amazed at the tangible shifts of energy it brought about. Then, a week later, she invited me to participate in a very different ceremony that involved the creation of an incredibly beautiful mandala about 3 metres in diameter, consisting of candles, colourizers**, and thousands of flower petals arranged on the floor. During that ceremony, I had one of the most powerful experiences of awakening ever, and I knew then that I wanted to learn all those skills myself.

A year later, we were living together in Bali, where I discovered a rich, spiritual culture that was very different to anything I'd ever known before. I found that if I was respectful, Balinese people welcomed me to their temples, without any need for indoctrination or beliefs. The more I engaged with them, the more unrestricted access I had to their temple network. It was an incredible time for discovering how spiritual forces truly work and how to consciously connect with them.

My spiritual practices moved to an entirely new level during the five years I lived in Bali, far beyond anything I knew to be possible. I experienced extraordinary states of being during meditation and exalted states of consciousness, completely out of my mind, emotions, and physical body.

In 2007, I took on the role of General Manager of the hotel and conference centre Karen had built, and I created the most sought-after restaurant in East Bali at that time. People would travel three hours from the other side of the island just to dine there. Karen and I also taught many workshops together in the conference centre, attended by thousands of people from around the world. It was a memorable period of my life, which I look back on fondly.

Then, in 2010 it was time for us both to leave Bali, so we sold up and moved to the UK, which is now our permanent home. I became a UK citizen and now feel more at home here than in Australia. I'm living exactly where I want to be.

People sometimes ask me if I miss the world of cheffing and hospitality that I was immersed in for over 16 years. My answer is not at all. The great thing about mastering any skill in life is that, with awareness, aspects of it can be transposed to other skills, which is exactly what I've done with space clearing and clutter clearing. And, of course, spending my time teaching people how to raise the level of consciousness in their lives feels to me to be a far more meaningful and fulfilling calling than cheffing ever was.

Space Clearing, Volume 2

I love the depth of my relationship with Karen and the work we do together in the world. I am truly grateful for her practical, no-nonsense approach to spiritual matters, and it is an honour to be able to share my space clearing and clutter clearing skills and know-how with others.

PART TWO

Deeper understandings of space clearing

8

About spiritual connections

In the space clearing workshops we teach, when we come to the part where we demonstrate activating a flower offering**, most people have nothing in their experience to relate this to. They enjoy the beauty of the candle and the flowers, and they can feel the tangible space of peace and stillness that descends in the room as the offering is activated. But we can see that they struggle to understand it.

It's a sad fact that most people alive today never consciously come into contact with a high-level spiritual connection*. The closest they get to this is visiting a sacred site or a place in nature that feels special.

Most people occupy unpresenced homes and live spiritually disconnected lives, searching for happiness in the best way they know through the acquisition of material possessions or experiences that offer a fleeting sense of fulfilment. Deep down, they have an unquenchable yearning for something more.

This "something more" is the spiritual connection that all traditional cultures and religions offer in one form or another. But now many cultures have lost their spiritual integrity and religions tend to ask their followers to rest on faith rather than giving people a direct experience of high spiritual presences.

About spiritual connections

It's said that you won't miss what you have never had. But when it comes to spiritual connections, we were at one with these before we were incarnated here on earth, and we *do* miss them while we are here. Deeply and unceasingly.

We find some comfort in the love that human relationships can offer. But however deep that love is, it's only a minor echo of the richness of connection to high spiritual realms. The current human condition is that most people do not know how to fill the gaping hole of the longing they feel or even recognize that they have it.

Some people turn to recreational drugs to get "high". The reason this type of experimentation usually begins during teenage years is because young people haven't yet resigned themselves to a life of disconnection. They actively long to find more meaning and purpose.

And they are on the right track in one respect because drugs *can* give access to higher astral planes that feel intoxicatingly profound. However, the feeling only lasts for as long as the chemical substance is in a person's body. When the effect wears off, they are then plunged back into everyday reality, which feels worse than ever, spurring them to take drugs again.

The problem with using an artificial method to get high is that the person does not have to put any effort into developing their subtle body structures, which is a large part of the purpose of incarnating in human form in the first place. It can be a complete waste of a life. The spaces that can be accessed artificially are also haphazard and difficult to navigate. Drugs tend to connect people to skewed astral* spaces that are fraught with dangers.

Others turn to alcoholic intoxication, antidepressants, sleeping pills, and so on, not as a way of ascending to higher spiritual levels but as a way of numbing themselves and blocking out the pain of disconnection. These behaviours often begin after a loss of some kind. All losses trigger the memory, to some extent, of the cosmic grief of being disconnected from our spiritual source.

Spiritual connections in Bali

We will be referring to Bali a lot in this part of the book because it's a place on earth where spiritual connections are a tangible reality in the everyday life of the people who live there. Energetic awareness is woven into everything Balinese Hindus do, and it has been for thousands of years. Spiritual connections live in their blood. You can see it in their eyes and in the radiance of their smiles. You can feel it in their hearts. Modern life, for most people, is a hollow shell compared with the richness of spiritual connection that Balinese people experience every day.

The reason we felt so at home in Bali when we lived there was that the island abounds with spiritual connections. Balinese people have highly effective methods of attracting high-level presences to their temples and providing them with an anchorage so that they can remain there. Balinese children are brought up to know and interact with spiritual forces as part of the fabric of their life. They learn how to recognize different connections and how to distinguish between authentic high spiritual presences and astral beings that imitate them.

Karen was married to a Balinese man for 12 of the years she lived in Bali, and on two occasions they travelled together to the UK. One day, she took him to Warwick Castle, which is one of England's best-preserved and architecturally impressive medieval castles. She hoped he'd be impressed or at least interested, but instead he was mystified.

About spiritual connections

"The furniture is very strange," he said, pointing to priceless antiques. "And these are not real people," he said, gesturing to the artfully crafted wax figures in period costumes. "Can we meet the people who actually live here?"

"It's a very old castle," Karen explained. "No one lives here now."

"Then why have you brought me here?" he asked. "There are no people and there is no spiritual presence. What's the point?"

Outside of everyday life, there are two main reasons why Balinese people make journeys – to visit people or to visit spiritual presences residing in temples. An uninhabited castle has neither, so is of no interest at all.

Some years later, Karen found herself in a very similar situation. Some people went to a lot of trouble to take her to visit Big Sur in California, which they felt sure would impress her. But she didn't meet anyone there and the land energies were devoid of spiritual presence. She found herself asking exactly the same question: "What is the point of bringing me here?"

By contrast, we once took a very sceptical man to visit a Balinese temple. He was a practical, down-to-earth type, an electrician by trade until he retired, with no interest in anything spiritual.

All Balinese temples have an invisible force field in the space between the two carved stone pillars of the entrance gate. Balinese people are fully aware of this and will silently announce themselves to the temple presences as they pass through a gate to enter a temple space. Some westerners are sensitive enough to feel something, although they don't know what it is. Most don't notice anything at all.

We made no attempt to explain this to the man. We simply suggested he looked at the palms of his hands before he entered the temple and then again after entering. We didn't tell him what to expect, so he had no preconceived ideas.

What followed is etched in our memories forever. He looked at his palms outside the temple. They were normal. Then he stepped inside and looked again. His palms were instantly mottled all over with white blotches.

Puzzled, he stepped back outside. The blotches disappeared. He stepped inside again, and the blotches reappeared. He did this again and again, staring at his palms in utter disbelief.

We explained to him that these white blotches (or pale-coloured blotches in people of colour) are one of the ways our body responds when we enter a space that is spiritually presenced. And one of the most impressive things about Balinese temples is that this effect happens in nearly all of them. The only exceptions we found, after visiting hundreds of temples around the island, were those that have heavy tourist footfall through them. Balinese people do their best but are not able to maintain the same levels of presencing in those places.

The story of this man is not an isolated incident. During the years we lived in Bali, we took many people to visit Balinese temples and they all experienced the same mottled-palms effect. If you ever visit the island, you can experiment with this yourself. You can also use it in any temple or sacred site you visit anywhere in the world to discover if there is a genuine spiritual connection in the place or not.

Communing with spiritual connections

Many people think of music and dance as forms of entertainment. In most traditional cultures, they have a very different purpose. They

About spiritual connections

have been developed very precisely as ways of summoning spiritual connections. Particular sounds, rhythms, and movements that resonate with a specific presence can have that effect.

There are still some places in the world where you can witness this today. The most powerful we have found is the sacred music and dance of Bali. By this, we don't mean the demonstrations performed in the main tourist areas of the island for camera-happy audiences. We're talking about authentic dances that usually only take place in remote villages.

To gain access to one of these, you have to know someone from a village who invites you to a ceremony that involves some kind of dance, and you will need to and wear full Balinese traditional dress, not just a sarong hastily tied over your clothes. Karen was fortunate to be invited to many ceremonies like this during the 20 years she lived there.

Such events begin with long periods of waiting while the priest or priestess performs rituals to invoke a spiritual presence. The musicians and dancers are anointed with holy water in a specific way to help them to enter a meditative or trance-like state.

There are two kinds of dances in Bali. There are the ones where the musicians connect to the spiritual presence and take the lead, with the dancers following. The other kind is where the dancers connect to the spiritual presence and take the lead, with the musicians following. The latter is much rarer, and only the most accomplished dancers can do it. Both are exceptional to behold.

Karen once attended a major ceremony in Batur temple, which is one of Bali's largest and most sacred temples, high in the mountains, located on the edge of a huge caldera containing an active volcano.

Hundreds of families arrived, carrying elaborate offerings to the gods on their heads, a woven leaf mat to sit on, and an entire day's food to eat, still in the pots it had been cooked in. She had been living in the village for several months and knew many of the people well. As the only westerner present, she was warmly invited by many of the families to join them and share their food. She moved from mat to mat, enjoying their company and sampling small portions of the feasts they had prepared.

Animated conversations continued for many hours as the assembled throng patiently waited for the necessary rituals to be performed. A gamelan orchestra struck up from time to time, and a group of twenty or so male Baris dancers assembled in lines and moved in square formation to the music.

In this particular temple, Baris dancing is a speciality. The men's costumes were the most elaborate Karen had ever seen, featuring triangular pointed headdresses adorned with tiny shells and white frangipani flowers. On their torsos they wore long tongues of red, yellow, black, white, and green cloth, intricately embroidered with gold thread, sequins, and beads. Each dancer also had an ornate *kris* dagger slung across his back.

The dance she witnessed was different to any she had seen in Bali before that day. The dramatic movements of the Baris dance, performed barefoot and in perfect synchronization, are evocative of Balinese-style martial art poses, the epitome of masculine strength and virility. Immersed in the high meditative state that had been induced in them by the priest, the dancers anchored themselves in the depths of the dragon forces of the temple space below and let their bodies move.

They did not dance. They were danced.

About spiritual connections

What started as repetitive movements designed to attract the specific presence for that ceremony quickly became the living embodiment of the presence itself as it danced through them. It began with the musicians playing and the dancers following, then transformed into the presence dancing the dancers, with the musicians following.

Balinese people have a name for this state. They call it *taksu*, which roughly translates as "channelling the Divine". They admire a person's ability to do this immensely and can spot a fake immediately. It has some similarities with the concept of surrendering to an artistic muse, but the Balinese version is much more than this. It is the art of communing with a specific spiritual connection and becoming the vehicle through which it can express itself and bestow its grace upon everyone present. Balinese people are so familiar with this that they will often appraise a performer among themselves and awards them points, on a scale of 1 to 10, for spiritual effectiveness.

Not all temples in Bali use music or dance to help to summon a presence before a ceremony begins. Some rely purely on the use of various types of offerings and spoken invocations, often accompanied by the priest or priestess ringing a bell in the prescribed manner. Music and dance are a powerful addition to the mix, and any Balinese person who has been trained in these arts is highly respected in their community. It takes many years of practice and very special talents.

Prepersonal people

There are still some cultures in the world that have a spiritually connected way of life to some extent because they remain immersed in what is known as the prepersonal stage*, which rests on group consciousness. As Samuel Sagan once said, "Prepersonal people smile because at the bottom of their heart it is easy to find connection." The difference between them and people who have been brought up in cultures that are mainly in the personal stage* is they do not have to forge these connections personally. They only need to be part of the group.

In ALTMC, Samuel Sagan explains:

> In the early prepersonal stage*, human beings were one with the Divine, but without any sense of individuality. Then comes the personal stage*, in which individuality is acquired at the expense of a near-complete disconnection from spiritual worlds. Finally, in the transpersonal stage*, human consciousness is to regain its unity with the Divine, while retaining individuality.

Most of us never experience this blissful union with spiritual connections even once in our life. It was lost to us when we started to move from the prepersonal to the personal stage, in which we are meant to take control of our own destiny. It's still possible to have spiritual connections in the personal stage, but it's no longer automatic. It has to be done consciously and is much more difficult to achieve.

Balinese people are now beginning to experience this too, as they move from the prepersonal stage of human consciousness to the personal stage, which is why their spiritual culture is no longer as vibrant as it once was. In our visits to Bali in recent years, we have observed a substantial decline in the level of spiritual presencing in some of the temples and in the ambient etheric* of the island. This is partly due to the encroaching influence of tourism and the modern world, but mostly because the younger generations of Balinese people do not hold the same level of spiritual connection that their parents had. It's highly likely that within a generation the prepersonal level of connection will be lost entirely. They will need to learn new ways of spiritual connection that are more suited to moving through the personal stage.

This, by the way, gives a deeper level of understanding of why techniques such as burning herbs or incense, which originated in prepersonal cultures, are not suited to westernized homes in modern times. We live in a personal culture, aspiring to be transpersonal. Our lifestyle is much more astralized (impacted by thoughts and emotional reactions) than the etheric-based lifestyles of indigenous ancestors ever were, because they lived much closer to nature. The space clearing methods we need in the twenty-first century for our more urbanized way of life are therefore very different. They have to be able to address much denser types of etheric energies and far more impacted types of astral imprints** than ever existed in bygone times.

Space clearing is a sacred ritual

Karen didn't describe space clearing as a ritual in the first book she published in 1996. That's because she was living in Bali at the time where, due to a quirk of translation, they call even their most profound rituals "ceremonies". Through living there and mixing with Balinese people, the terminology rubbed off on her.

We have continued to use the word ceremony because ritual has many occult connotations that we don't wish to be associated with. It's also common these days to use ritual to mean a mundane habit that has been repeated so often it has special status, such as a ritual cup of tea or coffee in the morning.

We therefore call space clearing a ceremony, but really it is a sacred ritual*. And the thing about a sacred ritual is that it is not created by humans at all. It is created by a spiritual connection as a way for humans to connect to it. Few people in the world are able to commune with spiritual presences and cognize at this high level, but it can be done.

Tibetan chanting is a good example of this. Its purpose is to invoke the presence of a specific deity. You won't get this effect from listening to a recording of a Tibetan chant sold for commercial profit, but there are still some temples in the world where the monks enter deep meditative states and use chanting in this way.

Other examples can be found in Balinese Hindu temples, where you can experience first-hand the powerful spaces created when high-level presences are invoked by the time-honoured temple rituals conducted by priests and priestesses. There has been a decline in the power of these ceremonies in recent years, but there are still temples where this happens, if you are prepared to take the time and put in the effort to look for them.

The reason we are including this information here is to explain that any form of authentic space clearing is never a set of techniques invented by humans. In all traditional cultures, space clearing methods are based on specific rituals that have been created by a spiritual connection and then cognized by humans.

This is why it's never a good idea to mess with a ritual. The steps of a space clearing method that has integrity are prescribed by the spiritual presence they are designed to connect to. They need to be done in a specific way and in a specific order to obtain a specific result. If you closely examine any form of space clearing in a traditional culture, you will find there are always unseen forces behind the ritual. If you change the order of the ritual or add extra elements to it, all you will have is a series of empty techniques that connect to nothing at all and have little or no effect.

The White Gold spiritual connection

The connection that lies at the heart of the space clearing ceremony we have developed is known as White Gold**. It's high level, non-denominational, and provides a platform on which other connections that have integrity can land.

We hasten to add that because it is called White Gold this does not mean in any way that it has the energetic appearance of being white or gold. If you ever think you see flashes of white or gold while doing a space clearing ceremony, this will be purely in your own imagination. The connection does have unique aspects that can be perceived in a number of ways, but colour is not one of them.

You may be wondering, as you read this, if everyone who does space clearing by following the instructions in *Space Clearing, Volume 1* will automatically be able to connect to the White Gold spiritual presence? Well, no. Of course not. Giving that kind of guarantee would be as ludicrous as suggesting that everyone who decides to take up yoga can instantly become supple.

What we can say, though, is that our books don't just pass knowledge. We write them in such a way that they also pass higher spaces of consciousness, which makes it possible to connect to the spiritual connection behind the words.

Samuel Sagan also excelled at this. If you want to know more about this aspect, and about the prepersonal, personal, and transpersonal journey of humankind, the best starting point we know of is his *Atlantean Secrets* and *Bleeding Sun* novels. They immerse the reader in spaces of connection in a way that no other books we know of do.

The integrity of spiritual connections

This section of the book would not be complete without emphasizing that there are astral beings that masquerade as high spiritual presences. These are unfortunately all too common, especially in relation to New Age teachings. Many people get tricked by them because they are not able to discern the difference between a spiritual connection that has integrity and an astral being that is mimicking this.

Spirit guides, angels, and channelled beings are all highly suspect in this respect, especially the ones that tell you to do things or feed you with information you have no way of verifying. They can be very convincing but are, in fact, astral beings that like to hijack human consciousness for their own purposes.

We therefore strongly advise you to have nothing to do with any non-physical beings that speak to you in words. High-level spiritual connections do not do this, as we explain in more detail in Chapter 24 about invocational energy clearing. Angels can communicate with humans, but only at extraordinarily high levels of consciousness, far above the level of words and the mind.

9

The main purposes of space clearing

In this book, we will be explaining how the space clearing techniques described in *Space Clearing, Volume 1* work. You don't need to know any of this information to be able to do space clearing in your own home, but most people find that deepening their understanding improves their skills and the results they are able to obtain. Besides, if you've read Volume 1 and are already this far into Volume 2, you're surely curious to know more!

The main purposes of space clearing are:
- Clearing and revitalizing energies in buildings
- Taking energetic ownership of a space
- Raising the level of consciousness in a space
- Facilitating spiritual connection
- Spiritually presencing a space

Here's more information about each of these.

Clearing and revitalizing energies in buildings

By following the steps of the Essential Space Clearing** or Full Space Clearing** ceremony, most people can revitalize stagnant energies** and clear recently formed, lightly embedded astral imprints** in their own home. With practice, deeper layers of astral imprints, including those resulting from traumatic events, habitual behaviours, or chronic

63

sickness, can also be cleared. We explain in this book and *Space Clearing, Volume 1* the many benefits this can have in your life.

Taking energetic ownership of a space

Another important use of space clearing is to help you to forge a much deeper relationship with your home by taking energetic as well as physical ownership of it. This will happen to a certain extent through decorating and furnishing a property, as well as keeping it physically well maintained, clean, tidy, and clutter-free. But there is much more to energetically owning space than that. It's one of the topics we plan to write an entire book about in the coming years.

In relation to space clearing, we will be explaining more about this in the chapters of this book to do with hand sensing, flower offerings, and harmony balls.

Raising the level of consciousness in a space

Most people have no idea how to live their life at a higher level than the mundane level at which it is generally lived. Space clearing is designed to raise the level of consciousness in our own personal spaces, which raises the quality of life it is possible for us to experience. This makes it easier to gain access to higher levels of consciousness that are always available to us all, yet rarely tapped into.

Those of you reading this who have taken our Seven Levels of Consciousness** online course will recall that we refer to the level of everyday life as Level 6. In the context of this book, we can explain that space clearing can be used to raise the energy in a space from Level 6 to Level 5, and depending on the skill of the person, to higher levels too.

If you want your life to be more meaningful and purposeful than the general level it is lived at by most people today, knowing how to change the energies of your home is a total game-changer. Space clearing can transform your home into a place that will deeply nurture and support your spiritual path and enhance your awareness.

Facilitating spiritual connection

One of the remarkable qualities of the White Gold spiritual connection that is associated with the space clearing ceremony we have pioneered and developed is that it can act as a platform for other spiritual connections that have integrity to land on. This is why it can be used by people from such a wide range of cultural backgrounds, religions, and spiritual beliefs.

Spiritually presencing a space

Most religions have rituals that are intended to temporarily give its devotees access to levels of consciousness they cannot easily attain by themselves, in order to experience enhanced states of being. To facilitate this, temples are constantly purified to maintain the energy of the space at high levels.

At its highest level, space clearing can be used to presence spaces to facilitate profound levels of stillness for meditation and spiritual practices. It encompasses the extraordinary art of landing Spirit into matter (infusing physical substances with high-level spiritual presencing).

Levels of space clearing

The four levels of space clearing are:
- Basic Space Clearing
- Essential Space Clearing
- Full Space Clearing
- Professional Space Clearing

Just about anyone can do Basic Space Clearing by following the instructions in *Space Clearing, Volume 1*.

We have also provided in-depth knowledge for those who wish to access deeper levels through Essential Space Clearing and Full Space Clearing. Both require more effort and skill, but the results are well worth it.

Professional Space Clearing is only for the very few. It requires the cultivation of specific subtle body structures, which can take many years of personal development work to build. Ultimately, it's a Point-dragon art. This may not mean much to many readers of this book, but you will be able to glean some initial understanding of it by looking up the terms "Point" and "dragon" in the ALTMC Glossary at the back of this book, and we will explain more about it in the coming pages.

Clients benefit enormously from having a Professional Space Clearing done in their home, and there are many benefits for the practitioner too. Professional-level space clearing is a fertile arena for spiritual development, once described by Samuel Sagan, founder of the Clairvision School, as the most complete subtle body workout he had ever seen.

To do space clearing at practitioner level requires enhanced etheric, astral, and superastral awareness, perception, and skills. So, to be able to explain more about how space clearing works, we first need to give you a basic explanation about the subtle body structures that are involved. That's what the next chapter is about.

10
Subtle body structures

The Fourfold Model developed by Samuel Sagan contains the most advanced insights into human subtle body structures we have ever found. It explains that there is much more to us than just a physical body. We have:

- A physical body
- An etheric body
- An astral body
- A Higher Self

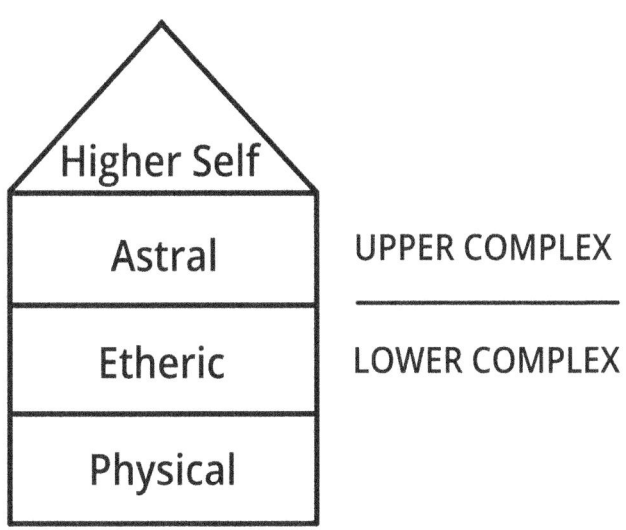

The Fourfold Model

The physical body

The physical components of a human body are the skeletal, muscular, nervous, endocrine, cardiovascular, lymphatic, respiratory, digestive, urinary, and reproductive systems, and the skin.

The etheric body

All humans, animals, and plants have an etheric body*, which permeates the physical body and extends beyond it. The Chinese call this *chi*. The Japanese call it *ki*. In India, it is known as *prana*. Elsewhere, it is often known as life force energy. The physical body and etheric body work closely together and form what is known as the lower complex*.

Western medicine takes no account of the etheric body, but traditional Chinese medicine is based on the knowledge that all diseases begin in the etheric before they manifest physically. Acupuncture acts directly on the meridians of energy to unblock and optimize etheric flows. Hence, in ancient China, it used to be that a person would only pay their doctor when they were well. If they became sick, it meant the doctor had not done their job, so they would stop paying until they were well again. It's the complete opposite of how medical care is structured today.

The astral body

All humans and animals also have an astral body*. It's the part of us that thinks, has emotions, reacts, feels stressed, gets confused, and so on. If you've ever tried to silence your mind* by meditating, your astral body is the part that keeps generating chitter-chatter inside your head. If unchecked, it can cause overthinking, neurotic behaviours, obsessions, addictions, and a range of other mental and emotional problems.

The astral body is also what makes our muscles contract and relax so that our physical body can move.

As a spiritual being incarnated into a physical body, we need to have an astral body to be able to function. We would be like a vegetable without one. But in our modern, fast-paced world, it's all too easy to become overastralized. When this happens, the astral body grasps parts of the physical body through the etheric, which causes us to feel aches and pains. Overastralization is the cause of many physical health problems.

The astral body also comes with countless latent or active samskaras (mental and emotional scars), created by traumatic experiences in this life or previous lives. One of the biggest illusions humans suffer from is that we are in control of our own life when, in fact, 99% of the time we are being unconsciously driven by samskaric charges in our own astral body.

Learning how to identify and resolve samskaras and how to maintain a good etheric–astral balance are both key to happily inhabiting a human body.

The Higher Self

A major difference between humans and animals is that we have a Higher Self. It's the essential part of us that can connect to high spiritual realms and has continuation from incarnation to incarnation. The Higher Self and astral body together form what is known as the upper complex*.

The great challenge for humans is that our Higher Self is veiled by our astral body, which is why all personal development work needs to have two distinct aspects:

1. Construction (meditation and other forms of subtle bodybuilding*)
2. Deconstruction (sourcing and resolving samskaras)

To learn more about the Fourfold Model than this brief introduction can provide, the best starting point is the Clairvision Knowledge Track titled *KT Subtle Bodies, The Fourfold Model*, which we highly recommend.

How we interact with our environment

Just as there is more to us than a physical body, so the atmosphere of the planet we live on contains more than just the physical air that we breathe. It also contains ethericity and astrality, which are sometimes referred to collectively by the vague term "energy". They are invisible, so cannot be seen with our physical eyes, but they can be felt.

We engage and perceive ethericity with our etheric body. If you have a favourite place in nature, for example, it will be somewhere that nurtures your etheric.

We engage and perceive astral spaces with our astral body. The dream spaces we go to when asleep are a direct experience of astral realms, and every waking experience that involves a thought or emotion has an astral component too.

The variety of astral spaces we can inhabit while incarnated in a human body is vast. It ranges from very low levels (the stuff of nightmares, horror films, and so on) to exalted levels of profound spiritual enlightenment. The higher levels of astrality, known as superastrality*, can sometimes be accessed by chance, such as having a spontaneous "Aha!" moment above the head, often symbolized in cartoons by an illuminated light bulb. Through meditation and other practices, it's possible to consciously cultivate subtle body structures above the head to access higher levels of consciousness and superastral know-how at will.

Subtle body structures and space clearing

Space Clearing, Volume 1 was written in such a way that most people will be able to get results if they follow the practical steps mechanically without having any etheric or superastral awareness at all. The changes won't be spectacular, but they will make a difference.

Doing the same ceremony with more etheric and superastral awareness is a completely different experience, with much better results.

And doing the ceremony at practitioner level, with the highly developed levels of etheric and superastral know-how that requires, is a different experience again, with vastly more substantial results.

It can take decades to develop subtle body structures, so simply reading this book won't be enough. What we hope it will do, though, is open the door to the first steps, which begin with developing more etheric awareness.

11

Etheric awareness

We explain earlier in this book that Balinese people are happy to follow traditional practices that invoke spiritual connections without understanding how the rituals work. They know the immense joy they feel in their hearts after a temple ceremony and the blissful etheric state that feels like walking on air as they leave.

People with enquiring minds from other cultures tend to take a different approach. They want to know how things work. And rightly so. There is far too much nonsense associated with energy work today, and we do not wish to add to that. We encourage everyone to develop their own perception so that they can see and know for themselves what has integrity and what does not.

The unseen worlds of energy

A common belief today is that humans are physical beings, living in a physical world, who have the option of having spiritual experiences, if they choose to. This is considered to be a sensible, educated, scientific approach.

The problem is that those who hold this view don't know what they don't know. Because they have no experience beyond the physical, they don't take into account the subtle body structures that all humans have. Viewed from the perspective of our Higher Self, we are not physical beings at all. We are spiritual beings having a human experience for a number of years. Our natural state of existence, while incarnated on earth, is not to lose ourselves in the materialism of physicality but to remain connected to the high spiritual realms from which we came and to which we will return.

Having a daily spiritual practice is helpful, but it's simply not enough in our stressful, fast-paced world. Much more is needed to be able to even glimpse what it feels like to be spiritually connected and navigate through life from that perspective.

Any genuine spiritual seeker must start by developing more awareness of etheric realms, and the only way to do that is to develop their own etheric body to a more awakened state. This is also an essential first step for anyone wishing to understand space clearing beyond beginner level, so it is a vital topic to include in this book.

What is an etheric body?

The world consists of much more than the physical things we can touch and see. Physicality is only the tip of the iceberg. Beyond this, there are worlds upon worlds of more rarefied fluid-dimensional and non-dimensional realities that are just as tangible as the physical realms, if you are able to discern them. They can't be felt with our ordinary physical senses, but it's possible to develop other organs of perception to do so. The level of functionality that can be built up is remarkable.

Imagine, for example, that you lived in a culture where for some reason it was taboo to use your arms. As you grew up, they withered and hung uselessly from your shoulders. Then supposing one day you meet someone who says, "Hey, do you know you can use those?"

"For what?" you ask, incredulously.

"For so many things!"

Then the person teaches you how to begin to move your arms. It would be nothing more than a few jerky spasms at first, but gradually, if you worked at it, you'd build some muscle and be able to move your fingers, turn your wrist, bend your elbow, flex your arm, and pick up objects. One miraculous day, you'd find you could use your previously pathetic appendages to feed yourself. And that's just the beginning. You could go on to learn how to write, create handicrafts, paint masterpieces… the list is endless.

There are parts of human subtle body structures that have fallen into just such disuse in modern times, to the extent that most people don't even know they exist, never mind how to use them. The focus these days is on accomplishing physical feats that will be entered in record books and anything that will push the physical body to new limits.

This all amounts to very little when compared with the vast unexplored worlds of human consciousness and subtle bodies of energy. It was this quest that led Karen, many years ago, to the discovery of etheric realms, and it was cultivating her own etheric body that led her to the development of space clearing and an in-depth exploration of higher levels of consciousness. Richard took a different route, primarily through meditation, mental and emotional deconstruction, mastering bodywork skills, and developing deep levels of dragon know-how. There is more than one path.

How to feel your etheric body

Everyone knows that unseen energies exist. We can't see electricity or microwaves, but we accept they are real because we can turn on lights and use our mobile phones.

Etheric awareness

Similarly, we can't see etheric energies, but we have proof they exist. Each time you feel tired at the end of the day, that's your etheric vitality wearing down, causing you to need to sleep to recharge it.

A similar process happens on a larger scale during your life. The boundless energy you had as a child was because your etheric vitality was strong at that time. It depletes as you age, so you have less energy as you grow older. Aging is the result of a wearing out of the etheric body.

You can see this in flowers too. Their etheric body is what makes them grow and gives them vitality. Flowers are at their most vital when in full bloom. Their ethericity gradually diminishes and fades as they die.

Your etheric body is closely connected to your breath. It's the part of you that loves to be in nature, breathe fresh air, and walk barefoot on the grass. Before the Industrial Revolution, the world was primarily etherically based. Most people lived in rural communities and had a natural connection to land energies. Some remnants of this can still be found in countries where industrialization and urbanization have not yet taken hold.

Your etheric body is also the part of you that can feel how eating fresh organic fruit and vegetables nourishes you in a way junk food never can. It's our astral body that craves junk food. The etheric body knows it is not nutritious.

One of the primary functions of the etheric body is the continuance of life through sexual reproduction. That's why there is such an emphasis in society on family life and reproducing yourself before you die. It's essential to our species. But it's a lower function of the etheric because the animal level of reproduction doesn't require any special skills other than to find a mate and have sex. All animals can reproduce. There are many higher levels of etheric functionality that humans can develop too.

A deeper way to experience your etheric body is through the type of meditation that is designed to awaken your third eye*. Learning how to still the mental chatter and emotional pulls of your astral body makes it possible to feel the etheric layer of life force energy in your physical body in a variety of ways, such as a beautiful tingling vibration in your skin.

The benefits of a strong etheric

The higher parts of you (your Higher Self and some parts of your astral body) continue from one incarnation to the next. The etheric body does not. It only exists for as long as you are alive in your current physical body. After death, your physical body and etheric body will both dissolve within a short time.

Like your physical body, your etheric constitution is largely determined by what you inherit from your parents. Some people have the good fortune to be born with a strong etheric body. They are robust, have good stamina, and tend to excel at physical skills and sports. They are often characterized by bushy eyebrows and have an ability to maintain good health, regardless of what they eat and drink.

Other people have a much weaker etheric and may have a shorter life. They tire easily, are prone to falling sick, and have to be careful about their diet.

The environment you live in and how well you maintain your physical and etheric fitness can help to improve your etheric strength. But there is only so far you can push this. The basic qualities you inherited from your parents will always be a major determining factor.

An awakened etheric

An awakened etheric body is a completely different matter. Regardless of whether you have a strong or a weak etheric, you can bring a degree of awakening to it, if you're prepared to work at it. The problem is that modern life is characterized by etheric numbness. Many people don't even know what their etheric feels like, never mind learning to consciously operate it.

Here are some examples of how different life can be if you start to awaken your etheric.

Bodywork

An awakened etheric body has a certain know-how and intelligence. For example, someone with an awakened etheric does not just lie passively on a massage table while a bodyworker massages them. They actively realign their own energies from the inside as the therapist works on them from the outside. With a capable bodyworker who has well-developed etheric awareness, superb results can be obtained through this type of non-verbal teamwork.

The more etherically awakened you are, by the way, the more discerning you'll become about who you have bodywork with. A massage therapist who does not have an awakened etheric will rely on set techniques rather than etheric know-how. They will also not know how to energetically cleanse themselves after working on clients, so they will pass a noxious mixture of energies from one person they work on to another. The more etheric awareness you develop yourself, the more you will be able to perceive this and will not want to receive bodywork from such people.

Feeling changes in ethericity

A very useful benefit of having an awakened etheric is the ability to feel changes in ethericity. A good example of this is something we witnessed countless times while sitting in Balinese temples waiting for a ceremony to begin.

Balinese people are very relaxed in such a situation. You won't see the type of false piety that you sometimes find in other religions, where everyone puts on their best holy look. They chat quietly among themselves while the priest or priestess performs the rituals to summon a specific spiritual connection.

This may go on for some time. Hours in some cases. No one ever complains. But when the spiritual connection starts to land, everyone feels it immediately. Nothing needs to be said. Each person can feel in their etheric that a presence has arrived. They immediately stop chatting, children are scooped up and put into prayer position in the laps of their parents, and everyone gets ready to start the ceremony.

Most revealingly, Karen remembers once attending a ceremony in a newly consecrated temple where the priest continued the rituals for over two hours before finally turning to everyone present and admitting what they already knew: "The presence has not descended."

The wonderful thing about a culture where everyone can feel spiritual connections is that no one takes anything on faith. The ceremony was abandoned that day, the priests reconsecrated the temple a few days later, and everything worked fine after that.

The kiss line

Having an awakened etheric opens whole new worlds of possibilities for intimacy too. There are two main types of loving relationships in which you can experience something we call the kiss line.

One is with a sexual partner, when you lie naked next to them, your bodies touching. The other is with a baby, child, friend, or close relative, when you have some part of your skin resting in contact with theirs. You both need to be very relaxed, comfortable with each other, and perfectly still.

With a sexual partner, it is easiest to feel the kiss line if you are lying side by side rather than physically intertwined, although with practice you can tune into it in any position.

Put your awareness on the line where your physical bodies touch and feel what is happening energetically in that space. If you and your partner both have a degree of etheric awakening, it will feel as if your skins are kissing each other all along that line.

It's as if every possibility that exists between the two of you is in that line, in a deliciously quintessential way. There is an intelligent knowing, with multiple exchanges of energies and information in each micro-second. The more love, openness, and honesty there is between you, the greater the exchange of energies and the level of bliss. Conversely, if one of you is hiding anything from the other, the effect will be diminished accordingly.

The exquisite feeling that can be experienced when breastfeeding a baby is a different version of the kiss line. It's more than the feeling of contentment that the release of oxytocin can create. It comes from a heightened awareness of the etheric contact with the baby.

The kiss line is not something you will find if you lie naked next to your pet, though. Yes, there is something that can pass in the love between humans and pets, but it can't be compared to what we're describing here. The kiss line is a human-to-human experience.

Personal chi

Have you ever wondered why the world is so fascinated by celebrities? In the case of sports stars, we admire the strong etheric they have inherited from their parents and forged through their personal will to excel. We love to watch them do things we cannot easily do ourselves.

But what about movie stars, singers, and other famous people? Why are we so captivated by someone acting a role, singing a tune, or publicly performing in some other way? To the logical mind, it makes no sense why we would value this so highly and pay them so well.

The answer lies in understanding that they have a degree of etheric awakening that shines through them in the form of personal chi (known in traditional Chinese medicine as *jing*).

There are five main types of personal chi:
- Sparkling chi
- Supportive chi
- Silky chi
- Magnetic chi
- Direct chi

All celebrities have at least one kind. Many have several types. Any spiritual teacher of substance will actively practise all five.

Developing personal chi is a natural result of etheric awakening, which is why we have included information about it here. Please be aware, though, that it is possible to use personal chi for the purpose of unethically manipulating others for your own gain as well as for the benefit of humanity. We therefore urge you only to cultivate your personal chi if you intend to use it with the highest level of integrity.

Sparkling chi

This is the most common type of personal chi. It is easiest to see in the charm of a small child or an adult who is happy and excited about life. Those who naturally have an abundance of sparkling chi are very charismatic and likeable. They laugh and smile easily. They are playful, fun-loving, and enthusiastic. Their eyes are bright and shiny, and they know how to turn this on at will.

Movie star Tom Cruise has mastered several aspects of personal chi, especially the sparkling kind. Jeremy Clarkson made an astute observation about this when welcoming him and an equally radiant Cameron Diaz to the Stars in a Reasonably Priced Car segment of *Top Gear* (Series 15, Episode 5). "Can I just say," he said, as they took their seats for the interview, "what staggers me, sitting here, is that it's almost like I've been joined by the genetic blueprint for the human race. Our evolution will reach a point where they look like THIS!"

Supportive chi

People who have highly developed supportive chi genuinely care about others. Their eyes and smiles are sweet and kind, and they have a wonderful, warm, all-embracing hug. They are very earthy and tend to work in caring professions. They are loyal, dependable, and love to dedicate themselves to a worthy cause.

Silky chi

This type of personal chi is associated with softness, refinement, and grace. People with silky chi have an openness and gentleness that attracts people to them and makes them want to help them. They are very sensual, sensitive, and often touch others deeply.

Magnetic chi

People who have magnetic chi are very captivating and alluring. They know how to turn on irresistible charm and project sexual energy through their eyes with great effect. They are sometimes said to have "bedroom eyes". When used with integrity, these people have great warmth, heartness, empathy, and compassion. Their depth of passion, feeling, and understanding makes people feel safe to open to them and confide in them. They are able to connect to others at a very deep level that goes far beyond words.

Direct chi

People who have highly developed direct chi are wilful and intense. They exude power and are natural leaders. You may not necessarily like them but feel drawn to them anyway. Their eyes are penetrating and forceful. They see through any superficiality and speak directly to your essence. They get straight to the point and are people of few words.

We encourage you to look for these five different types of personal chi as you go about your daily life and especially when watching movies, documentaries, or any media involving celebrities or people who excel in their field of expertise.

Space clearing is a dragon art

For completeness, we need to explain here that to truly explore and master the deeper mysteries of space clearing, what's needed is not just an awakened etheric but also a substantial degree of dragon* know-how.

By dragon, we don't mean the mythical beasts found in fairy tales or the animated creatures seen in movies. We're referring to the power of the lower chakras* that form the subtle body structure known as the column below*.

Etheric awareness

All humans have an energetic structure known as the column above*, which is located above the head and extends vertically upward. We also have a column below, which is located below the body and extends vertically down. Connecting these two is the principal etheric channel of the body, known as the central channel*.

The degree of development and awareness of the column below varies greatly from person to person and also from culture to culture. If you visit a region of the world where people are still very connected to land energies, just about everyone you meet there will have well-developed structure in their column below and know how to use it. It's as natural to them as breathing. In other cultures, and especially in urban environments, it's common for this structure to lack development and for people to be unconscious of it.

Something we've observed many times is that people who naturally live with their sleeves rolled up tend to be much more in touch with their personal dragon than those who do not. This was one of the main things that captivated Karen so much about Bali and why she decided to live there for 20 years – just about every Balinese person naturally lives with their sleeves rolled up, has an awakened etheric, and actively engages dragon forces. Exceptions are those who work in the air-conditioned offices of institutions such as banks. After a while, their connection to land energies tends to diminish, with the result that they live more in their head than in their etheric.

If you ever visit Bali, hoping to see and learn about this, you will need to understand that people who are born and raised in a prepersonal culture connect to a group dragon structure rather than the more individualized dragon structure that those raised in a personal culture tend to have. Nowhere is this more evident than when a group of Balinese people come together to play ceremonial music on a gamelan, which consists of percussion instruments played with metal hammers, together with gongs, drums, and sometimes other instruments too. It's loud, fiery, forceful, and unfathomably exciting because the sound is created by the musicians plugging their dragons directly into the subterranean forces of the Great Dragon and allowing it to play through them. Listening to it, it's possible to immerse your consciousness in the glorious torrent of sound and be plunged into spaces of profound underworld perceptions that are utterly beyond words and far beyond the comprehension of the mind.

Knowing this information about dragon structures makes celebrity watching even more fascinating. Some movie stars always have their sleeves rolled up, no matter what role they are playing, unless it's a very formal character or a victim. And that piece of information tells you something too. If you are the kind of person who feels life is unfair and bad things always happen to you, it can fundamentally change the way you engage with life and the types of experiences you attract to yourself if you start to live with your sleeves rolled up instead of rolled down. Of course, you have to fully embrace the can-do feeling that comes with this and not whinge about how cold it feels. The changes it can bring about can then be remarkable.

Interestingly, there is a very popular television programme in the UK called *Dragon's Den*, where savvy self-made entrepreneurs review business propositions brought to them. This programme perfectly illustrates some of the dragon qualities of the business genre – people who hold their own, are not easily swayed, and have a certain level of drive, intensity, and ability to get things done. In the American and Israeli versions of this show the dragons are called sharks instead, which carries a very different, predatory frequency.

Dragon-owning of spaces is an aspect of space clearing and a whole art in itself. There are people who naturally know how to do this in everyday life. They walk into a room and own the space. They move into a home and plant their dragon. They have arrived. They command attention and respect wherever they go.

Having someone like this come to stay in your home as a guest can be challenging. Without intending to or giving it any thought at all, they energetically take the place over. Often the space doesn't seem large enough for them, so it can feel overwhelming to have them there. If they are aware of this, they may try to make themselves smaller, but it rarely works. They are just naturally big people who make an impact on the energy of a space wherever they go. If you invite them to stay in your home, you will definitely notice they are there.

Awakening your third eye

The most important first step to start awakening your etheric is to awaken your third eye. It is the gateway to higher levels of consciousness. The best starting points we can recommend for this are Samuel Sagan's book *Awakening the Third Eye* and his introductory course Meditation, Portal to Inner Worlds, which (at the time of writing) is available at clairvision.org as a free audio download. If you want to go further, there is a substantial body of work known as the Clairvision Knowledge Tracks, which includes many practices that are designed to awaken the etheric.

The important thing to understand here is that awakening your third eye is not something to study when you feel like it, then drop it and revert to your old habits the rest of the time. It involves actively bringing more awareness and vision* to every aspect of your life, all the time. It's about notching up your consciousness to a completely new level, from where your perception of everything in the world looks and feels very different.

To give you a flavour of this, here are some practical changes we can recommend that will help you to start awakening your etheric and improve your space clearing skills at the same time.

Live with your sleeves rolled up

In *Space Clearing, Volume 1*, Chapter 8, we explain that people who naturally live with their sleeves rolled up generally have more etheric interaction with their environment and more etheric know-how than those who do not.

It will make a significant difference to the space clearing results you are able to obtain if you remember to keep your sleeves rolled up above your elbows throughout the ceremony. But more than that, if you want to develop more etheric awareness, it will help if you can learn to live with your sleeves rolled up most of the rest of the time too.

> **Richard**: When I trained as a chef, the uniform I was asked to wear was a traditional white jacket with 10 black buttons down the front and long sleeves with wide cuffs. Each time I put it on, I immediately rolled the sleeves up to above the elbow. My teachers were constantly telling me off for this, citing various safety regulations. But I took no notice because I do everything in my life with my sleeves rolled up, even when the weather is freezing cold. Since then, I've noticed that many top chefs naturally wear short sleeves or roll their sleeves up most of the time. It allows much more etheric interaction with the food they prepare.

Go barefoot when possible

Going barefoot can make a huge difference to your level of etheric awareness. Wearing socks may be necessary in some climates or situations, but it has the unfortunate side-effect of dulling your etheric.

> **Karen**: I remember once, when taking my usual early morning walk in Bali, coming across a white European man in his early 50s, squatting on the pavement with a Balinese man. They were smoking cigarettes, deep in conversation, smiling broadly, and laughing together. I had often seen the man around but hadn't taken much notice of him before. We would say good morning, nod at each other, and that was that. Like many westerners who live in Bali, he smoked and drank a fair amount of alcohol, so we didn't have a lot in common.
>
> But that day I happened to glance down at his bare feet and was amazed to see how etherically alive they were. The feet of westerners usually look astralized and energetically disconnected from the earth, but his were just like Balinese feet, interacting with the etheric of the land and fully participating in the conversation. They were as lively and expressive as his hands. This was very unusual.
>
> I spent some time watching him and could see that the relationships he had forged with Balinese people during the time he lived on the island had begun to awaken his etheric. He was halfway between the dull ethericity of most westerners and the vibrant ethericity of most Balinese.

Clean up your diet

The food you eat will have a huge effect on your level of etheric awareness and vitality.

> **Richard**: A good friend of ours was a personal trainer who was always very fit and in excellent health, but he got hit with such a fierce bout of meningitis that he had to be

> hospitalized. Most hospitals have no understanding of how essential good-quality food is to the healing process, so to aid his recovery, I cooked up a large pot of organic chicken bone broth. It's one of the most etherically regenerative substances you can consume, especially if you're unwell. I took it to him in thermos flasks and the change in him as he drank it was astounding. He said it felt like having an energetic transfusion. After he recovered, he immediately asked me to teach him how to make the broth himself!

Fresh organic fruit and vegetables nourish and support the etheric. Astralizing substances such as sugar, caffeine, alcohol, meat, dairy products, and all types of junk foods and ultra-processed foods (including vegan foods that are synthesized to resemble meat and dairy products) have the opposite effect.

We're not suggesting you cut these substances completely out of your diet. Just be aware each time you consume them that you will tilt the balance to being more astralized and less etherically aware. They don't just affect your physical body – they also impact you energetically.

Sugar, for example, is not a food substance at all. It's classified as a psychoactive drug. The rush from consuming sugar is not as intense as the high that comes from taking drugs such as heroin or cocaine, but it has some similarities. People crave sugar because it creates a thrill that can be felt in the bloodstream and brain within minutes. It also mimics some of the natural feelings of wellbeing that accompany high spiritual states of consciousness. However, it's a false high that is always followed by a crash, which makes the person want to consume more to experience the thrill again.

You may be interested to know that this roller-coaster effect is one of the main reasons why it's a prerequisite for the professional space clearing practitioners we train that they mostly eliminate sugar from their diet. If their blood sugar is constantly surging up and down, it will seriously skew their perception, and they will not be able to accurately sense, interpret, and work with energies in buildings. And if they rely on false highs to get them through the day, they will not be able to access the high-level spiritual platform from which an authentic space clearing ceremony is conducted. Excessive sweetness in the blood also puts them more at risk of picking up any perverse energies* in the buildings they clear.

Clear your clutter

The more you awaken your etheric, the less you will need, want, or tolerate physical, mental, emotional, or spiritual clutter in your life. It works the other way around too. The more you clear your physical, mental, emotional, and spiritual clutter, the more etherically vibrant you can become.

As Karen explains in *Clear Your Clutter with Feng Shui*, clutter is stuck energy. It can take the form of physical objects that clog the energy flows in your home or behaviours that keep you stuck in repetitive loops. Clutter in any form clogs your etheric and stagnates your life.

One of the main reasons clearing physical clutter feels so good is because it's etherically freeing. You start to feel more alive with each load of unwanted stuff that leaves your home.

It's about getting the right balance – not so many possessions that they burden you and hold you back, and not so few that you are unable to do what you have incarnated on earth to do. When you make decisions about what to keep or let go of from that standpoint, rather than what you mentally or emotionally want to cling onto, clutter clearing becomes a profound process of restoring integrity to your life, one item at a time.

12

Energetic protection

When learning how to do space clearing, many people worry about self-protection. This certainly was a concern Karen had when she first began. At that time, she used to protect herself by visualizing energy shields around herself, which she now regards as completely useless. This chapter describes the personal journey she has taken in this respect and the advice we can offer about it.

Sensitivity to energies

During the first years of developing her space clearing skills in England, Karen was so sensitive to everything around her that she couldn't comfortably ride on public transport. She found that whenever she was next to someone, she would immediately feel coated in their energies and swamped by their thoughts and emotions. She started to avoid crowded places and public transport.

At the time, she thought of this as an inevitable side-effect of having a heightened level of awareness. She considered it a measure of her progress and a price she had to pay. The more she picked up other people's frequencies, the more sensitive she thought she must be. She willingly endured it and persevered.

Then she went to live in Bali and discovered the utter folly of these assumptions.

Balinese people live very consciously in both the seen physical world (which they call *sekala*) and the unseen world of energies (which they call *niskala*). They see it as a sacred duty of humans to be a bridge between the two.

They are able to live very comfortably in both worlds because they have a unique subtle body configuration. They live energetically turned upward, devotedly serving the high spiritual presences that grace their island, resulting from hundreds of years of ritual practices. They are also deeply connected to the subterranean energies and forces that permeate the land.

> **Karen**: The 12 years I had spent in the UK developing my subtle bodies to be able to read energies meant that I already had a partially awakened etheric before I went to live in Bali. However, I had taught myself to live in a perpetually permeable, open state, which meant I was like a sponge, picking up all kinds of energies wherever I went. This meant I often felt terrible by the end of each day.
>
> I had developed personal purification methods to clean myself up each evening, but it was not sustainable. If I'd carried on like that, I would probably have become a recluse.
>
> What happened during the time I lived in Bali is that I learned to hold myself very differently because my etheric became much more awakened and robust.
>
> At first, I lived in Bali for six months of each year and spent the other six months in England, where I still kept some belongings and earned enough income to support my lifestyle. After a few years, I was able to get the necessary

Energetic protection

visa to become a resident in Bali, so it became my home base and I moved the few belongings I still had in the UK there. That deeper level of commitment allowed me to forge a much deeper level of immersion into the culture. Later, being married to a Balinese man for 12 years gave me even greater access.

I spent my time almost exclusively with Balinese people. I learned Indonesian and all three levels of the Balinese language. I got to know thousands of people, and many tens of thousands of people knew me, or had heard of me, because I was so unusual. I was a westerner who understood things that most Balinese understood but most westerners didn't.

A curious phenomenon I learned to live with was that if ever I went travelling somewhere on the island, by the time I arrived home at the end of the day, news of where I had been would already have reached my Balinese husband. This was long before mobile phones became widespread. Most communication was by word of mouth, passed from person to person along the Balinese grapevine.

Similarly, I once received a letter from someone in the United States who had read my book. It was addressed to "Karen Kingston, Bali" and it reached me, even though I lived in a small village that was three hours from Bali's main postal sorting office.

Balinese people have evolved the highest level of sensitivity to the unseen worlds I have ever found in any culture. Living among them for so many years had the effect of awakening my etheric and developing specific subtle body structures that had lain dormant. I saw how they naturally densified their energy in situations where this was needed, and I learned, by being with them, how to do this myself, as a child would learn from its parent. Eventually, I was able to automatically seal my energy, as they do, without needing to give it any thought. I could maintain my sensitivities while deflecting unwanted energies like water off a duck's back.

For many years, I travelled three times around the world every year, teaching workshops, conducting space clearing consultations, and doing media interviews. After acquiring this etheric skill, I actively engaged crowds rather than avoiding them. I have rarely felt energetically drained by people or places ever since.

Richard: I was very sensitive to people and places as a child, but I'm blessed to have inherited a robust etheric from my father, which came into fullness when I was about 21. Since that time, I have never suffered the type of energetic bashing Karen has described, but living in Bali for five years had a deeply transformative effect on my etheric too.

It began when Karen introduced me to an extraordinarily talented Balinese bodyworker, with the most awakened etheric I have ever encountered and a remarkable range of skills. I knew immediately that I wanted to train with him, but he took one look at the palms of my hands and pronounced them "dead".

His usual practice with Balinese apprentices was that they first had to go to a local temple each day to meditate until

Energetic protection

they reached the point where the energy centres (chakras) in the palms of their hands opened. If they didn't open, he couldn't and wouldn't train them.

I was already an experienced meditator, and we had a dedicated meditation room in our home in Bali, so the process was a bit different for me. The stillest and quietest time of the day in Bali is around 3 am, before the cockerels wake up. I started getting up at that time each day to engage the most involuted levels of meditation I could. It took me six months, but it worked. And because of the will I put into it, it wasn't just the palms of my hands that came alive. My entire etheric awakened and profound levels of dragon know-how were activated too.

When he saw this, he immediately agreed to work with me. To my knowledge, I was the first and only non-Balinese person he ever successfully trained. I subsequently became a professional bodyworker for a while in Australia and it's a skill I've maintained to this day, although the only lucky recipient of my massage skills now is Karen!

The benefits of an awakened etheric

Chapters 17 to 21 of Samuel Sagan's *Awakening the Third Eye* describe excellent methods for densifying your etheric while maintaining awareness. These are valuable techniques to learn for living in our modern world, whether you do space clearing or not.

In Chapter 1 of *Awakening the Third Eye*, Samuel Sagan explains, "Perception is the mother of protection", meaning that awareness is the best form of protection there is. We totally agree. If you can see something coming toward you, you can take action to deflect it. If you have no awareness of such things, you'll never know what hit you.

Someone who has an awakened etheric is able to perceive noxious energies and deflect them. The intelligence in their etheric will enable them to densify their personal energy field to do this.

For professionals who work with energies, more advanced methods are needed to avoid toxic dumping. The ultimate technique is known as the triangular seal, which can be instigated by someone who has developed the subtle body structure to operate Point* functionality. We realize the last sentence will be meaningless to anyone reading this who is not familiar with Clairvision techniques and terminology. We have included the information to give a helpful direction to those who are genuinely interested to know more and would like to explore this topic further.

Etheric perception

On many occasions when we lived in Bali, we would meet a Balinese friend while we were out and about, and when we asked them where they were going they would say, "Oh, I'm on my way to have an entity cleared".

Balinese people have enough etheric awareness to know when they have somehow picked up an entity*, and they know they need to have it removed as soon as possible by a local entity clearer before it can nest in their body and cause any real damage.

On other occasions, we would meet someone who would tell us they had picked up a perverse energy*. This is not such a big deal as an entity and much easier to clear, but it's uncomfortable nevertheless, so they would still seek help to get it removed as soon as they could.

Energetic protection

To clarify the terms we're using here, by entity we are referring to an astral fragment* from someone who has died, which can take the form of an energetic parasite. And by perverse energy we mean an etheric substance of some kind that doesn't belong inside the human body but has somehow got inside it (dampness or wind, for example). You can find more information about these types of energies in Chapter 4 of *Space Clearing, Volume 1*.

What a different world it would be if everyone had more awareness of this. So many physical, mental, and emotional health problems could be avoided if these occurrences were identified and dealt with energetically in the early stages, instead of being left to fester and develop into physical symptoms that doctors attempt to treat pharmaceutically.

If you ever find yourself in this situation, travelling to Bali to find an entity clearer is NOT a solution because the clearing techniques they use are only designed for people who have a prepersonal astral body configuration. A completely different approach is needed for the astral bodies of people from westernized countries (read *Entities: Parasites of the Body of Energy* by Samuel Sagan if you would like to know more about this).

Personal energy management

The information in *Space Clearing, Volume 1* and this book is for people who want to space clear their own home or business. It's not intended for professional-level space clearing because that requires in-depth training and subtle body development to prevent picking up unwanted energies while doing the ceremony in other people's homes. We've heard many unfortunate tales from various people who have gone ahead and set themselves up as space clearers without any training, or without a deep enough level of training. They eventually have to stop because they don't know how to handle this aspect.

There are many weird and wonderful formulas that are said to protect you from external influences. They include visualizing yourself being in a protective bubble, holding a crystal of some kind, or carrying a few pieces of orange peel or a sponge in your pocket (we're not making this up).

If you have believed and trusted in any of these methods, it may come as something of a revelation to you to discover that they have no basis in any known energetic principles. How they came into being we have no idea, but they have somehow been perpetuated and even become widespread in some circles. When we meet and spend time with people who have been using these so-called protection techniques, our general experience is that they have picked up unwholesome energies and are not even aware they have done so.

Some of the most common signs are:
- Being overweight or underweight
- Skin problems
- Feeling overwhelmed
- Neurotic behaviour
- Uncontrolled urges to do the kind of things they teach other people not to do

Of course, all these symptoms can have other causes, so this list is only intended to give an indication, not a diagnosis.

Providing you follow the steps of the ceremony described in *Space Clearing, Volume 1* and observe all the cautions, there's no need to worry about picking up unwanted energies when space clearing a home you have lived in for some time. There's a small possibility this can happen when space clearing a home you have just moved into, and there's a greater possibility if you space clear the home of a relative

Energetic protection

or friend. We have included many safeguards to prevent this, but we cannot cover every situation you may encounter or the subtle body capabilities you may or may not have. Space clearing skills never used to be taught to everyday folk, after all.

The most important thing to remember is never to attempt space clearing if you feel any fear or apprehension about doing it. Don't override those feelings if you have them.

How do professional space clearers manage? Well, firstly they need to do years of personal work to get to know themselves very well, so that they can immediately spot if something is out of whack in their energy. There are also particular practices they implement regularly. And they need to have someone they can go to from time to time to check their energy, or a group of peers who know them very well and have the perception to see when something has gone wrong. These are not the kind of people who tell you what they think but the kind who can open a space for you to be able to clearly see the problem for yourself and then help you to work through it.

13

Superastral awareness

Superastral awareness is an essential aspect of space clearing for anyone who wishes to understand it beyond beginner level. It is the ability to operate consciously from specific subtle body structures above the head rather than from the level of ordinary mental consciousness* (your astral body*, which is the vehicle of the mind and emotions).

You can do a space clearing ceremony mechanically while based in your astral body, thinking mundane thoughts about your next meal or what you heard on the news earlier that day. However, the changes it will bring about will be minimal. The ceremony is designed to be done while holding superastral awareness, which is why there are so many references in *Space Clearing, Volume 1* to involution, verticality, and transposing your awareness to above your head.

The limitations of your astral body

There's a great story that's been circulating the internet for years about a note that was supposedly left by a son to his father:

> Dear Dad,
>
> It's with great regret and sorrow that I'm writing to you. I had to elope with my new girlfriend because I wanted to avoid a scene with Mom and you. I have been finding real

Superastral awareness

passion with Stacy and she is so nice. But I knew you would not approve of her because of all her piercing, tattoos, tight motorcycle clothes, and the fact that she is much older than I am. But it's not only the passion. Dad, she's pregnant.

Stacy said that we will be very happy. She owns a trailer in the woods and has a stack of firewood for the whole winter. We share a dream of having many more children. Stacy has opened my eyes to the fact that marijuana doesn't really hurt anyone. We'll be growing it for ourselves and trading it with the other people who live nearby for cocaine and meth. In the meantime, we will pray that science will find a cure for her currently incurable disease so Stacy can get better. She deserves it.

Don't worry, Dad. I'm 15 and I know how to take care of myself. Someday I'm sure we'll be back to visit so that you can get to know your grandchildren.

Love from your son,
John

PS Dad, none of the above is true. I'm over at Tommy's house. I just wanted to remind you that there are worse things in life than a report card. It's in my centre desk drawer. I love you. Call me when it's safe to come home!

Why does this story make people smile? Because it's such an ingenious way of communicating to the father that things could be a whole lot worse than the poor report card he is about to read. It puts it in a whole new perspective so that the father will be glad the problem isn't more serious, instead of reacting to it in his usual way.

The truth is that most people have very predictable reactions to things. Their behaviour is mainly reactive, repeating the same patterns day after day, year after year. That's what life is like when you're entrenched in your astral body. Samskaras run your life.

What is a samskara?

Samskara is the Sanskrit word for the emotional imprint or scar that can be left in a person's psyche by an experience. Each time a similar incident takes place, the samskara gets triggered and the old emotions arise.

Suppose you trap your finger in a car door, for example. For the rest of your life, each time you get out of a car, the memory of the old pain may be triggered, and you'll be careful not to hurt yourself again.

Suppose you got hurt in love. You may carry that emotional baggage with you into a new relationship and just one wrong word from your partner can trigger the memory of the old hurt and cause a giant row out of nowhere.

There are endless variations of this.

Samskaric triggers

In the case of the son's report card, it seems likely there may have been other poor report cards in the past and the father's reaction to them had become predictable. Children intuitively know the samskaric triggers of their parents very well and deliberately play on them or try to avoid them, depending on how compliant the child is by nature or how safe it is to rebel.

The source of the father's emotions may not even have anything to do with the son or his report card. Each time this happens, it may trigger an event from the father's past, such as how certain things make him feel undervalued as a person or how his own father treated him when he was young. If the father did some personal work, he would be able to trace his emotions back to their true source and not have to subject his son to that type of reaction in the future. He would be able to discuss the situation calmly and objectively and give his son the support he needs to move forward.

Why it's important to source samskaras

Thoughts and emotions are the reactions of your astral body. When you're subject to reactions, any small thing can ruin your day. And when something major happens, it can throw you off-track for years or even the rest of your life.

In *Regression: Past-Life Therapy for Here and Now Freedom*, Samuel Sagan explains:

> A key realization is that the astral body is *made* of samskaras. Its very nature is grasping and reacting, and its substance is like a sea of samskaras, some big, some small, some more linked to emotions, others more to thoughts.

Karen decided in her late teens that there must be a better way to live than being thrown around by the random roller coaster of emotions, up one day and down the next. She set about searching for solutions and tried various methods of sourcing and resolving samskaras. It took her over 15 years to find one that really worked and then another 10 years to find an even better method (Inner Space Techniques, called IST for short) that we both use to this day.

It's not possible to resolve all your samskaras, not by a long way. But if you find a good IST practitioner to work with, or learn how to do IST yourself with a partner, you can take the smart approach, which is to tackle the major samskaras that many of the smaller ones rest on. When you resolve the biggies, the smaller ones connected to them will often melt away because they no longer have anything to gear into.

Sourcing samskaras is the pathway to moving beyond the limitations of your mind and emotions to be able to access superastral realms with integrity. It takes years of personal work. It's not a quick fix. It goes deep and is genuinely life-changing. It's therefore very worthwhile. The more you are able to navigate consciously through life with superastral discernment, the more you will be able to take control of your own destiny.

What is superastrality?

Superastrality means levels of consciousness that are higher than the astrality of ordinary mental consciousness.

Like radio signals that travel through the air and cannot be perceived without a radio receiver to translate them, superastral frequencies permeate the upper layers of astrality of our planet. Most people are unaware of them, but they are influenced by them all the time.

The reason most people have no awareness of superastral levels is because the mind cannot comprehend them. They can only be perceived through verticality, using the subtle body structure above the head known as the column above*. Being able to do this will move your experience of space clearing, your space clearing skills, and many other aspects of your life to a higher level.

Superastral awareness is essential if you are engaged in a spiritual path of any kind, to enable you to access higher levels of consciousness. The reason there are so many misconceptions about this in New Age teachings is because people mistakenly think they can access higher parts of themselves through their mind or emotions, which doesn't work at all.

Superastral awareness can give profound insights into many other aspects of life too. People who rise to the top of their field of expertise know how to access superastral levels at will. They don't painstakingly work things out in their mind. If you've ever watched a brilliant coder at work, for example, they transpose their awareness to above their head from where they can effortlessly tap into superastral streams. It's all done at the level of packed thoughts*.

Talented musical composers have a similar skill. They can plug into high superastral streams and create a new piece of music or a song in very little time. One of the things that was so exceptional about the Beatles was that John Lennon and Paul McCartney wrote nearly 300 songs together, all very different and each within the space of a few hours or a single day at the most.

One song Paul McCartney wrote by himself came into being in a very different way. In *The Lyrics: 1956 to the Present* he recounts that he woke up one morning with a tune that came to him in a dream. It felt so familiar that he thought it must be an old classic, but when he asked around, no one had ever heard it before. After a couple of weeks, he realized it was a brand-new song, so he put some words to it and claimed it as his own.

That song was "Yesterday", listed in *Guiness World Records* as the most recorded song in the history of pop music, and acclaimed by Sir Elton John, in a BBC interview with Michael Parkinson in 2008, as his definition of a perfect song. Its beauty comes from the purity of the archetypal superastral layer he plucked it from, which few composers know how to access.

Another example of superastral know-how can be seen when watching top Formula 1 drivers behind the wheel. They are moving at speeds the mind cannot compute, so they learn to cultivate and navigate from a superastral structure above the head known as the Point.

Richard used a similar technique in his cheffing days, when he ran busy kitchens in some of the top restaurants in Australia. Without needing to look, he would know everything that was happening in each cooking section by holding superastral Point awareness of the space. When driving a car from the Point, he would know before he could see it that he needed to take action to avoid a kangaroo that was about to jump out in front of him. And since starting to play golf after moving to the UK in 2010, within four years he had used his Point know-how to achieve a very respectable handicap of 4.

How to perceive superastrality

The column above is defined in ALTMC as follows:

> The column of energy that extends infinitely above the head, as in an upwards extension of the crown chakra... Just as the mind is the organ of ordinary astral consciousness, so the column above is the vehicle for superastral levels of consciousness and their corresponding functions of perception. Verticality, as a key quality of the column above, is a direct way to access these levels.

The column above is not physical, so you can't see it. And if you wave your hand above the top of your head, you won't be able to feel it. But everyone has a column above and can learn how to use it. It's one of the most important subtle body structures for anyone engaged on a spiritual path to develop because it is the means by which we can naturally connect to levels of knowing and high spiritual realms while incarnated here on earth. A well-developed superastral body is also essential for conscious navigation of modern technologies and lifestyles.

In *Awakening the Third Eye*, Samuel Sagan explains:

> Just as the third eye is a key piece in the edifice of subtle bodies, so there are energetic centers located above the head that have a regulatory effect over the interaction between the astral and etheric bodies. Just like the third eye, but on another level, these centers lend themselves to cultivation – resulting in a different positioning of astral processes...
>
> To match the future, a dual strategy is required. On the one hand, a mighty cultivation and awakening of the etheric body. On the other hand, a cultivation of the "superastral body", meaning a transformation of thinking toward supermind: super-fast, frictionless thought processes. Note the word "frictionless", here. It makes all the difference between a harmonious raising of the voltage of consciousness and a stressed, frantic lifestyle that can only result in an exhaustion of essential etheric energies.
>
> The Clairvision style of supermind work is called the "power of the Point". In the progression of our style of inner alchemy, it is what comes after the third eye work.

Superastrality in buildings

One of the easiest ways to experience superastrality is to visit a building that has a lofty ceiling, such as a magnificent cathedral or temple. These towering structures are designed to allow our consciousness to soar. The feeling of awe they engender is caused by our verticality being drawn up into the superastrality of the space.

This also happens to some extent in any high-ceilinged room, which is why people tend to feel more creative in such spaces. Low-ceilinged rooms, by contrast, often have a stunting, oppressive effect. Wealthy people intuitively know this and often incorporate high ceilings into the design of the buildings they occupy.

The command node

If you've ever had the opportunity to watch a building being built, there is something that happens as soon as the foundations have been put in place, or even just physically marked out. There are no walls yet, but the blueprint for the structure of the building has been established and there is an energetic "something" that is created in the fluid-dimensional centre above the space. It becomes more tangible as the outer walls are erected, and especially when the roof is put in place.

Fluid-dimensional structures are not easily discernible. They are midway between the physical and the non-physical, so they can only be cognized superastrally through verticality. In fact, a central energetic structure of this type exists in the upper space of every room and in the overall upper space of every building too. Learning how to consciously cognize it can radically change the way you do space clearing and your relationship to your home too.

Karen had been doing space clearing professionally for about 10 years before she first became consciously aware of this superastral "something" in the home of every client she worked with. We started exploring it together and with other space clearing practitioners, including a fascinating week-long intensive in the United States in October 2006 with Samuel Sagan and 24 space clearing practitioners and trainees, where the topic was mapped in depth. The name command node** emerged from that and has become an accepted term that is now used by professional space clearers and students of the Clairvision School.

Samuel Sagan described the command node at that time as "a metaphysical entrance into energetic aspects of a room". And in relation to space clearing as "a mediating position for celestial influences to interact with the physicality of a room".

A command node doesn't happen automatically or accidentally. It has to be consciously forged and owned, which requires superastral awareness and know-how, as well as a substantial engagement of will. Without this, the fluid-dimensional "something" will still be there, but it will be nebulous, vague, and of no use to you at all.

The first few times you space clear your home will help to clarify the energy of the space. This will then make it easier to start crafting the command nodes of individual rooms, if you have the subtle body structure to be able to do so. True MC-ship** begins when you are able to superastrally craft, engage, and hold the command node of your entire home, which will also greatly improve the space clearing results you are able to obtain.

Holding space

In life, holding space means the ability to hold a specific flavour of consciousness or heartness that others can tangibly feel and rest on. Examples of this are holding a space to help someone learn a new skill, recover from a traumatic event, undergo surgery, or navigate the process of dying.

In relation to space clearing, holding space is the ability to superastrally gear your verticality into the command node of a building or a room while doing the steps of the ceremony. This involves a heightened degree of superastral awareness as well as superastral know-how.

How to develop more superastral awareness

The first step to developing more superastral awareness is to learn to silence the thoughts and emotions of your astral body so that you can transpose your awareness to above your head.

As mentioned earlier in the book, to do this with integrity involves two aspects of spiritual work:

- Construction (techniques of involution and building subtle body structures)
- Deconstruction (sourcing and resolving samskaras)

You can find a wealth of knowledge about all these topics in Samuel Sagan's books and the Clairvision Knowledge Tracks. If you enjoy reading novels, a good starting point would be his *Atlantean Secrets* series, followed by *Bleeding Sun*.

Another helpful resource you may like to consider is Karen's Creating Conscious Space online course, which includes a substantial section on taking superastral MC-ship of your home.

If you wish to go deeper, The Seven Levels of Consciousness online course is about the levels of consciousness that are accessible to humans, and how to navigate them. It's a model that Karen has developed since 1978, based on her personal exploration of the unseen worlds of energy. We have developed it further together since 2005.

The levels of consciousness in this model range from Level 7, which is the lowest level humans can sink to, to Level 1, which is the highest level we can experience within the limitations of being incarnated in a physical body.

To give some examples, Level 6 is the level of everyday life and ordinary mental consciousness. Superastral awareness starts at Level 5 and is often accompanied by searching for more meaning or a smarter way of doing something. The rare and memorable "Aha!" moments of realization we have from time to time are superastral Level 4 experiences, which can be totally life-changing.

We warmly encourage you to explore the topic of superastral awareness further. It's the entry point to a much more visionful* and meaningful way of life.

14

How hand sensing works

Hand sensing** is one of the unique aspects of our space clearing ceremony that you won't find in other energy clearing systems. Anyone can learn to do it, although it takes many years of subtle bodybuilding to be able to do it with accuracy. Space clearing practitioners use it at the beginning of a ceremony to determine what problems exist in a place and near the end of the ceremony to check that the space has been cleared.

If you just want to do space clearing in your own home, the basic hand-sensing technique is much simpler and most people can learn it quickly and easily by following the instructions in *Space Clearing, Volume 1*. We are including this section here for those who wish to know more about how it works.

Reading energies

Reading energies in buildings has become as tangible to us as reading a book with our eyes. In fact, reading a book with your eyes is a very good analogy for explaining how hand sensing works.

The way we learn to translate characters on the page of a book into meaningful concepts through scanning them with our eyes is very mysterious, when you stop to think about it. The letters are just symbols, after all. How does our brain make sense of them? But it does.

There are specific subtle body structures that can be developed to do something very similar through hand sensing, to translate etheric energies and astral imprints in buildings into meaningful information.

If you had never seen anyone read a book before, you would stand open-mouthed in astonishment the first time you saw someone do that. This is exactly how many of our clients respond when we give them intimate details about their love life, finances, health, and what's working in their life and what's not, simply by reading the energies in the walls, furniture, and other objects in their home with our hands. The history of everything that has happened in the place is there to be read, if you know how.

Some people assume this must be a psychic skill, but it definitely is not. We consider psychic or clairvoyant readings of any kind to be highly unreliable. They form no part of our work, and we advise extreme caution if you are ever "told" something you cannot verify for yourself. We've met far too many people whose lives have gone off-track because they have tried to follow a path that has been suggested to them by a psychic, or have put their lives on hold, waiting for something they've been told will happen. The global astral layers that psychics draw from are far too polluted to trust these days.

Eyeless sight

While writing this book, we were fascinated to discover we are not the only people who have taught ourselves to read with our hands. There are several other well-documented cases of people who have developed aspects of hand-sensing skills, known by various terms such as paroptic vision, dermo-optical perception, hyperesthesia, fingertip sight, cutaneous vision, skin vision, and extraretinal vision.

The earliest recorded reference we have found is by Robert Boyle in *Experiments and Considerations Touching Colours*, published in 1665, in which he described a blind man who was able to discern colours by holding materials between his thumb and forefinger.

A French writer and philosopher called Jules Romains wrote an entire book about the topic in 1924, titled *Eyeless Sight: A Study of Extra-Retinal Vision and the Paroptic Sense*. He began by studying a number of people who were able to read with their hands, then spent up to six painstaking hours a day trying to develop the ability himself, with some success.

A more recent example is Rosa Kuleshova, a Russian woman from a family that included some people who were blind. She led drama classes for visually impaired people in her village and hit upon the novel idea of teaching them to read with their hands. She trained herself several hours a day over six years to be able to read colours, shapes, and printed text with the third and fourth fingers of her right hand, as proficiently as if she was seeing these things with her eyes. From 1962 on, she was tested extensively at the Soviet Academy of Science in Moscow and various other institutions, and her skill was found to be genuine.

News of her abilities prompted Dr Abram Novomeisky of the Nizhne-Tagil Pedagogical Institute in Russia to conduct a study with 80 graphic arts students wearing lightproof blindfolds. He discovered that about one in six of them could feel the difference between two colours. We used to do a similar practical in our Advanced Space Clearing workshop using six coloured cards, where the success rate was about one in three people (we created a Level 5 space in the meeting room, so they had some help with this).

In 1963, an American woman called Patricia Stanley gained public attention when she was found to be able to perceive colour through her fingertips. Richard P. Youtz, Professor of Psychology at Barnard College, New York, carried out over 60 hours of double-blind tests to verify this, and in further tests conducted with 135 psychology students, he discovered that around 10% of them were able to do it too.

Various scientific theories have been proposed to explain the phenomenon of eyeless sight. One is that some people may have cells in their fingertips that are similar to those we have in our eyes. However, Rosa Kuleshova and two of Novomeisky's students were able to read letters in a completely dark room, so this was discounted. Other theories have speculated that some form of electromagnetism is involved, such as infrared rays. No firm conclusions have ever been reached.

This doesn't surprise us because the key to understanding how hand sensing works does not lie in the realm of scientifically measurable data. It lies in the realms of subtle body structures. It's done through a combination of etheric sensing* and vertical knowing. For it to work, there needs to be a certain degree of awakening in a person's etheric body and they need to have honed their column above to the degree that it can function as a reliable organ of perception. A clean diet, healthy lifestyle, clear mind, and inner stillness are also essential.

Subtle body structure of this kind can be carried forward from one lifetime to the next, and in Karen's case, she was born with it. This is why she was able to learn to do hand sensing and develop other space clearing skills so easily and to such a high level. She didn't need anyone to teach her.

Richard has had the ability to rest on vertical knowing throughout his life. He awakened higher levels of this by learning the Clairvision techniques and practitioner-level space clearing skills.

Energies in buildings

The least reliable of all the senses we have is our eyes. Visual impressions can be very deceptive. A house can look very nice yet have a murky history. Conversely, a building may not be much to look at yet has wonderful vibrant energies that will provide a nurturing environment for the occupants. Hand sensing is one of the main techniques we use to go beneath surface appearances and discover the truth of the matter.

Energies in spaces can't be measured scientifically. Yet, most people can feel them to some degree, and they can distinguish between a clear space and one that has stagnant energies or is heavily imprinted. When you walk into a room that has clear energies, it feels refreshing and uplifting. A room that is laden with stagnant energies or layers of astral imprints feels uncomfortable and stifling.

When you move into a home that has had previous occupants, unless they were courteous and capable enough to space clear the property before they left, it will contain predecessor energies made up of their etheric residues and astral imprints, as well as the etheric residues and astral imprints of everyone who lived there before them. Hand sensing can reveal a range of information about previous occupants such as their state of health, fitness, prosperity, happiness, and many other aspects.

The problem with predecessor energies is that they tend to cause history to repeat itself. The beauty of our space clearing ceremony is that it revitalizes stagnant etheric energies and can also clear astral imprints, to give you a fresh start. Other clearing techniques may move energies around, but we've yet to find any other system that works at these deep levels or permanently changes spaces for the better.

The professional space clearing practitioners we train learn how to read both types of energies in order to determine the causes of problems in a client's home. It's one of our favourite parts when teaching a professional training because it's so visionful* and always surprising in some way.

Being able to read etheric energies through hand sensing gives a very useful indication of the effect a room will have on its occupants. To learn how to read astral imprints takes a lot longer – years in most cases – and only a few people we've trained have ever become expert at it.

Fortunately, it's not necessary to be able to read etheric energies or astral imprints when space clearing your own home. If you follow the steps of the space clearing ceremony described in *Space Clearing, Volume 1*, you will still get results.

Imprintability

There's a sliding scale we use in space clearing to measure the imprintability** of various household materials (the degree to which physical materials tend to become astrally imprinted or etherically coated). The least imprintable are dense substances such as metal in its solid state, glass, ceramic tiles, marble, and synthetic materials such as plastic. This, incidentally, is one of the main reasons why a front door made from metal, glass, or plastic is a feng shui no-no – these materials cannot anchor energies in the way that a front door is supposed to. Wood is a much better choice for the main energy portal to your home.

More easily imprintable materials are stone, brick, plaster, wood, carpet, and pottery. The most imprintable of all are items such as mattresses, which is why it's generally not a good idea to buy one second-hand.

The more porous the material (the more water it can hold), the more astrally imprintable it will be. Clothing, for example, picks up energies very quickly from the person wearing it, but all that's needed to clear those imprints is to launder the items, using warm or hot water and detergent (not dry cleaning). Mattresses are generally much more deeply imprinted and more difficult to clear because you can't put them through the wash.

Personal items

In his book *Supersense: Why We Believe in the Unbelievable*, Bruce M. Hood, a professor of Developmental Psychology in Society at the University of Bristol in the UK, recounts how he explores this topic in his own way in some of his lectures. He passes a fountain pen around the audience that he pretends once belonged to Albert Einstein. "The reverence and awe towards this object is palpable," he says. "Everyone wants to hold it. Touching the pen makes them feel good."

Then he produces a cardigan and asks who would be willing to put it on. Usually at least a third of the people in the audience volunteer to do so, until he reveals (another pretence) that it once belonged to Fred West, a vile English serial killer. Immediately most of the hands go down and people visibly recoil from those who adamantly keep their hands up. "Typically, they are male and determined to demonstrate their rational control," he says. "Or they suspect, rightly, that I was lying about the owner of the cardigan."

Hood takes a very scientific approach to such matters. "How and why should a cardigan come to represent the negative association with a killer?" he asks. "If I had chosen a knife or noose, the association account would have been adequate. A cardigan is not an item usually linked to murderers. It is something that offers warmth and comfort."

He concludes that "The Fred West cardigan stunt triggers mostly a sense of spiritual, not physical, contamination. You can't wash away such contamination as though it were dirt."

Our perception, after years of hand sensing objects of all kinds, is that putting on Fred West's cardigan would be no problem at all energetically, providing it had been freshly laundered. It would be a completely different matter if it hadn't been washed, though. If he wore it frequently, and even more so if he wore it recently and it hadn't been laundered for a long time, it would be saturated with his imprints. This would have an energetic effect on any wearer, as people intuitively know, without being able to explain exactly why.

Personal spaces

Beds are especially interesting to hand sense because most people spend a third or more of their lives sleeping, so their mattress becomes very imprinted with their energies.

This can sometimes give rise to delicate issues for a professional space clearer to handle. For example, if someone is having an affair while their partner is at work or away travelling, the imprints of a third person may be found in the marital bed. Then a decision has to be made whether to say something about it or not. And, of course, the space clearer's hand-sensing skills have to be accurate enough to know if the energies of the third person are from a visiting lover or a child who often sleeps with the parents. If the bed is second-hand or has been moved from another room in the home, the imprints of someone who previously slept in it may have a perfectly innocent explanation.

It's also possible, through hand sensing, to know when a child is regularly wetting their bed, or when someone has insomnia, nightmares, restless leg syndrome, and many other sleep-related or medical conditions.

A situation we have both come across at separate times in clients' homes is imprints of sexual abuse in a child's bed. Something has to be said, especially if the person who has requested the space clearing ceremony seems to be unaware of the abuse. It needs to be handled very sensitively.

Hand sensing can reveal marital problems too. In one family home, the only person Karen met was the wife, who assured her that everything in her life was fine and the only reason she wanted to have space clearing done was to give the energy of the home a boost. However, when hand sensing her bed, Karen could clearly feel that she was the only person sleeping in it. She said nothing at that point and continued hand sensing the rest of the house. There was no sign of the husband's imprints at all until she came across a single mattress on the floor of his study up in the attic. Hand sensing revealed he had been sleeping there for some time. When Karen mentioned this to the wife, her entire façade dropped. She had been pretending to the outside world for so long that her marriage was intact that the deception had become habitual. She realized she couldn't hide it in this situation.

In another home, after hand sensing both sides of a couple's bed, Karen remarked to the wife how sexual her husband was. "You've got that wrong," the woman said, so Karen sensed the bed again and got exactly the same reading. "We've been married for 15 years and, ever since the first night, he's had no interest in sex," the woman assured her. "It's been the biggest disappointment of my life."

Puzzled, Karen continued the space clearing, wondering how she could have been so mistaken. A week later she heard from the woman. Her husband happened to go out and leave his laptop open at his email inbox page, from which she discovered he'd been having an affair with another woman for years. She was stunned, of course, but grateful to Karen for alerting her to the fact that all was not as it seemed. Divorce followed soon after, leaving her free to start her life afresh and find a new partner.

A huge mansion Richard once space cleared had previously been a psychiatric hospital. Three couples in succession had purchased the property, ploughed huge quantities of money into renovating it, and had divorced before the job was complete. The fourth couple to buy it called him in to help, even though their relationship had deteriorated so much that they were getting divorced too. They sent their personal assistant to represent them during the ceremony instead of being present themselves.

Richard remembers it was an impressive building to look at architecturally, but hand sensing revealed a very different picture. Many years of violence and abuse of patients by hospital staff were embedded in layers in the walls. The most memorable part of the circuit was in the area of the property's new boiler. "This is what caused the divorce," he said to the personal assistant after hand sensing it. She confirmed this was true and explained the husband had bought a $100,000 top-of-the-range boiler the wife didn't like, so she had replaced it with this larger and more expensive one. The argument about it was the final straw that ended the marriage.

Space clearing didn't save their relationship (it was too far gone), but it did make a huge difference to the energy of the space. The personal assistant let Richard know that two days later, for the first time ever in that house, she was amazed to witness the family sitting down to have a meal together and talking to each other "like human beings", as she put it.

Energetically owning a space

Another important function of the hand-sensing circuit is to discern the energy flows around a space. This is known as "walking the chi". For many people, the hand-sensing circuit will be the first time they have ever walked around the inside perimeter of their home in the entire time they have lived there. It's a powerful way to start to take energetic ownership of a space.

Cats know a lot about this. It's the first thing they do when they move with you to a new place. In most cases, the tail will go up, the whiskers will start quivering, and the cat will walk around the inside perimeter of the entire home, brushing its fur up against the walls. Some cats continue to do this every day to re-establish and maintain their territory. They are proactively owning the space, physically and energetically.

It's possible for someone with an awakened etheric to take energetic ownership of a space at a much more refined level. When walking the inner perimeter to hand sense the walls, there can also be a cognizing through the chakras in the soles of the feet, an owning of the space through certain structures in the column below, and a simultaneous gearing into the superastrality of the space through the person's column above to start crafting a command node. These are not techniques we can teach through the pages of a book, but they can be developed, so we have included a mention of them here.

Advanced levels of hand sensing

In *Space Clearing, Volume 1*, we listed a few techniques that can be used to sensitize your palms. That's all that's needed when doing hand sensing in your own home.

How hand sensing works

The skills we teach to our practitioners are more advanced and can only be taught to those who already have a substantial degree of etheric awakening and a lifestyle that supports that (for example, no psychoactive drugs of any kind, including sugar, caffeine, and alcohol). It involves awakening the chakras in the palms of a person's hands and feet, together with a superastral cognizing that takes place in the column above, using the hand as an antenna for perceiving impressions.

If you would like to learn more about hand sensing, we recommend starting with the third eye meditation course called Meditation, Portal to Inner Worlds, available at clairvision.org. Then follow the Vision Path of the Clairvision Knowledge Tracks until you arrive at the one titled *Buzzing Forest 2*, where you will find an entire section about hand sensing, written and recorded by Karen.

15

How flower offerings work

Karen: In 1997, I taught a space clearing workshop in County Wicklow, Ireland. The wonderful warm reception I received from the Irish people made me decide, for the first time ever in a public event, to demonstrate the effect of landing a spiritual connection through a flower offering**, for everyone there to see and feel.

There were over 100 people in a large marquee tent that the organizer had hired. I spent the first day of the weekend workshop explaining the preparations needed for a space clearing ceremony. The second day was all about the techniques, which I taught in some depth. But the one thing I always glossed over was flower offerings. I explained how to make them, but I had never, until that day, demonstrated to an audience how to activate one.

Looking back on this now, I find it odd that no one had ever asked me about it. I had been teaching space clearing workshops for three years by that time and the question had never come up. Perhaps people didn't know how to put it into words.

How flower offerings work

Anyway, on this occasion, I set up a table in front of the audience and laid out my space clearing equipment. In the middle of the table, I placed a flower offering consisting of a small saucer with a tealight at the centre and assorted small flower heads arranged around it, pointing outward.

I announced I would be activating the flower offering. The audience hushed.

I lit the candle with a match. The silence deepened.

I picked up my space clearing water pot in one hand and a white mini carnation flower head in my other hand. I dipped the flower head into the space clearing water** and sprinkled the water onto the flower offering. I repeated this twice more, then with my attention focused on the flame of the flower offering to the exclusion of all else, I slowly performed the space clearing mudra** that I use to activate an offering.

When I do this, it's as if the entire physical world recedes into the background and the unseen worlds come to the foreground. All that is physical becomes ethereal and insubstantial. All that is unseen becomes tangible and clear.

The audience followed every movement. Many of them held their breath. The effect was electrifying. And the stillness, silence, and sacredness that landed in the space was phenomenal. The White Gold spiritual presence descended and filled the entire tent. It created what is known as an aquarium effect*, so-called because the experience is one of such depth that you feel completely immersed in it, like a fish submerged in water.

I checked to see how mottled the palms of my hands had become (see Chapter 8 for an explanation of this effect). On that day, my palms were more mottled than I had ever seen them when conducting a space clearing ceremony. I checked with the front row of the audience and their palms were mottled too. Then the next row, and so on, all the way to the back row. The entire marquee tent was flooded with spiritual connection, and everyone was immersed in it.

Over the years, I had activated many offerings when space clearing people's homes, but never on such a large scale before and never so publicly. The audience was awed, and I was too.

When I first started including offerings in space clearing ceremonies, I noticed that the effect would extend to the area immediately around wherever it was placed. As I developed my skills, I observed that it extended farther and farther. On that day in 1996, what took me by surprise was that it filled the whole marquee.

Nowadays, Richard and I know how to land spiritual connection through a flower offering in such a way that the effect can stretch even further than that, in every direction. Those of you reading this book who have attended the Advanced Space Clearing workshop we used to teach will have experienced this in person. In that workshop, we create a huge flower mandala on the floor, illuminated with dozens of candles. It fills the centre of the meeting room space and allows people to sit in a profound space of spiritual connection for several hours.

Here are some of the comments made by participants after experiencing this:

The beautiful ceremony in this workshop was a complete surprise to me. I know Karen says that space clearing creates sacred space, but I realize I had no idea before what "sacred" actually feels like. I don't suppose any person brought up in the West can possibly know unless they have an experience like this.

***

Today was amazing. The energy in the room was incredible.

***

There were some extraordinary moments in this workshop when time seemed to stop and I became aware of there being so much more happening in the unseen worlds than I have ever felt before. It felt real, tangible, actual, and so natural. I didn't want it ever to end.

***

I contacted sacredness for probably the first time in my life.

***

After that workshop in Ireland, demonstrating how to activate a flower offering became an integral part of each space clearing workshop I taught, and I also devoted a substantial portion of the day to teaching participants how to do this themselves. Now the instructions are freely available to all in Volume 1 of this book.

Energetically landing in a space

There was a time in history when people used to be born, live, and die in the same house. This still happens in some parts of the world, but for many people, moving home is now a part of life.

When we used to ask in our workshops how many people had moved home in the previous 10 years, nearly every hand in the room went up. When we dropped the period down to five years, half the hands stayed up. And when we asked who had moved in the past year, at least 10% of the hands remained in the air.

Balinese people have a unique approach to this aspect of life. Their family home never changes. It's where the family temple is located, so the home and temple are passed down through the generations. It can never be sold and at least one family member must live there.

Any person leaving home to find work or set up a new home with a partner will immediately do a ceremony when they arrive in their new home to connect the temple there to the temple in their family home. Not only this but, through the dragonweave (see Chapter 3), all family temples are connected to a local village temple, all village temples are connected to the main temple in that area, and all the main temples are connected to the mother temple on Mount Besakih. This means that any Balinese person can go into any temple on the island and connect through the temple matrix to the same powerful spiritual presences they have known all their life. It's a remarkable system that will survive as long as it remains practical for each family to maintain an ancestral home.

We do not know of any other culture that has such a sophisticated system. On top of this, people move so many times in their life now that their birth home no longer has much significance. What's important therefore is being able to land energetically wherever you live in the world, so you can feel a sense of belonging there. This is something that space clearing can help with enormously, and it's another reason why it's such a vital skill to learn in modern times.

When you move into a new home

If you live in an area you love but feel you haven't quite landed there yet, the part of a space clearing ceremony that can help you to consciously forge this is the activation of flower offerings. The combination of the flowers, candle, space clearing water, and the flower offering mudra can facilitate this to an astonishing degree. It is the fastest and most effective way we know to make a place feel like a home.

> **Karen**: I first discovered the importance of this aspect of flower offerings when I worked with a couple who had designed and built their dream house in a beautiful location in the United States. Try as they might, they and their two young children did not feel at home there. They liked the area but hadn't forged a relationship with the land energies. It was as if their home was floating energetically in mid-air with them rattling around aimlessly inside it.
>
> They called me in to help. There were a few feng shui issues that needed to be addressed, but it was during the space clearing ceremony that this problem became clear. There was good compatibility between the family and the land energies of the area, but they lacked the ability to fully land themselves there. I was able to facilitate this for them during the flower offering activations.
>
> I will never forget the moment at the end of the ceremony when the children arrived home and ran around the house,

exploring the changes. Children often feel the effects of a space clearing more than adults, and their children were especially receptive. They didn't know who I was or what I had done, but they excitedly reported to their parents, "It feels like home now! It feels like home now!" They could sense the transformation. The family lived there happily for many years after that.

Landing spiritual connection

When Karen added flower offerings to the space clearing ceremony, it introduced the completely new dimension of landing the White Gold spiritual connection.

At practitioner level, activating a space clearing flower offering is an invitational act of devotion to facilitate landing the White Gold spiritual connection onto the offering and from there deep into the infra-etheric* layers of the earth. This doesn't happen automatically, of course. It is a Point-dragon doing that can also create a platform on which other spiritual connections that have integrity can land.

In other words, activating a flower offering is the most profound part of any space clearing ceremony, when it is done by someone who can hold a deep enough level of involution and has the connection and know-how to do it.

Matrix flower offerings

Matrix flower offerings** are activated after all the other flower offerings have been activated. In *Space Clearing, Volume 1*, we explain that they look identical to the other flower offerings, but the method of activating them and the effect created is substantially different. They are used in a Full Space Clearing ceremony to create a fluid-dimensional superastral matrix.

How flower offerings work

As we explain earlier in this book, fluid dimensionality is a quality found in astral realms. You are sure to have experienced it in your dreams. It simply means the dimensions are not fixed, as they are in the physical world. Fluid-dimensional spaces are midway between the physical dimensionality you are familiar with while living in a human body and the non-dimensional space of consciousness you will return to after you die.

That's why there is no need to place matrix flower offerings vertically in a house according to the physical dimensions of the space. The matrix is created through a superastral linking of all the flower offerings, which is fluid, not geographically fixed. This is very different to using intention or visualization, which are weak imitations of superastral skills and know-how, so we don't recommend that.

The purpose of the superastral matrix is to create a structure that high spiritual forces can gear into during a space clearing ceremony. It vastly improves the effectiveness of a ceremony and how long the results last, so it's a skill that all professional space clearers have to learn and excel at.

This is not something we can teach you how to do through a book, so maybe you are wondering if space clearing will still work for you? The answer is that there are many levels of capability at which space clearing can be done. Our job is to open doors to show you what is possible. Your job is to do the best you can and improve on that as much as you want to or are able to. Follow the steps of the ceremony as closely as you can, including matrix flower offerings if you are doing a Full Space Clearing, to allow deeper levels to gradually unfold.

16

How space clearing water works

An essential part of the space clearing ceremony is using space clearing water** to activate offerings. In this chapter, we explain more about it and why it's so important.

About water

Water is one of the most plentiful substances on earth. It covers about 70% of the earth's surface and makes up between 45% and 75% of the human body, depending on a person's age, gender, and weight.

It's composed of two gases – hydrogen and oxygen – and is one of the most unusual substances on earth. Its most baffling feature is that it is a liquid in its normal state, unlike other chemical compounds with similar-sized molecules, which are all gases.

More curious still, water is the only naturally occurring substance that transitions between solid, liquid, and gas states at everyday temperatures (ice, water, and steam). Ice is also the only known frozen substance that floats on the surface of its liquid form instead of sinking. And water is known by scientists as a universal solvent because it dissolves more substances than any other liquid, which is why it's almost impossible to find pure water anywhere.

Most important of all, water is essential for the functioning of DNA, proteins, and cell membranes. Without water, there would be no etheric forms of life on earth, including humans.

Spiritual qualities of water

Holy water is an intrinsic part of many religions and spiritual practices, including Christianity, Hinduism, Islam, Judaism, Buddhism, Shinto, and Zoroastrianism. This is because water has another unique property that scientists are not aware of or able to measure – it can hold spiritual force. It facilitates the passage of Spirit into matter.

Now, that may not sound like much, but it's huge. It means that the force of certain high-level spiritual connections can be infused into water, which can then be used for blessing and purification purposes. This has far-reaching effects.

In Balinese Hindu rituals, the use of holy water is said to derive from Krishna's words in the *Bhagavad-Gita*: "If one offers Me with love and devotion a leaf, a flower, fruit, or water, I will accept it." In Bali, water is so central to the practice of Hinduism that the religion is also known as Agama Tirta, which translates as The Religion of Holy Water (*agama* means religion and *tirta* means holy water).

We have the ability to easily discern through hand sensing if water holds any spiritual presence and have consistently been impressed with the high level of presencing in Balinese holy water. Other types of religious holy water are often no more interesting than ordinary tap water.

Richard: A range of rituals are used in Balinese Hinduism to create various types of holy water for specific purposes. One extraordinary priest I met was connected to such deep levels of dragon forces that he could make holy water by using a special breathing technique to infuse it with spiritual presence. It was amazing to watch him do it.

Karen: Before I experienced the potency of Balinese holy water, the only type I rated was made by a female Indian guru called Sri Mata Amritanandamayi Devi (usually shortened to Ammachi or Amma). I once attended a *puja* ritual conducted by her in London and watched with great interest as dozens of large buckets of water were placed in front of her by her disciples for her to bless. She simply put her hands on either side of each bucket for about a second. Her disciples then ladled the water out of the large buckets into small plastic cups and placed a leaf over the top of each one. Later in the ceremony, they distributed the cups to the assembled throng of thousands of people.

As soon as I received mine, I removed the leaf and hand sensed the water, curious to know if it held any spiritual force. Ammachi had had such a brief interaction with it that I doubted it would. I was, therefore, very surprised and impressed to feel a substantial energy emanating from the water held in the cheap white plastic cup.

Space clearing water

The method you can use to make space clearing water is described in detail in Chapter 33, Step 15 of *Space Clearing, Volume 1*. It is compatible with all cultures, religions, and spiritual streams when used in a space clearing ceremony.

How it works is that the spiritually presenced droplets of water amplify the natural ethericity of the flower offerings to create an invitational landing platform for the White Gold presence. This is why we emphasize *gently* sprinkling a few drops of water from the flower head onto the offering, not jerkily tapping the flower head with a finger or shaking your hand from side to side to force some drops to fall, as some people tend to do when they first learn the technique. Gentle sprinkling is an etheric action. Jerky tapping or shaking is astralized, so it will not have the intended effect.

The unique combination of a flower offering and candle flame, the space clearing water, and the specific mudra used to activate the offering is designed to create an invitational space for the spiritual presence associated with the space clearing ceremony to land. The materials are essential, but it is the person's ability to do the flower offering mudra that determines how effective it is. This varies greatly from person to person, so we can offer no guarantees, but we have included as much information as possible in *Space Clearing, Volume 1* to help you.

17

How clapping works

The clapping** circuit is an essential preparation for the belling** circuit.

Its main purpose is to break up clumps of stagnant energies that accumulate in buildings, mostly in corners, in the gaps between things, and especially around clutter. Just as stagnant water in a pond can be revived by using an oxygen aeration system, so an important part of the remedy for stagnant energies in a building is to get them moving again. Clapping is the best way we know to break up the clumps and start to revitalize them.

The clapping technique can also be used to shatter recent surface-level astral imprints that have not yet become embedded in the walls, furniture, or other objects in a space.

How space clearing clears energies

A misconception that can sometimes arise about space clearing is that it clears energies out of a building in a similar way to how you might sweep physical dust out of a door. This can cause some people to feel concerned that space clearing their home might adversely affect their neighbours.

We want to make it very clear that it doesn't work like this at all. Space clearing doesn't move energies from one place to another. It transforms them. Stagnant etheric energies are not negative or bad. They just need to be revitalized, which is what clapping does. And astral imprints have no effect after they are shattered, which is what the combined effect of clapping and belling can do.

The clapping technique

There is a world of difference between the way you might appreciatively clap someone's performance as a member of an audience and the type of clapping that is needed for space clearing. Gentle or muffled clapping won't do a thing. To break up stagnant energies, the sound needs to be loud and sharp – the kind that cracks like a whip and would seriously startle someone nearby if you did it unexpectedly.

The best technique is to aim the four fingers of one hand into the cupped palm of your other hand to produce a loud, reverberating clap. We recommend you practise this until you are able to do it effortlessly and at will. If your skin tends to be dry, some non-greasy, unscented hand cream may help.

We need to explain, though, that some people, no matter how hard they try, will find it difficult to do this. That's because it can't be done while you are in your head. You need to be able to involute*, rest in the depths of your column below, and clap from there. That's the only way to put enough fire and oomph into it to make it effective.

Clapping needs to be consciously directed – not with your mind but by transposing your consciousness to your column above and directing the sound and its effect from there. Using this method, much less physical exertion is needed, and the clapping technique is much easier to do. At its most advanced level, clapping is a Point-dragon technique that requires a strong engagement of will.

Space Clearing, Volume 2

What to do if none of this makes any sense to you? We've included this detailed information for those who want to know. For everyone else, just make your clapping as loud and as sharp as you can and really get into all the corners!

18

How belling works

The purpose of the belling** circuit in a space clearing ceremony is to shatter astral imprints that have become embedded in the walls, floors, ceilings, fittings, furniture, and any other objects in a building. At practitioner level, there are also advanced techniques that are used to balance, harmonize, and reset the space at a higher level.

The problem with astral imprints

The physical materials a building is composed of can become astrally imprinted, layer upon layer. Traumatic or repetitive events create the most deeply embedded imprints and are the most difficult to clear.

If the history of a house has been a happy one, the astral imprints will reflect that. Probably, as you read this, you can think of a place you've walked into and really loved how the space felt.

But what if the history has not been so great? What if you live in a home where the previous occupants were unhappy, got sick, got divorced, went bankrupt, put on weight, suffered a tragedy of some kind, or had a run of bad luck while living there? Those energies will still be in the walls and will affect you, whether you realize it or not. Added to that will be layers of astral imprints of your own experiences in that home and anyone who shares the space with you. The most recent or traumatic imprints will affect you the most, and it is these that tend to cause history to repeat itself by triggering behaviours that cause new imprints to be generated.

The belling circuit, therefore, is often the most important circuit of all because it brings about the most change. That doesn't mean that it's the only circuit you need to do. It will be most effective if you do all the other steps of the ceremony too. Even the Basic Space Clearing ceremony, which is the quickest and simplest version of all, needs the clapping circuit to be done before belling, and the harmony ball circuit to be done after belling.

The belling technique

One of the most insightful questions Karen was ever asked about belling was posed by Samuel Sagan, soon after witnessing a space clearing ceremony for the first time. His question was: Would the effect be the same if a robot rang Karen's bell?

The answer, of course, is no. But what a brilliant question it was because it prompted years of subtle body mapping that continues to deliver deeper understandings about belling to this day.

The reason for this is that ringing a bell is not just a mechanical action. A top-of-the-range robot could probably be programmed to ring a bell perfectly, but it would not have the subtle body structures to use it as a human can. It would not have the etheric sensitivity to adjust the volume and type of ring to different densities of energies. It would not have the ability to feel when enough belling has been done in an area or more is needed. Most important of all, it would not be able to target and shatter astral imprints. And at the highest level, it would not be able to use the sound of a bell as a vehicle to carry spiritual connection.

How belling works

In truth, when most people start to learn how to ring a Balinese space clearing bell, they don't have any of these skills either. But the point we are making here is that a robot could never develop them, whereas a human can. It's a remarkable skill to have.

In Bali, they say it takes a priest or priestess at least a year to learn to ring a temple bell. Our experience of training space clearing practitioners is that it can take considerably longer than that for someone to become skilled in the range of belling techniques we teach them.

Thankfully, learning how to ring a bell to do space clearing in your own home does not require so much practice. It's not as simple as just picking up a bell and shaking it, but most people can learn how to ring a Balinese space clearing bell by following the instructions in *Space Clearing, Volume 1*.

For those who want to know more about this, it may help if we remind you that belling is essentially a superastral skill, which means it is designed to be done from above the head, not from your mind, or through intention or visualization. You hold the bell handle in your hand and ring the bell by rotating your wrist from side to side. The sound the bell makes then needs to be wilfully directed from your column above into the walls and other objects in a space in order to shatter the astral imprints embedded there. Holding an awareness that the purpose of belling is to shatter astral imprints will help you to more consciously direct the sound, which will improve your skills and the results you are able to obtain.

Like other space clearing techniques, belling is ultimately a Point* skill, so the belling circuit will be a very different experience for someone who has developed Point functionality and proficient belling skills. At that level, it can sometimes feel akin to spiritual ecstasy.

19

How personal belling works

Personal belling involves ringing a Balinese bell close to the front of your body, from your root charge* area to above your head, while receiving the sound of the bell in your central channel* (the energy channel that runs up the centre of your body). The combination of the sound and the vertical upward movement of the bell has a centring and uplifting* effect.

Uses of personal belling

Personal belling is an essential part of making space clearing water for use in an Essential Space Clearing or a Full Space Clearing ceremony.

You can also use it to centre and uplift yourself if you feel stuck, upset, scattered, or confused. When clutter clearing, many people find it helpful to do personal belling if they start to feel bogged down or overwhelmed.

It's important not to overdo personal belling, though, because it can make you feel ungrounded. We don't recommend doing it more than once a day. And don't use it so often that you depend on it to centre yourself or uplift your energy. It is not supposed to be a substitute for emotional therapy.

Why it's called personal belling

In her first space clearing book, Karen called this technique chakra balancing. She soon had to change that because she discovered that other people were using that term for very different techniques. In any case, it was a misnomer because chakras are energy centres in the body, and energy is always in motion. Energy can therefore never be exactly balanced.

Personal belling is a much better term for this technique because it is a way of giving yourself a personal version of the belling technique that is used to space clear a building.

What type of bell to use

The large Balinese space clearing bell works best for personal belling, although you can get some of the effects with a small space clearing bell.

Please don't attempt to do personal belling with any other type of bell. Only Balinese bells have the resonance and purity of tone that is needed. Other types of bells can leave you feeling like you have had a sheet of rough sandpaper run through your energy, which is not a good experience. They also do not have the ability to amplify energy blockages. Balinese bells are the only ones we have ever found that do that.

How to do personal belling on yourself

This is described in detail in Chapter 33, Step 15 of *Space Clearing, Volume 1*.

How to do personal belling on another person

Providing you don't overdo it, it's perfectly safe to do personal belling on yourself. Personal belling another person requires specific skills and protocols, as we've learned from several decades of teaching the technique to professional space clearers. There's a lot that can go wrong.

Because of this, we were in two minds about whether to include information in this book about it. We have decided to do so, for two reasons.

Firstly, we have taught the technique to a number of very skilled bodyworkers who really got it and have used it to obtain remarkable results with clients. We hope it will reach more people of that calibre.

Secondly, the information here will help anyone who receives a personal belling from a therapist to have better discernment about whether the technique being used is correct.

The technique

This technique is for competent therapists who regularly space clear their treatment room, own a large Balinese space clearing bell, and would like to offer personal belling as a service to their clients.

You must be able to involute, transpose your awareness to above your head, and listen to the sound of the bell from there.

You must also be able to ring your bell cleanly, with the clapper moving from side to side, not spinning around inside the dome, and be able to create EXACTLY the same resonant sound each time you ring it that lasts for at least 5 seconds. This takes practice. If you are not skilled enough to do it, the technique won't work and will probably feel irritating to the person you are belling.

The room you use for this needs to be quiet and as far away as possible from external sounds. Turn off any equipment that makes any kind of

How personal belling works

mechanical noise or causes a flow of air through the space (fans, air conditioning, etc).

Ask your client to sit on the edge of a chair with their legs shoulder-width apart, their arms uncrossed, and their hands resting loosely in their lap and not touching each other. They must be able to sit vertically for a few minutes without leaning against the back of the chair.

- The starting position is to hold your bell by the middle of its handle in your dominant hand and rest the dome on the flattened, upturned palm of your other hand.
- If you are right-handed, stand on the right side of the client. If you are left-handed, stand on their left side.
- Explain briefly what you are about to do. Then ask the client to close their eyes.
- Tell them to take a few deep breaths, as if they are inhaling all the way down to their toes and back up again. While they are doing this, synchronize your breathing with theirs, feeling what it feels like to breathe like them. Only breathe in and out through your nose, even if the client breathes through their mouth.
- Then tell the client to breathe normally, and at the bottom of your and their next out-breath, bend forward and ring your bell at the level of their knees, about 30 cm (12 inches) in front of them.
- While the bell is still ringing for the next 5 seconds or so, move it toward their root charge area and then vertically upward, following the contours of their body, keeping a distance of about 7 to 8 cm (3 inches) away from them. Slowly breathe in as you do so and put your awareness in your own central channel to feel how the sound of the bell interacts with the client's central channel as you move it upward.
- Continue the upsweep until the bell is as far above the client's head as you can comfortably reach.

- Keeping the bell perfectly vertical, twist the handle horizontally 90 degrees in a clockwise direction (as seen from above).
- Then, in a smooth motion and taking care not to let the bell ring, inhale a little bit more through your nose and stretch your arm to lift the bell vertically up and out of your client's energy field. Exhale through your nose as you move it in a wide semi-circular arc away from the person to return the bell to the starting position, resting it on the upturned palm of your other hand.

Repeat this sequence twice more, synchronizing your breath with the client's breath each time.

What personal belling reveals

If you ring the bell correctly, it will fade in and out as you move it up the front of the client's body and above their head, amplifying any blocks they have.

If someone is in good shape, physically and energetically, the bell will sound clear and resonant all the way up on each of the three rings. If there are aspects that need attention, the sound will waver on the first pass of the bell, change somewhat on the second pass, and can be very different on the third pass. In many cases, the sound becomes – to coin a phrase – as clear as a bell. Sometimes there is no change at all, which indicates there are deeper levels that need attention than personal belling can help with.

Mistakes to avoid

Please avoid these common mistakes.

Analysing with your mind

Personal belling is not about listening to the sound of the bell or analysing the sounds it makes with your mind, which may come up with all kinds of nonsense if you allow it to interfere. To do this technique, you need to place your awareness in your column above and listen from there.

Correctly interpreting the sounds is much more advanced and requires substantial development of the subtle body organ of perception known as verticality, which takes many years to cultivate. If you have not done that level of personal work, don't attempt it. Just do the technique and say nothing at all to your client. It will still have a beneficial effect if the belling technique is done well.

Psychic prophesying

Interpreting the sounds made by the bell during personal belling has nothing to do with intuition, psychic skills, prophesying, or saying the first thing that "intuitively" comes into your head. Any of these could be wildly inaccurate and could send someone off-track for years or even the rest of their life, which you would then be karmically responsible for.

Reverse personal belling

Personal belling is always done from the region of the base chakra to above the head, never the other way around. Reverse personal belling will have the effect of pulling a person's energy down, not the intended result of uplifting them.

Belling a pregnant person

Never do personal belling on someone who is pregnant. It can shock the baby.

Belling someone who is sick

It's fine for someone who is unwell to do personal belling on themselves, providing they don't overdo it (no more than once a day). However, we don't advise doing personal belling on someone who is sick unless you are a trained therapist and are already very familiar with their energy.

Belling children

Some children enjoy having a personal belling, but most don't need it. They usually do not have the level of astral impaction that teenagers and adults have, so it can feel like an uncomfortable intrusion into their energy. Be sensitive to this possibility if you decide to try the technique on your own children. Stop immediately if they show any sign of discomfort (they will usually wriggle or try to physically move away from the bell). Never do personal belling on other people's children.

Belling pets

Pets do not need and often do not respond well to personal belling because their spine is not vertical. The technique is for humans, not animals.

Practitioner-level personal belling

We want to make it very clear that personal belling other people is not part of Basic Space Clearing, Essential Space Clearing, or Full Space Clearing, but it is often part of a space clearing ceremony conducted by one of our certified practitioners. It allows them to work with each member of a household at a much deeper level.

Learning how to do this is one of the most challenging parts of our professional training. It can take some trainees a year or more to learn the basics and many more years to learn to accurately read and translate what the sound of the bell is amplifying in a person's subtle body structures.

Here are some poignant examples from our experience of doing personal belling on clients.

Karen: One person I remember very well was an architect. He and his wife had a beautiful home, and the space clearing ceremony I did for them was a gift to themselves to help them enjoy it even more. I had picked up some clues during the early parts of the ceremony that all was not well with the husband, but it was not until the personal belling that I realized the extent of the problem.

On the first ring of the bell, it rang as resonantly as always, but then the sound completely died as I moved it vertically up over the contours of his body to above the head. There was such an absence of sound that I looked inside the dome of the bell to see if the clapper had fallen out. It hadn't. The same thing happened with the second and third passes of the bell too. If I hadn't heard it with my own ears, I wouldn't have believed it possible.

At this point in my space clearing career, I had done personal belling on hundreds of people, enough to know that this was highly unusual and seriously worrying. Interpreting the sound of the bell, or rather the non-sound, it was clear to me that the man was totally exhausted. So, I didn't beat about the bush. I looked him in the eye and asked him, "How long have you felt this exhausted?"

What happened next was astonishing. His wife burst into tears, and he crumpled before my eyes. He dropped his convincing façade of everything being all right and admitted he was barely holding himself together. It turned out that since setting up his new business a year ago, he had been working 80-hour weeks with hardly a day off and he could no longer sustain it. His wife was very concerned about him and relieved I had brought this out in the open.

I explained to them both that I had never heard my bell reflect such a deep level of exhaustion in anyone before. I urged him to seriously consider taking some time off, sooner rather than later, and reorganize his business so that it would not take such a toll on him. By the end of the ceremony, he had made the decision to do just that. He told me that hearing for himself the way the sound of the bell died was what brought the reality of his exhaustion home to him.

Richard: A pattern I've seen in many clients is that on the first ring of the bell, the sound wavers in and out very noticeably as I move it upward. Then, in the area vertically above the head, just when you'd expect the sound to start fading toward the end of the ring, it unexpectedly becomes louder and more resonant. On the second and third rings of the bell, there is usually less wavering of the sound as the person's energy becomes more centred.

What this reveals is that the person has a well-established spiritual practice in their life that they find fulfilling, but their everyday life is chaotic or disorganized. A daily practice of doing personal belling each morning to centre themselves can be very helpful in this situation for a period of time.

Karen: Another personal belling I will always remember was with a middle-aged female client who had not given any indication of health issues during the ceremony. But when I rang the bell, the sound was perfectly clear and resonant until it reached her belly area, where it became completely mute. It then resumed as loud as before as I moved the bell over the heart area and upward, finishing above her head.

I knew from this that there could be something seriously wrong in the area of her belly. Sure enough, exactly the same thing happened on all three passes, so I asked her about it. She admitted she'd had severe pains in the last week and was thinking she perhaps needed to see a doctor. I encouraged her to do so that day. Three days later she called me from hospital to let me know she had taken my advice and had been rushed to hospital to have an emergency colostomy.

A personal experience of personal belling

To end this chapter, here's an account of a very memorable occasion when Karen once used personal belling on herself to great effect.

Karen: In the late 1990s, I flew to Dublin, Ireland, to teach a one-day space clearing workshop The Irishman who organized the event got me to the venue on time, but his idea of doing this was to drive at top speed down 20 miles of winding country lanes with me in the back seat hanging on for dear life while he chattered non-stop to his assistant in front. Taking it slower was not in his nature, nor an option, because we'd be late. By the time we arrived, I was in such bad shape that I went straight into the ladies' toilets and threw up.

Now, when I get travel sick, I get very travel sick. I usually throw up several times and need to lie perfectly still for an hour or two until normality resumes. It doesn't happen very often but when it does, it's totally debilitating.

In this situation, I had a group of about 100 people waiting for me to space clear and set the space of the room so that they could go in and take their seats for the workshop I was about to teach. It seemed impossible that I could turn this around.

While deciding what to do, I threw up again, and as I was washing my face and hands, I had an "Aha!" moment about how I could use my bell to recentre myself.

So right there, standing next to a washbasin in the ladies' toilets, with several very surprised workshop participants looking on, I took my bell out of my bag and did personal belling on myself. The first pass had some effect. The second pass helped a little more. And on the third pass, it felt as though my entire energy clicked back into alignment, from above my head all the way down to my root charge. The waves of sickness vanished completely.

I had never tried using personal belling to relieve travel sickness before and have never tried it since. But on that day, all that mattered was that it worked for me in that situation. I felt as good as new, space cleared the room, taught the workshop, and everyone had a great day.

20

How harmony balls work

Harmony balls** are used near the end of a space clearing ceremony to put new, higher frequencies into the area that has just been cleared. This is done by infusing specific frequencies into a harmony ball and then shaking those frequencies out into the space.

The origin of harmony balls

When Karen first started doing space clearing professionally, she would clear the stagnant energies and astral imprints from a person's home to leave them with a blank canvas on which to create their life afresh. It didn't take her long to realize that space clearing creates such a clear space that people feel compelled to immediately fill it energetically with what they already know and feel safe with.

This unconscious resting on the past is not at all what is needed to move forward. She therefore started including a harmony ball process in each space clearing to help her clients to consciously infuse the space of their home with new, higher frequencies, so that they would not lapse back into their old ways. This proved to be so effective that it is now a key part of every space clearing ceremony.

Harmony ball infusion

The harmony ball infusion process involves becoming very still, involuting*, and aspiring* upward. It is designed to facilitate opening to high spiritual forces that want to help humankind but are not able to do so when we are too immersed in the frequencies of everyday life and ordinary mental consciousness.

The key to asking for help from above is not to ask for specific things such as more money, finding a new partner, resolving a health issue, or any of the problems that people tend to use prayer to get help with. Spiritual connections exist at levels of consciousness that are far beyond words or worldly concerns. They can, however, receive and respond to aspirations* that come from a person's Higher Self.

This is why in Chapter 25 of *Space Clearing, Volume 1* we explain in detail the difference between making a wish list and clarifying a focus for a space clearing ceremony. A wish list, no matter how wrapped up in spiritual jargon and mystical longing it may be, is generated by the wantings of a person's thoughts and emotions (their astral body). It will therefore be limited to the level of ordinary mental consciousness, which we call Level 6 in the Seven Levels of Consciousness model we use. That's fine for everyday life, but real change doesn't happen there. Lasting change starts at Level 5 and above.

So instead of a wish list, we encourage you to create a clear, concise focus for each space clearing you do. This will help you to hold it as a silent, packed thought* above your head throughout the ceremony, without the interference of the noisy fluctuations of your mind and emotions. When done correctly, the harmony ball infusion process can connect you to higher parts of yourself that you rarely, if ever, have access to.

Harmony ball frequencing

The final part of the harmony ball process is to shake the frequencies out from your harmony ball into the layer of clean, clear ethericity that the clapping and belling circuits are designed to create.

It's a very joyful part of the ceremony that's likely to bring a huge smile to your face and a lightness to your step. It can have the effect of drastically changing your relationship to the place where you live by infusing it with qualities that will nurture and support you in every aspect of your life.

If you find yourself feeling tired or your arms start to ache during the circuit, that's usually a sign that you are putting too much astrality into it (the most common cause of this is trying to be too efficient). Putting astrality into the space will have the opposite effect to what's needed. Harmony ball frequencing is an etheric process, so breathe through your nose, not your mouth. Let your body become supple. Relax your shoulders and arms. Hold the harmony ball firmly but lightly. Use a fluid movement that's halfway between walking and dancing. You'll get the best results when it feels easy and enjoyable to do.

How harmony ball infusion and frequencing works

The reason Balinese harmony balls work so well for this part of the space clearing ceremony is because of their spherical shape and the beautiful jingly-jangly sound they make when shaken. They are specially designed for this purpose.

To gain a deeper understanding of how they work, a similar question to the one asked about space clearing bells in Chapter 18 is very helpful – would it be the same if a robot did the harmony ball infusion and frequencing?

The answer, of course, is no, because a robot does not have an etheric body or a Higher Self. It therefore would not be able to consciously infuse higher frequencies into a harmony ball or use it to put those frequencies into a home. It needs to be done by a human, and not just any human. The person who holds the main harmony ball for the ceremony needs to be the person who has overall responsibility for the energy of the space – the head of the household, or one of the heads of the household if it is jointly held by two people.

The spherical shape of a harmony ball and the conductive material it is made of make it an excellent temporary repository for higher frequencies. The chiming sounds that are created when it is shaken, made by the tiny ball bearings inside it striking against the bronze strips that line its inner surface, also provide a perfect medium on which those frequencies can ride. But the whole process only works when it is consciously directed by a human holding the harmony ball.

It also only works if the previous steps of the ceremony have successfully created clear space in the walls, furniture, and other objects in a home into which the new, higher level of frequencies can be embedded.

We've often seen that people who have more access to their Higher Self, because they have done a lot of personal work to deconstruct the samskaras of their astral body, get much more from this part of the ceremony than those who have never done any personal work at all or are just starting out. But everyone will get some benefit from it, at their own level. It's a beautiful, uplifting way to end a space clearing ceremony on a high note, and it makes the effects of the ceremony last much longer.

PART THREE

Energy clearing misconceptions

21

Why there are so many misconceptions about energy clearing

When Karen introduced space clearing to the world in her first public talk in London in 1991, most people were not aware that energies in buildings could affect them or that it was possible to change them. Some had heard about purification practices that have existed in traditional cultures around the world for centuries, but this was the first system they had ever heard of that was designed to clear and revitalize the types of energies found in buildings in the modern world.

Five years later, Karen published her first space clearing book, and it immediately became an international bestseller. But then something happened that she hadn't anticipated and certainly didn't welcome. Many variations of energy clearing practices sprang up and adopted the name "space clearing" too.

Karen accepts she is partly responsible for this happening. As a first-time author, under pressure from her publisher to offer cheaper options to those who couldn't afford to buy Balinese space clearing equipment, she listed various alternatives in her book. She sincerely regrets agreeing to that, and it has been a key factor in our decision to self-publish these new books about space clearing so we have full editorial control and the ability to make updates and clarifications whenever necessary.

Karen looked into trademarking the term space clearing at that time, but when she realized what would be involved in policing it, she decided she would rather spend her time developing higher levels of her work than being embroiled in litigations. The success of her book means there are now millions of pages on the internet about different forms of space clearing, ranging from the plausible to the utterly ridiculous.

We can understand why this has happened. We live in a world where people are looking for quick fixes in their busy lives. It's therefore not surprising they gravitate to methods that claim to effortlessly change the energies in their home in minutes, with no skill involved and very little effort or expense. Who wants to do all the preparations and conduct a lengthy space clearing ceremony if it can all be achieved in a few seconds using a much simpler method?

Another reason there are so many different forms of energy clearing is the lack of knowledge about how energies work. Many people who develop these techniques may do so with the best of intentions, but they don't know what they don't know.

We have already shared with you in this book our depth of knowledge about how space clearing works. Those who have attended our space clearing workshops and experienced first-hand the extraordinary high-level spaces we create know why we have the distinction of being the world's leading experts in this field. People whose homes we have space cleared have experienced on an even deeper level the remarkable transformations space clearing can bring about. Some tell us the changes are so profound that they date their lives pre- and post-space clearing ever after.

We therefore want to go one stage further in this book and share our knowledge about which energy clearing methods *don't* work, and why. Our wish is to help everyone to have better discernment. It's up to you what you choose to believe and practise, but we hope our insights into the effectiveness of these alternative methods will at least promote some healthy questioning.

While there are far too many examples of energy clearing misconceptions to comment on them all, we have included the main ones in this part of the book.

22

Intuitive energy clearing

Every so often someone contacts us to tell us we've got space clearing completely wrong. They say that all the decisions about what to do and how to do it can be arrived at through intuition. The person doing the clearing can intuit the best date and time, who needs to be present, which clearing techniques are used, in what order, and so on. All that's needed is a clear intention and doing what intuitively feels right.

Everything is made of energy, they say. Each person is on their own spiritual journey, so there is no right way or wrong way to do energy clearing. Whichever method feels right will be exactly what each person needs to do.

The problem with intuition

The problem with intuition is that most people don't know where their ideas come from or how to separate the notions that have integrity from those that don't. They may think an intuitive flash they have received is correct, but in fact it has been shaped by their personal samskaras* or influenced by external factors such as astral waves that are beyond their comprehension.

They don't even understand the mechanics of how intuition works. When asked, they will tell you they "just know". This can lead to someone feeling completely convinced they are right, with no way that anyone else can verify or challenge their beliefs. It can also lead to some very strange practices.

One example of an intuitive energy clearing technique we have heard of is to loudly pray, randomly clap, and then stamp your feet while ordering all negative energies to leave. A client who paid for a consultation of this type told Karen that she barely managed to keep a straight face while this was happening. She said the only thing it changed for her was her bank balance (she was too embarrassed to challenge the practitioner, so she paid for her services anyway).

Another example is a ritual that was added to the space clearing ceremony by one of the first people Karen trained in the 1990s. The practitioner got her client to walk three times around their local duck pond while chanting a particular word that was supposed to have magical properties. The man went along with this odd request but was so disappointed by the results of the space clearing that he called Karen to ask about it. When questioned, it emerged that this practitioner had been inventing all kinds of strange additions to the ceremony that she intuitively felt needed to be part of it. She wasn't willing to change this, so she left our network. This kind of thing no longer happens with our certified practitioners because they now take annual continuing professional development courses with us to maintain and develop their skills.

The difference between intuition and vision

We explain in Chapter 8 that the space clearing ceremony we teach has not been invented or intuited. It has been cognized from high archetypal* realms.

This means that when we are probed in depth by experienced people who have highly developed spiritual vision*, many reasons are revealed for why each step of the ceremony is needed and why the steps are in the order they are in. If you change the ceremony in any way because you intuitively feel this will improve it, what you will be doing is lowering it to your own level of comprehension and reducing its effectiveness.

By vision, we don't mean physical eyesight. We mean perception at levels that are substantially above the level of ordinary mental consciousness*, including awakening the third eye* and developing subtle body* structure* above the head. The space clearing practitioners we train have all developed their vision to a very high level and are able to conduct the ceremony from that standpoint. They don't follow the steps passively or intuitively. They understand exactly how the ceremony works and what needs to be done in each property they work in to obtain the best results for their clients.

23

Intention and visualization

Some people believe that intention is all that's needed to do energy clearing. You just have to close your eyes and visualize all the energies in your home being purified by white light, or all unwanted energies leaving.

We certainly agree that clarity of intention has an important part to play, as we explain in Chapter 25 of *Space Clearing, Volume 1* about establishing the focus of a ceremony. And, of course, what you do needs to feel right. Never surrender your own discernment and blindly follow instructions.

But we certainly do not agree that intention alone is enough. The fact is, most people do not have the willpower to resist a pastry, never mind bring about an energetic transformation in a space purely by intending it to be so. Believing in the power of intention is not at all the same as being able to use it to bring about actual changes.

It is theoretically possible to build one's personal subtle body structures to be able to access the profound level of involution that can affect astral fields at will. It would require a huge amount of personal development work and countless years of advanced meditation to do this. It's the level at which will and consciousness are one. We have never met such a person ourselves, but we believe it could be done.

For the ordinary person, though, no matter how strongly or earnestly they intend something, it will be a mere puff in the wind of their astral body and have no substance at all. Intention won't change a thing without corresponding physical actions to bring it about.

You can't sit on your sofa, for example, and expect all your house cleaning to magically be done just because you wish it to be so. Intention without action is nothing more than wishful thinking.

It would be equally absurd to imagine that space clearing – which is essentially a much higher level of house cleaning – can be done by intending or visualizing it to be so. For those who have the ability to perceive energy changes in a building before and after a space clearing, it's obvious that these types of techniques have no effect at all.

24

Invocational energy clearing

Some people claim to be able to invoke angels to do energy clearing. They usually call on big angels, such as Archangel Gabriel or Archangel Michael, who will come at a moment's notice to do their bidding, just because they are asked to or because a specific invocation is used.

We wish it were that simple. What a different world it would be if we could all connect to high spiritual beings at will and with such ease. And how easy energy clearing would be if angels could take care of it for us on request, without us having to do anything except call on them.

However, it doesn't work that way.

There certainly are angelic beings who shine their light onto human beings, and there are ways to connect and combinesse* with them. It requires the ability to hold a highly involuted state of consciousness and profound inner stillness. Most people never experience anything close to this state of consciousness even once during their entire lifetime. It's definitely not one that can be invoked by saying a few words.

It's also possible to summon angelic beings through powerful religious rituals, as Karen discovered during many meetings she had with the Reverend Christopher Neil-Smith, who used to be the top exorcist of the Church of England. When she first met him in 1979, he had been

Invocational energy clearing

doing exorcisms for 30 years, and he is believed to have completed over 3,000 exorcisms by the time he died in 1995. He certainly had the ability to invoke angelic forces.

We have met people who are convinced they are tuning in to an angelic presence when, in fact, they are only imagining it or are being influenced by an astral being that is masquerading as an angel. These types of experiences can feel very real and persuasive. But as a wise Balinese friend once said, "Not everything above is good and not everything below is bad". Perception and discernment are always needed.

The noise that runs through most people's minds all the time makes it impossible for angelic beings to get close to most humans. Unless you have learned how to silence your mind through meditation, it will chatter away all day long, like the babble of broadcasting stations that can be heard if you move the dial of a radio through its frequency bands. This noise will continue during the hours of sleep, taking you through a procession of astral spaces we call dreams. There are high-level spaces we are supposed to go to during sleep, but most people's dreams are a continuation of the astral spaces they inhabit during their waking life, so they usually never get beyond that.

If you're ever lucky enough to consciously experience being in the presence of an angelic being while incarnated in a human body, you will never forget it. The energy of the space in the room will become rarefied and your awareness of your physical body will recede. For a few precious moments, you will experience a profound state of stillness and have access to higher parts of yourself you have only glimpsed before or have never consciously been in contact with at all. For most, it is a life-changing event because it opens the door to restructuring your entire life top-down.

So yes, angels exist. And some do have an affinity with specific purification rituals. But simply calling an angel's name and expecting it to do energy clearing on demand won't change a thing. Angels are not available on speed dial.

25

Distant energy clearing

We've heard there are energy clearing professionals (not trained by us, we hasten to add), who sit at home, ring a bell over a floor plan of someone's home, and declare it to be energetically clear. That'll be $300 for a minute's work, thank you very much.

If distant space clearing were possible, we wouldn't have bothered to travel all over the world for so many years to do the ceremony in people's houses and apartments. We would have saved ourselves the time, effort, and expense of all the international travel and made a small fortune without ever bothering to leave home.

Attempting to do energy clearing from a distance is neither effective nor ethical. If someone claims to be able to space clear your home virtually, we're sorry to say they're either misguided, ignorant, or conning you.

The reason it doesn't work is because there has to be a direct engagement with the etheric and astral energies of a building in order to change them. This can't be done from a distance. It can only be done in person.

26

Purification with sound

We've experimented extensively with many types of sound-producing instruments to establish which work for energy clearing, which don't, and why. The topics covered in this chapter are:

- Bells
- Singing bowls
- Gongs
- Tuning forks
- Wind chimes
- Drums
- Clap sticks
- Shamanic rattles
- Chanting

Bells

Karen used bells made of brass or bronze for many years before she discovered Balinese space clearing bells. The most common types available are Tibetan bells and tingsha cymbals. They cost less than Balinese bells and do have some energy clearing capabilities.

The difference in composition and crafting means they can't be used to make space clearing water. They also don't have the purity of tone to be used for personal belling or the ability to amplify blocked energies in people or buildings. It therefore won't work to use these types of bells to do Essential or Full Space Clearing, but you could use one to do Basic Space Clearing. The results won't be as good as using a Balinese space clearing bell, but it will be better than nothing at all.

Bells made of materials such as glass, wood, ceramic, clay, or horn do not have the ability to shatter astral imprints so are not suitable to use for energy clearing.

Singing bowls

Singing bowls are very different to bells, both in the sound they make and in the effect they have.

A singing bowl consists of a metal bowl and a mallet. The bowl is usually placed on a cushion in the palm of one hand, and the mallet is held in the other hand. To produce a sound, the mallet is placed in contact with the lip of the rim of the bowl and slowly circled around it to produce a continuous melodic sound. It can be very beautiful to listen to.

However, it's not possible to direct the sound into the walls and corners to shatter astral imprints, as you can with a Balinese bell. They are also rather heavy and require the continuous use of both hands.

For all these reasons, we do not consider singing bowls to be an energy clearing tool and do not recommend their use. They don't clear energies in buildings. It's not what they are designed to do.

Another major difference is that the sound emitted by a singing bowl goes out in horizontal waves into the space, whereas the sound of a Balinese bell is more awakened. It has the effect of verticalizing and transforming both the horizontal and superastral space of a room.

Verticalization is an important principle in space clearing because it is through this that integrity is restored to spaces. You can see the two principles of verticality and horizontality very clearly in the shape and function of the two objects. A bell is vertical. It can be actively rung, and its sound can be wilfully directed to clear stagnant etheric energies and shatter astral imprints. A singing bowl is not vertical, and its sound cannot be directed – it ripples out in horizontal waves that travel where they will.

It's often claimed that singing bowls are made of a special alloy composed of seven metals that correspond to the seven major planets. This mystical combination sounds very alluring, suggesting that an object would be imbued with the powers of the solar system. Unfortunately, this is nothing more than a marketing ploy. Singing bowls have never been made from seven metals and experts say they would not produce a better sound even if they were.

Our Balinese bellmakers confirm this. Bells are made from a special type of bronze that contains more tin than normal bronze. They sometimes add a small quantity of 22-carat gold when making temple bells for Balinese priests and priestesses, but this is no guarantee of superior quality of sound. The best bells are nearly always those that are made of pure bronze. It takes a very high level of expertise to mix in any other metals.

So what are singing bowls good for? They are best used in situations where a sustained sound is required that bells are not capable of producing. They are also a helpful tool to disengage the intense grasping of the mind (the astral body) in order to become more fluid and yin.

We've heard that some people use singing bowls in a similar way to the personal belling technique we describe in Chapter 19. This won't have the same effect as a Balinese space clearing bell because the sound will remain constant rather than amplifying what's happening in your energy as you move the singing bowl vertically upward, but it can have an uplifting effect that feels very nice. If you decide to try this, be sure only to use a singing bowl that is of a high enough quality to emit a clear, resonant tone.

In relation to space clearing, the only possible use of singing bowls would be after a space clearing ceremony to help to maintain the space. Using a singing bowl for this creates a somewhat blissful, horizontal, unconscious effect. Refreshing the space by doing Basic Space Clearing with a Balinese bell is much more awakening, so that would always be our choice.

Gongs

When we lived in Bali, our conference centre owned a beautiful set of large gongs. We discovered at that time that the deep, sonorous tones of gongs are far too low to be effective for energy clearing and these items are also too heavy to carry around. We really enjoyed using them to open spaces of consciousness during our workshops, though, as those who experienced this will probably remember for the rest of their lives.

Tuning forks

We're not sure how the notion came about that it might be possible to do energy clearing by wafting a tuning fork around. It will vibrate when struck and emit a perceptible sound, but it's so weak it has no effect at all on stagnant energies or astral imprints in buildings.

Wind chimes

Wind chimes are not designed for energy clearing, and we don't recommend them for feng shui purposes either. The constant noise of wind chimes keeps people's minds full of chatter, so they never fully rest. They tend to make people busy, usually in unproductive ways. Outdoor wind chimes are the worst because they create noise pollution that can irritate neighbours. A UK poll named them as Britain's most hated garden accessory.

Drums

Those who advocate drumming as an energy clearing technique say it is based on Native American traditions. We question this because history tells us those indigenous people lived in circular tipis and were nomadic. Circular tipis don't have corners where stagnant energies can accumulate, and the tribes generally didn't stay in one place long enough for a tipi to accumulate stagnant energies anyway. They would not have needed the types of energy clearing techniques that we need today.

We can certainly see the attraction of drumming. It's great fun, for one thing, and can look and sound impressive. It's a lot easier than clapping. And no awareness or perception of energies is required. Anyone can pick up a drum and bang it, but at best all it does is vibrate surface-level energies.

It's possible that if you got one of those incredible Taiko drumming bands from Japan round to your home and let them rip, it would have some kind of energy clearing effect. That type of drumming was primarily developed for the purposes of presencing spaces, so it could have a clearing effect too.

Simply walking around a building while banging a drum does not clear energies. It may stir things up (for better or for worse), but it does not target stagnant energies or revitalize them in the same way that clapping can, and it doesn't clear astral imprints at all.

Using a drum also distances a person from directly experiencing the space. It's a sanitized approach because it doesn't require etheric engagement or know-how. We can understand some people would feel more comfortable with this, but it's not the real deal. Drumming is only minimally effective as an energy clearing method.

Clap sticks

Clap sticks are a type of percussion instrument, consisting of two wooden sticks that are banged together to produce a noise. The sharp sound clap sticks make can have some effect, depending on the technique used and the ability of the person using them. But the changes they can bring about are very limited. Clapping is much more effective.

Shamanic rattles

We've heard of people using shamanic rattles instead of clapping. We don't recommend this because instead of breaking up the lumps of stagnant energies as clapping does, a shamanic rattle has the effect of scattering it all over the room, only to gather in the corners again soon after. It may look and sound dramatic, but it doesn't do the job. It's not an effective energy clearing technique.

Chanting

The purpose of chanting is to create sounds that resonate with a specific high-level spiritual presence, to enter into a high state of consciousness and connect to it.

The best-known example of this originated hundreds of years ago with the Gyuto monks of Tibet, whose order still exists. They chant sacred texts using a base note that is two octaves below middle C, with a simultaneous harmonic that is two octaves and one third higher, and other fainter harmonics that are one fifth and one tenth higher. The base note they hold has been found to vibrate at an astonishing 75.5 cycles per second, which is nearly twice as low as the world's greatest operatic bass singers are able to go.

People who have heard the extraordinary sound of these monks chanting live say there are no words to describe it or the space that descends. We have never had the opportunity to experience this ourselves, but we're pretty sure it would have the effect of energetically clearing space and presencing it. It could, therefore, be categorized as a form of energy clearing, especially if repeated regularly in the same space.

Does this mean that chanting can be used as an energy clearing technique in people's homes? Well, no. It would take exceptional devotion, a remarkable teacher, and a lifetime of practice to even get close to the level of chanting that would be needed for that, and even then, it's not certain what the effect would be or how long it would last. The space clearing ceremony described in our books is a much easier and surer method.

27

Purification with aromas

Inhaling aromas can have the effect of raising or lowering the level of consciousness you can access. The smell of sewerage, for example, will instantly connect you to lower levels of astrality. Some aromas can connect you to higher levels.

In both cases, the effect only lasts for as long as the smell is in the air and you continue to inhale it. Aromas do not clear energies in spaces or bring about long-lasting changes. They only create a perception of change if you inhale them.

Knowing this, let's look at the four main types of aromas that are often claimed to have energy clearing properties:

- Incense
- Smudge sticks
- Essential oils
- Sprays and mists

Incense

Incense is used in most of the major religions of the world because it is a quick and easy technique. Many Asian cultures also believe that the upward movement of the smoke helps to waft the essence of their offerings and prayers up to the gods.

It is not an energy clearing technique because as soon as the aroma dissipates and you stop inhaling it, the effect is lost. That's why incense has to be burned repeatedly. If it had a permanent effect, that wouldn't be necessary.

Karen included the use of two non-toxic types of incense in her first space clearing book to offer as much help as possible to people doing space clearing for the first time or those who had a lot of clutter in their home. It's no longer part of the ceremony because it isn't a space clearing technique.

There is also an issue with incense that has come to light since then, which means we no longer recommend using it for any purpose. Many types these days are made of a cocktail of substances that are carcinogenic when burned, emitting a range of toxins such as carbon monoxide, sulphur dioxide, nitrogen dioxide, aldehydes, ketones, xylenes, diethyl phthalate, and polycyclic aromatic hydrocarbons, including formaldehyde.

This is not too much of a problem in places such as Bali, where the temples are all open air, or in your own home, if you only burn incense occasionally. But it is causing serious problems in indoor temples in countries such as Thailand and Taiwan, where multiple incense sticks are burned at the same time.

Each stick emits roughly the same level of toxins as a cigarette, so being in a temple with several hundred incense sticks burning simultaneously exposes everyone there to the same level of health hazard as being in a room with several hundred smokers puffing away. High levels of sickness in temple workers have led some temples to ask visitors to refrain from using incense sticks or to use short ones, burn them only while prayers are in progress, then extinguish them immediately.

It's rather ironic that what is widely believed to be a purification technique has such noxious side-effects. It's likely that incense used to be purer in the days when it was all made by hand. Perhaps the move to mass production has changed that.

Whatever the case, there is no need to burn incense to do effective space clearing. Richard and I no longer use it, the professionals we train no longer use it, and it is not part of the space clearing ceremony we describe in *Space Clearing, Volume 1*. Some types of incense are so toxic that burning it will bring the energy of a space down rather than raising it.

Smudge sticks

Smudging is a practice that comes from indigenous American Indian traditions. It involves lighting a smudge stick made of dried herbs (usually sage, cedar, or sweetgrass) and wafting the smoke around a space, sometimes using a feather.

We feel sure this must have had a meaningful purpose within the context of the wonderful etherically-based American Indian lifestyle many years ago, but how it ever came to be regarded as a clearing technique for the dense types of energies found in modern buildings is a mystery to us. We have experimented with many different types of smudge sticks. Like incense, it does not revitalize stagnant energies in buildings or have any effect on astral imprints.

When Karen published an article about this topic in 2018, a number of people contacted her to tell her about a study titled "Medicinal smoke reduces airborne bacteria", which was published in 2007 in the *Journal of Ethnopharmacology*. It seems a number of websites have cited the study as proof that burning sage is an effective energy clearing method because the material used reduced 94% of airborne bacteria in one particular room in a one-hour period.

When Karen looked into this, she discovered the experiment was conducted with a substance called *havan sámagri*. This is widely used in rituals in India and consists of a mixture of about 60 aromatic woods, medicinal herbs, and other ingredients, but not sage. And even if sage *had* been an ingredient used in the study, space clearing is on an entirely different level to physical purification, so it doesn't follow that any substance that has physical antibacterial properties has etheric or astral purification properties too. That would be like physically cleaning your home with disinfectant and expecting it to clear it energetically too.

If you like the smell of smudge sticks, it's fine to burn them in your home from time to time, providing the area is well ventilated and you don't use palo santo sticks (these emit a high concentration of limonene, which reacts with ozone in the air to form the carcinogen formaldehyde). Just don't expect smudge sticks to change the energies of your space in any way. The professional space clearing practitioners we train never use them.

Essential oils

Like other aromas, essential oils do not clear energies in rooms. Some types are believed to have healing properties when used in massage oil on the skin. Be aware, though, that a number of studies have raised concerns about oils interacting with ozone in indoor air to create toxins such as terpenes. These are known to cause eye irritation, headaches, and dizziness, and can aggravate breathing problems in people who have asthma or lung disease. It's therefore important to make sure that any room where essential oils are burned is well ventilated. We never burn oils in our own home, except to use gently warmed almond oil when doing massage.

Sprays and mists

It would be wonderful if a few quick sprays of an inexpensive liquid could clear the energies in your home. Some sprays have strong aromas and some are scent-free, said to work at more subtle levels. No skill is required except the ability to hold a bottle, point, and squirt.

We have tested many of these products to assess if they have any effect. Our conclusion is that some aromas may have a temporary uplifting effect when you inhale them, in the same way that some types of essential oils do, or they may improve the ionization in a room, in the same way that any atomizer spraying plain water droplets will do. But odourless sprays or mists have no effect at all, and spraying or misting of any kind does not revitalize stagnant energies or have any effect on astral imprints embedded in walls, furniture, or other objects in a space. Using them is not an effective energy clearing technique.

28

Purification with light

Light brightens dark places, so some people assume it may have energy clearing properties too. We have yet to find any evidence of this because, like aromas, as soon as a light is turned off, the space returns to how it was before.

The light purification methods covered in this chapter are:
- Shining a flashlight
- Using a salt lamp
- Burning a candle

Shining a flashlight

One method of energy clearing we have heard of involves shining a flashlight into the corners of a room to banish energies that may be lurking there. No skill and hardly any effort is required for this. You simply need to turn on a flashlight and wave it around.

We're sorry to say that whoever thought this up had no understanding of the nature of etheric and astral energies, or how energy clearing works. Shining a light into dark corners may be psychologically reassuring to young children, but it is not an energy clearing technique for adults. At best, it will reveal where there are cobwebs!

Even streaming bright sunlight into a room does not change much energetically. It can make a space feel warmer and look brighter for a while, but after the sunlight fades, it will return to how it felt before unless you also open the windows to let in fresh chi. That will help a bit.

Using a salt lamp

We are often asked about salt lamps. Many claims have been made about the miraculous health-giving properties they have, sometimes including the ability to change energies in rooms. In tests we have done, we have not found them to have any energy clearing properties. The best we can say is that if you happen to like the look of a salt lamp and want to use it as a decorative item in your home, fine. But in our experience, that's as far as the usefulness of these lamps goes.

Burning a candle

Some people claim that burning a candle in a room is all that's needed to do energy clearing.

It's true that lighting a candle can have a powerful effect. As we explain in Chapter 33, Step 16 of *Space Clearing, Volume 1*, this is because whenever you light a candle, it will always connect to unseen forces of some kind. It's the reason we use tealight candles in the flower offerings for Essential Space Clearing and Full Space Clearing. Their purpose, when lit, is to anchor spiritual forces to hold the space during the ceremony.

So yes, lighting a candle always has an effect. However, it will only last for as long as the candle is lit, and the nature of the effect will depend on what the person lighting it connects it to. This can sometimes raise the level of consciousness in a space, but it does not clear energies. As soon as the candle is blown out, the effect will dissipate.

29

Negative energy absorbers, repellers, and banishers

You may have noticed there are no references in any of our books to negative energies. It's a loose description used by people to describe anything unseen that makes them feel uncomfortable. One of the main reasons we included such a substantial section about energies in buildings in *Space Clearing, Volume 1* is to give everyone a better understanding of the different types, in order to avoid such generalizations.

The two main types of so-called negative energy absorbers, repellers, or banishers are:
- Crystals
- Salt

Crystals

It's claimed that if you put a few pieces of crystals such as selenite, black tourmaline, or black obsidian around your home, they will magically absorb, repel, or banish negative energies from the space.

Karen worked with crystals for a number of years in the late 1970s and found that some do have healing properties that can be used when doing bodywork on people. The person using the crystals needs to have done a lot of personal work to awaken their etheric and know how to direct force through the crystals. They also need to have a lot of knowledge and experience of which type of crystal to use for which type of ailment and which part of the body to apply it to. Even then, the results are so hit and miss that Karen donated her entire crystal collection to a charity shop long ago.

There's also the issue that crystals mostly come from parts of the world where slave labour or child labour is rife. The backbreaking work of mining them also does terrible, long-lasting damage to the health of the workers, the environment, and wildlife. Ethical mining is extremely rare and, in most cases, unprofitable.

We therefore don't recommend the use of crystals for any purpose, and especially not energy clearing. Our experience of placing crystals in rooms is that, no matter how big they are, how many of them there are, or how long you leave them there for, they do not revitalize stagnant energies or shatter astral imprints. They have no energy clearing effects at all.

Salt

One of the optional extras Karen included in her 1996 book about space clearing was to put sea salt in bowls in the corners of rooms for 24 hours. She stopped doing this herself a few years later when it became clear it wasn't necessary, and we never use salt now for energy clearing purposes.

We especially want to dispel the notion that it's a good idea for therapists to keep a bowl of salt permanently in their treatment area. The problem with this is that when salt becomes energetically saturated, it pulls the energy of a space down rather than raising it. We've seen therapy rooms where the bowl of salt hasn't been changed for a year or more. The effect is nauseating.

Salt, if used for purification purposes, must be changed every day. But why bother? It's effect is negligible and only in the immediate area where it is placed. It's far better to do a regular space clearing ceremony to keep the entire space energetically clear.

30

Dowsing

Dowsing is a method of locating areas of geopathic stress and underground water streams using L-shaped metal rods. Images of people doing this have been found in the art of ancient Egypt and ancient China, as far back as 2200 BC. Other methods include dowsing with Y-shaped wooden sticks and pendulums, although we find these to be less reliable, so we never use them ourselves.

Dowsing is an invaluable skill for finding healthy locations to place beds, desks, and other key items of furniture in a home. It's also essential for meditation, to be able to find a place to sit that is not on toxic earth lines or above energetically disruptive underground water streams.

To become a proficient dowser requires the development of what is known as "eye-belly" awareness, meaning simultaneous awareness in the third eye and the energy centre of the belly. The best dowsers are those who also have well-developed structure in their column below. One of the most proficient dowsers Richard ever trained was a personal friend who was an ex-Royal Marines Commando. Those guys have serious dragon know-how!

Dowsing can also be used to find water. In 2017, 10 out of the 12 major water companies in the UK admitted to sometimes using the technique to find water pipes because it's inexpensive and usually accurate.

Some of their engineers keep dowsing rods in their vans in case they are needed. We've used it very successfully for this purpose too, to find where to dig a well in the grounds of the hotel and conference centre we used to own in Bali, which was located in a very arid region of the island.

Unfortunately, it's very difficult to find accurate dowsers these days because the techniques have become muddled with New Age practices. Distant dowsing is the worst of all, and we strongly advise against it. We've received many requests for help from people who have hired a dowser of this type and found the results unsatisfactory. When visiting the property in person, we've discovered some appalling mistakes. People have sometimes been told to move their bed from a spot that was perfectly safe to one that puts them right over a geopathic stress crossing point, which quickly causes their health to go downhill. Or they have been sold an expensive gadget that is supposed to neutralize geopathic stress but doesn't.

Some dowsers have ventured into the arena of energy clearing and claim to be able to clear unwanted energies in buildings simply by asking for it to be so. One leading teacher of this method confidently told Karen that all he needed to do for the energies in a place to change was to be there. A few years later, he changed this to only needing to look at a floor plan of a place for it to be cleared. He didn't even have the inconvenience of needing to leave his armchair.

Of course, when you ask these people how this works, they don't know. They say it just happens. They also don't have the ability to hand sense the energies of a property before an energy clearing or check them again after a clearing, as we and the professional space clearers we train always do, so they don't know for sure if anything has changed. It all rests on their own beliefs and the trust their clients place in them, which in many cases can be the helpless being led by the clueless. We've been called in to space clear homes that have supposedly been cleared using this method and found no evidence at all that they have been.

Another way we've heard of dowsing being used is for the practitioner to dowse with a pendulum or other dowsing aid to discover what combination of energy clearing techniques needs to be used in a particular situation. Leaving aside the fact that space clearing techniques need to be done in a specific order to be effective, as we explain in Chapter 3 of *Space Clearing, Volume 1*, it's anybody's guess where this information is coming from. They may sincerely believe this enables them to connect to a wisdom-dispensing force of some kind, but if asked, they don't know what this is. It could just as easily be their own imagination or random thoughts.

The best dowsers are the old-school type who will visit your property in person and use L-rods to determine the best locations for beds, desks, sofas, and other key areas where you spend the most time. They will never offer to use dowsing to do energy clearing because they know that's not what it is for.

31

Reiki

Karen took a reputable Reiki training many years ago and experienced a flaring of energy in the chakras of the palms of her hands for a few days. Intrigued by this, she asked the teacher to initiate her cat into Reiki Level 1, which she did. For a few days after that, whenever the cat sat in Karen's lap, she could feel his paws fizzing too.

The reason Reiki initiation works with most people, no matter what their level of consciousness or even if they are a cat, is because no personal development is needed. Learning Reiki, up to and including the level of becoming a Reiki "master", depends on whether you can afford to pay to receive the transmission link to the astral being behind your chosen school of Reiki, which will operate healings through you, at least for a time. Some therapists keep it and others lose it.

The problem with this is that Reiki practitioners have no idea what they are doing. The methods are prepersonal*, so they simply place their hands on the client in the way they have been taught and let the Reiki being do the rest. They can be thinking about their last meal or what movie they plan to watch and it will still work.

This frequently results in the practitioner soaking up energies from clients. They do not perceive these energies or know how to clear them, so it can cause them to have health issues, gain weight, or unwittingly pass the energies on to other clients.

Some enterprising Reiki teachers have developed techniques they say can be used to clear the energies of rooms. This involves drawing invisible symbols in the air with a finger or sometimes an incense stick, usually in the corners and centre of a room. To learn how to do this requires another expensive training.

Does it work? Owning the corners of any room gives a feeling of greater ownership of a space, which makes it feel like something has changed. But Karen has been in many rooms where Reiki energy clearing has been done and it hasn't changed the stagnant energies or astral imprints at all.

32

Guardian spirits

It's a lovely notion that every house has a guardian spirit you can call on to maintain the energy of the home, so we want to include some information about this here.

Guardian spirit shrines in Bali

Karen first came across the concept of guardian spirits during the 20 years she lived in Bali. Each family compound has a roofed shrine called a *sanggah pengijeng*, which translates into English as "the shrine of the guardian". It is placed close to the centre of a family compound and is always the first structure to be erected when building work begins. At specific stages it is upgraded from bamboo to wood and then to the final structure, which is usually made of ornately carved concrete or stone.

The function of this shrine is to give a resting place to the land energies that are displaced by the disruption of the construction process. Balinese builders see it as their sacred duty to place flower offerings on this shrine every day. After the building work is complete, the shrine is then consecrated by a priest during an elaborate Balinese Hindu house consecration ceremony called *mlaspas*, and the house occupants continue to place offerings on the shrine every day forever after. The purpose is to maintain a harmonious relationship with the land energies of the property.

Guardian spirits

Karen had the opportunity to hand sense thousands of these guardian spirit shrines in Bali and found that each one, to a greater or lesser degree, hosted unseen energies of some kind. The energies are more amorphous than the spiritual presences that reside in the family temple shrines, which connect to the powerful network of temples in Bali, but they are tangible nevertheless.

Offerings are placed every day on every guardian spirit shrine in every family compound of the island. They are also placed in the family temple, on a shrine called the *palinggih taksu* (the shrine for god-given talents), and on smaller shrines called *plankiran*, located inside the home and in other locations around the property. Together they form a weave that holds the spiritual integrity of the family home in place.

Balinese people live with as much awareness of the unseen worlds as the seen worlds because they can feel the energies. People we met were fascinated to discover that we could feel this too and delighted that we took care to place offerings each day on all the shrines in our home, hotel, and conference centre.

This was Karen's daily practice at the time she wrote her first book, *Creating Sacred Space with Feng Shui*, so she included information in that book about guardian spirits and implied that every home has one.

It's turned out that this is one of several assumptions she made in that book that need to be corrected here. It's very clear to her now that homes don't have a guardian spirit at all, not even in Bali. The *sanggah pengijeng* shrine in each Balinese family compound is an anchorage for displaced land energies, *not* for some kind of benevolent being that looks after the home and the people who live in it. The perceived guardianship aspect comes from the belief that placing daily offerings on the shrine helps to maintain balance and harmony between the occupants of the family home and the land it is built on.

The consecration ceremony performed by a Balinese priest before a building can be inhabited is designed to weave specific spiritual forces into the structure of the building. In most of the world, people live in dead houses with no spiritual presencing of any kind and certainly no guardian spirit.

So why do some people feel they have a guardian spirit in their home?

Some people tell us they are sure their home has a guardian spirit. In most cases, what they are feeling is a natural resonance with the land energies of the place, which feels nurturing and supportive. This is perfectly well and good. Life always works better when you live in a place where you have an affinity with the land energies and feel nurtured by them.

Some people also feel affection for their home and vaguely talk to it in the same way that they might talk to a car or other inanimate objects. Providing there is no personification of the house or expectation of a reply, this is fine too.

We have heard of New Age practitioners who believe you can talk to your home and it *will* reply. We even know of one who claims to be able to dialogue with a home on behalf of a client to get its advice about what the person needs to do in their life, as if the house were some sort of oracle. We consider this to be a very misguided and risky practice. At best, the practitioner is imagining the entire dialogue. At worst, they are tuning into astral forces that hijack human consciousness for their own agendas. Either way, the method has no integrity and should not be trusted.

Guardian spirits

We have hand sensed and read the energies of thousands of homes around the world and never once found a guardian spirit in residence in any of them. It simply does not happen by default that every home has one, as some people fondly imagine or would like to believe to be the case.

This is actually a good thing. If every home had a guardian spirit, it would need to be energetically maintained. Who would conduct the rituals if you go travelling? Who would take care of it if you move house? What would become of it after you die? Once begun, these rituals must be continued, as has been done for centuries in Bali. Otherwise, it creates an energetic void that anything can come to fill.

How this relates to space clearing

What's different about the space clearing ceremony we have developed is that it's designed for our modern lifestyle, to clear and revitalize energies in buildings. It's very different to the shrine system that is used in Bali because it doesn't create an anchorage that has to be maintained.

The effects of a space clearing ceremony last longer if Basic Space Clearing is done between Essential or Full Space Clearing ceremonies, but daily purification rituals are not required. This is just as well because most people's lives are far too busy to take on such a responsibility.

PART FOUR

Personal uses of space clearing

33

The main personal uses of space clearing

In this part of the book, we will be exploring the many personal uses of space clearing, together with a recommended altar design for each type if you decide to do a Full Space Clearing ceremony.

To refresh your memory, the 12 main altar designs are:
- Single Focus
- Dual Focus
- The Accelerator
- Establishing Foundations
- Establishing Levels
- Crossroads
- Incarnation
- The Facilitator
- New Beginnings
- All Possibilities
- The Stabilizer
- Spiritual Aspirations

You can find detailed descriptions of how to create each of these altar designs in Chapter 33, Step 14 of *Space Clearing, Volume 1*.

The main personal uses of space clearing

The personal uses of space clearing covered in this part of the book are:

Home
- To facilitate clutter clearing
- To clear energies in objects
- When moving home
- Guest rooms
- When doing home improvements

Relationships
- Finding a new relationship
- Starting a new relationship in a new home
- Starting a new relationship in a home that one partner is already living in
- Revitalizing an existing relationship
- Harmonizing a fraught relationship
- Taking a relationship to a deeper level
- Getting clarity about whether to continue a relationship or end it
- After a divorce or break-up

Health
- During an illness
- After an illness
- To help lift depression
- To improve vitality

Special times of the year
- Springtime
- New year
- A birthday or solar return
- Other anniversaries

Major life events

- Marriage
- Pregnancy
- Birth
- Death
- Other major life events

After a disruptive experience

- After an argument
- After a burglary
- After an accident in the home
- After a party
- After a traumatic local or world event

When travelling

- Staying as a guest in someone's home
- Staying as a guest in a hotel
- Bed thwacking
- Other travel tips

To support personal development

- When you feel stuck
- To clarify a new direction in life
- To help overcome procrastination
- To deal with recurring problems or behaviours
- To promote prosperity
- To open new possibilities

Spiritual purposes

- To support you in your spiritual path
- To create and maintain a meditation space
- After a life-changing workshop, meditation retreat, or similar event

34

Space clearing to facilitate clutter clearing

Space clearing works best if you declutter, clean, tidy, and organize your home first. There's no doubt about that.

If you find it difficult to get started with clearing your clutter or are unable to complete it, you may like to know that it's possible to do space clearing first. This will have the effect of revitalizing the stagnant energies that accumulate around clutter and make it easier to clear it.

Of course, there has to be enough space for you to be able to walk around the inner perimeter of each room you space clear. It won't work, for example, to stand in the doorway of a junk room clapping and ringing bells. You will need to do some clutter clearing first, or at least move some items out of the way so you can walk around it.

It will also involve extra work because you'll need to do space clearing twice instead of once. The focus of the first ceremony will need to be on decluttering, and the focus of the second ceremony will be on what you aspire to in your life after you are no longer burdened by clutter. This is yet another example of how clutter makes everything in life harder work. But at least you will be moving forward, and that's what counts.

To help you get started with clutter clearing, the easiest version of the ceremony to do is Basic Space Clearing. There is no altar to set up. The only equipment you'll need is a space clearing bell and a harmony ball. And, if necessary, the ceremony can be done room by room, according to which area you are decluttering.

If you have already done a fair amount of clutter clearing but the process has stalled and you want to get it moving again, an Essential Space Clearing for your entire home will work even better.

Schedule the space clearing for the early part of the day so that you can immediately start clutter clearing after the ceremony, if you feel inspired to do so (many people do).

Choose a small, clearly defined area to begin with that does not contain any items you have an emotional attachment to. A drawer or shelf that will take you no more than 20 minutes to declutter, clean, and reorganize will work best, so you can easily achieve a clutter clearing success.

Other tried-and-tested techniques for clutter clearing can be learned from our books and online courses, and if you need more personalized help, you can book a session with Richard or one of our certified practitioners.

Recommended altar design

The Accelerator. For best results, use a red altar cloth, or a white altar cloth with a red colourizer in the central vertical axis position.

35

Space clearing to clear energies in objects

Space clearing techniques can be adapted to clear energies from specific objects you own. This can be especially useful for any second-hand things you acquire that may have a dubious history.

All objects become energetically imprinted by what happens around them. This is why the personal belongings of celebrities are so sought after. It's an attempt by people to capture a part of that person by owning an item that has been imprinted with their energy. It's also why some people like to keep objects that once belonged to someone they knew, and why children form such strong attachments to teddy bears and other items that they cuddle and pour their love into.

Brand-new factory-made items, where no human handling has been involved, will have no astral imprinting. Manufactured items that involve some human handling may have slight imprinting. Handcrafted items or pieces of art the creator had emotional involvement with will have considerably more imprinting. Second-hand items, and especially antiques, may be heavily imprinted.

You can save a lot of money buying second-hand things instead of new, and it's better for the environment too. The problem is that they are likely to carry the astral imprints of the previous owner and the experiences they went through. If an item was used a lot, used for a long time, or had very strong emotional connections for that person, the imprints will be correspondingly stronger. Unless you are skilled at hand sensing, you will have no idea what kind of imprints an item is embedded with or how this will affect you.

Space clearing your home will space clear all the objects in it too, but deeply imprinted or second-hand items may need a deeper level of clearing.

How to clear energy imprints in furniture

Equipment you will need
- Cleaning materials, suitable for the item
- A Balinese space clearing bell

Step 1: Roll your sleeves up above your elbows and clean the item to remove any physical grime and etheric debris**. Plain water is best unless it has a special finish that needs a particular type of cleaning product because water may damage it.

Step 2: Wash and dry your hands on a clean towel, paper towel, or tissues.

Step 3: Keeping your sleeves rolled up, clap all around the item to break up any stagnant energies surrounding it. If it has compartments, open them up and clap inside. If it has shelves, clap out each shelf. Gentle or muffled clapping won't work. The sound needs to be loud and sharp. If your skin is dry, a layer of hand cream may help you to create a stronger-sounding clap.

For soft items of furniture such as beds, sofas, and chairs that have padding, you can also use the bed thwacking technique described in Chapter 44, taking care not to accidentally damage any structural parts as you do this.

Step 4: Wash your hands again and dry them on a clean towel, paper towel, or tissues.

Step 5: Ring a Balinese space clearing bell around the item and above it, consciously directing the sound deeply into it. Don't be timid. Ring the bell loudly and strongly. Shattering astral imprints involves an engagement of will. The depth of clearing that can be achieved will depend on the level of oomph you can put into it.

Antique furniture is the most difficult to clear because its age usually means it's the most deeply imprinted. But it can be done, and it's well worth developing the skill to do this if you want to bring any second-hand things into your home.

While it's lovely to buy new things, when it comes to furniture or anything that outgasses, it's a curious fact that these days second-hand is often healthier. That's because modern furniture is usually made of materials such as wood laminates, particle board, plywood, treated upholstery fabrics, and foams, which can take several years to finish outgassing toxins such as formaldehyde. During that time, you'll be breathing in the fumes to some extent, depending on how well ventilated your home is. If you buy second-hand furniture, it's more likely to have finished outgassing by the time you get it.

How to clear energy imprints in small items and jewellery

Small household items

You can use the same technique we've described for clearing energies in furniture.

Clothing and other washable items

No special techniques are required to remove energy imprints from clothing or other washable items. Good old-fashioned laundering (not dry cleaning) is all that's needed. It will remove all imprints immediately.

Jewellery

Jewellery that has been worn for many years by someone will be more deeply imprinted than general household items, so it will need a deeper level of clearing.

The most effective method we know for this, apart from melting metal jewellery down and reforging it, is to use the space clearing water ritual to clear any energy imprints. Place the item in your space clearing water pot, fill the pot with still spring water, then follow the instructions for making space clearing water described in Chapter 33, Step 15 of *Space Clearing, Volume 1*. Leave the item in the water for about three minutes, then take it out and dry it on a clean towel, paper towel, or tissues.

Don't use the water to space clear your home too. Throw it away and make a fresh batch if you decide to do that.

36

Space clearing when moving home

One of the main reasons moving home can feel like such an upheaval is because we rest parts of our consciousness on the physical structure of the building we live in, all the items in it, and the energies of the land the property is built on. Uprooting yourself to move to another place can therefore feel like an enormous wrench.

Fortunately, there are several aspects of moving home that space clearing can help with to ease the whole process:

- Getting clarity about whether to stay or move
- Selling your home
- Finding a new home
- Leaving an old home
- Moving into a new home
- Clutter clearing when moving home

Getting clarity about whether to stay or move

Many people spend their lives working in a job they don't like, and that is sad enough. But few people even consider the effect of living in a place where they feel no real affinity with the land energies. It can hold you back more than you can imagine until you move to a place that is a better fit for you and can feel the difference this makes.

Deep down, most people *do* have a sense of whether they have found their place on earth. A space clearing ceremony can bring more awareness of this to the surface, which can be very helpful when making a decision about whether to stay or move.

Recommended altar design

All possibilities

Selling your home

When selling your home, you want to make it as attractive as possible to potential buyers. That's why it's essential to declutter it, tidy it, organize it, clean it, and repair or redecorate any parts that need attention. Removing personal items such as photos of yourself or your family can also help because it will allow potential buyers to more easily imagine themselves living there.

More effective still is a space clearing ceremony to remove your own energies and, if you've never space cleared the place before, the energies of previous occupants too. Many people can feel when a property is heavily imprinted, even if they are not able to explain it in those words. Space clearing will refresh and revitalize the space to make it feel more inviting.

We've received many messages from people telling us how quickly they have been able to sell their home after space clearing it. We certainly recommend it, although it's not a magical fix. There can be multiple reasons why a property takes time to sell. This can include factors such as a depressed property market when everyone is struggling to sell, a glut of properties being sold at the same time, or government legislation that makes it a difficult time to sell. It may also be that a property is being advertised at an unrealistic price, is in an undesirable location, is in poor condition, has strange décor choices, is too cluttered, and so on.

Your own attitude to selling and moving can be a major factor too. We've met people who have put their home up for sale without giving any thought to where they will go. Or they have so much clutter they dread moving because they know they will have to deal with it first. Some people are so sentimentally attached to their home they don't really want to sell it, even though finances or other factors dictate that they must. These and other types of issues can cause a home to remain unsold. Space clearing can help to highlight the problems and make it easier to work through the emotions that are holding you back.

If you feel you will miss your old home, a helpful tip is to find something you are really looking forward to after you move and focus more on that than on what you are leaving behind. It will make the transition much easier.

Recommended altar designs

If you are genuinely ready for a fresh start: New Beginnings
If there are obstacles that you need to overcome first: The Accelerator

Finding a new home

If you want to move but haven't been able to do so, it may be that you first have to complete your relationship with your current home. We're not suggesting you invest in expensive renovations that the next owner or occupier may not even like or appreciate. It's more about hanging pictures you've always meant to hang, making small repairs to things that have always niggled you, and generally owning the space and making it feel like your home. In other words, in order to leave, you first have to fully arrive.

In any case, putting these finishing touches to your home will help you to get more clarity about the new home you hope to find, and it will either speed up the process or make your current home a more enjoyable place to live if you change your mind and decide to stay.

Recommended altar design

The Accelerator

Leaving an old home

After you learn how to do space clearing, it's karmically responsible behaviour to physically clean and energetically clear the home you are moving out of, to leave a beautiful, clear space for the next occupants.

But let's face it. Unless you travel very light and moving home is no trouble at all, space clearing your old home probably won't be very high on your list of priorities on moving day, and there may not be time to do it anyway. The best time to space clear is much earlier, as soon as you're sure you want to move and long before you start packing.

If you own your home and need to sell it, this will usually help with the sale too. By starting to withdraw your own energies from the space, you will be energetically letting it go, which will allow prospective buyers to more easily feel what it will be like to live there themselves.

Whether you own or rent, the best focus for the ceremony will be making a smooth, easy transition to your new home while leaving a clear space in your old home for the next occupants. Instead of creating an altar that is personalized to you and anyone you share your home with, create one to welcome the new occupants. And during the harmony ball stage of the ceremony, instead of infusing frequencies into the space that will be helpful to you personally, focus on creating a high-level neutral space for the benefit of the next occupants too.

How to say goodbye to a home you are leaving

Loss takes many forms. Leading experts John W. James and Russell Friedman of the Grief Recovery Institute have identified over 40 life events that can cause feelings of loss, the most notable being the death of a spouse, a family member, or a pet.

What many people don't realize is that it's also possible to grieve for a home you once lived in. It can be as important to complete your relationships with places as it is to complete your relationships with people.

The two methods described here will give you a lovely feeling of completion when leaving an old home. Make this the last thing you do when leaving a place that has been your home for a while, after you have taken all your personal belongings out of the property and done any cleaning you need to do. Both methods will work best if you have space cleared the entire home recently. Choose whichever version most resonates with you:

- The happy memories method
- The closure method

The happy memories method

Go into each room and say goodbye by patting the walls, doors, or other fixtures in the place. If your home has stairs, it can feel very satisfying to stroke the banisters because you will have touched them many times while you've been living there.

If you're not a particularly tactile person, walk around your home and simply take one last look. Let any feelings come to the surface. It's better to cry a few tears at this time than to ache for years with emotions bottled up inside.

The closure method

This is the method we use ourselves whenever we move home.

1. Check that all the external doors to the property are closed.

2. Roll up your sleeves.

3. Wash your face and hands and dry them on a clean towel, paper towel, or tissues.

4. Go to the main entrance and position yourself as if you're going to do a circuit of hand sensing. Stand sideways to the door with the palm of your hand extended at heart level and your fingers pointing vertically upward. The ideal position is 3–5 cm (approximately 1–2 inches) from the door.

5. Keeping your hand free of tension, walk around the inside perimeter of your home with your hand at heart level and about 3–5 cm (1–2 inches) from the walls. Take exactly the same route you would take for a hand-sensing circuit.

6. Use your free hand to open and close doors as necessary, keeping it at your side the rest of the time, held in a loosely closed fist. This helps to accentuate what you will be doing with your active hand.

7. As you go around the inner perimeter, keep your head and spine vertical, engage throat friction*, and position your consciousness in your verticality above your head (in the central thread* of your column above*). Connect your active hand to your verticality and, instead of sensing energies in the walls, operate a closure of the space from your verticality, actively withdrawing the higher levels of your own energies from the space from there. Don't let your mind or emotions become involved in any way. To be effective, this has to be done entirely from above the head.

8. When you arrive back at the main entrance, take a deep breath in through your nose. On the out-breath, seal the circuit with a

stroking movement of the palm of your hand in the centre of the door where you started the circuit, splicing the energies into the etheric layer. (If you need to refresh your memory about how to do splicing, you can find a description in Chapter 22, Step 12 of *Space Clearing, Volume 1*.)

Recommended altar design

New Beginnings

Moving into a new home

One of the most important uses of space clearing is to clear out the energies of previous occupants. Unless you do this, your home will never truly be your space. There will always be residual energies from the past affecting everything you do there.

The best time to space clear

It's ideal to do space clearing before you move into a new home and again after you've moved in and unpacked, to fully land yourself in the space.

It's a lot quicker and easier to space clear an empty home than one that's full of stuff. It requires less hand sensing, less clapping, less belling, and so on. However, it's usually not possible to get access to a new home before you move in, so the first opportunity to do space clearing will usually be after you have moved in. That has some benefits too, because it means all your furniture and personal belongings will get space cleared at the same time.

How soon after moving in is it best to do space clearing?

Unless you can afford the luxury of hiring a moving company to pack and unpack everything for you, space clearing may need to be done in stages.

The first night

You're likely to be tired after moving home, so the best you may be able to do on the first night is to space clear your bedroom, so at least the area you sleep in will feel good. Keep your Balinese space clearing bell and a harmony ball with you during the move instead of packing them with your other things so you'll be able to find them quickly and easily.

After you have fully unpacked and settled in

Do a Full Space Clearing ceremony when you reach the point where you have fully unpacked and your new home is pretty much how you want it to be. This will help you and anyone who lives with you to fully land and take ownership of the space.

If it will take you some time to fully unpack and settle in

It can sometimes be chaotic after moving home. You may have workers coming in and out, fixing this and that. You may need to redecorate, have new carpets laid, or buy new furniture. It may take a while to simply decide where each item you own belongs in your new home.

When this has all been done and everything calms down, it will feel very different to when you first moved in, and you'll be different too. When your home is in chaos, parts of you will be in chaos. This is why it's important not to let this process drag on for years, as some people do. Weeks, okay. Months, understandable in some circumstances. Years? Life's too short to live in limbo for so long.

If it looks like it will take you a while to unpack and settle in, and especially if you embark on doing renovations that will take some time, we recommend doing Basic Space Clearing as soon as you can. It won't be as effective as doing an Essential or Full Space Clearing ceremony, but it will clear out the stagnant energies, which will make the moving-in process easier and will help the renovations to proceed smoothly. Do a deeper level of space clearing when all the renovations have been completed.

Moving into a brand-new home that has never been lived in before

You might think space clearing isn't necessary in this situation, but it usually is. It can make a huge difference to clear out any energies left by the builders and harmonize the space after the disruption of all the building work. It will also help you to fully land in the space so that it starts to feel more like home. Without space clearing, it can take much longer for this to happen.

This type of space clearing is usually reasonably easy to do. Put extra emphasis on the harmony ball circuit, where you put your own frequencies into the space.

Recommended altar design
New Beginnings or Incarnation

Moving into a new home that has been unoccupied for some time

If a property has been left vacant for a while, the air in it will have become stale and the energies will have stagnated. Space clearing can revitalize the space to make it feel much more welcoming and homely. If the property has physically deteriorated during the time it has been unoccupied, it will work best to do the repairs and cleaning first.

Recommended altar design
New Beginnings

Moving into a new home that has had previous occupants

If the previous occupants of your new home had a wonderfully happy, healthy, and prosperous life there, this increases the chances you will have a similar experience. In that situation, the main purpose of space clearing will be to forge an energetic relationship with the space to make it quickly feel like home. You can do this to some extent through decorating and furnishing it to your taste. Space clearing will help you to go much deeper.

If the previous occupants of your new home had failed relationships, health problems, financial difficulties, or any of the many other challenges that can afflict people, those energies will be imprinted in the walls, floors, ceilings, and any items they have left in the place. After you've lived there for a while and become immersed in those frequencies, it's likely you'll start to experience similar issues yourself without knowing why. Space clearing is therefore essential.

One word of caution. If you move into a home where traumatic events have taken place, such as a suicide, murder, or prolonged sexual abuse, we don't advise you to attempt to do space clearing yourself. The information in our books is not designed for that. Similarly, if you feel any fear or apprehension about doing space clearing yourself, this is usually a sign you are not equipped to handle whatever energies have been embedded in the place by previous occupants. We advise getting professional help.

Recommended altar design
New Beginnings

Clutter clearing when moving home

The longer you have lived in a place and the more nested in you are, the more clutter you are likely to have accumulated and the more challenging and time-consuming sorting through it can be.

For some people, decluttering before moving can involve thousands of decisions about what to keep, what to let go, and how to let it go. So, from the moment you know you are moving, start preparing by doing some decluttering every day. Go through everything you own, room by room, and discard anything you know you won't be taking with you. Start making plans to sell it, give it away, or dispose of it in some other way.

Get yourself to the stage where there are no more decisions to be made. When the time comes to pack, all you'll need to do is open your drawers and cupboards, take everything out, put it in boxes, and go.

When you get to your new home, unpack as quickly as you can so you can fully arrive and begin your new life there. Decide where each item you own belongs and put it there.

If you find yourself with boxes of things that have no home, you will either need to acquire some furniture to store them in or accept that these items are clutter and let them go. The same goes for pictures or mirrors that never get hung and anything else that turns out to be unneeded. No matter how much clutter clearing you do in your old home, you are likely to find there is more that needs to be done when you unpack in your new home.

If you find it difficult to get started with clutter clearing, here are some suggestions:

- Reread Chapter 34 of this book about space clearing to facilitate clutter clearing
- Read Chapter 29 of *Space Clearing, Volume 1* about clutter clearing
- Read our book *How to Clear Your Clutter*
- Read Karen's book *Clear Your Clutter with Feng Shui*
- Take one of our online clutter clearing courses
- Book a clutter clearing session with Richard or one of our certified practitioners

37

Space clearing guest rooms

It's all too easy for a guest room to become a dumping ground for things you no longer need or use but don't yet feel ready to let go of. You stash them away, believing that out of sight is out of mind.

The prospect of people arriving to stay can be a great motivation to clear out any clutter of this type that has crept into a guest room, followed by a space clearing to clear and revitalize the energies of the room.

Before your guests arrive

Space clearing your home before guests arrive to stay is a wonderful way to make them feel more welcome. If you have already done an Essential or Full Space Clearing within the past year, all that will be needed is an Essential Space Clearing just for your guest room if it has been used a lot, or a Basic Space Clearing to freshen the energy if it has not been used at all. It won't take long to do and can make a huge difference to how it feels.

Doing space clearing has the effect of setting the space of a room at a higher level, which will make it more likely you can have meaningful interactions with your guests. This can greatly improve how much you and they enjoy their stay.

Recommended altar design

The Facilitator

After your guests leave

Hopefully you won't have the type of guests who leave your home feeling like it needs a good space clearing to clear their energies out after they leave. But if this does happen, you now have the skills to do something about it.

If the only room affected is the bedroom the guest(s) slept in, just do a Basic Space Clearing in that room. If a large part of your home has been affected, an Essential or Full Space Clearing ceremony for the entire property will be needed.

Recommended altar design

New Beginnings

38

Space clearing when doing home improvements

Home improvements can really wear you down. It's not just the noise and dust, or the intrusion of having builders in the space. Even if you do the work yourself, doing home improvements can be very destabilizing, especially if substantial structural changes are involved.

The reason for this is that you are energetically connected to your home, and the longer you have lived there, the more connected you are likely to be. You may think you are simply making changes at a physical level, but the disruption it causes in your life goes far deeper than that. When a part of your home is being repaired or deconstructed and rebuilt, a corresponding part of you is being changed too.

Remodelling a kitchen is usually the most challenging of all because it involves ripping out and replacing the heart of nourishment of your home. Adding an extension is usually less disruptive because you will still have your kitchen and most of your living areas intact. Garden landscaping is generally the least intrusive, although this will depend on how connected you are to your garden, how much time you generally spend there, and how noisy the project is.

It can feel like your life is in limbo until the home improvements are finished, waiting for the parts of yourself and your life to come back together. It can make you feel scattered, exposed, and vulnerable while the work is in progress.

During the years we lived in Bali, we were delighted to discover that builders are very aware of these effects and take steps to alleviate them. They view any wood used in building construction, for example, as having been killed when the tree was cut down, and steel as having been killed when the iron ore and other materials it's composed of were mined. No Balinese person wants to live in a "dead" house, so they have devised highly effective consecration rituals to presence and bring the materials they are made of "back to life", as they put it. Before doing major repairs or remodelling, a special ritual is done by a priest to extract the spiritual presencing from that part of the building and move it to a temporary shrine. Then after the building work is complete, another ritual is performed to restore it. They liken this to the way a human is given anaesthesia before surgery to numb them to the pain.

We have personally experienced this ritual on a number of occasions in properties we owned in Bali, and it is by no means empty or symbolic. It has the very tangible effect of isolating the part of the building that is being worked on and minimizing the disturbance to the occupants. When asked about it, Balinese builders consider this to be such an obvious thing to do that they regard it as plain common sense.

How to minimize the turmoil of renovations or remodelling

Builders in other parts of the world generally do not have much awareness of energies. So, what can you do to minimize the turmoil if you decide to renovate or remodel your home?

It's ideal if you can have the work done before you move in. You will have no energetic connection to the property at that stage and can continue to live a normal life elsewhere.

The next best option is to hire a caravan, park it in the garden, and live in that rather than in the house.

If that's not possible, find a room or area in the property where you can create a personal sanctuary. Space clear it, then keep the doors closed as much as possible to keep dust levels down and create as much of a home environment in that area as you can. At the end of the project, space clear the entire property to connect it all back together.

Do the renovations or remodelling as soon as you can after moving into a home, while the motivation to do it is still fresh. Aim to complete the work within the first 6 to 12 months, if possible, then space clear it so you can fully land. We've met people who still have half-finished rooms a decade or two after moving in and, not surprisingly, their life feels similarly in limbo.

Another good tip is that if you have a number of projects to do, fully complete one and have a short break before beginning the next. This will give you welcome periods of sanity, which will allow you to rest and regather before the next onslaught.

If you hire professionals to do the work, it will be a lot easier to handle the whole process if you can find builders who are courteous and respectful, who you genuinely like and enjoy having in your space. Be sure to keep that in mind when hiring.

Home improvements before you move in

A little-understood reason why these types of projects can get very snarled up is what builders sometimes have to deal with when they tear a place apart to do improvements. It's not just dust that comes out of the walls. All the energies that have been imprinted over years will be released too, which can cause havoc in a space.

Some builders have a strong etheric and are able to deal with this. Others get overwhelmed, and that's where things start to go wrong. They may get sick or agitated, have accidents, or make mistakes, all of which can hinder the project and lead to unexpected delays and expense.

Our advice when this happens is to halt the building work, give everyone the day off, and space clear. Or better still, space clear before the renovation project begins, which is also much easier to do because you won't have to pick your way through builders' rubble. It's also wise to space clear again after all the building work has been completed to settle the energies of the space.

This topic brings to mind a property we once visited when we were house-hunting in the UK. The building had lovely high ceilings, plenty of space, and beautiful mature gardens. But the interior was very neglected, piled high with clutter, and desperately in need of space clearing. It had been used as a care home for the elderly for many years and was heavily imprinted with sickness and depression. And the energies weren't just in the walls. There were also perverse energies* floating in the space, which stuck to us as we walked around. This is called getting pancaked*, because it feels like the energetic equivalent of sticky pancakes landing on you.

We felt very sorry for the elderly residents who had lived there, but as professional space clearers we're used to sometimes dealing with grungy environments when we do consultations, so we have techniques we can use in such situations. It didn't take us long to clean ourselves up after our visit and feel fine again.

We couldn't help but wonder how the new owner of the property would cope. And what about the builders who would do the renovations? As well as having to deal with the energies imprinted in the walls, they would emerge at the end of each day covered in energetic pancakes, with no idea why they felt so bad or what to do about it. Many building projects are fraught with problems that get blamed on the ineptitude of the builders when the real source of the problems may be the energies they are having to deal with that they are not equipped to handle.

We don't advise attempting to space clear a heavily imprinted and pancaked house like this yourself. The information in our books is not designed to deal with that quantity or type of energies. It's a job for a professional space clearer, who will be able to take it in their stride. It's also best done by someone who is a trained entity clearer, since there are likely to have been a number of deaths in a property of this type. The most experienced practitioners we have trained are qualified to do both space clearing and entity clearing.

The good news is that most buildings *can* be energetically cleared. Owners of properties with this kind of history would benefit tremendously from having a Professional Space Clearing done before they put the house on the market. Otherwise, it can take years to sell.

Anyone planning to renovate or remodel such a place will also benefit from having it professionally space cleared before any building work is done. This small expense, relative to the cost of all the building work, can save months of hassles, aggravation, and frustration. We worked for many years with a UK-based property developer who knew what a difference this made, so she would always hire us to space clear each new property she acquired, before and after the renovations were done. It made sound business sense to her because she found that the building work proceeded more smoothly and the houses sold more quickly and for a higher price when finished.

Recommended altar design

Before renovations: The Accelerator
After renovations: New Beginnings

Home improvements after you've moved in

If you've lived in a property for a while and regularly space cleared it, an excellent way to minimize the effect of doing home improvements is to space clear before you begin and deliberately exclude the areas where changes will be made. This will have the effect of energetically separating your living space from the building areas. Then, after the renovations are complete, space clear the entire property to integrate those areas back into your home and reset the space at a higher level.

Recommended altar design

Before renovations: The Stabilizer
After renovations: New Beginnings

Repurposing a room or a building

When you change the purpose of a room, space clearing can be used to clear out the old energies and instill new frequencies that will be conducive to the new use. If you plan to redecorate, it will work best to do that before doing the space clearing.

Some examples of this are a junk room you have decluttered to make it into a study or bedroom, a garage you want to convert into a gym, or a bedroom that one child in your family is moving out of and another child is moving into.

If the entire home has recently been space cleared, there is no need to do a Full Space Clearing ceremony for this. A Basic or Essential Space Clearing ceremony just for the room that is being repurposed is all that's needed. Close the door to the room before you start the ceremony, and begin and end all the circuits at the door of the room, not the main entrance of the home.

More substantial changes of use, such as transforming a barn into a home or a home into business premises, are within the scope of the techniques described in *Space Clearing, Volume 1*. Heavily imprinted properties, such as buildings that have been used as hospitals, prison cells, and so on, will usually require Professional Space Clearing.

Recommended altar design
New Beginnings

39

Space clearing for relationships

Space clearing to improve relationships is one of the most frequent uses of space clearing, so we want to cover this topic in depth. The following aspects are covered in this chapter:

- Finding a new relationship
- Starting a new relationship in a new home
- Starting a new relationship in a home that one partner is already living in
- Revitalizing an existing relationship
- Harmonizing a fraught relationship
- Taking a relationship to a deeper level
- Getting clarity about whether to continue a relationship or end it
- After a divorce or break-up

Finding a new relationship

There are many complex factors involved in finding a new romantic relationship, so space clearing won't guarantee you will immediately attract a wonderful new partner into your life. It can substantially help, though, by clearing any residues in your home of previous relationships and setting the energy of the space to support you in finding a new one.

If you are planning to live with your new partner in your home or would like them to visit regularly and stay overnight, we also recommend proactively creating physical space for them, such as clearing out a

Space clearing for relationships

section of your wardrobe and some drawers for them to use. If your wardrobe is so stuffed full of clothes there is barely enough room for your own things, never mind someone else's belongings too, then some clutter clearing and reorganizing will be needed.

Recommended altar design

The altar design will be determined by the type of relationship you want and how quickly you want it. For example, if you want a passionate relationship and you're ready for it to happen soon, a good choice would be The Accelerator altar design with a triple-rippled pink colourizer in the central vertical axis position. If it's more important to you to find a relationship that brings stability to your life, choose The Stabilizer altar design and colourizers from the cooler end of the colour spectrum.

Starting a new relationship in a new home

An important use of space clearing is when you start a new relationship you feel has some serious mileage and you want to give it the best possible chance of success.

It's always best for a couple to live together in a home that neither person has ever lived in before so that each partner will have the same degree of energetic ownership of the space. Space clearing can be used in this situation to remove the stagnant energies and astral imprints of the previous occupants so that you can create a fresh new arena in which your relationship can flourish.

The best way to prepare for the ceremony is for each of you to get clarity about the relationship qualities you value the most. The best person to MC** the ceremony will usually be the one who has the most experience of space clearing. If neither of you have ever done space clearing before, the best person to MC will probably be whoever had the idea to do the ceremony.

Recommended altar design

New Beginnings

Starting a new relationship in a home that one partner is already living in

When one person has lived in a property for some time and a partner moves in to join them, the first occupant will always have more energetic ownership of the space and the second person to arrive will always be at a disadvantage because of this. It will be difficult for the second person to fully land themselves there because the home will not truly feel theirs.

This effect can be exacerbated if the first occupant had a partner who lived there and has now moved out. The longer they lived together, the more their relationship will be imprinted in the place, and the more likely it will be that a new relationship will go the same way as the old one.

However desirable it may be to start a new relationship in a new home, practicalities can often mean that this may not be possible for a while, or sometimes not possible at all. In this situation, space clearing is essential to clear out the history of the space.

It's ideal for the space clearing to be done first by the partner who has lived there for a while, to create a welcoming space for the person moving in. Then later, after they have unpacked and organized their belongings, the partner who has moved in can do another space clearing, which will help them to take more energetic ownership of the space.

Mattresses can become very heavily imprinted, so a new mattress is ideal. If that's not possible, the next best thing is to do bed thwacking (see Chapter 44).

These actions won't make the home the perfect place for a couple to live in forever. Space clearing can't change the visual and territorial associations of the partner who lived there first. But it can remove the imprints from the past, which will help a lot, so it's well worth doing.

Recommended altar design

New Beginnings

Revitalizing an existing relationship

Regularly space clearing your home to clear out old, stagnant energies can help a lot to keep all aspects of a romantic relationship vital. It can also help to revitalize one that has started to flag.

After a space clearing Karen once did for a middle-aged couple, they felt so much love for each other that they put on some music, waltzed together in their lounge, and had sex for the first time in five years. It opened a whole new chapter of their marriage.

Recommended altar design

Dual Focus or New Beginnings

Harmonizing a fraught relationship

Arguments and other types of personality clashes can occur in any relationship from time to time. If this happens too often, the frequencies will become embedded in the space and can become the cause of yet more quarrels and disagreements. If there is still a good foundation of love between you, clearing out these imprints can reset the space and help to restore harmony in the relationship. It can also help to bring any underlying issues to the surface to be worked through amicably.

Recommended altar design

New Beginnings or The Facilitator

Taking a relationship to a deeper level

Regular space clearing is one of the best ways we know to keep a relationship evolving and moving forward. It can also be very helpful when certain milestones are reached that take the relationship to the next level of commitment, such as agreeing to get engaged, married, share finances, and so on.

Recommended altar design

All Possibilities or New Beginnings

Getting clarity about whether to continue a relationship or end it

Space clearing clears out the past and instills new, higher frequencies in a home. The process of preparing for the ceremony, identifying the focus, and doing the space clearing can help to clarify if both partners truly want to continue the relationship and move forward or if it has run its course and it's time to part company.

Recommended altar design

The Facilitator

After a divorce or break-up

When a couple splits up, the person who moves out has to find a new place to live. That can be tough. But if you're the person left behind, you will have a different issue to deal with. You'll be left with all the astral imprints in the home of everything that happened during the relationship. The histories of good times and bad times will all be mingled together, and if the relationship did not end well, the residues of stress, arguments, and unhappy times will overlay everything else.

Space clearing for relationships

It's very difficult to pick up and carry on living in such an environment. There is also the problem that these imprints can cause history to repeat itself if you begin a new relationship while living in the same place.

When a relationship ends, it's ideal if each partner can start a new life in a new home, but there are many situations when this is not possible. If you have children, for example, it can be too destabilizing for them to have to move and perhaps leave their school and their friends. Moving can also be just too expensive, difficult, or disruptive to even consider.

This is where space clearing can help a lot. Clearing out the frequencies of the old relationship and infusing your home with new, higher frequencies will make it much easier to build your life anew. Be sure to include bed thwacking (see Chapter 44) to help to clear out the imprints from your mattress.

We also recommend you read Chapter 15 of Karen's book *Clear Your Clutter with Feng Shui*, which explains how to free yourself from negative or non-productive associations you may have with items in your home that are associated with an ex-partner.

Recommended altar design
New Beginnings

40

Space clearing for health

We've heard from many people over the years that space clearing has helped them to recover from a wide range of health problems. It can substantially boost the healing process.

The main uses of space clearing covered in this chapter are:
- During an illness
- After an illness
- To help lift depression
- To improve vitality

During an illness

Do not do space clearing if you are unwell

One of the times in your life you can benefit from space clearing the most is when you are unwell. But paradoxically, it is the time when you are least able to do it yourself. You need to be fit and healthy to do a space clearing ceremony, as we explain in Chapter 21 of *Space Clearing, Volume 1*.

This means that if you are physically or mentally unwell, you will need to seek the help of someone who already has some experience of space clearing to do it for you. This could be your partner, if you have one, a close friend, a relative, or one of our certified professional space clearers.

How to do space clearing for someone who is unwell

We all know that feeling of walking into a room where someone has been physically unwell for a while. There can be a heaviness in the air and often a distinctive smell, caused by the physical and etheric excretions of the sick person's body in its attempt to heal itself. If the person has been taking medications, those smells will be in the mix too, discharged through the skin and the breath.

Physical cleaning, changing the bedding, and opening the windows to bring in fresh air will revive the space to a certain extent. But it's not enough.

Layers of etheric debris build up in any room as a result of everyday living. Space clearing once or twice a year is usually enough to maintain a space in normal circumstances. When someone is sick, these layers build up much faster and thicker, and they create a residue in the room that can greatly hinder the healing process. The person has to fight not just the illness but their own energetic excretions lingering in the space too. Space clearing is one of the most effective ways to remedy this.

Of course, you will need the sick person's permission to do space clearing, unless they are a young child in your care or an adult who is mentally ill or so seriously physically ill they will not understand what you are suggesting or be able to make an informed decision about it. If someone does not want you to space clear, you must respect their wishes. If they are beyond being able to decide this for themselves, then do what you genuinely feel they would wish you to do.

The most important thing to remember is **NEVER** to do space clearing in a room where someone is unwell. In their weakened condition, they will be vulnerable to picking up some of the energies that are being cleared, which will make them feel worse, not better.

Space clearing is most effective when the entire home is cleared, so we have included instructions for that here. If the sick person's home has regularly been space cleared, it may only be necessary to space clear their room.

If the sick person can be moved out of the home
It's ideal if you can do the ceremony when the sick person is not at home (when they are attending a medical appointment, for example). If they are not too sick and it's a warm day, you may be able to move them to the garden while you do the ceremony.

If the sick person cannot be moved out of the home
If the sick person cannot be moved out of the home, keep the door to their room closed while you space clear the rest of the property, then move the person to another room while you do a smaller version of the ceremony in their room.

If you're doing a Full or Essential Space Clearing ceremony, there's no need to create a separate altar in the sick person's room. Just take the equipment you need from the main altar and put the items on a small table in the room:
- A space clearing bell and stand
- A harmony ball and stand
- A flower offering
- A space clearing water pot containing space clearing water
- Matches
- A flower head to activate the offering

If you happen to have a small altar cloth to place underneath the equipment and the offering, that will add a lovely touch, but it's not essential. Nor is it essential to use additional neutral harmony balls, although you can if you wish to.

Begin and end each circuit of the ceremony at the door to the person's room rather than the main entrance of the home. The steps are as follows:

1. Roll your sleeves up above your elbows.
2. Wash your face and hands, then dry them using a clean towel, paper towel, or tissues (not a towel that has been used by the person who is unwell).
3. Enter the room and close the door.
4. Open a window.
5. Do a circuit of hand sensing.
6. Activate the offering.
7. Do a circuit of clapping.
8. Wash your hands (quickly leave the room to do this if there is no washbasin there).
9. Do a circuit of belling.
10. Do a circuit of harmony ball frequencing. The harmony ball will have already been infused when you did the main ceremony for the home, so there is no need to infuse it again, although you can if you want to.

This space clearing will only take about 10 minutes, then you can move the person back into the room. Leave the candle of the offering to burn out, if you can safely do so. This will help to fully integrate the changes in the space.

How to do space clearing for someone who is chronically unwell

If someone's illness continues for a long time, it will be very helpful to do Basic Space Clearing in their room every few weeks, to refresh the energy of the space. Always move the person to another room while you do this.

Recommended altar design
The Facilitator

After an illness

It's important to space clear after any serious or chronic illness because it can leave particularly dense and enduring imprints in the walls, furniture, and other objects in a room.

Thoroughly clean the sick person's room, then space clear the entire home to clear out the residual energies and reset the space. Basic Space Clearing will usually not be sufficient in this situation. You will need to do an Essential or Full Space Clearing ceremony.

If the person's treatment involved chemotherapy or radiation, a series of additional space clearings may be needed to clear the etheric excretions that result from that.

If you are the person who has just been sick, don't attempt to do the space clearing yourself. You will need to ask someone you know to do it for you, who is in good health and already has experience of space clearing their own home.

Recommended altar design
New Beginnings

To help lift depression

Space clearing is not a cure for depression, but the effect it has of raising the level of energy in a person's home can often have a beneficial effect for its occupants.

One man told us, "I had been depressed for years and nothing had helped. A close friend came and space cleared my home. The energy lift it gave me was incredible. Now I'm back at work again and am enjoying my life. I just have to remember to space clear at the first sign of depression setting in, before it gets a grip on me."

You may be interested to know that we see depression as a spiritual condition, not a medical one, usually triggered by life events. In many cases, it's caused by a person moving too far away from their true path. Their Higher Self shuts them down, so they no longer feel any joy or enthusiasm until they create a life that has more meaning.

Most people who are depressed accumulate clutter in their home, which makes them feel even more stuck, so some clutter clearing will be necessary too. It will then become easier to do the essential personal work of sourcing why the depression occurred and what changes need to be made.

We're not claiming that space clearing is a quick fix for depression, but a combination of space clearing and clutter clearing can certainly help a lot.

Recommended altar design
Incarnation or The Facilitator

To improve vitality

When stagnant energies accumulate in a home, either because it is not regularly space cleared or because there is a lot of clutter, it will have a stagnating and fatiguing effect. You will feel stuck in your life and too tired to do anything about it.

Space clearing is a great remedy for this type of tiredness, and it's also very helpful to aid the recovery of convalescents. It works because clearing and revitalizing the energies in a home has a corresponding revitalizing effect on the occupants too.

If there is any room in your home where you habitually feel more tired than usual, or if you often wake up feeling as if you need a good night's sleep, we also recommend you check you are not spending long periods of time exposed to high levels of electromagnetic fields or geopathic stress. You can find more information about these topics on our website at www.clearspaceliving.com.

Recommended altar design

For tiredness and fatigue: The Accelerator
For convalescence: The Facilitator

41

Space clearing at special times of the year

There are certain times of the year when space clearing can be more effective than usual because it coincides with the beginning of a new cycle. The main times are:

- Springtime
- New year
- A birthday or solar return
- Other anniversaries

Recommended altar design

New Beginnings is the best altar design to use when doing space clearing at any of these times. Choose the altar cloth and colourizer colours that best represent the new frequencies you wish to bring into your life in the coming year.

Springtime

This is always one of the most effective times of the year to do space clearing. The bursting buds and flowering blossoms awaken deep instincts in us to emerge from winter hibernation, dust everything down, and begin a new cycle.

It's also easier at this time of year to do clutter clearing and spring cleaning because the impulse from nature supports us in letting go of the old and welcoming the new. The best order is to declutter, spring clean, and then space clear your entire home to clear out old energies and bring in new, higher frequencies.

New year

The new year is another very effective time to do space clearing because you can ride on the wave of new beginnings that ripples around the world as the calendar changes from one year to the next. It creates a momentum for change.

It's also a time when many people feel inspired to make resolutions for the coming year. The history of everything that happens in your home is recorded in the walls, furniture, and objects in the space, influencing everything you do, so if you want your new-year resolutions to succeed, it makes very good sense to start with a deep and thorough space clearing to remove the imprints of all your old habits from your home. Otherwise, no matter how sincere your intentions, they are likely to come creeping back again.

A birthday or solar return

Once a year, the sun returns to exactly the same position it was in at the time of your birth, known as your solar return. This is another very useful time to do space clearing, to clear out the old and bring new, high-level frequencies into your home to support you in the best way possible in the coming year. It's especially helpful for changing ingrained habits that no longer serve you.

Your solar return is often on the same date as your birthday, but not always. Other factors such as where in the world you happen to be on your birthday and discrepancies between the Gregorian calendar and astrological calculations can mean it may fall on the day before or after your birthday. If you want to know the precise date and time, an astrologer will be able to calculate this for you each year. But for space clearing purposes, it doesn't matter too much. The calendar date of your birthday is close enough.

Other anniversaries

Space clearing can be done to honour any other type of anniversary that is meaningful to you, such as a religious event, a life-changing moment, a wedding date, and so on.

42

Space clearing for major life events

Space clearing your home creates a supportive environment to help you to move through life's changes with more clarity and ease. Clearing out the past and resetting the space of your home at a higher level will help you to take whatever life throws at you more in your stride.

We therefore recommend doing space clearing whenever you find yourself immersed in a major life change.

The topics covered in this chapter are:
- Marriage
- Pregnancy
- Birth
- Death
- Other major life events

Marriage

Richard is Australian, so he thinks nothing of travelling 450 miles (about 725 km) to Scotland to buy a car and then driving home the next day. For Aussies, that kind of distance is like a stroll around the block.

On his way back to England on one such expedition, he decided to find a hotel for the night and called to say he'd been able to get a suite with a huge bed and a jacuzzi for a very reasonable rate. It turned out

Space clearing for major life events

he was in Gretna Green, the elopement capital of the UK, and he'd been given the hotel's penthouse wedding suite because no one had booked it that night. Being Australian, he'd never heard of the place or its reputation. He just thought he'd got a great room at a bargain price.

This suite had seen a lot of passionate lovemaking in its time, as Richard quickly discovered. Hand sensing revealed it was deeply imprinted with those frequencies, as well as all the stress and exhaustion of getting married and the drunken revelry that often accompanies it. Richard always takes his bells with him when he goes travelling, so he space cleared the room, thwacked the bed, and had a great night's sleep.

For energetically aware people who don't want to spend the first night of their marriage sleeping in the honeymoon suite chaos of so many other people's wedding night imprints, a Basic or Essential Space Clearing and some vigorous bed thwacking (see Chapter 44) is therefore a must.

When we got married in Australia in 2007, we hired a house for a few days and booked a celebrant who agreed to travel to the property to conduct the ceremony. This allowed us to give the house a deep and thorough space clearing and create a high-level space for the wedding.

Nothing can guarantee a lasting union between two people, but getting a marriage off to the best possible start will certainly give it the best chance of success, so we highly recommend doing this. It's usually not practical for weddings performed in premises that are specially licensed for marriages, where the time window allowed is not sufficient or permission would not be given, but it's a very viable option if you hire a private venue. Space clearing the marital home before or soon after the wedding is also a wonderful way to set the space for your new life together.

Some couples have asked us to conduct a special ceremony for their marriage or for a renewal of vows ceremony. But here we draw the line. Restoring integrity to the energy of a space is very different to orchestrating the forging of lifelong vows between two people. That's not what space clearing is for.

Recommended altar design
New Beginnings or Dual Focus

Pregnancy

Welcoming and facilitating the birth of a new human being into the world is one of the most important uses of space clearing.

If you have made a conscious decision to have a baby, space clearing your home with this as the main focus of the ceremony helps to set your intention in the space. It won't guarantee you conceive, but it will help to create a welcoming space for a spirit who is preparing to incarnate.

The space clearing will work best if both partners are present, with one person conducting the ceremony and the other assisting.

Recommended altar design
The Stabilizer or The Facilitator

Birth

Preparing a space for a birth

During pregnancy, many people instinctively feel the urge to clean and tidy their home, to create a nest to prepare for the birth of their baby. Space clearing can be an important part of this, to make the environment as energetically clear as possible. It helps to ease the baby's transition from the warm, safe space of the womb to the harsh reality of incarnating into a physical body on earth.

Doing a space clearing ceremony while pregnant is a complete no-no because a baby in the womb is very etherically open and vulnerable. Everything that happens to the parent washes through the baby, so care needs to be taken not to expose the baby to energies it is not equipped to handle. The space clearing techniques described in this book are perfectly safe, but they are not designed to be done when pregnant.

The best person to do space clearing at this time is the pregnant person's partner, if they have read this book, have the right space clearing equipment, and feel confident to do the ceremony. Other options are to ask a close friend who already has experience of space clearing their own home or hire a professional space clearing practitioner.

It's fine for a pregnant person to be present during the setting-up stage of the space clearing ceremony (hand sensing, creating the space clearing altar, and activating the flower offerings around the home), as well as during the harmony ball process at the end, but not during the clapping and belling circuits.

So, what *can* you do when you're pregnant? Clutter clearing! Pregnancy is a wonderful time to clear out the old to make room for the new, and it will really help to satisfy the nesting instinct too.

Recommended altar design
The Stabilizer

Cleansing a space after a birth

The energies surrounding a birth can be chaotic because there is an astral shattering that takes place when a baby's astral body is separated from its parent. The astral fragments* that are released at that time are often the cause of post-partum depression in the birthing parent (you can find more information about this in Chapter 7 of *Entities* by Samuel Sagan). For a home birth, it is therefore important for the room to be space cleared before the birth and again soon after, by a partner, a close friend, or a professional space clearer.

Recommended altar design
The Stabilizer

Death

Space clearing is a superb way to support the dying process of someone who has a terminal illness. It can also be used to cleanse the space after someone has died.

Death is a natural part of life. It will happen to us all sometime, although even talking about it is largely taboo in many societies. We discovered a very different attitude to this when we lived in Bali, where the topic is openly discussed and understood.

Karen's introduction to this came early on in her relationship with the Balinese man she was married to for 12 years. They were sitting in a restaurant, waiting for a meal they had ordered.

"Have you ever seen a dead body?" she asked (she's well known for unusual conversation starters).

"Hundreds," he replied.

This took her by surprise. She was expecting him to say no or, at the very most, one or two. She began rifling through her mental filing cabinets looking for an event in Balinese history that would explain this.

"Were you in a massacre or an earthquake or something?" she asked.

"No."

What had started out as an idle inquiry had suddenly become very interesting.

"What then?"

"Well, every time someone in my village dies, we all go to the family's house and keep vigil all night with the body. Then we help the family wash the body, prepare it for burial or cremation, and organize all the death ceremonies. This happens everywhere in Bali. Doesn't it happen in England, where you come from?"

"Well, no. If someone dies, the family pays undertakers to do that."

"What? You let strangers handle the body?"

"Yes."

He gave her one of those kind-yet-withering Balinese looks that says, "Don't you westerners know anything about anything?"

"Death is a sacred event," he explained. "If someone in your family dies, you can't leave it to people who don't even know the person to take care of what happens to their body and the journey of their eternal spirit. If someone in my village dies, we all go to help. Everyone wants to touch the body one last time to say goodbye." He patted her arm repeatedly in different places, imitating a group of people clamouring for one last touch. "No one feels quite right if they're not able to do this. It feels like you haven't finished the relationship properly."

This casual, pre-dinner conversation gave Karen much pause for thought and began in-depth research into death and grieving practices that continues to this day.

What happens energetically at death

Death is the transition from this physical world back into the energetic realms – a returning to our source. Learning how to do this well is a great art.

It's not just a person's physical body that disintegrates after death. Their astral body also goes through a process of shattering and their etheric body gradually dissolves, eventually leaving just their Higher Self, which is the eternal part of themselves. It's not quite that simple because it can sometimes happen that fragments of an astral body (called entities) may linger in a space and can even nest inside people and pets, parasitizing their energy.

If you are interested to learn more about the death process, we highly recommend reading *Entities* by Samuel Sagan, which explains in detail how entities are formed, how you can catch one, how it can affect you, and what you can do about it. This is the first of Samuel's books that Karen read. It's a voice of sanity in an ocean of nonsense about this topic.

We also highly recommend the Clairvision Knowledge Track *Death, The Great Journey*. It's invaluable to read to prepare for your own eventual death, or if you are currently facing your own death or the death of someone dear to you. It explains many of the mysteries of death and includes a section titled "Book of the Dead for Modern Times", which is designed to be read to a person soon after they die, to assist them in navigating the astral realms they find themselves in after departing their physical body. It can be used by people of all religious, non-religious, and spiritual beliefs. Karen read it to her mother after she died and found it to be one of the most beautiful and uplifting experiences of her life. In addition to helping her mother on her way, she experienced a much higher dimension of the woman she had known and a rich completion of her relationship with her.

Death, The Great Journey explains that the techniques for death are the same as the techniques for life, so the best time to read this book is while you are still very much alive. Put simply, the more you understand about dying, the more you will understand about living and how to make the most of every day you have.

At the time of writing, it is published in the form of a downloadable audiobook, together with a PDF copy of the text that you can read onscreen or print out, if you prefer. It's self-published so is more expensive than a mass-produced paperback, but the content is priceless. As Karen wrote in *Clear Your Clutter with Feng Shui*:

> I rate this as the most important book I've read this lifetime, and highly recommend you get a copy and read it yourself. It's totally inspiring, and will give you a profoundly insightful perspective, not just on death, but also on life.

Space clearing before a death

If someone is very ill and their death looks inevitable, space clearing is an excellent way to prepare the space, to facilitate the highest possible exit from this world to spiritual realms.

You will need to temporarily move them out of the room while you are doing the space clearing, of course, and be sufficiently reconciled to their impending death that you can remain emotionally calm and balanced while doing the ceremony. If you are not able to maintain equilibrium, do NOT do the space clearing yourself. It could create chaos in the space that would hinder rather than help the dying person.

Recommended altar design
Spiritual Aspirations

Space clearing after a death

All religions have well-defined funeral practices, and most traditional cultures also have prescribed methods of space clearing to cleanse and purify a building after someone has died in one.

Space clearing can clear the etheric debris that results from the death process. At the same time, depending on the skill of the space clearer, it can clear out imprints of sickness that will have accumulated if the person who died was ill for some time in that place. It can also remove the residues of grief and all the other mixed emotions that can accumulate after the death of a loved one.

If someone close to you has died, space clearing is not something to rush into, though. There usually needs to be a grieving period first, and the length of time this takes will be different for each person. We don't recommend doing space clearing yourself while you are still in the early stages of grieving, and if the death was a violent one or a suicide, we advise seeking the help of an experienced professional space clearer instead.

Here's what one American woman told us about her experience of having her home professionally space cleared:

> After my mom passed, I really wanted the energetic support to sort through her belongings because the energy felt like mud, so I hired one of Karen's certified space clearers to space clear her house. After the space clearing, I decided just to wait and see how things unfolded. The following morning my cousin showed up unexpectedly to help, and my brother volunteered to start on the attic. I was so amazed at the instantaneous result. We spent about three weeks clearing and going through everything, giving most of it away. It was very freeing. When we sold the house a year later, it sold in a week with multiple offers. The space clearing definitely helped on many levels. I felt very grateful for this.

Recommended altar design
The choice of altar design will depend on the intended use of the space by the future occupants of the home. If the property is being sold, use the New Beginnings altar design.

Other major life events

Major life events take many forms. They can include new beginnings such as starting a new form of education or a new job, or starting your own business, as well as endings such as graduating, leaving a job, or retiring.

They can be associated with wonderful successes, traumatic disappointments, or other types of situations where stress or loss is involved. Many people think that winning the lottery will be the solution to all their problems, for example, but in fact this can be one of the most stressful life events of all.

Space clearing can help to ease you through all these situations.

Recommended altar designs

For joyous life events: New Beginnings
For stressful life events: The Stabilizer

43

Space clearing after a disruptive experience

A traumatic or disruptive experience can leave you feeling very shaken. You may not be in a fit state to be able to do space clearing yourself, but the information in this chapter will enable someone who has experience of space clearing to do it for you in these types of situations:

- After an argument
- After a burglary
- After an accident in the home
- After a party
- After a traumatic local or world event

After an argument

An argument happens between two people when their astral bodies lock horns and a battle ensues about who is right. Sometimes the argument is verbal and noisy. Sometimes it takes the form of stonewalling or silent seething. Both types can leave a bitter astral frequency hanging in the space that is tangible. Repeated arguments in a home can create deep astral imprints in the walls, floors, ceiling, and objects in a space, which can then make it likely you will have more arguments.

We're not suggesting you need to reach for your space clearing bell whenever you have a disagreement with someone. That's not necessary at all. But knowing how to do Basic Space Clearing after a serious row is a very useful skill to have, and an Essential or Full Space Clearing can remove the imprints that accumulate as a result of recurring quarrels.

Recommended altar design

Choose the altar design that most closely relates to the cause of the arguments. For example, choose Establishing Foundations if you need to go back to basics or Establishing Levels if you need to separate various aspects of your life such as work and home. The Stabilizer can also work well in this situation.

After a burglary

A traumatic event such as a burglary can leave an astral imprint in a home, in a similar way to how your skin can become scarred as a result of a wound. And just as the skin can be open and painful for a while, with the risk of an infection, so a distressing event can make you feel vulnerable and hurt for a while, with the possibility of deep-seated emotions (samskaras) being triggered. It can have a significant impact on your emotional wellbeing and sense of security.

How space clearing can help

Your home is an extension of yourself. Its physical boundary marks the perimeter of your space and the area you permeate with your energy. When an intruder breaks in, it causes an energetic violation of the space, and this feeling can linger long after the event. In some cases, especially if there has been a physical confrontation with the burglar, a person can feel so traumatized by the event that they never feel safe in their home again.

Space clearing won't magically bring back any valuables that were stolen, but it can restore something equally precious – a sense of safety and a settling of emotions.

How to space clear after a burglary

An Essential or Full Space Clearing ceremony is needed for this, with special emphasis on the belling and harmony ball circuits. The belling circuit is the part when the astral imprints of the event can be cleared, and the harmony ball circuit is when new, higher frequencies are instilled in the space.

Whether you do the ceremony yourself or have someone else do it for you will depend on how experienced you are at space clearing and how traumatized you feel by the burglary. If you've never done the ceremony before, this is not the best time to start. If you are familiar with it, already have a space clearing kit, and feel confident about doing each of the steps of the ceremony, it can be very empowering to do it yourself to re-own your space.

Another option is to ask a friend or relative to do the space clearing for you, providing the person knows you very well, is a frequent visitor to your home, and has already space cleared their own home successfully. Someone who is just willing to have a go will not do. That can cause more problems than it solves.

The best remedy of all is to have a professional space clearing done to fully remove the imprinting caused by the burglary and quickly restore integrity to the space. All our certified space clearing practitioners have done extensive training to be able to work with clients at this deep level. The sooner it's done, the better, but the ceremony can also be conducted months or even years later, if necessary.

Can you be present during the ceremony?

If you feel very affected by the burglary, it will be best for someone else to do the ceremony for you and for you to step outside the building during the clapping and belling circuits. It's fine to be present during the rest of the ceremony, and it can be emotionally healing to witness the part where offerings are activated in each room of the home and to participate in the harmony ball circuit near the end of the ceremony.

Other types of support

In addition to the help that space clearing, friends, and family can provide, there are victim support organizations in most countries that offer free counselling and practical help to people who've been traumatized in some way. We suggest you do some research to see what's available in your part of the world. Life can bring its challenges at times, but there's help available these days, if you know where to look.

Recommended altar design

The Stabilizer

After an accident in the home

An accident in your home can create a physical injury and an emotional scar, as well as an astral imprint of the trauma in that part of the property. By removing the imprint of the accident, space clearing can help to relieve any anxiety you may have about it happening again.

If the accident was caused by something that needs altering or mending, such as a slippery bathroom floor or a loose stair tread, a physical repair will, of course, be essential too.

Recommended altar design

New Beginnings

After a party

The type of parties that involve consuming intoxicating substances such as alcohol or drugs can leave a space feeling energetically trashed.

After the physical mess has been cleaned up, space clearing can help to reset the energy of the space at a higher level.

Recommended altar design
The Stabilizer or New Beginnings

After a traumatic local or world event

External events you have no control over can impact the energy of your home if you bring them into your space by worrying about them.

It's important to be aware of what's happening in the world. Just ignoring it is not a solution. But there's a big difference between keeping abreast of the news and anxiously checking it many times a day out of fear.

We observed this happening on a global scale after events such as 9/11 and during the Covid pandemic. Many people let us know that space clearing helped them a lot during and after those times to maintain stability and a space of sanctuary in their home. It can also be very helpful during and after local events, such as contentious elections, civil disorder, or natural disasters.

Recommended altar design
The Stabilizer

44

Space clearing when travelling

Space clearing is a wonderful skill to have when travelling. You can use it to create a feeling of being at home wherever you go, and it will usually allow you to enjoy a much better quality of sleep too. This chapter includes:

- Staying as a guest in someone's home
- Staying as a guest in a hotel
- Bed thwacking
- Other travel tips

Staying as a guest in someone's home

If you invite someone to stay in a guest room in your home, space clearing the room will help to create a welcoming space for them. You can find more information about this in Chapter 37.

But what if the situation is reversed and you go to stay in a friend's home as their guest? Is it OK to space clear the room you stay in?

The answer is no. Not unless your host invites you to do so or you ask their permission and it is freely given.

The reason is that space clearing permanently changes the energy of a space. You may only be there for a short time but the clearing will have a lasting effect. Depending on the techniques you use and your level of skill, the changes may be dramatic, and while you may enjoy the results, your host may like the room just the way it is. Since you're there as their guest, it's right that you respect their wishes.

Staying as a guest in a hotel

You pay money to stay in a hotel room for a night, so it's fine to space clear it. No permission is required.

There's a traveller's version of Basic Space Clearing that can be used in this situation to improve the energy of a space you stay in for a short time. The only equipment you'll need is a Balinese space clearing bell and a harmony ball. If you arrive late at night, please be considerate of other guests and don't disturb them by clapping and ringing bells at some unearthly hour. Wait until the next day to space clear.

How to do a Basic Space Clearing ceremony when travelling

1. Refresh your energy after travelling by taking a bath or shower and putting on clean clothing. If you don't have time to do that, at least wash your face and hands.
2. Put a "Do Not Disturb" sign on the outside of your door.
3. Put any food and open drinks away in the fridge, if there is one, or in a plastic bag.
4. Open a window a little to allow a gentle flow of fresh air (you can still do space clearing if it's not possible to open a window, but it won't be as effective).
5. Turn off all devices, including your phone, and any loud or droning equipment such as a fan or air conditioning (if it's not possible to turn off the air conditioning completely, turn it to the quietest setting).
6. Remove any metal you are wearing or carrying in your pockets.

7. Take off your shoes and do the ceremony barefoot, if it is practical to do so.

8. Roll your sleeves up above your elbows and keep them rolled up throughout the ceremony.

9. Set up your space clearing equipment.

10. Starting at the door, do a circuit of hand sensing that includes all the walls, furniture, and the bed. End the circuit back at the door.

11. Starting at the door, walk around the entire inside perimeter of the room, clapping in each corner as you go, from high to low. Clap out the mattress too, from head to foot, about 3–5 cm (1–2 inches) above the surface of the bed. Finish with a loud, crisp clap at the door.

12. Wash your hands and forearms and dry them on a clean towel or paper tissues.

13. Pick up your space clearing bell and go to the door. Stand facing in the direction you will walk. Ring the bell once in the centre area of the door, then walk around the entire inside perimeter of the room again, ringing your bell and consciously directing the sound into the walls and furniture to shatter any embedded astral imprints. Never allow the sound of the bell to completely fade. When you arrive back at the door, complete the circuit by doing a horizontal figure of eight (the symbol of infinity) at heart level in the air with the bell. Finish with a brisk ring in the centre of the figure of eight where the two loops cross.

14. Infuse your harmony ball with higher frequencies, then walk around the inside perimeter of the room, shaking the frequencies into the walls and furniture.

If you need a reminder about how to do any of the techniques, please refer to the relevant steps of the ceremony in Chapter 33 of *Space Clearing, Volume 1*.

Bed thwacking

In addition to space clearing, something else you can do when travelling is bed thwacking.

To understand why this is necessary, next time you stay in a hotel, take a look around the room when you go for breakfast in the morning. How many of those people would you want to share a bed with? In most cases the answer will be none, but in fact you just did. Not with those exact same people sitting around you, but with people very similar to them who slept in your bed before you did and left their imprints in it.

Depending on the age of the mattress and the popularity of the hotel, hundreds or even thousands of people may have slept in that bed before you. And since sleep is a time when you are very energetically open and permeable, it is highly likely you will be affected by this in some way.

If you're starting to feel nauseous, help is at hand. Bed thwacking is an invaluable skill for the modern traveller.

How to do bed thwacking

First, peel back the bedcovers to reveal the mattress. Then open a window, if it's possible to do so, to create a gentle circulation of fresh air and chi in the room.

Next, find a sturdy implement you can use to do bed thwacking. A baseball bat or cricket bat works wonderfully well for this purpose when you're at home. In a hotel room, a wooden coat-hanger is a good choice or a telescopic umbrella, if you happen to have one with you. Pummelling with your fists is a good emergency measure, although not as effective as using a sturdy thwacker of some kind.

Methodically thwack the whole mattress for a few minutes to dislodge the energy imprints from it (and usually quite a bit of dust too).

Now here's a very important tip: Don't do this the first night you check in. When you do bed thwacking, all the etheric debris will go up in the air and will take a few hours to come back down again. If you do this and then jump into bed, it will all land on top of you.

In fact, it's not worth doing bed thwacking at all if you're only staying for one night. Just put up with it. But if you are staying for a second night or longer, do bed thwacking the next morning, put in a request for housekeeping to clean the room, then go out for the day. By the time you get back, all the energetic debris will have been wiped from surfaces and vacuumed up from the floor, leaving you with a sleeping space that is much clearer.

In your own home, you can go even further. Give your mattress a thorough thwacking several times a year to keep it energetically fresh. If possible, also drag it outside, into the garden if you have one, at least once a year on a sunny day to air it and purify it with sunlight.

Important note: Bacteria can survive on bed linen for several days but can only make you sick if you ingest them or they enter your system through an open wound. Bed thwacking is therefore highly unlikely to put you at any risk of bacterial infection. However, if respiratory viruses are present, bed thwacking will aerosolize them. If you then breathe them in, you can become infected. If you think there is any possibility of this type of contamination in the mattress, do not do bed thwacking when travelling.

Memory foam mattresses

The way memory foam mattresses are constructed means that bed thwacking doesn't work on them, which is yet another reason why we don't recommend buying one (they are made of polyurethane foam, which out-gasses toxins such as formaldehyde, benzene, acetaldehyde, styrene, and toluene diisocyanate).

Other travel tips

Here are some other travel tips we practise ourselves that you may find helpful.

Fully unpack to arrive

This is usually not worth doing if you check into a hotel late at night and are leaving the next morning. But if you're staying longer, unpacking your suitcase will significantly change your relationship to the location, the people you meet, and the quality of the experiences you have there. It can change a superficial engagement into one that has depth. Cumulatively, this can mean the difference between idle drifting or a life well lived.

This is why, whenever we teach a residential workshop or professional training, we always ask our students to fully unpack the first night they arrive. We know we'll be able to work with them at a much deeper level if they do so, and they will get much more from the event as a result.

How to make a place feel more like home

It can make an enormous difference when travelling for long periods to bring something with you from home that has no useful function other than to warm your heart and bring a smile to your face each time you see it.

When Karen used to travel extensively around the world to teach her workshops, she would always do this. Usually, it was a small fox ornament or a tiny teddy bear. These items weighed very little and took up almost no room in her luggage, yet they made any hotel room instantly feel more like home. Of course, there is always the risk, when travelling, that you may lose something along the way, so it is best not to take a treasured item with you.

When staying in one location for a week or more, buying a bunch of fresh flowers or a flowering plant can have a similar uplifting effect (most hotel housekeeping departments can usually supply a vase for flowers, if you ask them).

Know the geographical direction of your loved ones

Another travelling tip we can offer, learned from decades of flying all over the world to teach events, is to take a few moments when you arrive in a new place to figure out the geographical direction your loved ones are located in.

Holding a peripheral awareness of the direction during the hours of sleep will allow you to feel emotionally nurtured and connected to them, no matter how far away you are. It will also enable you to fully arrive and engage at a deeper level, because you will feel connected, not separated, from those you hold dear.

This technique works particularly well if you're travelling alone and visit a place you've never been to before.

45

Space clearing to support personal development

A major use of space clearing is to facilitate personal development. It can help in many ways:

- When you feel stuck
- To clarify a new direction in life
- To help overcome procrastination
- To deal with recurring problems or behaviours
- To promote prosperity
- To open new possibilities

When you feel stuck

A primary use of space clearing is to help you to move forward when you feel stuck in some way.

The reason it works so effectively is because everything in your home is a reflection of some aspect of yourself. If you feel stuck, there will always be a corresponding energetic stagnation that has been building up in a part of your home for some time. This will usually be accompanied by an accumulation of clutter, so the most effective remedy is a deep and thorough clutter clearing, followed by space clearing. The changes this can bring about is remarkable.

One couple we heard from had been wanting to buy the apartment they lived in for eight years, but the freeholder had refused to sell it. After they space cleared it, the freeholder contacted them the next day and said he was willing to sell.

Another woman wrote to let Karen know she had been trying to find a new house to rent and was getting desperate after several weeks of no progress. She was willing to pay a good price for something nice in the right area, but each time she found a house that suited her, it got let to someone else before she was able to clinch the deal. The situation was becoming urgent because the lease on her present home had nearly expired. She didn't think it would do much good, but she decided to space clear her house anyway. Within 24 hours she had signed a new agreement for a place that was everything she wanted. She said, "It was as if somebody let out the cork and a whole river of success flowed into my life!"

We've heard many similar testimonials over the years. One of the great things about space clearing is how empowering it is. After you've learned how to do it, you can take personal responsibility for clearing your own stuckness whenever you need to. And don't wait until it gets to the proportions described in the examples given here. At the first sign of feeling stuck, roll up your sleeves, clear your clutter, and space clear your home. You need never feel stuck in your life again.

Recommended altar design
The Accelerator or The Facilitator

To clarify a new direction in life

Creating energetic clarity in your home can help to bring more clarity to your life too.

One woman, who ran her own business, said about this:

> I had a big decision to make and just couldn't decide what to do. Then I remembered Karen's advice and started cleaning, tidying, and decluttering my home, followed by a space clearing. As I did so, I distinctly felt my inner confusion dissolve. By the time I had finished I was so clear about what I wanted to do that I could hardly wait to begin!

Recommended altar design
Incarnation or Crossroads

To help overcome procrastination

Procrastination is a form of stuck energy. You decide to do something but then put off doing it, which can sometimes result in unfortunate consequences for you and others.

A combination of clutter clearing and space clearing will clear out the stagnant energies in a home that encourage procrastination. Without realizing it, you will have been unconsciously resting on these frequencies. It may have felt comfortable and safe to do so, but it will also have been holding you back from doing things you really want to do. Clearing out these old energies and replacing them with new, higher frequencies will energize your space and energize you. Many people find that after space clearing, they are effortlessly able to achieve things they have been putting off for years.

If procrastination is a big issue for you, it's a good idea to set the main focus for your space clearing ceremony as one particular thing you want to achieve but have been procrastinating about. The breakthrough of completing a task you have been stuck on for a while will usually make it easier to continue after that to tackle and complete other tasks too.

Space Clearing, Volume 2

Recommended altar design

Single Focus or The Accelerator
Use a large red colourizer as the central vertical axis. Add one ripple to the colourizer if you want to progress slowly and surely, two ripples if you want to move faster, and three ripples for high speed. Bear in mind that faster is not always better but may sometimes be necessary.

To deal with recurring problems or behaviours

Whenever there is a recurring problem in your life, it's likely there will be imprints that correspond to this in your home. Sometimes they will have been put there by you. Sometimes they will have been created by people who have lived there before you.

Space clearing will not remove the cause of recurring problems or behaviours, but it can remove the imprints and give you a fresh start so you can tackle the issues without the hindrance of the past.

One woman whose apartment Karen space cleared had a daughter who had broken off communications with her many years ago. Halfway through the ceremony, the daughter called to talk to the mother and arranged to meet up. From that day on, they enjoyed a close mother-and-daughter relationship again.

Another woman Karen heard from was married to a man who was prone to sulking for weeks on end if he didn't get his own way. This had been going on for years and the wife was really fed up with it. The next time it happened, she space cleared the house, paying particular attention to the Relationships area of the *bagua* (you can find more information about how to locate this area in your own home in Karen's book *Clear Your Clutter with Feng Shui*). A few hours later, for the first time ever, he phoned to apologize and came home to talk the problem through. A year later she called to tell Karen, "He hasn't stormed off in a huff ever since. We sit and discuss our problems now like reasonable people. There's no doubt in my mind that space clearing saved my marriage."

Recommended altar design
New Beginnings

To promote prosperity

Space clearing does not offer a quick fix for financial problems. The way it can help is to reset the energies of your home at a higher level to make it easier for you to see and address the factors that are preventing you from becoming more prosperous.

Clutter clearing can also help enormously to unblock energy flows in your home, as Karen explains in detail in *Clear Your Clutter with Feng Shui*.

Recommended altar designs
The Accelerator or Single Focus. Use a purple altar cloth, or a white altar cloth with a purple colourizer in the central vertical axis position.

To open new possibilities

A very specific use of space clearing is to help you move to the next level in some aspect of your life, to become all that you can be. This will involve a serious engagement of will and a letting go of limitations. The results can be extraordinary.

Space clearing helps because it can remove the astral imprints of old ways of thinking from your home, which opens the door to new possibilities and makes you more receptive to them. For the best results, prepare for the space clearing by thoroughly decluttering your entire home and letting go of anything that no longer fits with who you are.

Recommended altar design

All Possibilities

This altar design is only recommended if your life is already working well and are ready to step up to a new level of engagement. If you're not sure you're ready for that, use New Beginnings instead.

46

Space clearing for spiritual purposes

Some people do space clearing for spiritual purposes more than for any other reason.

Of course, every space clearing has a spiritual element because it raises the level of consciousness in a space, which make you more spiritually connectable. There are also some specific applications we have included here:

- To support you on your spiritual path
- To create and maintain a meditation space
- After a life-changing workshop, meditation retreat, or similar event

To support you on your spiritual path

A common belief in modern times is that humans are physical beings who can choose to engage a spiritual path or not. This is what's known as a bottom-up approach. It's how things may appear to the tiny specks of existence that we are when trying to fathom the meaning of things from the limited standpoint of the human biped. It can be likened to an ant-like view of existence.

A top-down view of our life on earth has a completely different perspective. It perceives physical incarnation as a human experience that spiritual beings choose to have for a specific purpose.

A spiritual path usually starts with an exploratory phase. If that goes well, next comes a period of looking for more depth and meaning. This can then lead to a more serious commitment to spiritual practices.

Regular space clearing is essential for a spiritual way of life. It clears out the past so you can be more present in the now. It keeps the energies in your home clear to give you the best possible environment for spiritual work. And if you develop your space clearing skills sufficiently, you can use it to permanently raise the level of consciousness in your space.

Recommended altar designs

When focused on a particular aspect of spiritual development: Single Focus
For periods of deconstruction: The Stabilizer or The Facilitator
For periods of construction: Spiritual Aspirations or All Possibilities

To create and maintain a meditation space

Space clearing can be invaluable if you have a dedicated room in your home that is used primarily for meditation.

The purpose of meditation is to access higher states of consciousness. A meditation room therefore needs to be as clear of everyday frequencies as possible so that the space will be conducive to stilling the mind.

Without space clearing, it can take years to build such a space of stillness in a room. Even for a very experienced meditator, it can take months. Space clearing can hugely speed up the process. It can also help you to access more advanced levels of meditation quicker, depending on your level of commitment and the meditation techniques you are using, of course.

How to space clear a meditation room

If you have never done an Essential or Full Space Clearing ceremony in your entire home, do that first, earlier in the day or on a previous day, to set the energy of the space at a higher level.

Then establish a routine of doing Basic or Essential Space Clearing in your meditation room every week, with the door to the room closed in order to separate the energy of the space from the rest of your home.

Do this for a sustained period until you reach the stage where you can tangibly feel, each time you walk into your meditation room, how much stiller the space is than in the other rooms of your home. The speed and extent to which this happens will depend partly on your space clearing skills and partly on how deeply you are able to involute during meditation.

After this, do Basic Space Clearing from time to time to continue to build the clarity and stillness of the space and a Full or Essential Space Clearing ceremony at least once a year for your entire home.

Other ways you can build the space in your meditation room are:
- Don't use the room, or allow it to be used by others, for anything other than its designated purpose of meditation or related spiritual practices
- Dust all surfaces and clean the floor of the room each week to prevent etheric debris from accumulating
- Never wear outdoor shoes in the room
- Keep the room well ventilated so there is a good circulation of chi
- Keep the space clutter-free (only have items that directly relate to your meditation practice)

Recommended altar design

Spiritual Aspirations

After a life-changing workshop, meditation retreat, or similar event

If you attend a workshop or a meditation retreat that is truly life-changing, the way you integrate the changes into your life after you leave is very important. The precious hours and days that follow will determine whether you are able to hold the new level or fall back into your old ways.

We've attended events of this nature, for example, where the first thing participants did after they left the property was to noisily babble and shout among themselves, gorge on emotional suppressants such as pizza, chocolate, and ice cream, and quickly undo all the changes they had spent days or weeks cultivating.

A wiser approach, if you truly value your spiritual path and want to make the most of the experience you've just had, is to stay as involuted as possible on your journey home and after you arrive home. Ensure you have a few peaceful days with no worldly commitments so you can integrate the changes before being immersed back into your everyday life. Space clearing your home at the start of this integration period can set the space at a higher level, which can be a great help during this period.

Recommended altar design

Choose the design that fits best with the changes you are integrating into your life.

PART FIVE

Business uses of space clearing

47

Space clearing business premises

The three levels of the space clearing ceremony described in *Space Clearing, Volume 1* can all be adapted for business use. Please read all the topics covered in this chapter before proceeding:

- Space clear your own home first
- Types of businesses that can be space cleared
- Types of businesses that cannot be space cleared
- How to clarify the focus of a business space clearing
- When to do a business space clearing
- Who can be present during a business space clearing
- Space clearing equipment and materials
- Where to position the space clearing altar
- Where to place the second flower offering
- Where to place other flower offerings
- After the ceremony

Space clear your own home first

Before space clearing your business, be sure to do a Full Space Clearing ceremony in your own home first. The reason for this is that your business is an extension of you, not the other way around. In our experience of working with clients around the world, we find we are often able to locate the source of a person's business problems in the energy of their home, so that is always the most important place to space clear first.

If you run your business from home

If you run your business from home, you will need to decide whether to do one ceremony that encompasses both your home and business, or two separate ceremonies.

We recommend doing one combined ceremony if you live alone, have a good work–life balance, love the work you do, the area used as a workspace is relatively small in comparison with the rest of your home, and it is under the same roof.

Do two separate ceremonies if you share your home with others who are not involved in your business, your work commitments tend to intrude too much into your personal time, or the workspace area is relatively large, such as occupying an entire floor of your home. Always space clear the residential areas first, then the work areas. It's fine to do the two ceremonies on separate days, if it's more practical to do so.

Recommended combined altar design

Choose an altar design that incorporates both your personal and business focus for the space clearing.

Recommended separate altar designs

Create an altar for your home space clearing that relates to the focus of that ceremony. Create a different altar for the business space clearing that relates to the focus of that ceremony.

Types of businesses that can be space cleared

A business you own

You can use the information in this part of the book to space clear any business that you own, whether it is located in a property that you own or one that is leased.

A business you manage on behalf of the owner

If you're a CEO or manager who has overall responsibility for running a business, you can space clear the property yourself, although it is best to get the agreement of the owner first, whenever possible.

If that's not practical – for example, because the business is so large that the owner has no interest in being involved in that level of detail – then you will need to consider how you would feel if they were to unexpectedly arrive at some point during the ceremony. If you would feel uncomfortable in that situation, that's an indication you would probably be going against the owner's wishes, which would be unethical.

A business in which you are a partner

It is best to get the agreement of any partner or partners before doing the space clearing.

Types of businesses that cannot be space cleared

A business you do not own

Space clearing a business you do not own or manage requires much more advanced skills than we can teach in a book. If the space clearing is not done right, it can affect the running of the business and its profitability, so please don't attempt it, no matter how sincerely you may want to help the business owner.

Hospitals, hospices, and other places where sickness or death are common

Please read the information about this in Chapter 23 of *Space Clearing, Volume 1*.

How to clarify the focus of a business space clearing

The method for establishing the focus when space clearing your own home is described in detail in Chapter 25 of *Space Clearing, Volume 1*. A different approach is needed when space clearing a business because there are other aspects to consider, such as the welfare of your staff and customers, your relationships with suppliers, the direction you wish your business to take, specific problems you are dealing with, and so on.

If you are self-employed, the decision about the focus for the ceremony will be yours alone. If you work with others, it's wise to consult them, to get their insights and input.

Look for the key issue that needs to be addressed, which will help to bring about all the other changes that are needed too. Condense the focus into one short sentence of seven words or less so you can hold it in your awareness in packed* form while you do the ceremony.

When to do a business space clearing

If you run your business from home, follow the instructions in Chapter 27 of *Space Clearing, Volume 1*, including choosing a date when you will be able to stay at home for the rest of the day and sleep at home during the following week to integrate the changes.

If your business has its own premises, choose a time when all activities can come to a complete standstill and all equipment can be turned off while the ceremony is in progress. This usually means that the best time to do a business space clearing is on a public holiday or at some other time when no employees are present, such as at the weekend. If the only time you can do it is in the evening, start the ceremony before dusk, if possible (the reasons for this are explained in Chapter 27 of *Space Clearing, Volume 1*).

If your business operates 24/7 every day of the year, it will not be possible to space clear the property unless you close the business for a few hours so you can bring all activities to a stop.

If the property has smoke detectors that could trigger fire alarms and/or sprinkler systems if candles are burned, it will only be possible to do Basic Space Clearing (not Essential or Full Space Clearing).

Who can be present during a business space clearing

If you would like other people to be present, only invite those who are key to the management of the business and want to be fully involved in the ceremony, not those who are itching to get on with some work. All equipment will need to be turned off, including computers, routers, and phones. Do not do space clearing while cleaners or maintenance people are working in the place.

Space clearing equipment and materials

Plates for flower offerings

In addition to the usual space clearing equipment (see Part Three of *Space Clearing, Volume 1*), check that there are enough plates on the premises for the flower offerings. If not, bring some from home to use for the day.

Harmony balls

We usually recommend having one harmony ball you use for space clearing your home and another you reserve for space clearing your business premises. This is because the frequencies you will be putting into each harmony ball will be very different. If you are the sole owner of your business and you prefer to blend these frequencies by using just one harmony ball, that's fine too. It's a matter of personal choice.

It works well to use additional neutral harmony balls when space clearing business premises because they add extra volume and oomph. It's fine to use the same neutral harmony balls you use in your home because they don't become imbued with specific frequencies.

If you invite business partners or staff to be present during the ceremony, you will need to make a decision about whether to share a harmony ball or have one each. Individual harmony balls are usually best so that each person can take responsibility for their part in the business and can infuse the harmony ball with their own personal aspirations for the success of the venture.

Where to position the space clearing altar

If you do an Essential or Full Space Clearing, the location of the altar will vary from business to business.

The best place is usually the reception area, if there is one. If this would make the altar too visible to curious passers-by, you may prefer to choose a location that is more concealed but still close to the front entrance.

If there is no reception area, choose a location that is reasonably close to the main entrance, which is where each circuit of the ceremony will begin and end.

Where to place the second flower offering

When doing a Full Space Clearing ceremony in a residential space clearing, the second offering is always placed in the kitchen because that is the heart of nourishment of the home. This isn't applicable to a business space clearing, even if there is a kitchen, because the emphasis is on the success of the business, not personal nurturing. Depending on the layout of the business premises and the nature of the business, the best location for the second offering is usually on your own desk or work area, in recognition of your responsibilities as the owner or manager of the business.

Where to place other flower offerings

Other flower offerings can be placed on the desks or in the work areas of key employees, and in shared communal areas, including the kitchen or refreshments area. If you have a business that manufactures items, also place offerings on the most important pieces of machinery. If you have a shop, be sure to place an offering on or near the cash register.

After the ceremony

One of the ways a business space clearing differs from a residential one is that you don't need to sleep overnight in the place to integrate the changes (unless you run your business from home, as explained earlier).

If it's possible for you to remain on the premises until all the candles have burned down, the best way to spend your time is not to carry on with your normal everyday work but to use the freshly cleared space to gain an overview of the business. Get clarity about where your business is headed and how best to achieve that. How does it fit with your own personal life goals? What course corrections need to be made?

If it is not practical for you to stay in the building until all the candles have burned down, that's OK too. It's not as essential to do that as it is when you space clear your home. Be sure to blow all the candles out before you leave.

48

Space clearing your own business

The main ways space clearing can help if you run your own business are:
- When you move to new premises
- To help launch a new phase of your business
- To improve team spirit and harmony
- To improve productivity
- To prepare for an important business meeting
- To boost profits

When you move to new premises

Moving into new business premises is a wonderful opportunity for a fresh start. Whether you are starting a new business or continuing one that has existed for some time, space clearing is one of the quickest and most effective ways to take energetic ownership of the new space.

A brand-new property

If the property has just been built, space clearing will enable you to settle the chaotic energies of the construction process.

Premises that have previously been occupied

If the property has previously been occupied by another business, space clearing will enable you to clear out the energies of the previous occupants. This is especially important if the property has a history of business failures. Those energies will still be there and will affect you.

Premises that previously had a different use

Space clearing can be used to remove the old frequencies so you can instill new frequencies that are more conducive to your business.

Recommended altar design

New Beginnings

To help launch a new phase of your business

A new phase of your business can include streamlining it, expanding it, taking a new direction, or undertaking a major new project. It will usually work best if the focus of the ceremony is on gaining clarity about the new phase and the best way to implement it.

Recommended altar design

Single Focus or Establishing Foundations

To improve team spirit and harmony

Space clearing can be very helpful to foster the development of team spirit. There can be personality clashes in any business, so it is not a miracle fix-all, but regular space clearing does help to break the cycle of recurring conflicts. After a space clearing, it's common for staff to report feeling much happier in their work, even though they may not know why this is.

In a school Karen once space cleared, there was a high level of delinquency and most of the pupils came from broken homes. The headmistress was astonished to find, in the weeks following the ceremony, that the usual daily outbreaks of playground fights and bullying stopped completely, and the teachers and pupils were happier than she had ever seen them.

One business owner we knew who started space clearing regularly said, "People come in and say the atmosphere feels much clearer and happier. I think space clearing makes a tremendous difference. We all enjoy coming to work much more these days."

Recommended altar design

The Facilitator

To improve productivity

Space clearing creates a smoother flow of energies, which tends to result in better productivity. This is especially noticeable in creative environments where workers need a clear head space and benefit from a fertile collaboration of ideas.

Recommended altar design

All possibilities

To prepare for an important business meeting

A very tangible and productive use of space clearing is to prepare for an important meeting.

One client Karen used to work with in the UK would call her in before any important board meeting to space clear the room. She noticed consistently that when she did this, board members tended to make decisions faster, with fewer arguments, and for the greater good of the company instead of pursuing their own personal agendas.

Recommended altar design

The Facilitator

To boost profits

Space clearing is an excellent way to give a business a boost if profits ever start to drop beyond the usual seasonal ups and downs. The best preparation is to do a thorough clutter clearing of the premises first, to let go of everything that is no longer needed or relevant. Clearing out the old makes room for the new.

One company Karen space cleared in London requested this because business had become so slow. A month later, they contacted her to ask how to stop the phone calls coming in so thick and fast because they couldn't keep up with demand.

Some businesses contract our professional space clearing practitioners to space clear their premises annually. One of Richard's long-term clients, when he lived in Sydney, was a well-known and very successful financial advisor. She booked him to space clear her home and business every year without fail after discovering the remarkable level of clarity this brought, which enabled her to keep both her personal and business life beautifully on track.

For non-profit organizations, space clearing can be used to boost the success of the venture in other ways.

Recommended altar design

The Accelerator

49

Space clearing if you work for an employer

We want to be very clear about this, because it's a topic we are often asked about. If you work for an employer, it is NOT okay to sneak in at the weekend or stay on after working hours to space clear the premises, no matter how well intentioned you may be. It would be unethical to do this. You will need to wait until you are in a position to create your own business that you have full control of.

Here's what you *can* do if you work for an employer.

If you have your own private office

If you have your own room and you don't share the space with anyone else, it's fine to space clear just that area, providing you would feel totally comfortable if your boss happens to arrive unexpectedly while you are doing it.

But don't be tempted to space clear your boss's office too, no matter how difficult they are to work with or how much you'd like to fix or help them. That would be manipulative and out of integrity.

If you work in an open-plan office

We're sorry to say there is no space clearing solution for this situation. Even if there are partitions that delineate your personal space, it is pointless to space clear it because there will always be a seepage of energies over the tops of the partitions, to and from your space. It's a communal space that is not yours to control, so it also wouldn't be right to attempt to do so.

If you work in a hot-desking office

Hot-desking (multiple people sharing the same desk at different times of the day) means that no individual has responsibility for the desk space. If it's located in a self-contained area with its own door and you have access to it at a time when no one else is around, you may be able to get permission from the office manager to space clear it. If it's located in an open-plan setup, there is nothing you can do.

Recommended altar design

There is no recommended altar design for any of these situations. It will depend on the reason for doing the clearing.

PART SIX

Specialized uses of space clearing

50

Other uses of space clearing

In this section of the book, we cover four specialized uses of space clearing that will be of interest and relevance to some readers:

- Space clearing to complement feng shui
- Space clearing meeting rooms
- Space clearing treatment and therapy rooms
- Space clearing before and after an entity clearing

51

Space clearing to complement feng shui

Space clearing works beautifully in conjunction with feng shui and can be used in several ways:
- To enhance energy flows
- To clear the energies of previous occupants
- To clear the energies of current occupants
- To give a deeper level of insight into any feng shui changes that are needed

To enhance energy flows

Feng shui is the art of balancing and harmonizing the flow of natural energies in our surroundings to create beneficial effects in our lives. Many traditional cultures have a form of feng shui. What we are referring to here is the best-known system, which originated in ancient China and is still in use today.

> **Karen**: About 10 years after I first started developing space clearing, a friend showed me a book they had found. It was a huge illustrated volume, containing a chapter about something I had never heard of before called feng shui. "Look at this," he said to me. "The Chinese were on to all this stuff about 3,000 years before you!"

> I read the information with interest, but it was based on complicated calculations that didn't make a lot of sense to me at that time. However, it was wonderful to know that some research had already been done into energies in buildings, and when I studied feng shui myself later on, parts of it confirmed many of the understandings I had already arrived at by myself.

There are several schools of Chinese feng shui, some of which are entangled with Chinese superstitions that have no relevance to most people's lifestyles. There are also other schools of feng shui, some of which use random intuition or incorporate various kinds of New Age teachings. It's therefore very challenging to find a good feng shui consultant these days (please don't ask us for recommendations because we don't have a list).

The information in this chapter is for anyone who already has some knowledge of feng shui that they feel works well for them, such as furniture placement and balancing the elements of earth, water, fire, metal, and wood. These types of improvements can be very beneficial, and we certainly use them in our own home.

Space clearing engages a much deeper level because it directly addresses the energy flows that all feng shui knowledge is based on. It therefore helps to make all feng shui enhancements work better.

There have been many occasions when Karen has been called in by top feng shui consultants whose recommendations have failed to produce results because space clearing needs to be done. The two work beautifully together.

Clutter clearing is essential too, of course. A deep and thorough decluttering of a home will greatly improve energy flows, which will make feng shui enhancements and space clearing both work better, faster, and at a much deeper level.

Recommended altar designs

The Facilitator or The Accelerator

To clear the energies of previous occupants

"Predecessor energies" is a feng shui term used to describe the energetic residues left by previous occupants of a building in the form of stagnant energies and astral imprints.

Stagnant energies are the easiest to clear, and most people can do this by following the steps of the Basic, Essential, or Full Space Clearing ceremony in *Space Clearing, Volume 1*. Clearing astral imprints requires more skill but can be done too. Clearing both types of energies will give you a beautiful, fresh canvas on which to write your own future.

Recommended altar design

New Beginnings

To clear the energies of current occupants

Layers of stagnant energies and astral imprints will build up over time, even if you live in a brand-new home. Any feng shui changes you make will only be minimally effective unless you do regular space clearing too.

Recommended altar design

New Beginnings

To give a deeper level of insight into any feng shui changes that are needed

Space clearing allows you to get to know the energy flows in your home very intimately, which makes it easier to determine any feng shui adjustments that are needed. It therefore always works best to do space clearing before feng shui. In some cases, doing space clearing may even remove the need for any feng shui changes at all.

Recommended altar design

Choose the altar design that is the most relevant to the issues you need to address.

52

Space clearing meeting rooms

Space clearing a meeting room to set the space for a talk, seminar, workshop, or other type of presentation can make a huge difference. We have a great deal of experience in this area, having led events in many locations around the world. We always arrive early to make sure we have time to space clear the room before anyone else arrives.

We have taught these techniques to other speakers, teachers, and workshop leaders with excellent results. After they have tried it, they never want to lead an event again without first space clearing the room. It makes it easier for them to do their job, and easier for participants to stay focused and receive the knowledge and skills they have come to learn.

How to prepare

Before space clearing a meeting room, it's essential to space clear your own home and get good results. You need to be familiar with the basic techniques first.

Space clearing a meeting room requires different techniques because space will usually be much larger than any of the rooms in your home. Your relationship to the space and the purpose of the space clearing will be very different too.

When you space clear your own home, you clear out old energies and set a space that will nurture and support you and anyone who lives with you. It's personalized to the occupants of the home and designed to last for as long as possible.

When you space clear a meeting room, you also clear out old energies, but the space you set will be for a finite time, to facilitate a specific group of people having a specific experience in that place. The ceremony is therefore not personalized, and the effects are only designed to last for the duration of the event.

The method you are about to learn will work for space clearing a meeting room in which you will be teaching an event yourself. It won't work for an event that someone else will be leading because more advanced skills are needed to be able to do that.

Permission to space clear a hired meeting room

If you have hired a public meeting room for your event, this includes the energetic space as well as the physical space. No permission is required to space clear it unless it is specifically prohibited in the terms of your agreement, which is highly unlikely, or the space has been consecrated for use by a religious or spiritual organization (see Chapter 23 of *Space Clearing, Volume 1* for more information about this).

Please be considerate if there are any meetings being held in adjoining rooms. It's courteous to let the speakers know that any clapping and belling sounds they may hear will only last a few minutes.

Permission to space clear a borrowed meeting space

You must always get permission to space clear a borrowed space. To avoid misunderstandings, it's preferable if the host has already personally experienced space clearing in their own home so they know what they are agreeing to when you ask if you can space clear the meeting room.

Space clearing equipment

The only equipment you will need is a large Balinese space clearing bell (preferably on a bell stand). A small Balinese space clearing bell usually will not be sufficient, unless the meeting room is very small.

Personal preparations

There is likely to only be limited time to do space clearing before any event you are leading, so be sure to make these preparations in advance:

- At least a few days before the event, clarify the purpose of the event and the results you want the participants to get
- Polish your space clearing bell the evening or morning before the event
- Ideally, take a bath or shower and put on clean clothing before the event

Physical cleaning of the space

Space clearing needs to be done after the room has been cleaned and before the group arrives.

When teaching in a place you have never been to before, it is wise to arrive early to check that the cleaning has already been done. If not, you will need to do it yourself and also remove any clutter from the room.

If your event runs for several days, the space will need to be cleaned and space cleared daily. The cleaning can either be done at the end of each day or early the next morning. Space clearing needs to be done after the cleaning and immediately before the start of the event (not the evening before).

Set up the chairs and equipment

After cleaning and before space clearing, set up the chairs for participants and any equipment you or the group will need.

Who can be present during the space clearing

Do the space clearing without any spectators present and take steps to prevent interruptions. Put a sign outside the door telling people not to enter until invited in. This includes any assistants helping you during the event who are not familiar with space clearing.

Prepare the room

- Put any food or drinks away in a fridge or in sealed containers.
- Open at least one window so there is a gentle circulation of fresh air in the space. If there are no opening windows, you can still go ahead but the ceremony will not be as effective.
- Stop all other activities in the space.
- Turn off any fans and other loud or droning machinery. If the meeting room is air conditioned or uses a forced-air heating system, it will work best to turn it off while space clearing, if you can.
- Work in silence without any background music or other sounds.
- Turn off any devices such as computers, projectors, and phones.
- Set up your space clearing equipment near to the main entrance of the room (the one participants will be using to enter and exit).

Prepare yourself

- Remove any metal you are wearing or carrying in your pockets.
- Do the ceremony barefoot, if the floor is clean and it is practical to do so.
- Roll your sleeves up above your elbows and wash your face and hands.

How to space clear a meeting room

1. Keep your head and spine vertical the entire time.

2. In packed form above your head, hold an awareness of the purpose of the event and the results you want the participants to get.

3. Start and end each circuit at the main entrance to the room.

4. Pick up your bell and go to the main spot in the room from where you will be teaching the event. Do personal belling on yourself three times, from your root charge to as far above your head as you can reach, to centre and uplift your own energy. Keep your head and your bell as vertical as possible while doing this. Then place your bell back on its stand.

5. Starting at the main entrance, walk around the inside perimeter of the space, hand sensing the walls as you go and expanding your awareness to take energetic ownership of the entire space. Some meeting rooms can be very energetically trashed, especially the type that are frequently used for wedding parties, where copious quantities of alcohol are consumed. Fortunately, you will only need to take a very general reading during the hand-sensing circuit, to get an idea of the history of the space. It's not necessary to go into any depth because the emphasis is on establishing the territory. Stay objective and – most importantly – do not react to anything you find.

6. The clapping circuit is identical to Step 17 of the Full Space Clearing ceremony, except that you don't just clap in corners, you also stop along the way to clap out any hotspots you discovered during the hand-sensing circuit. To be effective, your claps will need to be loud and sharp.

7. The belling circuit is identical to Step 19 of the Full Space Clearing ceremony, except that if the room is a large one, you will need to ring your bell much louder and more vigorously than usual, and

there is no need to do belling on the participants' chairs or any other furniture in the room. Complete the circuit at the main entrance by ringing the bell once and using it to trace a horizontal figure of eight in the air at heart level. As always, finish with a brisk ring in the centre of the figure of eight where the two loops cross.

You can now put your shoes back on, roll your sleeves down, if you wish to, turn the air conditioning back on, if it's needed, and turn on any other equipment you'll be using.

If possible, leave a window open during the meeting to create a flow of fresh chi in the space. We don't recommend doing this in an area where the outdoor air is very polluted or where there is a lot of external noise, but it is something we always do, even when teaching in very hot or cold locations, where air cooling or heating is needed. This is because the stream of fresh air adds etheric vitality to the space, which is essential for participants to be able to access the higher levels of consciousness we pass through our teachings.

53

Space clearing treatment and therapy rooms

Next time you have a therapy session, a dental treatment, or some other kind of healthcare, consider how many people have been in that chair or on that table before you. Why? Because mingling with your energy at that moment will be all the etheric and astral residues they have left behind, including all their anxieties and fears. Even the seats in a dentist's waiting room can be like this. If you weren't nervous before you went in, it's likely you soon will be after you sit down.

Karen remembers once walking into a therapy centre to make an appointment and walking straight out again without booking. The density of etheric sludge in the reception area and waiting room was so thick that she didn't want to go any further. There was also an occasion when she sat up and climbed off a massage table after only 10 minutes because the therapist was so saturated in energetic gunge herself that she was oozing it into Karen's body with every stroke she made. Worse still, the masseuse wasn't a novice. She was a well-known massage teacher who didn't have the first idea about how to manage the energies she was exposed to each day.

The main purpose of massage is to relieve the areas of compaction where your astral body is grasping your etheric too intensely, which is what causes stiffness or pain. You will therefore want to open your energy as much as possible so the therapist can work with you as deeply as they can. If they do a good job, when you get up off the table your etheric energies will circulate more freely and your physical body will feel more supple. The etheric and astral energies you release during the session, as a natural part of the process, will remain in the room and the therapist may also absorb some of them.

Then in comes the next client and lies down in your freshly excreted energies, as well as those of all the clients who have received treatments before you. It's no wonder that so many massage therapists suffer periodic burnouts or that it's possible to get off a massage table feeling worse in some ways than when you got on it.

The rest of this chapter is specifically addressed to therapists, doctors, dentists, and anyone who works as a healthcare professional. If you are a client or patient and you work with a professional who may not have heard of space clearing, we encourage you to share this information with them.

Why space clearing is an essential skill for health professionals

An essential part of taking care of clients or patients is to create and maintain an environment that is energetically clear and supportive to their healing process. The most effective way we know to do this is by space clearing. This will benefit your clients and also help you because it will clear the energies released by the people you treat instead of you having to process them yourself.

All health clinics and therapy centres can benefit from regular space clearing. If you work with clients in your own home, space clearing will be most effective if you have a dedicated room that you use only for that purpose. Never work with clients on your own bed or in your bedroom, even when you first start offering therapy sessions, because you will absorb their energies while you are sleeping.

Where you can do space clearing

If you work in a health clinic or therapy centre and have exclusive use of a room where you see clients or patients, that's ideal. You can take full energetic ownership of the space and do space clearing on a regular basis.

If you rent a therapy or treatment room that is also used by other practitioners, it will work best to space clear it at the beginning of each block of sessions you do, with the explicit intention that the results will benefit everyone else who uses the space too.

How often to do space clearing

When you first start using a therapy room, do an Essential Space Clearing to clear out the residual energies in the space and reset it at a higher level.

Then do Basic Space Clearing each day for the first month or so to remove the etheric and astral excretions of clients, until you reach the point where you find you are no longer absorbing these energies yourself because the room is handling it for you.

After that, a weekly Basic Space Clearing will usually be enough, together with an Essential Space Clearing once a year, or more frequently if the room is used intensively.

If you have an exceptionally heavy session with a client from time to time, where a lot of energies are discharged, it's fine to do a quick Basic Space Clearing before your next client, if it's practical to do so.

The goal is to never let energies build up to the point where they impact you or your clients/patients. Don't overdo space clearing, though. It is possible to space clear too much, as we explain in Chapter 37 of *Space Clearing, Volume 1*.

The best time of day to do space clearing is in the morning, when your energy is at its freshest.

Supportive practices

- Daily vacuuming can really help to maintain the space of a therapy room. It removes physical debris and revitalizes floor-level stagnant energies through the vibrating, sweeping, sucking action of the machine. Use the type of vacuum that filters out dust, pollen, mould, bacteria, and other airborne particles. They cost a bit more but are well worth it.
- Always wash your hands and arms up to your elbows between clients/patients to reduce the energies you pick up and to limit the transfer of energies from one client/patient to another.
- Work with a window open to allow a circulation of fresh air and chi.
- Wear white or light colours, never black, and natural fabrics, not synthetics (see Chapter 33, Step 6 in *Space Clearing, Volume 1*).
- Use the bed thwacking technique each week (see Chapter 44) on treatment tables, treatment chairs, waiting room chairs, and so on.
- If you're a bodyworker, learn the channel release techniques described in Chapters 4, 6, and 8 of *Awakening the Third Eye* by Samuel Sagan. They can help you a lot.

54

Space clearing before and after an entity clearing

An entity is a non-physical parasite that can form from a fragment of the astral body of a person who has died.

Entities mostly attach themselves to humans or animals, but they can also become attached to a place. This is more likely to happen when the person who dies has lived in their home for a long time and has a strong connection to it. It's also more common in properties that have strong earth lines or underground water streams running through them (also known as geopathic stress), which an entity can feed off.

The space clearing ceremony described in our books is not designed to clear entities, but having a professional space clearing done in a property before and after an entity clearing can greatly facilitate it. It's also a very useful skill for any entity clearer who works with clients in a therapy room. We are therefore including specialized information about this here.

Space clearing before an entity clearing

In a residential property

The reason it's so helpful to do space clearing before doing an entity clearing in a property is exactly the same reason why cleaning layers of physical dust and cobwebs from a room will help you to see what condition it's in.

Cleaning at the physical level makes everything more physically visible. Space clearing does the same thing energetically. It gives an entity nowhere to hide. To give a cartoon image analogy, it leaves an entity looking like someone caught naked in a spotlight, clutching their genitals, and transfixed by the glare. The enhanced clarity of vision* this brings makes it much easier for the entity clearer to get a lock on the entity and clear it.

In the therapy room of an entity clearer

If you are an entity clearer who works with clients in a therapy room, regular space clearing is essential. It will create an energetically clear space that will benefit your clients enormously and make your job much easier too.

Space clearing after an entity clearing

As all capable entity clearers know, there is always some astral fallout after an entity clearing. It's an unavoidable part of the process. Space clearing is the best way we know to clean this up.

In a residential property

If an Essential or Full Space Clearing has already been done by a professional space clearer before the entity clearing, just do Basic Space Clearing in the area where the entity clearing has been done.

In the therapy room of an entity clearer

If Essential Space Clearing has been done regularly to maintain the energy of the space at a high level, a Basic Space Clearing will be all that's needed to clean up after an entity clearing.

55

The future of space clearing

This book and *Space Clearing, Volume 1* are about space clearing the types of buildings we currently live in.

But what about the future? Are there space clearing methods that will work if we live far from our beautiful planet, on other planets, or on space stations? In these places, there may be no space clearing equipment such as bells or harmony balls, or space clearing materials such as flowers. Is the human race doomed to live a spiritually impoverished life in these scenarios?

There are specific space clearing techniques we are currently developing to be able to clear spaces and create spiritually presenced environments in any location. We see this as being essential to the survival of humans, to ensure the spiritual wellbeing of our species in whatever future awaits us.

You'll be happy to hear it is much easier to do space clearing in the beautiful ethericity of our planet than it is likely to be in off-world environments, so we warmly encourage you to make the most of it here and now!

PART SEVEN

Resources

56

What next?

This book and *Space Clearing, Volume 1* are the first two books in our Conscious Living series. We have several more titles in the pipeline on a range of related topics.

Join our mailing list

If you'd like to know when new books and articles are published, and new events or special offers are announced, the best way is to join our mailing list to receive Karen's monthly newsletters.

www.clearspaceliving.com/newsletters

Explore Karen Kingston's blog

Karen's blog features a wealth of insightful articles about space clearing, clutter clearing, conscious living, and related topics.

www.clearspaceliving.com/blog

Explore our online courses

We teach a range of online courses that are open to anyone wishing to improve their quality of life. They are also the entry point to our teachings for anyone who is interested to train as a clutter clearing or space clearing practitioner.

www.clearspaceliving.com/courses

What next?

Purchase space clearing equipment

Our online shop has the finest-quality space clearing products available anywhere in the world, including individual items (bells, harmony balls, etc) and a range of space clearing kits.

www.clearspaceliving.com/shop

Find a practitioner

You can find an up-to-date list of our certified clutter clearing and space clearing practitioners in our International Directory of Practitioners.

www.clearspaceliving.com/practitioners

If someone claims to have been trained by us but their name does not appear in our directory, they either did not train with us, were not able to achieve the standard required for certification, or have not been able to maintain their skills by taking annual continuing professional development trainings. If in doubt, you are welcome to contact us to check a person's credentials.

57

Recommended reading

Books by Karen Kingston

Clear Your Clutter with Feng Shui (Piatkus, 1998) – the 25th Anniversary Edition of this book was published in the UK in 2024 in paperback and ebook. It has sold over 2 million copies in 26 languages. It is also available in audiobook format, narrated by Karen.

Books by Karen Kingston and Richard Kingston

How to Clear Your Clutter (Clear Space Living, 2023) – this concise book is designed as a quick and easy introduction to the clutter clearing methods described in detail in *Clear Your Clutter with Feng Shui*.

Space Clearing, Volume 1: The art of clearing and revitalizing energies in buildings (Clear Space Living, 2024)

Articles by Karen Kingston

You can find a wealth of articles about space clearing, clutter clearing, conscious living, and related topics at www.clearspaceliving.com/blog.

Recommended reading

Books by Samuel Sagan

Awakening the Third Eye (Point Horizon Institute, 2013)

Entities: Parasites of the Body of Energy (Clairvision School Foundation, 1994) – published in the United States as *Entity Possession: Freeing the Energy Body of Negative Influences* (Destiny Books, 1997)

Regression: Past-life Therapy for Here and Now Freedom (Clairvision School Foundation, 1996)

Atlantean Secrets, Volume 1: Sleeper Awaken! (Clairvision School Foundation, 1999)

Atlantean Secrets, Volume 2: Forever Love White Eagle (Clairvision School Foundation, 1999)

Atlantean Secrets, Volume 3: The Gods Are Wise (Clairvision School Foundation, 1999)

Atlantean Secrets, Volume 4: The Return of the Flying Dragon (Clairvision School Foundation, 1999)

Bleeding Sun: Discover the Future of Virtual Reality (Clairvision School Foundation, 1999)

Planetary Forces, Alchemy and Healing (Point Horizon Institute, 2016)

Samuel Sagan's books are available online from clairvision.org, which ships from the United States. We also stock all these titles in our online shop at www.clearspaceliving.com, which ships from the UK.

PART EIGHT

Glossaries

58

ALTMC Glossary

A Language to Map Consciousness (known as ALTMC for short, pronounced alt-em-see) is available to read at clairvision.org. For ease of reference and with the kind permission of the Clairvision School on behalf of Samuel Sagan, we have listed here abridged definitions to explain terms that we have included in this book, with information in brackets, where necessary, to add small clarifications.

What is ALTMC?

The introduction to ALTMC explains:

> This book presents some of the discoveries made by the Clairvision Foundation, as well as a set of principles that can be used by anyone interested in engaging in an exploration of consciousness based on direct experience. Note that the power of what is presented here lies in the fact that it isn't the product of one individual trying to share his/her vision of the world, as is often the case with books of esotericism, but the result of a collective "mapping". No view was adopted until it could be confirmed and objectified through the experience of the whole Foundation, as well as hundreds of students following the courses of the Clairvision School.

ALTMC definitions

Aquarium effect

A form of connection in which you are immersed in the presence. Rather than sitting in your column above, the connection floods the room, sometimes giving you the impression of floating in an "aquarium of presence".

Archetypes

Archetypes are the perfect prototypes out of which the seeds of things and beings originate.

Aspiration

Turning upwards in an attitude of active receptivity. Aspiration creates a receptacle for high spiritual beings to give help.

Astral body

The astral body is the subtle body that is the vehicle of thoughts and emotions.

Astrality

In the Fourfold Model of subtle bodies developed by Samuel Sagan and the Clairvision School, the astral body is the vehicle of thoughts and emotions, sometimes referred to as ordinary mental consciousness. Astrality is the fabric of this consciousness.

Central channel

The central channel of energy that extends from the top of the head to the root of the body (the perineum). It is the principal channel of the etheric body.

Central thread

The line of energy at the centre of the column above that begins at the vertex (the top of the head) and from there ascends vertically.

Chakra

In Sanskrit texts, chakras are wheel-like structures that govern subtle bodies and a whole range of functions of consciousness.

Column above

The column of energy that extends infinitely above the head, as in an upwards extension of the crown chakra. Ordinary astral consciousness is synonymous with the mind and personality. Superastrality is the more subtle frequencies of higher consciousness, accessed through the centres above the head. Just as the mind is the organ of ordinary astral consciousness, so the column above is the vehicle for superastral levels of consciousness and their corresponding functions of perception. Verticality, as a key quality of the column above, is a direct way to access these levels.

Column below

The column of energy that extends below the body. The column begins just below the perineum and extends infinitely down.

Combinessence

A oneness of essence. A coalescence of beings. A state of unity shared by two or more high spiritual beings.

Connection

A link of consciousness to a non-physical being or beings, or their world. A connection is experienced as a presence. Connections can also take place with your Higher Self, or higher parts of yourself.

De-exvolution

A de-exvolution is an involution. Calling it de-exvolution emphasizes the fact that in its original state, human consciousness was far more involuted than it is now. So in de-exvoluting, there is a return towards more primordial and less fallen states.

Dragon

On the individual level, the dragon is the power of the lower chakras, which manifests in the potential of life force and desires, passions, belly drive, raw energies, including the sexual force, intensity, underground vitality, and resources, and ultimately will power. Behind and beyond the individual dragon lies the universal Dragon, the unlimited power that is the matrix of the entire creation.

Individual dragon = the power of your lower chakras, the power in your column below.

The Dragon = the universal Dragon power, of which your dragon is an emanation.

Elementals

Tiny beings that conglomerate to form matter. Classically, it is elementals that form the four elements of earth, air, fire, and water.

Entity

A term used to refer to parasites of the body of energy. Most entities are fragments, issued from the astral body of the dead. To speak of parasitic entities, many healers use the term "attachment".

Etheric

See: Etheric body and Ethericity. (When used as a noun, etheric is short for "etheric body". When used as an adjective, it means relating to the etheric body or qualities of ethericity.)

Etheric body

The vehicle of life force. The etheric body can be equated with the *prana-maya-kosha*, "envelope made of *prana*" of the Hindu tradition, and with the *qi* (also known as *chi*) of the Chinese tradition.

Ethericity

The quality of the etheric or life force. Anything that is alive has an etheric body and therefore a quality of ethericity. Ethericity can also refer to the subtle substance of life force, distinct from an etheric body. For example, a plant has an etheric body that gives it life. A garden has ambient ethericity that can be felt apart from the life force of any individual plant.

Etheric sensing

A form of perception based on sensing energetic characteristics of plants, animals or people through your own etheric body. Etheric sensing is a resonance from etheric to etheric. The knowing coming through etheric sensing is therefore primarily related to life force.

Exvolution

A turning outwards of consciousness, towards grosser levels of existence. The opposite movement of involution. Excessive exvolution is one of the central characteristics of the present human condition. Dwelling in a human body, consciousness is constantly drawn outwards through the senses, towards the material world. Consciousness loses touch with its inwards essence, its non-manifested roots. This engrossment in the senses is an exvolution, an extroversion by which consciousness forgets its own nature of infinity and becomes assimilated to physical limitations. Human beings forget they are immortal Spirits, they believe themselves bipeds bound by the constraints of a three-dimensional universe. Consequently, to know itself consciousness must follow a path of involution.

Fragment

Fragments are issued from the shattering of the astral body of the dead. Made of astral substance and sometimes coated with etheric energy, they can act as entities.

Infra-etheric

Levels of the etheric body that lie closest to the physical and are beyond the present range of perception.

Involution

A turning inside of consciousness. Consciousness letting go of the senses and internalizing itself, turning towards its source and cognizing itself. The opposite of involution is exvolution. Just as a glove can be turned inside out, so consciousness is turned outside in through involution. However, it would be more accurate to say that consciousness is turned inside out through exvolution, and that involution brings it back to its original state. Hence the key direction: consciousness knows itself through involution.

Lower complex

Because the etheric body remains tightly bound to the physical body until death, the two are often grouped together under the term "lower complex" when discussing subtle bodies. See also: Upper complex.

Mind

The layer of thoughts and emotions. The astral body is the vehicle of the mind.

Ordinary mental consciousness (OMC)

The waking consciousness of present-day human beings. The discursive mind.

Packed thought

A condensed thought, the content of which is not explicit or expressed but concentrated into a seed. Ordinary mental consciousness operates with unpacked thoughts, supermind with packed ones. For example, when you turn towards a glass, you immediately identify its shape and know that it is a glass without having to repeat to yourself, "this is a glass". The instant silent knowing that identifies the object is an example of packed thought. If, after this, your mind indulges in commenting, "this is a glass", then this commenting is an unpacked thought. Abstract intelligence operates through packed thoughts.

Pancake

A Clairvision term for a perverse energy that lands on your face or some other body part after floating in the etheric environment.

Personal stage

The present stage of human evolution in which human beings have developed a sense of individuality and a certain degree of self-determination, but have lost their unity with the Divine and are disconnected from spiritual realms. See also: Prepersonal stage and Transpersonal stage.

Perverse energy

An etheric substance that has crept into the human system and nested in it, to the detriment of vitality and health.

Point

Perceived above the head, the Point is the standpoint from where consciousness can operate non-dimensional functions of superastrality as well as resonate with higher angelic frequencies. The Point is like a prism through which the non-dimensional astral body is projected into the dimensional etheric and physical bodies.

Power of the Point

Super-focused states of consciousness. The power of the Point operates with packed thoughts and can access archetypal forces and superastrality. It can therefore resonate with the supermental consciousness of gods and angels.

Prepersonal stage

A stage of existence in which human beings have a poor sense of their own individuality, or no sense of individuality at all. In the early prepersonal stage, human beings were one with the Divine but without any sense of individuality. Then comes the personal stage, in which individuality is acquired at the expense of a near-complete disconnection from spiritual worlds. Finally, in the transpersonal stage, human consciousness is to regain its unity with the Divine, while retaining individuality. See also: Personal stage and Transpersonal stage.

Presence

The flavour of consciousness that characterizes a being, whether a high angel or a small parasitic being such as an entity.

Ritual

A practice through which a connection is established with non-physical beings. This definition contrasts with the loose modern use of the term "ritual", which covers circumstances such as losing your first tooth or burning your personal journal. These may have symbolic significance but, strictly speaking, they do not qualify as rituals.

Root charge

The root charge is the powerhouse behind all emotional charges and desires. It is held in the toroid, a doughnut-shaped master structure of energy located just below the perineum and the anus. The voltage held in the root charge is a limited manifestation of the power of the Dragon.

Samskara

Samskaras are imprints left in the psyche by emotionally charged experiences.

Structure

Structure refers to "the ability to go from A to B", meaning to carry out elaborate tasks, manage complex situations, solve problems, and organize. Structure brings a know-how of achieving. In the supermind work, structure is equated with superastrality.

Structures

Structures refers to various subtle organs or structures such as chakras, gateways, etc.

Subtle bodies

The non-physical layers which, together with the physical body, constitute a human being. Subtle bodies form the non-physical hardware of consciousness.

Subtle bodybuilding

In the present condition of human beings, subtle bodies aren't completely shaped – not unlike unused atrophied muscles that do not respond to the conscious will. The term "subtle bodybuilding" adequately reflects the sustained effort by which subtle bodies and their constituting structures are perceived, shaped, crystallized, made operational, integrated to your consciousness, and submitted to the rulership of your Higher Self.

Superastrality

Superastrality refers to levels that stand above ordinary mental consciousness. It is accessed through verticality. Structure and superastrality are one and the same thing.

Third eye

Organ of inner vision and command centre of the body of energy. The third eye gives direct perception of non-physical realities, leading to first-hand experiences instead of having to rely only on theories. Rather than a patch of energy on the forehead, the third eye is a tunnel that extends from the back to the front of the skull. It includes several centres of energy, including the frontal eye (between the eyebrows) and the atom (at the very middle of the third eye tunnel).

Throat friction

A simple but extremely powerful technique that consists of making a friction sound while both inhaling and exhaling. Its effect is to crystallize structures of energy and to induce high states of vision and connection. The throat friction technique is described in detail in Chapter 2 of Samuel Sagan's book *Awakening the Third Eye*.

Transpersonal stage

The prepersonal, personal and transpersonal stages are three phases in the evolution of human consciousness. In the prepersonal stage, human beings have little or no sense of individuality, but there is union with the Divine. In the personal stage, a sense of individuality has appeared, but at the cost of a loss of connection with the Divine and with spiritual worlds. In the transpersonal stage, the sense of individuality is retained and unity with the Divine has been regained. See also: Prepersonal stage and Personal stage.

Unpacked thought

A thought expressed in some form of inner discourse, as opposed to a silent knowing. The discursive mind (ordinary mental consciousness) operates through unpacked thoughts.

Uplifting

Uplifting consists of pulling energies up along the central thread of the column above. It is one of the cardinal techniques taught by the Clairvision School.

Upper complex

The astral body and the Higher Self working together. See also: Lower complex.

Verticality

Verticality is simply the quality of being vertical. It is easily perceived in the vertical column of energy (known as the column above) that extends upwards above the head. Superastrality is accessed through verticality. See also: Column above

Vision

A superior function of consciousness. A direct perception of reality, which bypasses the senses and cognizes the essence of things.

Visionful

An object of perception is said to be visionful when it engages subtle vision through the richness of its qualities (inner light, vibration…) or because of the archetypal forces behind it. It is a very useful concept for developing non-physical perception.

59

Space Clearing Glossary

Ambient etheric

See Ethericity* in the ALTMC Glossary.

Astral imprint

An astral frequency that is embedded in a physical substance. The technique used in space clearing to read astral imprints is called hand sensing. The primary technique used in space clearing to clear astral imprints is called belling.

Basic Space Clearing

An abridged version of space clearing, described in detail in *Space Clearing, Volume 1*. It is conducted using a Basic Space Clearing kit and is the version most people start with.

Belling

A range of techniques using the unique sound of a Balinese space clearing bell to clear astral imprints** and revitalize energies in buildings during a space clearing ceremony.

Clapping

A range of techniques involving striking the palms of one's hands together to break up clumps of stagnant energies and surface layers of astral imprints in buildings and objects.

Colourizer

A strip of handwoven gold-threaded material, available in a range of colours. Used in the creation of an altar for a Full Space Clearing ceremony.

Command node

A superastral* structure that can be consciously crafted in the upper space of any room or building. It can be used during a space clearing ceremony to facilitate top-down MC-ship* and spiritual presencing of a space. The term emerged during a mapping session between Samuel Sagan, Karen Kingston, Richard Kingston, and a group of space clearing practitioners and trainees in 2006.

Essential Space Clearing

This version of space clearing is described in detail in *Space Clearing, Volume 1* and is conducted using an Essential Space Clearing kit. It is more effective than Basic Space Clearing and not as comprehensive as a Full Space Clearing, although it is quicker and easier to do.

Etheric debris

Elemental* energies resulting from the energetic excretions of living organisms. Etheric debris feels cruddy and unclean. It is often intermingled with stagnant energies and may have a physical component such as dust, grime, mould, or grease.

Flower offering

When activated during a space clearing ceremony, the purpose of a flower offering is to create an anchor for spiritual forces and help to facilitate taking energetic ownership of a space. A classic flower offering consists of a small saucer or plate with a tealight candle at the centre and small flower heads placed around the candle, pointing outward. A rose petal flower offering consists of a small saucer or plate with rose petals placed around a tealight candle and a few flower heads on top of the rose petals, pointing outward.

Full Space Clearing

The most effective version of space clearing, described in *Space Clearing, Volume 1*. It is conducted using a Full Space Clearing kit.

Hand sensing

The art of sensing etheric* and astral* energies with the palm of one's hand and interpreting them through specific subtle body structures that can be developed above the head.

Harmony ball

A small brass-plated ball that makes chiming sounds when shaken. It is used in the final part of a space clearing ceremony to facilitate putting new, higher frequencies into a space.

Imprintability

The degree to which physical materials tend to become astrally* imprinted or etherically* coated.

Island

An independent floor-to-ceiling structure found in some homes, such as a freestanding fireplace in the centre of a living room or sometimes an entire room within a room.

Matrix flower offering

Matrix flower offerings are used in a Full Space Clearing ceremony to create a superastral* matrix that links all the flower offerings on each floor horizontally and all the matrix flower offerings to each other vertically. The method of activating matrix flower offerings is substantially different to that of other flower offerings.

MC

MC is short for Master of Ceremonies. The MC of a space clearing ceremony is the person who takes overall responsibility for it, practically and energetically.

MC-ship

Holding the position of MC.

Personal belling

A centring and uplifting* technique using the sound of a Balinese space clearing bell.

Space clearing flower offering mudra

The ritual movement used to activate a flower offering in a space clearing ceremony while holding a flower head between the forefinger and middle finger of one hand.

Space clearing water

Water that has been ritually presenced for use in a space clearing ceremony.

Stagnant energies

Etheric* energies that stagnate in areas where energies do not flow well, similar to the way water can stagnate in a pond. Stagnant energies often accumulate around clutter.

The Seven Levels of Consciousness

A model created by Karen Kingston and Richard Kingston of the levels of consciousness that are accessible while incarnated in a human body.

White Gold

The spiritual connection that facilitates the space clearing methods described in this book.

Index

Page numbers in *italics* relate to photographs and illustrations.

A

Accelerator (altar design) 202, 209, 210, 226, 229, 240, 268, 270, 271, 288, 295
accidents in the home, space clearing after 258
acupuncture 68
Agama Tirta (Religion of Holy Water) 133–134
alcohol 88
All Possibilities (altar design) 208, 232, 272, 274, 287
altar designs
 listed 198
 after a burglary 258
 after a death 253
 after a divorce or break-up 233
 after an accident in the home 258
 after an argument 256
 after a party 259
 after a traumatic local/world event 259
 after illness 238
 before death 252
 business premises 279
 clarity about a new direction in life 269
 clarity about a relationship 232
 clarity about moving home 208
 clutter clearing 202
 convalescence 240
 dealing with recurring problems or behaviours 271

deepening a relationship 232
feeling 'stuck' 268
feng shui 295
finding a new home 210
finding a new relationship 229
guest rooms 219, 220
harmonizing a fraught relationship 231
home renovations 226
improving productivity 287
integrating changes into your life 276
joyful life events 254
lifting depression 239
marriage 246
meditation rooms 275
meeting rooms 287
moving business premises 286
moving in with a new partner 231
new homes 215, 216
opening new possibilities 272
overcoming procrastination 270
pregnancy and childbirth 246, 247, 248
profit boosting 288
promoting prosperity 271
repurposed rooms/buildings 227
revitalizing a relationship 231
saying goodbye to your home 213
selling your home 209
sick person's room 238
special times of year 241
spiritual development 274
stressful life events 254

team spirit and harmony 287
tiredness and fatigue 240
altars
    in business premises 283
    in sick person's room 236-237
ALTMC (A Language to Map Consciousness)
    definitions (glossary) 319-329
    introduction to 318
    stages of human evolution 58
ambient etheric. *See* ethericity (ambient etheric)
Amritanandamayi Devi, Mata (Amma) 134
angels
    astral beings masquerading as 62, 167
    communication with 62, 166-167
    and entity clearing 166-168
    and power of the Point 325
animals, connecting to 43-44
anniversaries, space clearing on 243
aquarium effect 125
    definition 319
archetypes (definition) 319
arguments, space clearing after 255-256
aromas, purification with (misconceptions) 177-181
aspiration
    definition 319
    during harmony ball infusion 153-154
astral beings, masquerading as spiritual connections 62, 167
astral body
    and birth 248
    and death 250, 323
    definition 319
    and engagement with astrality 70
    overastralization 68-69
astral/energy imprints. *See also* perverse energies
    buildings 116-117, 136-137, 139-140, 216, 224-225, 227, 230, 231, 232-233, 238, 245, 252, 295
    definition 329
    mattresses 118, 119-121, 263
    second-hand objects 203-204
astrality. *See also* superastrality
    definition 319
    engagement with 70
astral travelling 3
atom (centre of energy) 327
attachments. *See* entities
Awakening the Third Eye (Samuel Sagan) 85, 95-96, 107, 306

B

Balinese colourizers. *See also* altar designs
    definition 330
    ripples 270
Balinese harmony balls. *See* harmony balls
Balinese people
    death traditions and rituals 27-28, 248-250
    dress 56, 83
    entity clearing 96-97
    group dragon structure 83-84
    home improvements 222
    homes 128, 192-194
    languages 29
    music and dance 54-57, 83-84
    spiritual connections and practices 12-23, 46-47, 52-58, 78, 92, 128, 133-134
    western influences on 58-59
Balinese purification rituals 21-24
Balinese space clearing bells. *See also* belling
    for meeting room clearing 299
    suppliers 33
    verticality 171-172
Balinese temple bells 27-32, 57, 141, 172

Balinese temples and shrines 16–20, *18*, 128. *See also* churches and sacred places
  dance in Batur temple 55–57
  guardian spirit shrines 192–194
  palm mottling effect 53–54
  poleng use 14, *15*
  presencing in 60, 78
barefoot 86–87, 262, 300
Basic Space Clearing
  accessibility 66
  definition 329
beds and mattresses
  energy clearing 204–205, 230, 233, 245, 263–264
  imprintability 118, 119–121, 263
  memory foam mattresses 264–265
  placement, and dowsing 187, 188, 189
bed thwacking 204, 230, 233, 245, 263–264, 306
belling. *See also* Balinese space clearing bells; Balinese temple bells
  bells used for 26–27, 31–33, 143, 170–171
  definition 329
  furniture clearing 205
  hotel room clearing 262
  meeting room clearing 301–302
  personal belling. *See* personal belling
  purpose and explanation 139–140
  technique 140–141
bhuta kala (evil spirits) 21, 22
birthday, space clearing on 242–243
bodywork (massage) 77, 94–95, 184, 303–304, 306
bowls, singing 171–173
Boyle, Robert 114
breastfeeding, and kiss line 79
breathing
  and etheric body 75
  during harmony ball frequencing 155
  during personal belling 145, 146
  throat friction 212, 327

building work. *See* home improvements
burglaries, space clearing and support after 256–258
business premises, space clearing 277–289
  home rooms used for business 279, 281, 304–305
  meeting rooms 287, 297–302
  treatment and therapy rooms 304–306

C

caffeine 88
candles 183
ceilings, high 108
celebrities, personal chi of 80, 81
central channel 142
  definition 319
central thread
  definition 320
chakras
  "balancing" 143
  crown chakra 106, 320
  definition 320
  lower chakras 82, 321
  in palms 95–96, 123
chanting 60, 175–176
chi 68, 322. *See also* personal chi
children
  etheric awareness of 129
  personal belling on 148
Chinese medicine, traditional 68, 80
churches and sacred places. *See also* Balinese temples and shrines
  incense burning in 177–179
  spiritual connections in 54
  superastrality in 6, 108
circular buildings 174
Clairvision Knowledge Tracks 70, 85, 110, 123, 250–251
Clairvision School 37, 39–40, 42, 46. *See also* Sagan, Samuel

clapping
    alternatives (advice against using) 175
    definition 329–330
    furniture clearing 204
    hotel room clearing 262
    meeting room clearing 301
    purpose and explanation 136–137
    technique 137–138
clap sticks 175
clarity, space clearing for 268–269
cleaning. *See also* washing
    meeting rooms before space clearing 299
    objects before energy clearing 204
    therapy rooms 306
Clear Your Clutter with Feng Shui (Karen Kingston) 36, 42, 89, 233, 251, 270, 271, 314
closure method (saying goodbye to a home) 212–213
clothing
    Balinese dress 56, 83
    imprintability 118–119
    light colours 306
    rolled sleeves 83, 84, 86, 204, 212, 237, 262, 300
    washing 206
clutter, and stagnant energies 332
clutter clearing
    Clear Your Clutter with Feng Shui 36, 42, 89, 233, 251, 270, 271, 314
    and depression 239
    and feeling 'stuck' 267
    and feng shui 295
    guest rooms 219
    help with 218
    How to Clear Your Clutter 314
    importance of 89–90
    when moving home 208, 217
    and opening new possibilities 271
    and pregnancy 247
    and prosperity 271
    space clearing before 201–202
    in springtime 241

colourizers. *See* Balinese colourizers
colours, sensing using hands 114–115
column above. *See also* verticality
    definition 106, 320
    and dragonweave 19
    and prayer 19–20
    and superastrality 104, 106–107
column below
    definition 320
    and dragon 83–84, 321
combinessence (definition) 320
command node 108–109
    definition 330
connections (definition) 320. *See also* spiritual connections
consciousness
    in a space, raising level of 64–65
    ordinary mental consciousness 324
    presence. *See* presence(s)
    seven levels of. *See* seven levels of consciousness
    subtle bodies. *See* subtle bodies/subtle body structures
    turning inwards (involution). *See* involution
    turning outwards (exvolution) 322–323
construction, in personal development work 69, 110
convalescence, space clearing for 240
Creating Sacred Space with Feng Shui (Karen Kingston) 35, 193
creative productivity, space clearing for 287
Crossroads (altar design) 269
crown chakra 106, 320
crystals 184–185

D

dance 54–57
death
    Balinese traditions and rituals 27–28, 248–250

337

preparation for 250–252
shattering of astral body 250, 323
space clearing before/after death 252–253
violent 252–253
Death, The Great Journey (Clairvision Knowledge Track) 250–251
debris, etheric. *See* etheric debris
deconstruction, in personal development work 69, 110
de-exvolution (definition) 321. *See also* involution
depression 239
  post-partum depression 248
diet. *See* food and drink
direct chi 82
distant (remote) energy clearing 169, 188
divorce and relationship break-up 232–233
doors/entrances to your home, materials of 117
dowsing 187–189
dragon
  definition 82, 321
  group vs individualized dragon structures 83–84
  and root charge 326
dragon-owning of spaces 84–85
Dragon's Den (TV show) 84
dragon space, at Clairvision School retreat centre 39–40
dragonweave 19, 128
dreams 70, 105, 131
drugs, recreational 5–6, 45, 51
drumming 174–175
Dual Focus (altar design) 231, 246

E

electromagnetic interference 240
elementals (definition) 321
energetic ownership of a space 122
energetic protection 91, 95–99

energy imprints. *See* astral/energy imprints
entities
  clearing (Balinese people) 96–97
  definition 307, 321
  exorcisms 166–167
  space clearing before/after entity clearing 307–308
Entities: Parasites of the Body of Energy (Samuel Sagan) 37, 97, 248, 250
equipment suppliers 33, 313
essential oils, burning 180–181
Essential Space Clearing
  accessibility 66
  definition 330
Establishing Foundations (altar design) 256
Establishing Levels (altar design) 256
etheric awareness
  importance of 72–73
  in Bali. *see also under* Balinese people
  of Richard 43–44, 94–95
etheric body 73–74
  awakened etheric 77–79
  awakening (starting points for) 85–90
  definition 321–322
  in different cultures 68
  and energetic protection 91, 95–99
  feeling and experiencing 70, 74–75
  strong/weak etheric 76, 94
etheric debris
  and death 252
  definition 330
  and illness 235, 238
ethericity (ambient etheric)
  of the countryside 6
  definition 322
  engagement with 70, 77–78
  of flowers 75
etheric sensing (definition) 322
etheric vitality 75
exorcisms 166–167
extraretinal vision 113–115

exvolution (definition) 322–323. *See also* involution
eyeless sight 113–115

F

face washing 212, 237, 261, 300
Facilitator (altar design) 219, 231, 232, 238, 239, 240, 246, 268, 274, 287, 295
fatigue, space clearing to improve vitality 240
feet, bare 86–87, 262, 300
feng shui
   Clear Your Clutter with Feng Shui 36, 42, 89, 233, 251, 270, 271, 314
   Creating Sacred Space with Feng Shui 35, 193
   introduction to 293–294
   Relationships area of the *bagua* 270
   space clearing as complement to 294–296
financial success, space clearing for
   profitability 288
   prosperity 271
flashlight, as energy clearing method (misconception) 182
flower offering mudra 125, 135
   definition 332
flower offerings
   activation (in workshops) 124–127
   activation (water sprinkling method) 135
   in Bali *16*, 16–17
   in business premises 283
   definition 330–331
   explanation of 130–131
   matrix flower offerings. *See* matrix flower offerings
   in new homes (and energetic landing) 129–130
   and White Gold 125, 130
fluid-dimensionality 108, 108–109, 130–131

focus of the ceremony, clarifying 154, 281
food and drink 75, 87–89
Formula 1 drivers, superastral awareness 106
Fourfold Model *67*, 67–70
fragments
   and birth 248
   definition 323
fragrance. *See* aromas, purification with (misconceptions)
fresh chi, and open windows 183, 302, 306
frontal eye 327
Full Space Clearing
   accessibility 66
   definition 331
furniture. *See also* bed thwacking; beds and mattresses;
   clearing energies of 204–205, 306
   new vs second-hand (energy imprints) 203–204
   placement 187, 188, 189
future of space clearing 309

G

geopathic stress 187, 188, 240, 307
ghosts. *See* entities
gods, and power of the Point 325
golf 106
gongs 173
grief
   on saying goodbye to a home 211
   space clearing after a death 252–253
guardian spirits in homes (misconception) 193–195
guest rooms
   in someone else's home 260–261
   in your home 219–220, 260

H

hand cream 204
hand sensing. *See also* eyeless sight

and building energies 116, 121
definition 331
examples of 119–121
explanation of 112–115
further resources 123
hotel rooms 262
Karen learns and develops 7–11, 115
meeting rooms 301
hand washing
  and clearing energy imprints from objects/furniture 204, 205
  and closure method 212
  and hotel room clearing 261
  and meeting room clearing 300
  and sick person's room clearing 237
happy memories method (saying goodbye to a home) 211
harmony balls
  for business space clearing 282
  definition 331
  frequencing 155–156
  infusion 153–154, 156
  purpose and explanation 153, 155–156
health issues. *See* illness
health professionals 303–306
herbs, burning 179–180
Higher Self 69, 76, 154, 156
holding space 109–110
holy water 133–134
home improvements 221–227
Hood, Bruce M. 118–119
hospitals and hospices 280
hot-desking offices 290
hotel rooms 244–245, 261–266
How to Clear Your Clutter (Karen and Richard Kingston) 314
human evolution, stages of
  personal stage. *See* personal stage
  prepersonal stage. *See* prepersonal stage
  transpersonal stage. *See* transpersonal stage

I

illness
  avoiding space clearing when unwell 234
  detection using hand sensing 9, 11, 120
  and personal belling 147–148, 150–152
  space clearing for convalescence 240
  space clearing for others who are unwell 235–239
imprintability (of materials) 117–122
  definition 331
imprints. *See* astral/energy imprints
Incarnation (altar design) 215, 239, 269
incense burning 177–179
infra-etheric 40
  definition 323
Inner Space Techniques (IST) 103–104
integrity of ritual, maintaining 60, 162–163
intention (misconception about) 164–165
intuitive energy clearing 161–162
invocational energy clearing 166–168
involution
  after life-changing workshop/retreat 276
  clapping 137
  definition 323
  flower offering activation 130
  harmony ball infusion 153
  in Nyepi ritual, Bali 21, 22–23
islands (definition) 331
IST (Inner Space Techniques) 103–104

J

jewellery, energy clearing 206
jing. See personal chi

K

kaja orientation 19–20
kangaroo 106

ki 68
Kingston, Karen
   in Bali 12, 17-19, 20-21, 23-24, 27-33, 36, 46-47, 52-57, 78, 87, 91-94, 173, 192-193, 222, 248-250
   blog 312
   develops space clearing 9-11, 26-27, 38, 153
   early years 2-6
   learns and develops hand sensing 7-11, 115
   media appearances 34
   online courses and services 37-38, 110-111, 312
   publications 34-36, 42, 89, 158-159, 193, 233, 251, 270, 271, 314
   Reiki training 190
   relationship with Richard 39, 46-48, 245
   space clearing workshops 32, 34, 36, 40, 47, 114, 124-127, 151-152, 173
   subtle body structure development 6
   work with Samuel Sagan 37-39
Kingston, Richard
   in Bali 46-47, 94-95
   bodywork training 94-95
   cheffing 44-45, 86, 106
   early life 43-44
   in Gretna Green 244-245
   learns and develops space clearing 40-41
   publications 314
   relationship with Karen 39, 46-48, 245
   superastral awareness 106
   work at Clairvision School retreat centre 39-40, 42, 46
kiss line 78-79
Kuleshova, Rosa 114

L

life events, space clearing for 244-248
life force. *See* etheric body; ethericity (ambient etheric);
life force energy 68
light, purification with (misconceptions) 182-183
lower chakras 82, 321
lower complex 67. *See also* upper complex
   definition 68, 323

M

magnetic chi 82
marriage, space clearing for 245-246. *See also* relationships, space clearing for
massage. *See* bodywork (massage)
matrix flower offerings 130-131
   definition 331-332
McCartney, Paul 105-106
MC (Master of Ceremonies) and MC-ship
   and command node 109
   definition 332
   and new relationship in a new home 229
meditation
   and Balinese bodyworkers 94-95
   courses in 85, 123
   retreats 276
   spaces for 274-275
   as subtle bodybuilding 69, 70
   and third eye awakening 76
meeting rooms 287, 297-302
memory foam mattresses 264-265
mental health issues 239, 248
mind (definition) 323
misconceptions about energy clearing 158-160
   aroma use 177-181
   distant (remote) energy clearing 169, 188
   dowsing 187-189

guardian spirits 193–195
intention 164–165
intuition 161–162
invocational energy clearing 166–168
light use 182–183
negative energy absorbers 184–186
Reiki use 191
sound use 170–176
moving business premises 285–286
moving home
  clutter clearing for 208, 217
  and home improvements 223–225
  moving in with a partner 229–231
  prevalence in society 128–130
  saying goodbye to your old home 211–214
  space clearing for 207–210, 213–216, 229–231
mudra. See flower offering mudra
music 54–57, 83–84
music composition
  and archetypal forces 4–5
  and superastral awareness 105–106

N

negative energy absorbers (misconceptions) 184–186
Neil-Smith, Rev. Christopher 166–167
New Beginnings (altar design) 209, 213, 215, 216, 220, 226, 227, 230, 231, 232, 233, 238, 241, 246, 253, 254, 258, 259, 271, 272, 286, 295
new home. See moving home
new possibilities, space clearing for 271–272
new year, space clearing in 242
niskala 92
Novomeisky, Abram 114
Nyepi ritual, Bali 21–24

O

objects, astral imprints and clearing 203–204, 206. See also furniture

open-plan offices 289–290
ordinary mental consciousness (OMC) (definition) 324
ownership of space, energetic 64

P

packed thoughts. See also unpacked thoughts (definition)
  and peak performance 105
  definition 324
  glass of water example 324
  and power of the Point 325
palms of hands
  chakras in 95–96, 123
  mottling 54, 126
  sensitizing for hand sensing 122–123
pancake effect 224
  definition 324
parasites. See entities
paroptic vision 113–115
parties, space clearing after 258–259
permission/agreement to do space clearing 235, 280, 290, 298–299
personal belling
  accounts of 149–152
  on another person 143–151
  bells used for 143
  definition 332
  purpose and explanation 142–143
  and uplifting 142, 332
  on yourself 142–143, 150, 151–152
personal chi 80–82
personal development, space clearing for 267–272
personal objects, imprintability 118–119
personal stage 58–59
  definition 324
perverse energies
  care home example 224–225
  clearing 96–97, 225
  definition 324
physical body 68

342

Point
    and belling 141
    definition 324–325
    and energetic protection 96
Point-dragon art, Professional Space Clearing as 66, 130
poleng patterned material, Bali 14–15, 15
power of the Point 107
    definition 325
practitioner-level space clearing. *See* Professional Space Clearing
prana 68, 322
prayer, and verticality 18–19
pregnancy and childbirth
    avoiding personal belling on pregnant person 147
    avoiding space clearing while pregnant 247
    space clearing after 248
    space clearing for 246–247
prepersonal stage 57–58
    definition 325
presence(s)
    in churches and sacred places 6
    definition 325
    in spaces through space clearing 65
procrastination, space clearing for 269–270
productivity, space clearing for 287
Professional Space Clearing
    benefits 66, 257
    Directory of Practitioners 313
    personal belling 148
    practitioner attributes 66, 89, 163, 257
    practitioner energetic protection 99
Professional Space Clearing Practitioner training 40
profitability, space clearing for 288
prosperity, space clearing for 271
psychic readings 113, 147
purification rituals, Balinese 21–24

Q
qi 322

R
rattles, shamanic 175
recurring problems/behaviours, space clearing for 270–271
Regression: Past-Life Therapy for Here and Now Freedom (Samuel Sagan) 103
Reiki 190–191
relationships, space clearing for 228–233, 270–271
    getting married 245–246
    team spirit and harmony 286–287
remote energy clearing 169, 188
renovations. *See* home improvements
repurposing rooms/buildings 226–227
ritual(s)
    Balinese purification rituals 21–24
    definition 325
    space clearing as 59–60
    and spiritual connections 59–60
Romains, Jules 114
root charge 142
    definition 326
rose petal flower offering (definition) 331

S
Sagan, Samuel. *See also* ALTMC (A Language to Map Consciousness); Clairvision School;
Awakening the Third Eye 85, 95–96, 107, 306
and command node 109
and dragonweave 19
Entities: Parasites of the Body of Energy 37, 97, 248, 250
Fourfold Model. *See* Fourfold Model
Karen works with 37–38, 140
novels 61, 110
on Professional Space Clearing 66

publications (list and suppliers) 315
Regression: Past-Life Therapy for Here and Now Freedom 103
Richard works with 46
salt, in rooms 185–186
salt lamps 183
samskaras
   definition 326
   identification and resolution of 69, 103–104, 110
   and 'intuitive' energy clearing 161
   and overastralization 69, 102–104
   and triggers 102–103, 256
sanggah pengijeng (guardian spirit shrine) 192–194
sekala 92
selling your home, space clearing for 208–209
seven levels of consciousness 64, 110–111, 154
   definition 333
sexual abuse, imprints of 120
sexual partners
   kiss line 79–80
   marital problems 119, 120–121
shamanic rattles 175
sight, eyeless 113–115
silky chi 81
singing bowls 171–173
Single Focus (altar design) 270, 271, 274
sleep
   dreams 70, 105, 131
   problems with 240
sleeping orientations, Balinese 19–20
sleeves, rolled 83, 84, 86, 204, 212, 237, 262, 300
smudge sticks, burning 179–180
solar return, space clearing on 242–243
space clearing. *See also* Basic Space Clearing; Essential Space Clearing; Full Space Clearing; Professional Space Clearing
   additional resources 312–315

before/after entity clearing 307–308
business premises. *See* business premises, space clearing
equipment suppliers 33, 313
with feng shui 294–296
focus of ceremony 154, 281
future of 309
Karen develops 9–11, 26–27, 38, 153
levels (overview) 65–66
maintaining integrity of ceremony 60, 162–163
meeting rooms (procedure) 299–302
misconceptions. *See* misconceptions about energy clearing
for personal development 267–272
personal uses (overview) 199–200
purposes (overview) 63–65
as a sacred ritual 59–60
sick person's room (procedure) 236–238
for spiritual development 274–275, 276
and subtle body structures 71
when travelling (procedure) 261–262
treatment and therapy rooms 304–306, 308
space clearing teaching
   blog 312
   online courses 37–38, 312
   Professional Space Clearing Practitioner training 40
   workshops 32, 34, 36, 47, 114, 124–127, 151–152, 173
space clearing water
   definition 332
   jewellery clearing using 206
   making 134, 142
   sprinkling on flower offering 135
sparkling chi 81
spirit guides 62
Spiritual Aspirations (altar design) 252, 274, 275
spiritual connections
   absence in uninhabited places 52–53

in Bali 12–23, 46–47, 52–58, 78, 92, 128, 133–134
and dance 54–57
feelings of disconnect 50–52
masquerading by astral beings 62, 167
and rituals 59–60
in sacred spaces 53–54
and space clearing 65
White Gold. *See* White Gold (spiritual connection)
spiritual development 273–276
splicing 213
sprays and mists, aromatic 181
springtime, space clearing in 241–242
Stabilizer (altar design) 226, 229, 246, 247, 248, 254, 256, 258, 259, 274
stagnant energies. *See also* etheric debris
  clearing 116–117, 121–122, 136–137, 295
  definition 332
  and 'stuck' feeling 9, 267
Stanley, Patricia 115
structure
  definition 326
  and superastrality 326
structures
  definition 326
'stuck' feeling. *See also* procrastination, space clearing for
  and stagnant energies 9, 267
  space clearing for 267–268
subtle bodies/subtle body structures
  carrying forward from previous lifetimes 115–116
  definition 326
  Fourfold Model *67*, 67–70
  Karen's development of 6
  and space clearing 71
subtle bodybuilding 69
  definition 326–327
sugar 88–89

sunlight, as energy clearing method (misconception) 183
superastrality. *See also* astrality
  awareness 70, 100, 104–111
  and high ceilings 108
  command node 108–109, 330
  definition 104, 327
  matrix flower offerings. *See* matrix flower offerings
  and structure 326
  and verticality 104, 106–108, 327
supportive chi 81

T
taksu 57
team spirit and harmony, space clearing for 286–287
temple bells, Balinese 27–32, 57, 141, 172
temples. *See* Balinese temples and shrines; churches and sacred places
third eye
  awakening 76, 85, 95–96
  definition 327
thoughts
  packed thoughts. *See* packed thoughts
  unpacked thoughts 328
throat friction (breathing technique)
  and closure method 212
  definition 327
Tibetan chanting 60, 176
tiredness, space clearing to improve vitality 240
toroid 326
transpersonal stage 58, 59
  definition 327–328
traumatic events, sites of 216
traumatic local/world events, space clearing after 259
travelling
  bringing uplifting item with you 265–266

345

guest rooms. *See* guest rooms
hotel rooms 244–245, 261–266
knowing the geographical direction of loved ones 266
unpacking 265
treatment and therapy rooms 303–306
triangular seal 96
triggers, samskaric 102–103, 256
tuning forks 173

U

unpacked thoughts (definition) 328. *See also* packed thoughts
unpacking when travelling 265
uplifting
   definition 328
   and personal belling 142, 332
upper complex 67. *See also* lower complex
   definition 69, 328

V

vacuuming 306
verticality. *See also* column above
   in Balinese culture 18–19
   of bells 171–172
   definition 328
   and prayer 19–20
   and superastrality 104, 106–108, 327
virtual energy clearing. *See* distant (remote) energy clearing
vision. *See also* eyeless sight
definition 328
versus intuition 162–163
visionful (objects) (definition) 328
visualization. *See* intention (misconception about)
vitality, improving by space clearing 240

W

"walking the chi" 122
Warwick Castle, lack of spiritual presence in 52–53
washing
   clothing 206
   face 212, 237, 261, 300
   hands. *See* hand washing
water
   chemical properties 132–133
   space clearing water. *See* space clearing water
   spiritual qualities and holy water 133–134
White Gold (spiritual connection) 61, 65, 125, 130
   definition 333
wind chimes 174
windows, opening 183, 302, 306

Y

"Yesterday" (song) 105
Youtz, Richard P. 115

Printed in Great Britain
by Amazon